Comical Co-Stars of Television

Comical Co-Stars of Television

From Ed Norton to Kramer

ROBERT PEGG

McFarland & Company, Inc., Publishers
Jefferson, North Carolina, and London

Library of Congress Cataloguing-in-Publication Data

Pegg, Robert, 1954–
    Comical co-stars of television : from Ed Norton to Kramer /
Robert Pegg.
        p.   cm.
    Includes bibliographical references and index.
    ISBN 0-7864-1341-7 (softcover : 50# alkaline paper) ∞
    1. Television comedies— United States.   2. Television actors
and actresses— United States— Biography.   I. Title.
    PN1992.8.C66P44 2002
    791.45'028'092273 — dc21   2002002398

British Library cataloguing data are available

Manufactured in the United States of America

*Cover photographs of Art Carney and Michael Richards ©2002 Photofest
Cover photograph of television set ©2002 PhotoDisc*

McFarland & Company, Inc., Publishers
  Box 611, Jefferson, North Carolina 28640
  www.mcfarlandpub.com

For Marg, who is and always will be
Top Banana in my heart

Acknowledgments

There's an old episode of *The Munsters*, in which Lily Munster is worried about what would happen to her husband, Herman, if his new career in show business should go to his head. She has a vision of the big ham on stage at the Academy Awards making an acceptance speech. He tells the audience, "I'd like to thank all the little people who made this award possible." In his most smug and condescending voice, he continues, "I'd like to thank them, but I can't — because I did it all myself." He then lets loose with that big, goofy laugh.

I'll try not to sound quite so full of myself. While it is true that sitting down to write this book was a solitary job, the entire project certainly was no one-man effort. In fact, the research, the interviews, the publishing and editing — all the fun stuff — involved many other people. And none of their contributions were little.

First off, of course, I have to thank all the actors who granted me interviews. Max Baer, Jim J. Bullock, Tim Conway, Ann B. Davis, Jamie Farr, James Gregory, Pat Harrington, Don Knotts, Tom Lester, George Lindsey, Dave Madden, Don Most, Ken Osmond, Ron Palillo, Michael Richards, Jack Riley, Rose Marie, Ronnie Schell, Larry Storch and Fred Willard — all of them were generous with their time and memories and patient when it came to answering questions they've already been asked many times about events which often happened decades ago. All of them are marvelous actors and in my eyes, there isn't a second banana in the bunch of them.

In particular, I'd like to thank Tim Conway, who went to the trouble of working up some material just for his interview; Jack Riley, who sent some *Rugrats* merchandise to my young son when he heard he was a fan; and Don Knotts, who had just published his own autobiography at the time of our interview — and so really didn't have to talk to me.

A special thanks has to go to Joyce Randolph, Stan Livingston and

Lucie Arnaz — all actors themselves who were happy to be interviewed not about themselves, but about *other* actors. It just shows that in addition to being wonderful actors, they're also exceptional human beings.

I'd also like to thank the staff of the London Public Library in my hometown as well as Ebon Brown and the helpful staff at the Museum of Television and Radio Broadcasting in New York for their assistance in the Scholars' Room where I did a great deal of my research.

On a personal note, thanks to Herman Goodden, as always, for encouragement and friendship. Thanks to Brian "Al" Richards for riverbank consultations and his insights into the differences between Gomer and Goober Pyle.

Love and many thanks to my kids, Heather, Courtney and Fraser — all of whom selflessly sacrificed personal computer time so that the manuscript could be typed and filed.

And a big thank you to my wife, Marg, who is the most supportive player in my life and who also never fails to smile and roll her eyes whenever I do my own imitation of Herman Munster making that "I'd like to thank all the little people" speech.

Table of Contents

Introduction

The creation of the second-banana character is one of the most enduring achievements of that great American art-form known as the television
sitcom.

Although some scholars credit William Shakespeare with creating the
"first" second banana in the form of that Falstaff guy in *Henry IV* and later
reviving him for the sequel, *Henry IV — Part 2,* most TV historians agree
that the second-banana phenomenon was born on that historic occasion
in the early 1950s when Art Carney as Ed Norton first burst into the Kramden's apartment and greeted Jackie Gleason with a "Hey, Ralphie-boy!" on
The Honeymooners.

Usually in the guise of a wacky neighbor, goofy co-worker or dorky
best friend, the second-banana character has contributed to the success of
some of the most beloved situation comedies of the past half-century. *The
Honeymooners* would be just another husband-and-wife domestic comedy
if not for Norton. If not for Kramer, *Seinfeld* would just be a show about
three mean-spirited, unlikable losers. And all you have to do is look at
The Andy Griffith Show in the years after Don Knotts left the series to know
that Andy wasn't having any fun after Barney Fife left town.

There have been some memorable TV stooges over the years. Some
of the classics, like Carney, Knotts and Tim Conway, have gone on to
become top bananas in their profession. But just as memorable are the
one-hit wonders like Max Baer as Jethro on *The Beverly Hillbillies,* Tom
Lester as the handyman from *Green Acres* or even Skip Young as plump,
jolly Wally Plumbstead on *The Adventures of Ozzie and Harriet.*

Most often, the second banana is just one character among many who
serve as foils to which the star can react. But sometimes the stooge character becomes *so* popular that *he* becomes the star. Can a second banana
carry a show by himself? The answer to that can be found in one word —
Urkel. Jaleel White as ultra-nerd Steve Urkel on *Family Matters* is one of

the biggest success stories among the television collective of second bananas for going from one-shot cameo to series star in one season.

Although the concept of sitcom second banana was first immortalized by Carney as Norton, one of the biggest influences on the majority of stooges to come was *The Steve Allen Show* of the late 1950s. On Allen's Sunday night variety program was the troika of supporting players—Louis Nye, Tom Poston and Don Knotts. In their own individual ways, each of these actors inspired many other young comics to get in on the act. They are the standard to which all other second bananas compare themselves.

Of that bunch, Don Knotts is universally acknowledged—by fans and his peers—to be the ultimate TV stooge. His influence can be seen in everything associated with wacky sidekicks—from supplying the industry standard body-type model (the majority are string bean geeks) to the wild, broad acting style he later pioneered as Ralph Furley on *Three's Company*.

However, Knotts' greatest contribution is in making a real person out of what was originally a cartoon character. Knotts' three-dimensional characterization of Barney Fife is a form of perfection which all TV stooges have strived to achieve in the successive four decades of second bananadom.

There are certain prerequisites which help in the creation of a TV stooge. The character can't be too bright—although his actual level of intelligence can be quite deceptive. There is something childlike and innocent about these stooges. Incompetence, ineptness and klutziness are personality traits. They tend to be mildly eccentric or quirky. They may not be certifiably nuts but they also aren't too well connected with reality. They march to the beat of a different drummer. They live in their own little worlds and operate on a different wavelength than the rest of us. They tend to show their individuality with a distinctive non-conformist fashion sense. In some cases, the more outrageous the wardrobe, the better—although this gimmick is often used just as a lazy way of getting a cheap laugh. A snappy catch phrase is also an easy identifying feature. If the character is popular enough, the general populace will go about their everyday lives emulating the latest TV dork and peppering their speech with "Dy-no-mite!" or "Up your nose with a rubber hose!" The preferred body type is unnaturally thin, but if a suitable actor of that weight isn't available, round and chubby is a good alternative. Quite often a big ego accompanies that pathetic body. Surprisingly, most TV stooges are also very successful with the opposite sex.

Until the late 1970s, most second bananas were white and male. There weren't many black, Hispanic or female stooges. There are two possible explanations for this. One is that during the first three decades of television, all sitcoms were written and produced by white males. The other possi-

The Holy Triumvirate of Second Bananas: from left to right — Louis Nye, Don Knotts and Tom Poston on *The Steve Allen Show.*

bility is that those white writers were simply reflecting their times and there was a disproportionate percentage of geeks and dorks in the Caucasian race during those years. Happily, today we live in a world where all races and genders are given the opportunity to make fools of themselves on television. Nevertheless, because many of the characters discussed in this book come from shows of the 1950s through the mid–1970s, there is an unavoidable shortage of women and non-white characters.

The book is intended as a broad sampling of the period from the Golden Age of Television (1950s) through the appearance of the last great TV stooge, Michael Richards, who played Kramer on the 1990s series *Seinfeld*. It is a subjective inventory, which is to say that the list which makes up the Table of Contents contains all of the author's personal favorites. If your own favorite is absent from that list, it should be pointed out that *everyone* was invited to participate. Most responded. Others didn't.

The book is not exclusively about TV stooges. Second bananas are an offshoot of that larger branch of central casting known as Supporting Players. Wackiness isn't always necessary in the creation of a memorable character on a sitcom. Actors like James Gregory and Ann B. Davis don't fit into the second-banana stereotype, but they created strong, original characters without the benefit of pratfalls, mugging or saying something like, "Eat my grits!" every five minutes.

Today's actors are a funny breed. They often mistake their big egos for talent, and some think they're just the greatest thing since the invention of processed cheese. Since the days when Kramer went from being a peripheral character to a full-fledged equal and co-star, television has changed. Starting with *Friends,* no one on a sitcom wants to play support anymore. They all want to be a star. As a result, support has become a dying art. The role of the second banana used to be an honorable position in the show business industry. None of the veterans who know the tradition have any objections to the term, and some even wear the label with pride. But the new kids on TV don't know their history and would be offended if they were to be called a second banana — even if it was in the form of a compliment. "Second banana?! Sir, I am an Actor!"

During the 1960s, every sitcom had a second-banana character, and all of the shows from that era which are still popular in reruns had strong supporting casts. Today, the tradition continues, but not as strongly, and it seems that the torch is being carried by actors who are also students of comedy. Recent candidates for the Second Banana Hall of Fame include Andy Dick from *Newsradio*, French Stewart from *3rd Rock from the Sun*, and *Suddenly Susan's* Kathy Griffin.

Luckily for TV viewers, there will always also be a demand for strong supporting players who deliver the goods week after week. Alfonso Ribeiro, who played Carlton Banks on *The Fresh Prince of Bel Air,* consistently stole scenes from Will Smith, and he's always the best thing about the many second-rate sitcoms he's appeared in since those days. On *Newsradio,* Phil Hartman was a prime example of a supporting actor at the top of his craft. Television just doesn't get any better than his portrayal of the insufferable Bill McNeal.

It's a shame that the new generation of television actors, writers and producers don't know the history of their profession. As the saying goes, you can't know where you're going unless you know where you've been. Unfortunately, half a century after its birth, it's obvious that the television sitcom of today is going nowhere.

Yet the legacy of second-banana figures has had a far-reaching effect on TV. Before Bob Denver became a star with *Gilligan's Island*, he played television's first beatnik, Maynard G. Krebs, on *The Many Loves of Dobie Gillis*. That character can still be seen years later in Shaggy on *Scooby-Doo* cartoons and Screech on the kidcom *Saved By the Bell*. Andy Dick's character Matthew on *Newsradio* is like a slightly older Arnold Horshack from *Welcome Back, Kotter*. After *Seinfeld* became a big hit, there was a succession of Kramer clones. And of course all great second bananas have a little bit of Don Knotts in them.

All of that is good. As Groucho Marx once said, "Television is the sincerest form of flattery."

Max Baer

Jethro Bodine on *The Beverly Hillbillies*

"Acting is all bullshitting," explains Max Baer. The actor, best known as Jethro Bodine on *The Beverly Hillbillies,* continues, "It's all about salesmanship. You have to sell yourself to the producers that you can do that role and then you have to sell yourself to the audience that you are that character. Being a good actor is the same as being a good salesman."

His appraisal of the art of acting should not be surprising. Even back on *The Beverly Hillbillies,* Baer was known for being outspoken. His reputation for being brutally honest and frank has not diminished. "When I do radio interviews, they never know what I'm going to say," he admits. However, his comparison of acting to sales work also should not come as much of a surprise to anyone who knows his life both before and after the *Hillbillies.* First and foremost, Max Baer is a salesman. Before becoming an actor, he studied business in college. After his series ended and he couldn't get work as an actor because he was typecast as Jethro, he became an independent movie producer. He invested his life savings of $110,000, a partner put up a similar amount and they made *Macon County Line,* a movie that went on to make $35 million. With the profits he bankrolled more movies, invested in real estate and became a rich man. Although he was once bitter about what "Jethro Bodine" did to his acting career, he has come to embrace the character and his connection with the show that made him famous. Today he owns various licensing rights to *The Beverly Hillbillies* name and is in the process of putting it on generic food products, slot machines ("Strike it rich, like the Beverly Hillbillies!") and plans to open up a casino-hotel in Nevada named *Jethro's Beverly Hillbillies Mansion and Casino.* Clearly, if there is one thing that Max Baer knows about, it's how to sell.

Maximilian Adalbert Baer Junior was born December 4, 1937, in Oakland, California, the son of world champion heavyweight boxer Max Baer and his wife, Mary. When he was three years old, the family moved to Sacramento, where his sister Marian and brother Jim were born.

Max Jr. attended Christian Brothers High School in Sacramento. While there he won the Sacramento Junior Golf Championship two years in a row and was later runner-up in the men's competition. At the time, he seriously considered becoming a professional golfer but instead enrolled in Santa Clara University where he studied business administration and minored in philosophy. Despite his later success in the business world, Baer says that business administration was not his first choice and he would have been personally happier if he had majored in philosophy.

"Going to college and studying business was something I did to please my parents," he says. "My parents had both lived through the Depression and knew what it was like to be poor. I was the first in our family to go to college and that was very important to them. My father had been a boxer and later worked in pictures but he wanted us to get a good education so we could get a real job after college."

However, when Baer graduated from Santa Clara in 1959, after a six-month stint in the Air Force Reserve, he headed for Hollywood with $300 and a vague interest in becoming an actor. Both his father and uncle Buddy Baer had acted in movies years before. Yet Baer says his family background had nothing to do with his decision. As he saw it at the time, acting would be a nice way to make some money and meet girls.

In Los Angeles, he hooked up with Steve Cochran, an old family friend who had acted in a number of Westerns. Through him, he met Pamela Duncan, who had been in numerous B-movies, mostly Westerns and science fiction flicks, and she began to coach him in getting acting jobs.

Prior to this, Baer had never acted or shown any interest in acting. In high school and college he wasn't a member of the drama club and didn't take any theatre classes and instead spent his spare time involved in sports. However, when *The Beverly Hillbillies* made it big, all articles and interviews with Baer mention his involvement with the college players at Santa Clara and that he had appeared in their student production of *The Male Animal.*

Not so, Baer admits today. He made it up to have something to put on his resume. "When you come to Hollywood and start auditioning for work, they all want to know what you had done before. So I said that I had been in *The Male Animal* at college. No one was going to check or know about it because it was out of town. But I knew that our school had put it on so I put it down on my resume. I'd never even seen the play."

Duncan coached him on the basics of acting and how to look natural on camera. She began taking him around and introducing him at the various studios in town. It was on one such visit that an executive saw him walking from a distance and mistook him for James Garner, then starring as TV's *Maverick.* That led to a screen test, and a one-year contract as a studio contract player with was the result.

That was in 1960 and he began appearing frequently as different characters on a number of television shows produced on the Warner Bros. lot. At six feet, four inches and with an athlete's build, Baer was a natural for cowboy shows and he made multiple appearances on both *Cheyenne* and *Maverick.* But of greater benefit was the solid training Baer received as an actor — voice and diction training and how to carry himself (he has the best posture of anyone in the business). However, although the experience also gave him some real genuine credits he could put on a resume, he was underused and Warner Bros. did not renew his contract when the year was up.

Baer wasn't unemployed for long. In 1962, he landed his first full-time job as an actor with *The Beverly Hillbillies*, the CBS series which would supply his paycheck for the next nine years.

The Beverly Hillbillies was the brainchild of producer-writer Paul Henning, who had previously worked on *The Bob Cummings Show*. The premise of a family of Tennessee mountain folk who become multi-millionaires after oil is discovered on their land and then move to Beverly Hills, California, was the classic fish-out-of-water scenario which would fuel the series' long run. The Clampett family was headed by the Abe Lincoln-like patriarch Jed, played by Buddy Ebsen. Irene Ryan played Jed's cantankerous mother-in-law, Granny, who was set in her ways and longed to return to the hills. Donna Douglas was widower Jed's daughter Elly Mae and Baer played his nephew, Jethro Bodine, who made the move West with them so he could get a good education. He eventually did get one. Even though he was in Grade 3 when he started at a private school in Beverly Hills, it took him six years to graduate from the sixth grade.

Once he graduated, Jethro was all set to conquer the world. Unfortunately, he could never make up his mind on what career path he wanted to follow. One day he would have his heart set on being a fry-cook, the next day he'd have decided on becoming a brain surgeon. Jethro was impressionable and drawn to occupations based on the latest fad, which gave Henning plenty of material to spoof. When he saw his first James Bond movie, he wanted to become a "double-naught spy." He also experimented with becoming an astronaut, a bullfighter and movie star. With all of these occupations, he had an ulterior motive — they were all glamour jobs which would attract girls.

Girls and food (not necessarily in that order) were Jethro's two main passions in life. Sometimes he managed to combine the two in his quest for a career. His motivation in wanting to become an astronaut came from a comic book — he wanted to be the first man up there to find all that cheese and all those "Moon Maidens." When he opened a restaurant named "The Happy Gizzard," it featured topless waitresses. Under the misconception that topless meant hatless, he recruited Elly Mae and Granny as his topless servers. Even Uncle Jed went topless at The Happy Gizzard. Jethro, of course, wore a big chef's hat.

That was just one of many hats Jethro would wear over the years. To his credit, he had plenty of drive and ambition and wanted to put his sixth grade education to work. At various times he toyed with the idea of becoming an atomic scientist, brain surgeon and general in the U.S. Army. His uncle owned a movie studio and that gave him the chance to be movie producer and "star-maker"—under the name C.B. DeBodine.

Yet, he was also a simple man with simple interests and goals. The glamour jobs were always just phases—what he really wanted to be was a streetcar conductor so he could wear one of those "nickel-squirter" change dispensers on his belt.

Perhaps what Jethro was most qualified for was being an international playboy. He had his uncle's millions at his disposal, lived in the right neighborhood, had no real job to hold him down (once his chores were done for the day) and he had an undeniable effect on women—although it was seldom positive. Mostly, what he had going for himself was ego. There was no question in his mind that he wasn't cut from the same cloth as his hayseed relatives. Once he arrived in California, all that Beverly Hills sophistication wore off on him. He took love lessons from Dash Riprock; he read the Playboy Adviser for tips on how to be a swinger. He had all the potential to be a Hugh Hefner in denim.

The problem was—no one else shared his inflated opinion of himself. For all his newfound sophistication and higher education, in his checked shirt, jeans and rope belt, he still came off as a country boy. But Baer never played him as a hick. The movie cliché of a hillbilly was as a slow-witted, drawling lay about. Baer's Jethro was anything but that—he was a high-energy character and despite what was going on up there, his brain was always ticking. It was a portrayal completely opposite to the popular conception of a hillbilly.

Most of the credit has to go to Baer for choosing to play Jethro that way simply because of his own contrary nature. In life, as with his fictional alter-ego on *The Beverly Hillbillies,* Max Baer was a non-conformist. As originally written, Jethro, like all the other characters, was a total hick and they were defined by their dialogue. In the first season of the show, dialogue was mostly connected with the misconceptions they encountered on their arrival in luxurious Beverly Hills which they had never experienced in the hills of Tennessee. There were stock jokes about the "fancy eatin' table" in the billiard room and one regular set piece was the doorbell gag. Every time the doorbell rang, the Clampetts would wonder where the music was coming from and how sure enough, every time the music played, someone would show up at the front door. These lines could have been said by any member of the Clampetts. In that first season all the dialogue was written in support of such gags and could have been delivered by any slow-witted character.

Baer put his own spin on the character. Jethro may not have been the brightest light in Califorry, but he was not completely dumb. Baer portrayed him as more naïve than stupid.

He says that this approach came about quite by accident during his audition for the role. "I was drunk at the time," he says and then stresses that he isn't much of a drinker. "I was early for the audition and Irene Ryan (Granny Clampett) took me across the street to a restaurant and we had a few martinis. I was still pretty young and wasn't used to martinis and so when we got back for my screen test, I was feeling pretty good –although not noticeably drunk or anything. For the screen test I was supposed to walk into the log cabin and when I did, I accidentally walked into the door and just laughed and said 'excuse me.' And that's what got me the part. They all thought it was hilarious that I would say 'excuse me' to a door. So from then on, the way I would play Jethro was to just laugh at everything."

Under normal circumstances, producer Paul Henning, a veteran of Hollywood and one of the few regular churchgoers in the industry, wouldn't have tolerated someone on his set with liquor on his breath regardless of the innocent circumstances. But Henning was not present for the screen test. When he saw the film of the audition and how everyone laughed, that clinched the deal for Baer. "Paul Henning is a brilliant writer and one of the best producers but when he would watch the dailies and people were laughing, he always assumed they were laughing at his script. If Paul saw people laughing, he'd think he was a genius— so of course he liked my screen test. Paul was his biggest fan."

Baer says that he had a few problems with Henning over the course of the series' run but admits that they were largely due to his own stubborn personality. "I'm a very contrary person. If I thought there was a problem with Jethro's dialogue in a script, I wasn't afraid to let my opinion be known. I was hired as an actor; if they had wanted a puppet they should have hired one. But that doesn't mean that I didn't respect Paul or that I was even right."

Not that Baer would deliberately hold up production. "The problem was that Paul was always upstairs writing and any disagreements were on the set. But there was no time for arguing about 'what's my motivation.' The term show business says it all, it's a *business*. It's like a production line and things have to run smoothly. But me, being me, I would occasionally throw a wrench that would end up holding up the line for a while."

As the series went on and the characters began to gel, Henning and his writers were able to move past the hillbilly clichés and next to Granny, Jethro was the character with the most comic potential. Initially, Baer stuck with his original interpretation of the character knowing that's what the producers wanted. "Jethro was just a big innocent kid. He didn't know any better than to laugh at life. So that's what I did — laugh at everything."

Gradually, the character became less of a reactor and more of an initiator whose misguided ideas and misunderstandings helped propel many of the episodes in which Jethro was the lead comic character. Jethro's gung-ho enthusiasm, his innocence and self-confidence that he could do anything made him a perfect vehicle for episodes which showcased just how inept and unqualified he actually was for most occupations in life. His unwarranted self-confidence and sixth-grade education also made him a bit of a deluded know-it-all and that, combined with his all-round naivete, lent a child-like quality to the character.

Baer compares Jethro to another great childlike sitcom character. "If you watch closely, you can see that Jethro is a lot like Barney Fife on *The Andy Griffith Show*. He's all cocky self-confidence, especially around women and he thinks he knows everything. I didn't realize it at the time but there are a lot of similarities in Jethro and Barney Fife in how they behave."

For the audience, Jethro's most enduring quality was his wide-eyed optimism and that was all Baer's invention and contribution to the character. Henning provided the dialogue and the outrageous situations, but Baer provided the attitude. He pulled it off by delivering those lines with such a big goofy grin on his face that you just knew he meant it. "And that's all about selling yourself," says Baer. "Jethro thought he could do anything and that's what I had to sell in playing him."

The series ran for nine years and it remained popular with television audiences throughout its run. However, in 1971, like all of CBS's rural comedies, it was cancelled by executive Fred Silverman in spite of its still-strong ratings.

The series was getting increasingly silly in its last years, as Henning and company were finding it harder to come up with new ideas. In attempts to revive ratings and reinvent the fish-out-of-water premise there were road trips to England, New York and many trips to Hooterville, the home of Hennings's other sitcoms, *Petticoat Junction* and *Green Acres*. Still, Baer was sorry to see the show go. "It was a fun show to do and I can appreciate it a lot more today. It was a good place to work and it was steady work. I would have been happy to keep going and would have rode that horse to death."

When the show was cancelled, Baer found himself with the inevitable typecasting problems and a lack of job offers. In 1974, he took matters into his own hands and wrote the script for a feature film, *Macon County Line*, on the back of an old *Beverly Hillbillies* script. He put in $110,000, which was all the money he had at the time, and a partner put in $127,000. Baer produced the movie and took a small role as a redneck Southern police deputy. It went on to make $25 million at the box office and $10.5 million in rentals. "That was all because of not being able to get any work as an actor in the three years after *The Beverly Hillbillies* was cancelled," he says. "It came out of frustration and the realization that if I wanted to get my career going again, I would have to do it myself."

He took the profits from *Macon County Line* and made more films, *The Wild McCullochs* in 1975, *Ode to Billy Joe* in 1976 and *Hometown U.S.A.* in 1979 — all of which he directed as well. Of the three films, *Ode to Billy Joe*, starring Robby Benson and Glynnis O'Connor, was the most success-ful. As an independent film-maker with a limited budget, Baer pioneered the idea of bringing brand marketing to the movie business. He bought the rights to a popular song title and had a script (by Herman Raucher) written around it. In making the song title the star and the draw, he was the first to use what has become a standard practice today. In his case, he took country singer Bobbie Gentry's haunting hit pop song and told the story behind the mysterious circumstances of why Billy Joe McAllister threw himself off the Talahatchie Bridge. Made for $1.1 million, the film made over $25 million at the box-office alone.

During the 1980s, Baer still acted, doing a few pilots such as a cop show called *The Asphalt Cowboy*. Mostly he tended to business and real estate interests but did some acting just to keep up his membership in the Screen Actors Guild. He played a Vietnam war vet on a two-parter of the private eye drama *Matt Houston*, and like all recognizable faces from past TV series, he also guest-starred in a couple of episodes of *Murder, She Wrote*.

These days, Baer is again involved with *The Beverly Hillbillies*. Uti-lizing his knowledge of brand marketing, he has bought various licensing rights to the show and is in the process of putting them on generic food products. "*The Beverly Hillbillies* has been shown on 61 countries all over the world and has been on television for the past 40 years— the name has world-wide recognition value. Now, if you were in a supermarket and had to choose between a generic product and a product of similar quality at the same price with the name *The Beverly Hillbillies* on it, what are you going to choose? People buy things they are comfortable with and *The Beverly Hillbillies* is something everyone has seen on television. Just the novelty aspect alone makes it a winner."

He also has a line of *Beverly Hillbillies* slot machines, each one fea-turing a different likeness of either Jed, Granny or Jethro. He plans to use the same brand-name appeal in opening a *Jethro's Beverly Hillbillies Man-sion and Casino* in Nevada. Plans call for a 240-foot-tall oil derrick emit-ting a 70-foot flame every 20 minutes. Inside will be an authentic recreation of the Clampetts' Beverly Hills mansion which will lead to a casino and Hillbillies-themed spin-off rooms—an All-You-Can-Et Buffet, Granny's Shotgun Wedding Chapel and a Cement Pond.

Since retiring from the acting side of show business, Baer has proven to the entertainment industry that unlike Jethro, he's no dummy and is, in fact, a sharp businessman.

However, there are a few undeniable similarities. When describing his business plans for *The Beverly Hillbillies* brand name, Baer takes on a Jethro-like enthusiastic zeal in selling the concept. More importantly, however, it must be noted that the interview for this book was conducted over an early-morning breakfast. A *big* breakfast.

Max Baer Jr. Credits

FILM CREDITS

1. *The Wild McCullochs;* 1975; Culver
2. *Macon County Line;* 1974; Deputy Reed Morgan
3. *A Time for Killing;* 1967; Sergeant Luther Liskell

TV CREDITS

1. *The Birdmen;* TV movie; 1971; Tanker
2. *The Beverly Hillbillies;* TV series; 1962–1971; Jethro Bodine

NOTABLE TV GUEST APPEARANCES

1. *Murder, She Wrote;* State Trooper Boone Willoughby; 2/10/1991
2. *Murder, She Wrote;* Johnny Wheeler; 10/29/1989
3. *Matt Houston;* 11/9/1985
4. *Matt Houston;* 11/2/1985
5. *Vacation Playhouse;* 9/9/1963
6. *Cheyenne;* 3/20/1961
7. *Cheyenne;* 2/27/1961
8. *77 Sunset Strip;* Luther Martell; 2/3/1961
9. *Maverick;* Ticket Taker; 12/4/1960
10. *Maverick;* Cowboy; 10/30/1960
11. *Maverick;* Brazos; 9/18/1960

Jim J. Bullock

Monroe Ficus on *Too Close for Comfort*

If "wackiness" is a marketable commodity in the world of sitcoms, Jim J. Bullock has cornered that particular market over the years. Introduced to television audiences as Ted Knight's own personal second banana, Monroe Ficus on *Too Close for Comfort*, Bullock later parlayed his national profile into becoming a regular on a revived syndicated version of *Hollywood Squares*. With his off-the-wall sensibility and over-the-top delivery, it was obvious to all that Bullock was the heir apparent of that show's late, great center-square, Paul Lynde.

Although he also played a third banana on the furry sitcom *ALF*, what confirmed Bullock's place in the pop-culture firmament was his participation in what is surely one of the bravest and most surreal bits of programming in television history — *The Jim J. and Tammy Faye Show*. It was a daily talk show hosted by the openly gay Bullock and former TV evangelist Tammy Faye Messner, best known for her overuse of mascara, the scandal that saw her first husband, Jim Bakker, end up behind bars, and her own considerable flair for wackiness.

Bullock's own greatest asset is his knack for unpredictability. Not too surprisingly, that's what landed him the role of Monroe on ABC-TV's *Too Close for Comfort*. Called in to audition before the show's producers and a roomful of network executives, the 25-year-old Bullock made an unforgettable impression. After being kept waiting for an hour to be called in, when he was finally summoned in to read for the part, Bullock impulsively stormed indignantly into the room of network suits, flung his script at the producers' feet, threw a hissy fit saying that he never should have been kept waiting so long and then stormed out of the audition.

Seconds later he returned on his hands and knees, asking their forgiveness and begging for the job. Everyone started laughing and Bullock got the job.

"Fortunately, *thank God* it worked for me because it so easily could have gone the other way," Bullock remarks. "It's not anything I would advise anyone to try. They could have thought I was crazy and just as easily called security. But — it was meant to be."

Undoubtedly it *was* meant to be. Although he was not a newcomer to Hollywood, prior to *Too Close for Comfort*, Bullock had absolutely no television experience. His previous work in Los Angeles had been as a stand-up comic — one who specialized in improvisation. His act was bound to attract attention because it involved Nancy Sinatra, a stuffed rabbit and giant go-go boots. A disembodied voice introduced it to the audience as "a tasteless unnatural example of *The Twilight Zone*."

That sounds like a far cry from the boy who originally intended to become an evangelistic singer. Although he once claimed to have been raised by "a group of musical nuns in a small abbey somewhere in Austria," the truth behind Bullock's upbringing in a strict Baptist household is a little more pedestrian — but seemingly just as unlikely.

Born February 5, 1955, in Casper, Wyoming, James Jackson Bullock's formative years were spent in the small west Texas town of Timber City before the family moved to Odessa, Texas, when he was in the ninth grade.

In high school he was drawn to the drama department, and it was in a school production of the musical *Bye Bye Birdie* that we can get a glimpse into Bullock's future. He played the part of Harry MacAfee, the role made famous on Broadway and on film by Paul Lynde.

"I imitated him completely," admits Bullock. "I used to do a really good Paul Lynde impersonation."

In fact, throughout his *Hollywood Squares* days, the comparison between the two glib, gay icons was inevitable. "It is kind of weird how our careers have sort of paralleled," says Bullock. "Growing up, I always found Paul Lynde to be so funny. He was such an original character, he truly was and he had always been one of my favorite actors. So, of course I'm always flattered by those comparisons."

As fate would have it, at the time of Bullock's debut in the Odessa production of *Birdie,* one of Lynde's former personal assistants had moved back to the area and caught the show. Bullock continues, "He called up Paul Lynde and said, 'You have to come and see this kid doing you — of all the impersonations I've ever seen, this kid has you down pat. You've got to come see this!'"

Unfortunately, Lynde was then taping *Hollywood Squares* in Las Vegas and couldn't get away. "But he did send an autographed picture to my high school and I think it is still hanging there to this day," says Bullock.

Although an appearance by his idol would have been the icing on the cake for the whole *Birdie* experience, just being in the production had already been a life-changing experience for Bullock.

"It is very clear to me when I was hit by the showbiz bug and it was in that high school production of *Bye Bye Birdie.* Something clicked inside me and I thought, 'This just fits *so* well.'"

At the time, however, he didn't take the idea of a career as an actor too seriously for a number of reasons. "Because of my religion and upbringing, I was led to believe that a career in show business wasn't a very Christian thing to do and I didn't feel I could serve the Lord properly by being an actor."

Nonetheless, just being on stage had an effect. He knew he could entertain, he liked the experience and since he was blessed with a strong baritone singing voice, he applied for and got a scholarship to the

Oklahoma Baptist University to major in music. His dream was to become an evangelistic singer.

Prior to this, in his senior high school years he had spent summer vacations touring with the religious singing groups The Continentals and The Brighter Day Singers. "It was very much like Up With People but it was more gospel-oriented — not gospel as you think of it today in that soulful way. This was Christian music but very sanitized and pasteurized."

It was at the Oklahoma university that he made the decision to become an actor. "I had gone there with the intention of becoming an evangelistic singer but in my second year I got into a production of *Godspell* and that was it! I knew in my heart what I had to do and so I left college at the end of that year."

Before leaving, however, he had confirmation of his talents by winning the Best Actor Award in the school's production of *A Midsummer Night's Dream*. He played Bottom.

"I went home and told my parents about my decision and they were just *shocked*. This was so alien to them to be coming from their son. I was the only son who had gone to college and they were really proud of me and my choice in life to go into the ministry. And now I was telling them that I was quitting school to go to Hollywood!

"My mother wasn't very happy about it but my Dad was more laid back and easy going. My mother had read something in the tabloids to the effect that at the time there were a million members in the Screen Actors Guild and only two percent of them were working.

"But those statistics didn't mean anything to me. You know — you're young, you're dumb and full of hopes and dreams and I didn't let any of those statistics hold me back. I just said, 'Well, that's just not going to apply to me.'

"It was like I was on a crusade. I knew I was given these talents and this was the avenue that I was obviously meant to go down."

On arriving in Los Angeles in 1977, the 22-year-old Bullock studied briefly at the Lee Strasberg Institute and then immediately started landing jobs "waiting on tables in restaurants."

"I came out here to be a *serious* actor," says Bullock. "So I stayed at the Strasberg Institute for a while but everything I did there was a comedy. It seemed that even if I tried a serious piece it would come out funny.

"But after being there a while and working in a restaurant — and *every* waiter in this town is a hopeful actor — I thought, 'You know what? I don't want to be like everybody else' and I started showcasing my singing.

"That was short-lived because the stand-up comedy thing came up. I was doing yet another production of *Godspell* out here and this agent, Jo

Ann King, saw me and I kind of owe my career to her. If it had not been for her, I would have never done stand-up—*ever*, ever ever done stand-up. She's the one who suggested and *forced* me to go into stand-up. Every day she would literally make me perform improvisations for her and she'd say, 'Write that down, that's good!'

"She took me by the hand to my audition on amateur night at the Improv and I got up on the stage and did my three minutes of I-don't-know-what but they liked it and I became a regular there and then began at the Comedy Store a week later."

In retrospect, the move to stand-up comedy seems only natural for the quick-witted Bullock. "Comedy was always a way of getting attention for me when I was a kid and I always knew I was funny," he explains. "So when Jo Ann suggested I go into stand-up, a part of me thought, 'Why not? This is what I've been doing all my life anyway.'

"But the idea of it also scared me. I'm just not a competitive person and she would take me around to the clubs to check out the other comics and later we'd go out for coffee and I'd say, 'Jo Ann, I can't do what these people do—Letterman and Leno, their jokes are clever and intelligent,' And she'd tell me, 'Well, that's not what you have to do. You just do whatever you do and it'll be funny because you're a *funny* person.'"

At the time, the late 1970s, largely due to the phenomenal success of Steve Martin and Robin Williams, everyone and their dog thought they had what it takes to be a stand-up comic and in Los Angeles they were a dime a dozen. Anyone would have to be quite "different" to stand out from the rest.

Bullock's act was certainly different. Even today, he describes it as "bizarre." The house lights would go down and as the theme music from *The Twilight Zone* was played, a Rod Serling imitator would introduce Bullock's act as "a perfectly tasteless, unnatural example of *The Twilight Zone.*" The music would then segue into Nancy Sinatra's *These Boots are Made for Walkin'* and the curtain would open to reveal the young baby-faced Bullock in a long blonde wig, a short mini-skirt, a pair of giant homemade go-go boots and lip-synching *Boots.*

"It was *stupid,*" Bullock admits. "But I was very funny and really unique at the time. And then I would go from that to doing the dying scene from *Romeo and Juliet* with a stuffed rabbit and I would make out with it and almost screw it onstage. It was really *weird* stuff."

Considering his own description of his act, we can see no reason to doubt him. Much of his act was also improvised. "I was very different because I was not a joke-teller. I was more improvisational. I would keep certain things in my act but to the audience it would look like I just came up with these things.

"A large part of my act was just kind of going off and taking a risk. The whole improv thing is so horrifying to me now and I don't know how I had the courage to do it because you either *are* on or you're not and there's no middle ground in between. You either killed or you totally died in front of them."

Bullock didn't have any trouble getting noticed. After a year, he was "discovered" at the Comedy Store by an ABC-TV talent scout and signed to a development deal. Bullock explains that although "I was *already* fully developed for my age," the development deal simply meant that ABC had exclusive rights to use him in any television property for which he might be appropriate.

During that year while signed to ABC, Bullock auditioned for the part of Monroe Ficus on Ted Knight's sitcom *Too Close for Comfort*. Originally the part was intended to be temporary. Monroe was to be a boyfriend of Lydia, one of the two daughters of Knight's character, Henry Rush. The producers were looking for a Woody Allen–type and told Bullock's agent that he was all wrong for the part, that he was too fat and too gay. "*I* didn't even know I was gay at the time but *whatever!*" says Bullock.

However, he lost 40 pounds and when the part still hadn't been cast three months later, the network insisted that the producers see him again — but this time at a network audition in front of a roomful of network executives.

"It was a network reading and they're terrifying to begin with," says Bullock as a way of explaining what was to follow. "I was terrified. I'd never been to a network reading before. It's not the same as reading for two or three producers. It's a roomful of 30 or 40 of the top brass *and* the show's producers.

"I was *so* nervous. And I don't think this was a conscious decision, I think it was the survival instinct — but I knew I had to break that ice because I had to go in and get comfortable somehow because it was such a tense situation for me.

"So that's what I did. It just came out of my mouth. They kept me waiting and waiting and so I walked in and walked up to the producers and in front of all these people from the entire network, I threw this fit and threw the script down on the floor and left and then I *immediately* came back in on my hands and knees and they all started laughing."

When he got home that day, his agent called to say that he had the job.

At the time of Bullock's audition, *Too Close for Comfort* was well into its first season. Before his arrival, the show revolved around Ted Knight's Henry Rush character and his problems as an over-protective dad coping with having his two independent college-age daughters living in the apartment above him and his wife Muriel, played by Nancy Dussault.

Originally, Bullock's character, Monroe Ficus, was only intended to be a two-episode role. However, the producers saw the instant chemistry between Bullock and Knight and the comic possibilities, and so the character kept turning up every couple of episodes until they finally signed Bullock as a regular near the end of that first season.

Monroe was one of those people who has the habit of turning the most minor of problems into big trouble and inadvertently involving everyone around him. Like many second bananas, being inept and incompetent were his strongest characteristics. Of course, all his troubles were the result of his good intentions. Needless to say, his chaotic life was a thorn in the side of organized, efficient and easily exasperated Henry Rush.

The addition of Bullock was just what the show needed. In fact, his character had a definite purpose — as a foil for Ted Knight. "Unbeknownst to me, Ted was ecstatic with what I brought to the show," says Bullock. "At the time, the show was in trouble because with Henry Rush, his brand of humor was sarcastic and you can't have him being mean to his daughters or wife. He needed a sounding board, someone for him to pick on for it to work."

If TV audiences could not relate to Henry Rush bullying his own family, they had no trouble understanding his impatience with Monroe Ficus, who just sort of followed one of his daughters home from school one day. "Monroe was a friend from school of Lydia Rush. She took pity on this puppy. He was like a lost puppy who just latched onto the Rush family."

Monroe was a lost soul, a bit of a naif — and according to Bullock, not terribly different from himself, a relative Hollywood neophyte. When he finally got his chance to read for the part at the infamous audition, Bullock honestly points out that "Monroe was not some ingenious concoction of my own. I just read the script and how I did it seemed to fit. I didn't sit there and think, 'How am I going to play this character?' It's just what happened, it's just the way I read it — sort of geeky and dorky. And it was very much how *I* was at that time in my life."

Bullock's youth and innocent nature played well on the show in his relationship with the star, Ted Knight — both on screen and off. If Henry Rush and Monroe were opposites, it was a similar situation between Knight and Bullock. "I was scared to death of him," admits Bullock.

"In the first script that I had, it was Monroe's Doctrine and it was a huge script for a guest star. It was like the major lead of that episode and whether that episode was successful or not all depended on who they hired as Monroe to pull it off. So I had all this wonderful stuff and wonderful business in that first episode and it was so funny for me and I was the star of it.

"But I had heard all these horror stories about *Laverne and Shirley* and how guest stars would come on and they'd have all this great funny stuff but by the end of the week, the two stars had vultured it and split it among themselves so basically it was just down to extra business for the guest actor.

"And I was afraid that Ted might be like that. So I went into that first reading just mortified of Ted — afraid that he would rip off all my funny stuff. Secondly, he was *Ted Knight!* Ted Baxter from *The Mary Tyler Moore Show* and I was just this little nobody from West Texas. And Ted was very good at instilling that fear and keeping that fear going. He made no bones about the fact that he was the star of the show and that he was the reason the show was a hit.

"He had quite an ego. There was a presence about him that was very intimidating and that really worked to the benefit of our on-screen relationship because Monroe was not only intimidated by Mr. Rush but Jim Bullock was intimidated by Ted Knight."

His initial fear of Knight also made for another unintentional contribution to the character by Bullock — Monroe's high voice. Bullock remembers that during his first week on the show, he was sick, but rather than let anyone know, he didn't say anything out of fear that Knight or another actor might insist that he not be allowed to stay on the set, spreading his germs around.

"I had a high fever, I was sweating and my voice went up in range. So on that first episode, my voice was high because I had a cold and it was all up in my head. I did not intentionally give Monroe that high voice but they loved it! From that moment on, it would drive me crazy when they would come up to me and say, 'Get your voice up, your energy is down!' My energy wasn't down, it was just that my voice had dropped back to its normal level which is normally really quite low."

Although his part was originally intended as a very limited run, Bullock ended up outlasting his co-stars on the show. By the fourth season the two daughters were gone from the storyline, and when the show's setting was changed and Henry and Muriel Rush moved from San Francisco to Marin County, Monroe made the move with them.

"About the forth season, they had Monroe renting a room upstairs in the Rushes' house and I moved in and was there constantly because they had a hard time justifying the fact that 'Hey, this guy must not have any life whatsoever, he's always over here!' So they moved me into the house.

"Neither of the girls were part of the show after it became *The Ted Knight Show* and was in syndication. By then it really was kind of Ted's and my show. I hope that doesn't sound too egotistical—I don't want to sound like a typical egomaniac actor insisting, 'It was *my* show!' but over the years, people talking about *Too Close for Comfort* will say to me, 'Oh, it was that show with you and Ted Knight.' Never have I heard anyone describe it as the show with the mother and two daughters. Everyone always remembers Ted Knight and Monroe when they think of the show and their relationship and the things that they got into."

The show came to an abrupt end with Knight's unexpected death due to cancer in 1986. Although the show was entering its sixth season, Knight's untimely demise probably only hastened the inevitable. With the change of setting and premise came new characters—particularly a new baby for Henry and Muriel in its last season. A sure sign that a sitcom is in trouble is when a middle aged couple have a baby in an attempt to revive ratings with a plot twist guaranteed to generate new storylines.

Following his six-year run on *Too Close*, Bullock had a big enough national profile to land a regular gig on a revived version of *Hollywood Squares*. The game show was the perfect vehicle for exploiting his naturally spontaneous personality and indulge his knack for improvisation. The new exposure gave TV audiences the chance to see a side of Bullock they could have only guessed at or seen briefly on the talk show circuit.

Considering his background in improv, *The New Hollywood Squares* was the best of both worlds for the former stand-up. "One of the best things about *Hollywood Squares* was the freedom they gave me. They trusted me and my instincts and the writers also wrote specifically for me. It's great when they know you and your kind of humor but they always said, 'If you think of something better, then go for it.'

"The beauty of that is—if the muses aren't with you that day or if you didn't have anything witty to come up with—and a lot of times you don't—then you had something already written right there in front of you that was clever. So you *always* looked good."

Bullock enjoyed the social aspect of *The New Hollywood Squares* so when he got a job on the sitcom *ALF* in 1989, he was surprised by the complete change in atmosphere on that set. Although it had been a genuine national phenomenon when it began, by the time they recruited Bullock for *ALF*, the show was on its last legs and that had taken its toll on the cast.

"Just going on that show from *Hollywood Squares*, which was absolutely such a party, to such a miserable group of people was a shock. On the breaks all I can remember is the sound of dressing-room doors slamming. No one hung out together, no one talked on the set, there was no camaraderie. It seemed like everybody hated everybody."

Still, at the time, he was thrilled to get the job. *ALF* had been a high-profile Top 10 network show. "I was ecstatic to be back on a network show. *Too Close for Comfort* had ended up as a syndicated show and *Hollywood Squares* was also syndicated. It's not that way today, but at the time, a network show was 'Hey, you've made it!' And syndication at that time was like, 'Oh, that's nice, you're working.'

"So just to get back on a network show was a big deal for me — and I fought for that part and my manager fought to get me that part."

The part was that of Neal Tanner, brother of Willie Tanner (played by Max Wright), head of the household and main caretaker of that furry alien life form known as ALF. Then in its fourth and final season, Bullock had the thankless job of playing third banana on a show where everyone else was getting tired of playing straight man to a smart-aleck in a puppet suit. If anything, Bullock fulfilled the same role as that new baby on *Too Close for Comfort*— something to inject new life into the storylines.

Brother Neal was a bit of a variation on Monroe Ficus in that he was one of those eager-to-please, guileless and overly dependent types. As the long-suffering Willie, Max Wright had for years been getting exasperated at ALF on a daily basis. Now, he had the unenviable eye-rolling task of dealing with his troublesome kid brother as well. Of course, Neal moved into the Tanner household. Structurally, it was a totally unnecessary addition to the show.

"I really wasn't right for that part," says Bullock today. "But I got it and then I came onto this set where they took what I brought to the table and said, 'Jim, just do it straight okay?' They really made me very plain and vanilla as far as what I felt I could have brought to the show, so I was very frustrated in that sense. I just blacked out that period. I was definitely serving time on *ALF*. But the show itself was very funny. It *worked!* It was so bizarre in the fact that it did work. It was very cleverly written."

In 1994, Bullock went to Canada and shot two seasons of a syndicated teen show called *Boogies Diner*. It was one of those "kidcoms" made from the same mold as *Saved by the Bell*. It was about a group of teens working in a mall and their wacky adventures as they play havoc on The Establishment, here represented by Bullock as a store manager.

On *Boogies Diner* Bullock found himself in the unlikely position of playing straight man to a bunch of second bananas. Here, he was the Ted Knight or Max Wright type and Bullock played the exasperation with high, manic energy. Unfortunately, he was working with kids, young actors, and to do high energy right you need strong characters and actors to react off of, something to ground that energy, and on *Boogies Diner* he didn't have that.

Taken for what it was—a show aimed at 12-year-olds—*Boogies Diner* was not a bad show. Says Bullock, "*Boogies Diner* came at a time when I really needed work. Just the same, I had a good experience with it."

In 1996 came another shot at his own show, this time co-starring with former TV evangelist Tammy Faye Bakker who with her disgraced husband, Jim Bakker, had been head of the *PTL* Network in the 1980s until fallen by sex and financial scandals. The *Jim J. and Tammy Faye Show* was one of the more surreal and original offerings ever to hit daytime television. Just like Bullock's being cast in *Bye Bye Birdie*, his audition for Monroe, and seeking out his natural birthright on *Hollywood Squares*, he was once again cast in a part he was born to play: a straight man to an off-the-wall, heavily mascaraed ultra-conservative who has become a gay icon.

When the producers came up with the idea of a talk show for Tammy Faye, they knew that a co-host was of vital importance. "They realized it had to be a co-host situation because just Tammy on her own would be … well, you know. She was used to *PTL* where there were no commercial breaks and they had to get someone in there who could reel her in," says Bullock.

Bullock was the only one considered for the job. The two did a screen test together and much to their surprise the show actually sold to the syndication market. However, once again, Bullock found himself working for producers who didn't know what to do with him. What was probably the most original talk show around became just another daytime gab-fest.

"It was so weird and frustrating because the company that bought the pilot knew what it was when they bought it and then tried to turn the show into something it wasn't. They tried to turn Tammy into Kathy Lee Gifford and me into Mike Berger. Why on earth would you pay for Jim Bullock and Tammy Faye and then try to turn it into the same show as everyone else? They destroyed the show by snuffing out the life of what the show could have been.

"I thought it was a wonderful message in that here are two people who truly are from two different worlds. I *came* from Tammy's world and I think that's why I worked with her and understood her so well. And my world is so different from hers but that didn't matter. I thought that was such a good message to put out.

"But they didn't do it like that and that was *the* most frustrating experience of my whole life. Every day was a struggle and every day was fighting for what you are and what's right for you. Tammy would come into my dressing room crying and it was horrible.

"When they fired her they told the press that she left on her own accord because of her husband's health problems but she didn't. They fired her and it was just really awful and unjust. I've never walked off a set in my life — but I did that day. The way they did it was so cruel and I love Tammy too much to sit around and see her be treated like that. She also found out the same day she had colon cancer."

Not too surprisingly, Bullock says, "We got a lot of hate mail — given Tammy's background and my sexuality, but it wasn't all like that. There was a huge amount of people who loved her. Tammy has a gift for drawing out people's sympathy and people sympathized with her. You watch her and you can't help but think, 'Oh, bless her little heart.' She's sort of like a child and you want to take care of her."

The producers replaced Tammy Faye with Ann Abernathy, a well-known Los Angeles television personality. It was a good move as far as Bullock was concerned because Abernathy was a seasoned professional at the talk show format. "With Tammy, it had gotten to the point where I had to be the straight man reeling her in. I had to be the one to worry about the timing and commercial breaks and the questions to ask. And really that's not *my* place. I should be the one who's left to go free and someone else should be the straight man. And Ann was completely competent at doing that and that allowed me the freedom to be funny again and let my mind go."

Still, without the marquee value of Tammy's name, the show lost its syndicated audience and so only lasted the one year.

Around this period, dampening Bullock's usually high spirits was the death of his lover of six years, John Casey, whom he had been caring for all this time. With his death, Bullock took some time off.

Bullock hasn't done much television since the talk show. He doesn't blame it on typecasting although to some extent that's always a problem. "There was a time when I definitely had become typecast as Monroe, but then *Hollywood Squares* came along and it allowed me to be myself and show people that I wasn't that character that I came off as on *Too Close for Comfort*. But I *still* fight typecasting. There are still people in the industry who still think of me as just Monroe, or as that funny guy on *Hollywood Squares* who really can't do anything else. But it's like, 'No, no— there are other things I can do if given the chance.' But that's all part of the business."

Since the talk show, Bullock has gone back to musical-comedy theatre. Even during his days on *Too Close for Comfort*, he kept involved in what could fairly be called his first love by directing a one-woman show which combined music and comedy, called *Outta Werk.*

In 1996, he had a major role in the Lost Angeles production of *End of the World Party,* a dramedy about gay issues in the late 1980s. "That play was really good for me because it gave me the opportunity to be funny but also have some moments of reality too. I wasn't just a character in it, I was a real person."

In 2000, Bullock won the award for Best Performance in a Musical for his work in Howard Crabtree's *When Pigs Fly.* In that 1999 production, Bullock sang three songs. In one he was dressed up as a vanity mirror, in another he was a near-sighted Cupid. But his third song was the show-stopping closer called "Laughing Matters."

"The good thing for me in that show was that *I* had the only serious number in the show. Normally I never get those parts, I usually get the character parts. 'Laughing Matters' is a really sweet song and very poignant with a lot of truth in it and that was my solo."

With his rekindled interest in musical theatre, you might suspect that, as it was when he was a kid, a Broadway musical would again be the ultimate goal. "That *was* my dream," Bullock laughs. "But the reality is that although it's a great dream to have, before this I had never had a major singing role in a show that's done eight times a week. It's a lot of work and it's all about your voice. After the show you have to go home and get some sleep. You can't go out and have some fun. It was like I had no life for five months. So being in *When Pigs Fly* gave me a whole new perspective on that Broadway musical fantasy. I want to enjoy my life and I wasn't enjoying my off-stage life too much while doing that play. And on Broadway the pressure is even worse."

Just the same, you know you can only half believe him when he says, "Right now, I don't really care to be in a Broadway musical." With typical Bullock irreverent aplomb he adds, "You know what? Just gimme a game show. I'm really fine with a game show."

Time to call those producers of *The New Hollywood Squares.*

Jim J. Bullock Credits

FILM CREDITS

1. *Circuit;* 2001
2. *Get Your Stuff;* 2000; Tom
3. *The Eyes of Tammy Faye;* 2000; Himself
4. *Lost and Found;* 1999; Jewelry Store Clerk

5. *Switch;* 1991; The Psychic
6. *Spaceballs;* 1978; Prince Valium
7. *Full Moon High;* 1981; Albert Flynn

TV CREDITS

1. *The Jim J. and Tammy Faye Show;* TV series; 1996; Host
2. *Boogies Diner;* TV series; 1994; Gerald
3. *ALF;* TV series; 1989–1990; Neal Tanner
4. *The New Hollywood Squares;* TV series; 1987–1989; regular; substitute host
5. *Too Close for Comfort;* TV series; 1980–1986; Monroe Ficus

NOTABLE TV GUEST APPEARANCES

1. *Duckman;* (voice); 5/21/1994
2. *Seinfeld;* Attendant; 11/25/1992
3. *Body Language;* Himself; 1984
4. *Hot Potato;* Panelist; 1984

Best Wishes
Art Carney

Art Carney

Ed Norton on *The Honeymooners*

"In the supporting cast, Art Carney almost runs away with the show.... Mr. Carney has the important gift of knowing when to throw away a line and of keeping his clowning always under control. He should have a bright future in TV."
— Television critic Jack Gould reviewing
The Morey Amsterdam Show,
New York Times, January 16, 1949

Art Carney went on to have a bright future not only in TV but on Broadway and in the movies as well. When *The Morey Amersterdam Show* was cancelled in October 1950, Carney had already hooked up with Jackie Gleason on *Cavalcade of Stars*. By this time he was already an established second banana, having served in that capacity for a number of stars such as Bert Lahr, Milton Berle, Edgar Bergen and Henry Morgan — as well as being the principal stooge for both Amsterdam and then Gleason.

In the fall of 1951, Gleason and his writers came up with a regular skit called *The Honeymooners* about a forever arguing married couple, Ralph and Alice Kramden. After the first sketch aired, they decided that Ralph needed a best friend and so was born sewer worker and upstairs neighbor Ed Norton. When Art Carney slapped that old felt hat onto his head and made the first of thousands of memorable entrances into the Kramdens' tenement apartment, his future was assured. His days as a supporting player would also soon be coming to an end.

Despite all the acclaim and accomplishments to follow in the years ahead, and due to the perpetually running syndicated reruns of the "Classic 39" episodes of *The Honeymooners* from the 1955 season, Carney will always be foremost remembered as Gleason's stooge. In fact, he was the first of the classic second bananas in sitcoms and his influence can still be seen today every time Kramer bursts into Jerry's apartment on *Seinfeld*. But at the time those *Honeymooners* episodes were filmed, Carney was technically still a second banana and supporting player — after all, it *was* Gleason's show. However, Carney often more than equaled Gleason in getting laughs on the show. The audience thought of them as a comedy team and critics compared them to others — Abbott and Costello and Laurel and Hardy.

Although Carney loved Ed Norton and always claimed that it was his favorite character, he also hated being thought of as only a second banana. As early as the days of doing skits on the Gleason show, he began denying that he was even a *comedian*. He started insisting that he was just an *actor*.

That may be true and his career has certainly borne that out. But in the late 1940s and early '50s, Art Carney was first and foremost a comedian. He even got his start in show business as a comic. Years later, his

Honeymooners co-star, Joyce (Trixie Norton) Randolph, would say of him, "I think he was just *born* to be in show business. He's a funny fellow."

Actually, most of Carney's family seemed to have been destined for the entertainment world. His eldest brother Jack went on to become a producer for *Arthur Godfrey's Talent Scouts*. Another brother, Ned, went into dentistry and according to Randolph had a reputation as being the funniest dentist in Manhattan. All of Carney's brothers were involved in the drama club throughout high school. Their father, a former newspaperman, worked for a bank in their hometown of Mount Vernon, New York, as the head of public relations. His kids nicknamed him "Civic Virtue" for his work in community events.

Art Carney was born November 4, 1918, in Mount Vernon, the youngest of six boys. The first inkling that Art had a comic touch for entertaining the public came in grade school when, going up to sharpen his pencil, he stopped and made an elaborate production of pulling out a handkerchief and pretending to blow the nose of a bust of Beethoven. The teacher was not amused — but the stunt cracked up his classmates.

While still in public school, young Carney won a talent contest by imitating the popular comic Ned Sparks. It was in A.B. Davis High School that Carney honed his skills at mimicry. He began working on teachers and friends. He got so good at imitating his five brothers that years later he would often phone home pretending to be one of his siblings and get them in trouble with their mother.

In a more public venue, he often performed at school dances and assemblies, knocking them dead with his impersonation of President Franklin Delano Roosevelt. His brother Ned, the dentist, had made him a pair of fake teeth and Art would put on a jacket and eyeglasses and use a long cigarette-holder as a prop. During his days in radio in New York during the 1940s, he made a large part of his living by exploiting his talent for impersonating F.D.R.

Carney once recalled that as a child he had always been "fascinated with actors and personalities who were in the public eye. I had this intuitive ability to mimic famous people. I would go to the newsreels to study the people who were making the headlines. I'd listen to the radio and study their voices. I didn't *really* do caricatures of famous people. I really zoomed in on them, getting voice mannerisms and inflections."[1]

At the age of 15, in 1933, Carney made his professional debut as an entertainer. "I fancied myself hot stuff as an impersonator," he later recalled for *TV Guide*. "When my brothers became fed up to the ears with my impersonations, they figured that a night before the critical eyes of Mount Vernon's Brother Elks would do me a world of good."[2]

It did — but not in the lesson in humility that his brothers had hoped. Despite what Art thought of his performance — a bad case of stage fright made his impersonation of football player Bronko Nagurski sound like a high-pitched girl — the Elks liked the show enough to invite him back again. Soon, other local civic clubs were asking him to perform. To flesh out his act, he expanded his repertoire to include Edward G. Robinson, Lionel Barrymore and radio comic Colonel Stoopnagle.

A newspaper notice for a performance at a 1936 civic club function noted that "Arthur W. Carney, one of the entertainers, will give impersonations and eccentric dancing."[3] Anyone who remembers the elastic contortions of a dancing Ed Norton can imagine what this "eccentric dancing" was like.

Carney graduated from high school in January 1937 after winning a second talent contest with his impersonations. He was also voted "Wittiest boy in class" by his classmates.

In a 1955 *TV Guide* article, "The Man in the Manhole," Carney said that his first big break came in 1937 when band leader Horace Heidt saw his Edward G. Robinson imitation at a performance before the Mount Vernon Rotarians. According to the article, when Heidt caught Carney's act, he was so impressed that he "took him along when he left town later that same night."[4]

A *TV Guide* from over a decade later gives a more accurate but less romanticized account. In the summer of 1937, Art's eldest brother Jack was working at the talent agency MCA and took Art to audition for band leader Heidt, who was looking for a comic-announcer for his touring big band. The impersonations were enough — "It was a pretty poor act but Horace liked it," Carney told the magazine in 1967.[5]

Horace Heidt's touring big band was as good a break as any kid just out of high school could expect. Although not too well remembered today, at the time, Horace Heidt and his Magical Knights were a very popular and well-respected outfit. Along with a couple of novelties like a blind xylophonist, the other band members included Frank DeVol (who would cap off his career years later as Happy Kyne, the house band leader on *Fernwood 2-Night*), guitarist Al Rey, pianist Frankie Carle and the King Sisters.

During his three years with Heidt, Carney's job was to do a "Battle of the Impersonators" with another company mimic each night. His takes on Lionel Barrymore and Edward G. Robinson were always popular but it was his self-penned imitations of politicians Al Smith and F.D.R. which brought him his first newspaper notices. The influential trade paper *Variety* noted on November 18, 1938, that Carney's political mimicry was "right on the nose and benefiting additionally by excellent material." One F.D.R. bit was about a make-work project to help the unemployment problem by moving the Atlantic Ocean into the Pacific Ocean by means of a nationwide bucket brigade.

Frank DeVol, a very funny man in his own right, recalled of the recent high school graduate that "Art was a funny, funny man who saw fun in so many things."[6] Carney was the youngest member of the troop and excelled at practical jokes.

In 1941, after three years of constant touring, Carney decided to break out on his own and try his luck as a nightclub comedian. He had earlier married his high school sweetheart, Jean Myers, and had wanted to settle down and start a family.

Carney had first started dating Jean in his senior year of high school. He later described their drawn-out courtship in the dry wit that typified his humor. "She made pretty good fried-egg sandwiches, and pretty soon I was dropping around to play duets with her father who was a concert pianist. Things rocked along like that for a while, and then one day I said to her: 'You know, I don't come around here just to play double piano with your father.'"[7]

A couple of months before his 22nd birthday, Carney married Jean on August 15, 1940. She traveled with the band until he decided to strike out on his own a few months later in early 1941.

Carney spent a couple of miserable years trying to make a living as a nightclub comic. He didn't like the freelance job and was often out of work. At one point, he and his wife had to move in with his in-laws and he began applying for work as a shipping clerk in the big New York department stores.

The world lost a shipping clerk on the day Carney's brother Jack, now with CBS radio, arranged a job as an actor for him at CBS, where he could put his political impersonations to work on *Report to the Nation,* a current events docu-drama which used actors to recreate events in the news.

Between 1942 and being drafted into the Army and sent overseas, Carney worked on a number of radio shows—soap operas, current events programs, crime dramas and children's shows on all the radio networks based in New York. His most notable and regular work was with *Gangbusters* and *March of Time.*

He even found the time to team up with an old Mount Vernon school friend, Larry Haines, who was also working in radio, and try to write a comedy series entitled *Bobo and Gigi* which they planned to pitch to the networks. Haines later told Carney's biographer, Michael Seth Starr, "It was just two guys, more or less the kind of character Art played on *The*

Honeymooners, but there were two of us. We were the same kind of nutsy guys based primarily on guys we knew as kids in Mount Vernon. We did this audition show and we kept breaking each other up; it never got off and we never finished it. But we both ad-libbed most of it. I think the whole recording was more us laughing at each other than the audience laughing at us."[8]

Before getting a chance to pursue a writing career, Carney was drafted and was shipped out to Normandy, France, on July 15, 1944. A month later, shortly after arriving, he was shot in the leg by a sniper and spent the remainder of his World War II days in a military hospital—first in England and then back in the States in Richmond, Virginia. The wound took nine months to heal and Carney was left with a permanent limp. Upon his discharge, he was awarded the Purple Heart for bravery. However, always the modest fellow, Carney summed up his brief wartime experience this way—"Never even fired a shot and maybe never really wanted to. I really cost the government money."[9]

Discharged in April 1945, Carney—now an established radio actor—had no trouble reviving his career in New York. He went back to doing the rounds of a variety of programs and proved so versatile in secondary roles that CBS signed him to an exclusive contract. It was the beginning of the second banana phase of Carney's career. He was teamed with people like Milton Berle, Bert Lahr and Edgar Bergen. He even worked as a stooge for Colonel Stoopnagle — one of his earliest subjects for impersonation back in high school.

"The Colonel was delighted to have me," Carney later told *TV Guide*. "The word had gone around that I was available—cheap." The Stoopnagle show featured a whimsical sort of wackiness—such as a revolving fishbowl for lazy fish. According to *TV Guide,* Carney and Stoopnagle often made up the whole show as they went along. "Sometimes it was terrible," Carney admitted.[10]

As for his work as a stooge, Carney said he would only work for people with whom he felt comfortable. Like he did when doing his preparation for his impersonations, first Carney would study the comic's style. "I observe his nature and his temperament and let them observe what I have to offer. If they like it, they buy it," he told one magazine during the early 1950s.[11]

One of his most popular bits as a second banana was a baseball act he did with Bert Lahr which they performed on a number of radio programs and later three times on Ed Sullivan's *Toast of the Town* alone. Carney described Lahr as "one of the old-school baggy-pants comedians—there aren't too many around these days."[12] But even though he credited

Lahr with being "a classic comic, a very great red-nosed clown," he also said that "Bert Lahr is a nervous worker, a very exacting guy."[13]

In fact, their baseball routine almost never happened. Carney explained how "Bert Lahr once hired me for a baseball sketch. I was a sports announcer interviewing him as a player. To me, the script was a perfect take-off on sports announcer Bill Stern and I read it that way, but Lahr didn't like it. He wanted the comedy to be broader. When I read it his way I didn't feel comfortable and told him I'd have to step out of the role. Finally, we compromised. Even if his original interpretation was right and mine was wrong, I still couldn't do it that way."[14]

He put the whole business of being a second banana in perspective when he said, "The stars always know that I'm not trying to top them. If they're capable, they know they have to have people around them who work well — people they can trust and rely on. I'm easy-going — not quick to make suggestions or blow up in rehearsal, although I never take a job if I have any doubts about the character being for me."[15]

At work was a specific sort of character which was gradually developing into an "Art Carney–type character"—a dense, uncomprehending dolt who would first show up on Morey Amsterdam's radio show, then Henry Morgan's show and finally burst out full-blown on *The Honeymooners* where Carney would define and polish the character for a number of years.

You can see a lot of Ed Norton in the character Carney played on *The Morey Amsterdam Show*—dimbulb Charlie the doorman, who later evolved into dimbulb Newton the waiter. The show began on radio and then made the jump to television shortly afterwards, giving Carney his first TV exposure. The show was hosted by Morey ("Yuk-a-puk") Amsterdam, a man of a million jokes and best known today as Buddy Sorell on *The Dick Van Dyke Show*. His show was a variety format set in the Golden Goose Café, a fictional Manhattan nightclub where musical acts would drop by and do a song or two. In between, Amsterdam would play his cello and banter with Carney's character or the equally vacuous cigarette girl who was played by the producer's wife, Jacqueline Susann.

Carney recalled his 1948 audition this way: "When I tried out for this job, I tried to impress Morey with my by-now slightly creaky impersonations. But he was not completely convulsed. 'Tell you what,' said Morey. 'I need a dumb doorman named Charlie. You look like just the fellow to me.'"

With that backhanded compliment, Carney got the role and played Charlie for a few months and when the show made the jump to television and later changed networks, the Golden Goose Café became the Silver

Swan and Charlie the doorman became Newton the waiter. However, the name change and a white towel which he kept draped over one arm was the extent of the change in his personality. As Newton, for the benefit of the new television audience, the tuxedo clad Carney slicked down his hair and parted it in the middle and wore a thick, dark, fake mustache.

In terms of personality, "goofy" pretty well sums up Newton. He responded to Amsterdam's steady barrage of one-liners with a moronic laugh. His catch-phrase, "Va-va-va-voom," was his way of describing a good-looking woman — accompanied with curving hand gestures. One early edition of *TV Guide* described Carney's va-va-va-voom as having "all the enthusiasm of a male seal greeting a female arctic explorer who used to have a featured spot at Leon and Eddies"—whatever that means.[16]

That article, entitled "Art Carney Rates as Top Comedy Stooge on TV," was a foreshadowing of the next few years to follow. It went on to say that Carney as Newton "is always good for his quota of laughs. And he comes to life without any of the standard tricks of the trade."[17]

During the same period, television critic Jack Gould pointed out Carney's natural scene-stealing abilities—"In the supporting cast, Art Carney almost runs away with the show. Playing the doorman at the nightclub, he has an excellent sense of timing and, if only by reason of his much greater height, practically overwhelms Mr. Amsterdam." This was the same review which went on to predict that Carney "should have a bright future in TV."[18]

As for Carney's scene stealing, Amsterdam was happy to oblige — as long as it made the show funny. Of his time on the show, Carney later said, "Morey Amsterdam taught me a lot about humor. Morey's a stand-up gag-man. He's not afraid to pass along a gag to another fellow. He's not afraid you're going to steal his act from him. The good ones aren't scared to let you have a laugh or two of your own."[19]

Despite Jack Gould's optimism about Carney's future in television, when *The Morey Amsterdam Show* was cancelled in October 1950, he went back to radio, again as a stooge — this time for the star of *The Henry Morgan Show.*

Carney first worked with Morgan in radio on *The Henry Morgan Show* on ABC in early 1950. It was a stock company where the regular characters were interviewed by Morgan, who would use his trademark sarcasm and acerbic wit. Carney's major character was The Athlete, someone as empty-headed as Newton the waiter. Whatever the skit, whichever athlete he was playing, Carney would preface all of his answers to the host's probing questions with, "That's right, Mr. Morgan." When Morgan made the jump to television in 1951, Carney returned along with the rest of the radio cast and did his Athlete character until the show ended a few months later.

While doing both *The Morey Amsterdam Show* and *The Henry Morgan Show,* Carney found additional work as resident stooge on yet another TV series. However, this was no mere few months' work. It resulted in an association which would last for as long as people owned television sets. A little-known comic named Jackie Gleason had been named host of a TV variety show called *Cavalcade of the Stars.* Carney was "borrowed" from the Amsterdam show one day to fill in on a sketch and that's when it all began.

In the sketch, Carney played a prim and proper advertising agency photographer who was shooting a whiskey ad featuring Gleason's "Man of Compunction" character, Reggie Van Gleason. The sketch was a take-off of Calvert Whiskey's advertisement featuring a Reggie-like "Man of Distinction." In demonstrating to Reggie the proper way to drink, both men get so totally drunk that Reggie ends up taking the photographer's picture. The skit went so well that Gleason hired Carney to come back the next week even though there was nothing written for him. From that point on Carney began appearing on *Cavalcade* on a weekly basis.

On October 5, 1951, the first *Honeymooners* skit was aired. Although Carney appeared in it at the end, it was not as Ed Norton. Gleason had wanted a running sketch which would be similar to the popular radio and TV series *The Bickersons,* about a combative married couple — she was always nagging and he was always criticizing. The result was *The Honeymooners* and it depicted the bleak lives of bus driver Ralph Kramden and his wife Alice, who spent her days in their sparsely furnished tenement apartment.

The first sketch involved an argument about making bread for dinner. Ralph inevitably throws a bag of flour out the window where it lands on a cop below walking his beat. The skit ends with Carney showing up at the Kramdens' door covered in flour.

Gleason decided that in order for *The Honeymooners* to become popular as a running feature, it would need more than just marital combat between the two characters. He and the writers decided to give Ralph a best friend in the form of an upstairs neighbor. Art Carney, who was already a *Cavalcade* regular cast member, was the obvious choice. Carney later said, "We invented Norton when Gleason was doing his *Cavalcade of the Stars* on the old Du Mont network. I became Norton, the one guy in the world who was even dumber than Ralph Kramden, the boob Gleason played."[20]

As Donna McCrohan, author of a couple of books about the show, pointed out in her book, *The Honeymooners' Lost Episodes,* "A contributing factor to the Kramden-Norton chemistry was certainly what Art Carney brought to the role. The writers had created an upstairs neighbor. But it was Carney who created Norton."[21]

That's the Norton that we are all familiar with from the "Classic 39" half-hour episodes which are forever running in syndication. But when *The Honeymooners* began as short four to 10 minute sketches on *Cavalcade,* the tone of the sketches was different. Compressed into only a few minutes of screen time, they were full of cynical, acerbic squabbling and slapstick pratfalls courtesy of Gleason and Carney and the humor was much broader.

Carney played Norton as broad as possible too at that time. He described his character his way: "Norton was a fifth cousin, once removed, to Charlie in Morey Amsterdam's show."[22] In later years, by the time they were doing the Classic 39, Norton was still dim, but more stupid in a naïve and innocent way, not just a one-dimensional dope as were Newton and Charlie.

The rough and tumble by-the-seat-of-your-pants sketch comedy of the early skits can be appreciated through this statement by Carney in 1955: "We used to get together and holler dialogue back and forth until we struck upon some lines that fit. Now we get some outside help, but we still kind of work our way through the chatter until the show falls together."[23]

When *Cavalcade of the Stars* made the jump from the Du Mont network to CBS in 1952, Carney decided to make the move with the show. Later Carney said that one of his main reasons for staying with the Gleason show was the free rein he was given to create Norton. "Of all the roles I played with him, and maybe of all the roles I ever played, Ed Norton was my favorite. I developed the costume and movements. I developed a lot of the character's attitudes. Norton was extroverted, where I'm shy, so it was great to get out of myself that way."[24]

Norton's standard uniform was also all Carney's idea. His choices give you an idea into his insight to the character. Of the white tee-shirt and pinstriped vest combination, he once remarked, "Did you ever see anything jerkier?"[25] As for the battered hat with which he would be forever identified, it was a felt hat which he had bought in his high school days. Carney once told columnist Earl Wilson, "It was the first felt hat I ever bought, it cost me five dollars and I haven't cleaned it since, not in 30 years. That hat is the only prop I still use. It still retains its shape."[26]

The hat wasn't the only part of Norton which had its origins in Carney's youth. He created one running gag on the show which he credited to his father. On the show, whenever Norton sat down at the table and took pen in hand to write something, he made a big production of it. In almost ritualistic fashion, he would studiously uncap the pen, put it down, adjust the piece of writing paper before him so that it was perfectly aligned in front of him, maybe move something on the table, pull his chair in better and shake his wrists a bit to loosen them up for the physical task at hand. Just as he was about to start writing, he would stop and pause and then start the process all over again. Ralph — who had been silently fuming and rolling his eyes in disbelief all through this — would finally explode and start yelling.

According to Carney, this whole routine was something he borrowed from his father, who would follow a similar routine whenever young Art brought home his report card to be signed. "He loved to move things around, my father. Like I'd bring him my report card and he couldn't just look at it and sign it. He had to lay it on the table and then he'd take out his glasses and clean the lenses and put the glasses on and move the report card up an inch further and then he'd adjust the salt and pepper shakers over there and he'd straighten his cuffs and take out his fat, long Waterman fountain pen and unscrew it and move around the sugar bowl and restore the salt shaker to its original position."[27]

What we don't know is if this was a genuine eccentricity of his father's — or if Dad Carney was simply dragging out his kid's agony. Young Art was not known for bringing home good report cards.

The other aspect of Norton which was all Carney's invention was that distinctive voice. Carney was a soft-spoken man by nature and Norton was anything but quiet. Carney himself described the voice as a cross between Marlon Brando and Slapsy Maxie Rosenbloom, a boxer-turned-comic-turned-nightclub-owner and all-round New York celebrity at the time.

But to those who worked with him, none of these things were known at the time. They weren't stories that he shared with his cast mates. According to Joyce Randolph, who played Norton's wife, Trixie, the cast was too busy working on the show to do much analyzing of their characters. Besides, she says, it just wasn't in Carney's nature. "Art did not talk to people. I'm sorry but Art did not talk much." Although he was friendly, she sums him up by saying, "Yes, he certainly is shy."

Unlike some actors, who, just before going into character will undergo a subtle bit of physical transformation in their posture and how they move and carry themselves, Joyce Randolph saw no such evidence in Carney's preparation. "I don't think he had to prepare a great deal. I never saw any preparation," she says. "But when he came through that door, he was Ed Norton."

Unlike many actors and their characters, there was not a lot of Ed Norton in Art Carney — just enough that Carney would let Norton come out. But there were certain of Carney's eccentricities and affectations in Norton. In her memoirs, *Love Alice: My Life as a Honeymooner,* Audrey Meadows, who played Alice Kramden, recalls a ritual which Carney performed every time they were about to go out and do the show live. She says that Carney would come into her dressing room, and not saying a word would go to her sink, turn on the faucet, bend over and flick water over both shoulders. He would then dry off his fingers and silently leave. Meadows thinks it has to do with superstitious rituals which actors can fall into — "Possibly he had a great audience response one night after he had gone through this ritual," she suggests.[28]

But more likely, it wasn't superstition or some personal eccentricity at all. It sounds a lot like Carney's own story about his own father's finger-play before signing his report card. Like that ritual, the one in Meadows' dressing room was probably meant to be just a performance for an audience of one. If nothing else, Meadows' story reminds us just how much of a physical comedian was Carney. As Norton, he was constantly in motion. He was unable to sit still for even a few seconds.

Carney was adept at broad slapstick — his tall, lean body made him a natural at pratfalls. He also incorporated his own little bits of business into Norton's body language — the finger-drumming, the elaborate hand gestures and just the ballet-like way he had of walking around a room, gracefully twirling from the refrigerator to the table.

Of course, Gleason himself was no slouch at physical comedy and the difference in their body sizes made the two men a perfect comedic team. In episodes like the one where they try to dance the mambo, just the sight of rotund and round Gleason rolling his hips is funny in itself. Combine that with Carney's limp and elastic dance contortions and you have a complementary team of comics — each funny in their own way, but dynamite together.

As Randolph says, "Art is a genius. He and Gleason were magic *together.* I don't think Gleason would have gotten as far as he did without Art. Art was just marvelous."

Carney himself probably summed it up best when he put it this way: "There was always a special chemistry between us. We brought out the best in each other."[29]

Gleason himself was well aware of how important Carney was to his success. In 1952, when he made the jump from the Du Mont network to CBS and changed the name from *Cavalcade of the Stars* to *The Jackie Gleason Show,* Gleason asked his regulars to join him. Their loyalty was well rewarded. Carney, who had been making $200 a week on *Cavalcade,* was enticed to join Gleason with a hefty raise. He was offered $750 a week and that was increased to $1000 shortly afterwards.

Gleason's gratitude was shown in other ways. Carney was given more sketch work and greater freedom in creating characters. As well, the part of Norton was beefed up on *The Honeymooners* segments. Previously, in the sketches, Norton was just used as comic relief, a few minutes of diversion from the running battle of wills in the Alice-Ralph stories. But by 1953, Carney's on-screen time was about equal to the star's. Gleason was also shrewd enough to realize Carney was good for the show. "Because he was very, very funny and the audience liked him, I wanted them to see him as much as possible," he said.[30]

Jack Philbin, a producer on the show, said that "Gleason loved Carney, and anything that Art wanted to do, he could, as far as the show was concerned. Their relationship was good that way. They weren't what I would say personal, intimate friends, but as an artist, Jackie admired Art greatly."[31]

For his part, Carney said, "Gleason knew that I wasn't out to upstage him or steal his thunder and he let me do and say anything I wanted to because he trusted me. That's the way it was and that's the way it always has been."[32]

Much has been written about Gleason's jealousy of Carney's laugh-getting skills and the affection the audience gave him. Yet a pure, undistilled example of what he truly thought of Carney's talents can be found in his reaction to a Carney ad-lib in the Bert Weedemeyer episode from the "Classic 39" season. Ralph and Norton have taken their wives for a coffee visit with Bert Weedemeyer, a newlywed co-worker of Ralph's from the bus company. When the actor playing Bert brings in the coffee, he accidentally bumps into the coffee table and spills the milk and coffee onto the floor. As if on cue, Carney pipes up, "Don't worry, the cat will get it."

Immediately, Gleason breaks up — and as if it was the funniest thing he ever heard, in character as Ralph, he repeats the witticism twice to Alice, howling with laughter the whole time until she fixes him with one of her I'm-not-amused glares. Both Meadows and Randolph stay in character throughout this impromptu bit of funny business, but Gleason's reaction is one of such genuine delight that you know he's responding not just as Ralph but as himself.

However, despite Gleason's professional respect for Carney's talents, his ego was too big to think of him as an equal and he hated when people called them a team or compared them to Laurel and Hardy. As far as Gleason was concerned, it was *his* show and that made him the Top Banana.

Joyce Randolph concurs with Gleason's status as "boss" even with his fellow actors. "Jackie ran everything," she says. "Everyone deferred to Jackie. He ran it all." On a more personal note, she reaffirms what two full-length biographies have already confirmed, "Mr. Gleason was not a really nice man and you never knew how he'd be on the day of the show. He could be wonderful and jolly or in a black Irish mood."

Carney himself told Gleason biographer William Henry, "He was the boss and I never said or did anything to challenge him as the boss and we got along fine."[33] With Gleason as Top Banana, that made Carney his stooge, a role that he didn't relish. "I always hated that second banana business and wanted to get away from it," he told Henry.

At the time, however, it was a role he was stuck with — and one which was bringing him praise. A piece on him in the *New York Times Magazine* on October 18, 1954, ran with the headline, "TV's Number 1 Second Comedian: Art Carney is to Jackie Gleason What Tonic is to Gin and Tonic." The headline to a May 23, 1954, article in *Pictorial Review* read, "TV's Most Contented Comedian: It's Not That Art Carney Lacks Ambition — He just Isn't the 'Top Banana' Type."

Perhaps the sub-headline to a May 28, 1955, article in *Televiewer Magazine* entitled "Carney's a Character" best sums up his own feelings about all this—"An actor first, then a comedian — Content to play 'secondary comic.'" In that article, Carney made pains to point out that he was not Norton, he was not even a comedian — he was an actor. "I figure myself as an actor. I'm an actor who has majored in comedy." He went on to say that he was proud that people actually believed that he was Norton — this meant he was doing his job in creating a believable character. His greatest asset as an actor, he thought, was his "ability to create and do different characters with Gleason. And Jackie's biggest talent is his ability to observe and capture the humor of any situation."

Still, during the Gleason years of the early 1950s, to the majority of the audience, Art Carney was a comedian. A March 8, 1954, article in *Newsweek* entitled "Art Carney Weighs In" focused on his laugh-getting abilities. "The comic's name is Art Carney and his growing gift has pushed him fast and loose to the top TV talent class. He has the talent of a scene-stealer, the talent of a natural comic with a face of pure rubber."

To increase his reputation as an actor and show people his range, Carney began appearing in other TV programs in roles vastly different from Ed Norton. His contract with Gleason allowed him to appear in two other shows every 13 weeks. On the advice of his agent, Bill McCaffrey, he began appearing in dramatic roles on television so that he would have more to choose from when the Gleason show eventually ended. Beginning in 1953, he began starring on anthology series like *Lux Video Theatre, Studio One, Kraft Television Theatre* and *Playhouse 90*.

By taking these steps early in his career, Carney proved that he was more than just a stooge and spared himself the typecasting problems which plague most second bananas.

Fortunately for Carney, he was able to appear in dramatic parts while still doing the Gleason show. If he had waited until after the show to prove his range it probably would have been too late — he would have already been identified too exclusively with the Norton character.

Another favorable factor was simply the time period. The early 1950s being the beginning years of television, there were not yet any preconceived notions as to typecasting. As well, the large number of dramatic anthology shows meant there were enough different roles available so that if an actor wanted to prove himself, he was given the chance. At that time, the opportunity was there for a well-known second banana to play a stooge on one comedy show one week and the next week to showcase his dramatic talents in a sober melodrama. This period did not last long and if *The Honeymooners* had debuted 10 years later, it is doubtful that the TV industry would have indulged Carney's dramatic acting ambitions when the show finally ended.

Luckily, this was not the case for Carney. When *The Jackie Gleason Show* was not picked up for the 1957–58 season, he went almost immediately to Broadway in *The Rope Dancers* — a serious look at alcoholism — and from that moment on, no one ever doubted that Art Carney was an *actor*, not just a comedian and certainly not just a TV stooge.

At the time, Carney summed up his career this way — "You know, I used to be a mimic. Then I was a comedian. Now I'm an actor. But, as an actor, I don't know how you could classify me. I'm not a 'method' man, I know that. And I don't think I'm Sir Henry Irving or Sir Herbert Beerbohm Tree. I think my friend and agent Bill McCaffrey hit it one day when I asked him what kind of an actor *he* thought I was. 'As an actor,' Bill said, 'you're a primitive — like Grandma Moses.'"[34]

For his time on *The Jackie Gleason Show,* Carney won his first Emmy Award on February 11, 1954, for Best Supporting Actor of 1953. He was up against an impressive list of supporting players — William Frawley from *I Love Lucy,* Tony Randall from *Mr. Peepers* and Carl Reiner from *Your Show of Shows.* Carney accepted the award with a Nortonesque "Who me?" That was the first of three consecutive Emmys for his work as a second banana. The next time he would win, it would be in 1959 for his work as the top banana in his own series of variety specials for NBC. *The Art Carney Specials* won the Emmy for Outstanding Program Achievement in the Field of Humor.

In the decade following the Gleason show's cancellation in 1957, Carney's career was predominantly highlighted by his work in theatre and on Broadway. After *The Rope Dancers*, he did long runs in *Take Her, She's Mine* in 1961 and was the original Felix opposite Walter Matthau as Oscar in the premiere run of Neil Simon's *The Odd Couple*.

However, despite his growing reputation as a serious dramatic actor, Carney always had a soft spot in his heart for Ed Norton and never turned down a chance to team up with Gleason for infrequent *Honeymooners* reunions. The first was as a guest star in 1962 on the debut episode of *Jackie Gleason and his American Scene Magazine*. In 1966, Carney again became a regular for the four-year run of a new *Jackie Gleason Show* broadcast live from Miami. Many of the one-hour shows were *Honeymooners* stories. But unlike the originals from the 1950s, which were mostly set solely in the Kramdens' tenement apartment, the new episodes were largely musical versions of reworked old scripts and often set in different locales around the world as bus driver Kramden and sewer worker Norton took their wives on European vacations. The unlikely premise wasn't helped by the fact that Audrey Meadows and Joyce Randolph had been replaced by the younger and more glamorous looking Sheila MacRae and Jane Kean as Alice and Trixie. One just has to look at these episodes to fully appreciate what a great contribution Randolph and particularly Meadows had made to the original *Honeymooners*.

However, the chemistry between Gleason and Carney was still there and this is what people tuned in to see. Whereas many of the old episodes were based on Ralph and Alice stories, the new versions concentrated on the misadventures of Ralph and Norton. For Carney, it was a chance to work again on what he called his favorite character.

In 1970, against his own better judgment, Carney was talked into doing a pilot based on Norton's work life in the sewer as a possible series for Gleason's production company. By all accounts it was a disaster. Carney had always said that he wouldn't want to be solely responsible for carrying a series and that a spin off of Norton would not be a good idea. "How many shows can you base around sewer jokes?" he once asked.[35]

When the first Gleason show ended in 1957, Carney was asked about his future plans. "I've been offered three series of my own, but I've turned them down. I'd rather be a second banana with a big show than carry the burden all by myself. I'd rather not have the full load of responsibility."[36]

However, for whatever reasons, some 13 years later he changed his mind. The pilot was to show Norton's life at work, away from Trixie and Ralph. Strong supporting character actors were brought in — veterans Al Lewis (from *The Munsters*), Phil Leeds (last seen as Judge Happy Boyle on

Ally McBeal) and a young Ron Carey (Officer Levitt from *Barney Miller*) were brought in. But the taping before a live audience didn't go well. It was obvious that Carney's heart just wasn't in it — and that was the end of the project.

It was probably just as well. The 1970s saw Carney return to long runs on Broadway in *The Prisoner of Second Avenue* in 1972. It also marked the beginning of a respected film career as a lead actor at the age of 56 for his Oscar-winning performance in *Harry and Tonto.* None of those accomplishments would have likely happened if a Norton TV series actually made it onto a prime time schedule.

For his part in the pilot debacle, it should be pointed out that Carney never aspired to be one of the world's top comics. He could have had his own series years before, but admits he "lacked that terrific drive to get to the top. Gleason is a natural. Gleason has in-born leadership qualities that I lack."[37]

Instead, he gradually built a career as a solid all-a-round actor by taking on a variety of roles over the years. As he said so many times since first gaining notice as Norton — he was an actor first, not a comic. *Honeymooners* writer A.J. Russell agreed. He told Carney's biographer, "It was always quite amazing to me that this guy was credited with the talent of a clown, because he was nothing of the sort. I believe Artie viewed the human condition and he responded to it. He knew people and he seemed to know what would make them laugh because he was empathetic to their faults and anything else that might have flawed their reputation."[38]

Carney also lacked an enormous ego like Gleason's — which may explain why he was better liked by his co-workers. It also suggests that he never knew how beloved his work as Norton was and how highly his performance was regarded by the audience and his own industry.

Joyce Randolph says, "I don't think Art had a tremendous ego. Years later when Art and Audrey and I were asked to participate in Comic Relief at Radio City Music Hall, the three of us walked out and the whole audience rose and gave us a standing ovation and he whispered to both of us, 'Geez, you'd think I was George C. Scott!' And so I said to him, 'You're *better.*' So you see, he doesn't have a tremendous ego."

Carney's influence can be seen today in a number of later second bananas, including the earlier mentioned Cosmo Kramer on *Seinfeld.* Actor Michael Richards not only has Carney's knack for physical comedy, but also his great sense of timing. All you have to do is look at a succession of slow, slack-jawed stooges from Maynard G. Krebs on *Dobie Gillis* to Screech on *Saved by the Bell* to see Carney's dimbulb influence.

However, Carney's greatest influence was on *The Honeymooners* itself. It is probably safe to say that without Art Carney, there would be no *Honeymooners*. Not to downplay Audrey Meadows' contribution as Alice, but as the series evolved, more storylines were devoted to the relationship of Ralph and Norton. Today, what people remember is the chemistry between Gleason and Carney. The most obvious sign of Carney's importance to the show is the fact that although Gleason later replaced Meadows and Randolph with younger versions of Alice and Trixie, not for a second would he ever consider casting a new Ed Norton.

Over the years much has been written about Gleason's jealousy of Carney's laugh-getting abilities and the affectionate applause with which he was greeted by the audience. This was surely often the case. However, there was one occasion when The Great One publicly thanked Carney and revealed how proud he was of his former sidekick. It was a few years after the first Gleason show had ended and Carney was doing a guest appearance on the debut episode of *Jackie Gleason's American Scene Magazine* in 1962.

After the show's final skit — one of the first *Honeymooners* reunions — Gleason came back out on stage to let the live audience know how grateful he was for Carney's support by appearing on the show.

"I want you to know how much of a kick it is for me to work with a guy like Art Carney. I've been in show business about 30 years now, and in all that time I've been appearing in shows all over the country, I have never worked with a comedian who has as great a comic sensitivity, as fine a delivery as Art Carney. And besides being a great comedian, he's also one of the finest dramatic actors I've ever seen. In other words, what I'm trying to say is, to me, Art Carney is one of the great performers in show business."[39]

It was a heartfelt and sincere public acknowledgement of how important Carney had been to his own show. It was a rare and uncharacteristic gesture for Gleason and one which he went out of his way to make.

Over the years, TV critic Jack Gould's 1949 prediction certainly came true. Carney had a bright future not only on TV but on the stage and then movies as well. Although he began as a comic, he became an actor. By nature a shy and modest man, nonetheless, he himself was aware of his talents and made no bones about leaving the second-banana roles behind long ago.

Carney put the whole thing in perspective and summed it up best in a 1967 interview in *TV Guide*. His Oscar win for *Harry and Tonto* was still a few years away and he had just reunited with Gleason for a new *Honeymooners* revival after a run on Broadway in the original *Odd Couple*. In typically succinct terms, Carney told the interviewer, "I'm not a stooge anymore. I used to be."[40]

Notes

1. *Art Carney: A Biography*; by Michael Seth Starr; Fromme Publishers; New York; 1997; page 13.
2. *TV Guide*; May 19, 1955; "The Man in the Manhole"; by Frank DeBlois.
3. *Art Carney: A Biography*; by Michael Seth Starr; page 19.
4. *TV Guide*; May 19, 1955; "The Man in the Manhole"; by Frank DeBlois.
5. TV Guide; January 14, 1967; "Carney on a Second Honeymoon"; by Ted Crail.
6. Art Carney: A Biography; by Michael Seth Starr; page 27.
7. *Ibid.*; page 18.
8. *Ibid.*; page 40.
9. *Ibid.*; page 41.
10. TV Guide; March 19, 1955.
11. Televiewer; May 28, 1955; "Carney's a Character"; by Evelyn Bigsby.
12. *Ibid.*
13. TV Guide; March 19, 1955.
14. Art Carney: A Biography; by Michael Seth Starr; page 46.
15. *Ibid.*; page 45.
16. Television Guide; "Art Carney Rates as Top Comedy Stooge on TV"; April 27, 1949.
17. *Ibid.*
18. New York Times; January 16; 1949.
19. TV Guide; March 19, 1955.
20. TV Guide; November 28, 1959; "A New Perspective for Art Carney."
21. The Honeymooners' Lost Episodes; by Donna McCrohan and Peter Crescenti; Workman Publishing; New York; 1986; page 153.
22. TV Guide; November 28, 1959.
23. Televiewer; May 28, 1955.
24. The Great One: The Life and Legend of Jackie Gleason; by William A. Henry III; Doubleday; New York; 1992; page 135.
25. Art Carney: A Biography; by Michael Seth Starr; page 68.
26. *Ibid.*; page 18.
27. *Ibid.*; page 12.
28. Love Alice: My Life as a Honeymooner; by Audrey Meadows; Crown Publishers; New York; 1994; page 198.
29. The Great One; by William Henry III; page 135.
30. The Honeymooners' Lost Episodes; by Donna McCrohan and Peter Crescenti; page 87.
31. Art Carney: A Biography; by Michael Seth Starr; page 64.
32. *Ibid.*; page 87.
33. The Great One; by William Henry III; page 135.

34. TV Guide; November 28, 1959.
35. Art Carney: A Biography; by Michael Seth Starr; page 163.
36. Art Carney: A Biography; by Michael Seth Starr; page 86.
37. TV Guide; January 14, 1967.
38. Art Carney: A Biography; by Michael Seth Starr; page 73.
39. *Ibid.*; page 120.
40. TV Guide; January 14, 1967.

Art Carney Credits

FILM CREDITS

1. *The Last Action Hero;* 1993; Frank
2. *The Emperor's New Clothes;* 1987
3. *Night Friend;* 1987; Monsieur O'Brien
4. *The Muppets Take Manhattan;* 1984; Bernard Crawford
5. *The Naked Face;* 1984; Morgens
6. *Firestarter;* 1984; Irv Manders
7. *Better Late Than Never;* 1982; Charley Dunbar
8. *St. Helens;* 1981; Harry Truman
9. *Take This Job and Shove It;* 1981; Charlie Pickett
10. *Defiance;* 1980; Abe
11. *Roadie;* 1980; Corpus C. Redfish
12. *Steel;* 1980; Pignose Moran
13. *Going in Style;* 1979; Al
14. *Ravengers;* 1979; Sergeant
15. *Sunburn;* 1979; Marcus
16. *Movie Movie;* 1978; Doctor Blaine/Doctor Bowers
17. *House Calls;* 1978; Dr. Amos Willoughby
18. *Scott Joplin;* 1977; John Stark
19. *The Late Show;* 1977; Ira Wells
20. *Won Ton Ton, the Dog Who Saved Hollywood;* 1976; J.J. Fromberg
21. *W.W. and the Dixie Dancekings;* 1975; Deacon John Wesley Gore
22. *Harry and Tonto;* 1974; Tonto
23. *A Guide for the Married Man;* 1967; Technical Adviser
24. *The Car That Became a Star;* 1965; (uncredited) Himself
25. *The Yellow Rolls-Royce;* 1965; Joey Friedlander

TV CREDITS

1. *Where Pigeons Go to Die;* TV movie; 1990
2. *Jackie Gleason: The Great One;* TV special; 1988; Guest Star
3. *The Cavanaughs;* TV mini-series; 1986; James "The Weasel" Cavanaugh
4. *Miracle of the Heart: A Boys Town Story;* TV movie; 1986; Father O'Halloran
5. *The Blue Yonder;* TV movie; 1985; Henry Coogan

6. *Izzy and Moe;* TV movie; 1985; Moe Smith
7. *The Undergrads;* TV movie; 1985; Mel Adler
8. *The Honeymooners: The Lost Episodes;* TV series; 1984; Ed Norton
9. *The Night They Saved Christmas;* TV movie; 1984; Santa Claus
10. *A Doctor's Story;* TV movie; 1984; Harry Wickes
11. *Terrible Joe Moran;* TV movie; 1984; Tony
12. *Bitter Harvest;* TV movie; 1981; Walter Peary
13. *Fighting Back;* TV movie; 1980; Art Rooney
14. *Alcatraz: The Whole Shocking Story;* TV movie; 1980; Robert Stroud
15. *Letters from Frank;* TV movie; 1979; Frank Miller
16. *You Can't Take it with You;* TV movie; 1979; Grandpa Martin
17. *Ringo;* TV movie; 1978
18. *The Star Wars Holiday Special;* TV special; 1978; Saundan
19. *Lanigan's Rabbi;* TV series; 1977; Police Chief Paul Lanigan
20. *Christman in Disneyland;* TV special; 1976; Gramps/Dr. Wunderbar
21. *Lanigan's Rabbi;* TV movie; 1976; Police Chief Paul Lanigan
22. *Katherine;* TV movie; 1975; Thornton Alman
23. *Death Scream;* TV movie; 1975; Mr. Jacobs
24. *The Snoop Sisters;* TV movie; 1972; Barney
25. *The Jackie Gleason Show;* TV series; 1966–1970; Ed Norton/Regular Performer
26. *That Was the Week That Was;* TV series; 1964; Himself
27. *A Day Like Today;* TV movie; 1964
28. *Art Carney Meets Peter the Wolf;* TV special; 1959; Himself
29. *Panama Hattie;* TV movie; 1958
30. *The Honeymooners;* TV series; 1955; Ed Norton
31. *The Jackie Gleason Show;* TV series; 1952—1957; Regular Performer
32. *Cavalcade of Stars;* TV series; 1950—1952; Ed Norton and various characters
33. *The Morey Amsterdam Show;* TV series; 1948; Charlie the Doorman/Newton, the waiter

NOTABLE TV GUEST APPEARANCES

1. *Fame;* Tim; 4/15/1982
2. *Alice;* Himself; 12/9/1979
3. *The Carol Burnett Show;* Himself; 1/4/1971
4. *The Virginian;* Skeet; 10/7/1970
5. *The Carol Burnett Show;* Himself; 2/19/1968
6. *The Carol Burnett Show;* Himself; 11/6/1967
8. *Jackie Gleason and His American Scene Magazine;* Ed Norton; 1/8/1966
9. *The Andy Williams Show;* 5/31/1965
10. *Jackie Gleason and His American Scene Magazine;* Narrator; 1/4/1964
11. *The Andy Williams Show;* 9/24/1963
12. *Jackie Gleason and His American Scene Magazine;* Ed Norton; 9/29/1962

13. *The Twilight Zone;* Henry Corwin; 12/23/1960
14. *Alfred Hitchcock Presents;* Cyril T. Jones; 11/23/1958
15. *Playhouse 90— Charley's Aunt;* 3/28/1957
16. *Suspense;* 4/20/1954
17. *Suspense;* 12/29/1953

Tim Conway

Ensign Charles Parker on *McHale's Navy*

52

Tim Conway has achieved what most of us only dream about — he's remained a big kid at heart. His style of comedy, even his approach to life show that this is a man who is still able to see life through a child's eyes. He also loves kids, he had six of his own, and his offbeat, harmless characters and sketches are all based on a child's foremost preoccupation — having fun.

Everything about Tim Conway, the man and the comedian, can be traced back to his childhood in small-town Ohio— where he was known as Tom. He was born Thomas Daniel Conway on December 15, 1933, in Willoughby, Ohio. His father, Dan, was an Irish immigrant. Sophie, his mother, was from Romania.

Being an only child, Conway never lacked for attention and he also had lots of opportunities to observe the mysteries of the adult world. He was lucky in that his parents were a constant source of amusement. "My father was Irish, so you couldn't tell him anything," recalls Conway. "As an example, he had a doorbell that he hooked up himself. But he hooked it up backwards, so that it rang all the time *except* when you pressed the doorbell. I told him that the wires were obviously crossed but he'd say, 'No, no. Leave it alone.' So we would sit around at night listening to this constant 'Bzzzzz …' and when it would stop, he'd say, 'I'll get it.'"

Conway says that this is the sort of thing that went on in the Conway home. He also tells how one time his mother got tired of hearing the sound of a new cuckoo-clock. Instead of just taking it down and losing a wall clock, his father's solution was to tape the door shut so the bird couldn't come out. On the hour you would hear the sound of the bird knocking on the door, trying to get out.

Shortly after Conway was born, the family moved to the wonderfully named Chagrin Falls, a small postcard town built around a picturesque little waterfall in the town center. "Chagrin Falls is an old Indian name," explains Conway. "The story is that the Indians were coming down the river in a canoe and as they approached the falls, they thought it was much bigger than it really was because of the noise it made. So they were very chagrined. And if you believe that, you would also believe the word 'falls' too."

It should be pointed out that with many of the things Conway says, they have to be taken with a small grain of salt. Although his anecdotes are all based on the truth, if he sees an opening for a joke, he can't help himself and he will go for it.

"It's a Tom Sawyerish type of town. It's *unique,* it really is. The main industry in town is a popcorn shop and that gives you an idea of just how industrial the whole town is," he adds.

Actually the town is so "unique" that the truth is stranger than Conway's memory. Well-known radio news commentator Paul Harvey did a report in 2000 about Chagrin Falls. It seems that for the last hundred years, every fall, the kids in town would slide down the biggest hill in Chagrin Falls on the bottom half of pumpkin shells. However, what made it into Harvey's newscast was the fact that due to a couple of youngsters being injured the previous year, the town passed a by-law so that a permit was needed in order to slide down a hill on a piece of pumpkin shell.

It all sounds exactly like the sort of town that could produce and nurture the mind of a Tim Conway. It also begs an obvious question and Conway is quick with his denial — "No, I have never slid down the hill on a half of a pumpkin."

Maybe there is just something about Ohio itself that makes people funny. Conway is just one of a disproportionate number of comedians who got there start in that state. Jack Riley, Fred Willard, Martin Mull, Pat McCormack and Kaye Ballard are all Ohio natives.

"There are a number of comedians who come out of Ohio — because nobody wants to stay in Ohio," Conway jokes. "I think it's the Midwest itself that makes us funny. We just seem to go for the simple humor. We seem to relate to people and things. We look at situations in a much funnier way than someone from Los Angeles or New York. They would try to make a situation a lot more sharp and chi-chi — like, 'Wouldn't it be a lot more funny if the guy was doing drugs?' And no, it wouldn't. We just look at folks walking down the street and try to have funny things match funny people."

Of course, Conway didn't even have to look out the window of his own house to see something funny. As he already pointed out, his father had an offbeat way of doing things. But he also did them for the amusement of his wife and son. "I thought my Dad was the smartest guy in the whole world," Conway has said. "He'd be driving down the street and look into the rear-view mirror and say, 'Isn't that a dime back there?' He'd back up and stop the car and get out and come back with a dime — and I thought he had amazing vision. It took me years to figure out that he would go out there and put a dime on the ground himself."[1]

Although he didn't figure it out till years later, it was a great lesson in comedy. The magic doesn't just happen. If you want to amuse your kid or entertain people, you have to do it all yourself. You make the effort. You secretly put the dime down so they'll look at you with awed wonder and disbelief. That's much like Conway's approach to comedy. He writes most of his own material and what he might do in rehearsals wasn't necessarily all of what he intended to do once the cameras were rolling. In that respect, he was certainly his father's son. Conway's relationship with his audience is such that he always puts the dime down but doesn't let us see him doing it. The setting up of the joke is as important as the payoff. And it was probably no accident that his father hooked up that doorbell backwards and then just left it that way. The deadpan poker face that Conway wore when doing the most absurd stunts on TV was undoubtedly inherited. "Yes, my father did have a sense of humor," Conway admits.

From his mother, he inherited a practical side. Not surprisingly, his thoughts of her are connected with memories of home.

"I didn't like Hollywood when we first came out here," confesses Conway. "I still don't particularly like Hollywood. I don't consider it my home. I consider Chagrin Falls to be home even though I haven't lived there in close to 40 years. But you always 'go home,'—that's where your life began so why wouldn't that be home?

"Anyway, my mother called me once when I was in my second year of *McHale's Navy*, and she said, 'You know, one of the Schutt boys is leaving the hardware store.' And I said, 'Yeah …?' And she said, 'Well, there's an opening. You know the other boys so if you could apply for that job it would probably be to your benefit.' And I said, 'You mean you want me to come home and work in the hardware store rather than do *McHale's Navy* on television?' And she said, 'Yes—because the hardware store is a much steadier job. At least you know where you're going to work in the morning and how long you're going to be there.' So my parents didn't take to the fact that show business was going to be a career."

From his mother, Conway inherited a strong sense of family values. It is reflected in the sort of career he has had and the sort of material he does—family-friendly, inoffensive, nothing that he wouldn't want his own children to see. Or his mom. In addition to learning practicality from his mother—again, in relying on himself for material instead of others—she also taught him how to knit and sew. Conway put his own twist on this skill, though, in his own unique way. He once made a suit with the same pattern as his wallpaper so that he could blend into the background and disappear. He also sews up the loudest, tackiest sports jackets he can imagine for when he and Harvey Korman go out to dine in Beverly Hills' fanciest restaurants.

Sophia Conway needn't have worried too much about her son going to Hollywood at too early an age. That was never a big goal and he says that he would have been happy just staying and working in Cleveland television and radio for all of his life.

While at Chagrin Falls High School, although he was the class clown on a consistent basis, Conway concentrated on sports and had hoped to become a physical education teacher. However, upon graduating in 1952, he enrolled at Bowling Green State University and figured that a career in radio and television was even easier than teaching gym and so he signed up for their radio and television broadcasting course. He also became a disc jockey on the college radio station, won a school talent contest and quickly established himself as the campus clown.

After graduating in 1956, Conway enlisted in the Army and was placed with the Eighth Army Assignment Team. His misadventures in the Armed Services made him uniquely qualified to play the inept and bumbling Ensign Charles Parker a few years later on *McHale's Navy*. While doing publicity for that show, Conway told one reporter, "I was stationed in Seattle in a section that was responsible for sending out troops as replacements to bases in the Far East. I was a private at the time but had to keep the books on all the shipments.

"In one month I lost 7,500 men but that was my worst month. In the average month I lost only about 1,500. Of course I had other troubles too. There was a time when a unit in Korea needed two cooks. Somehow they received 350 of them."[2]

Remarkably enough, even after all that, the VFI named Conway as Veteran of the Year in 1999.

When Conway's two-year tour of duty was over, he returned to Ohio and took the television and radio community in Cleveland by storm. He was first hired by radio station KYW, where he wrote comical material for the promotions department and jokes for DJ Big Wilson, the popular morning man. After six months he moved to WJW-TV where he was to direct the morning movie program, *Ernie's Place,* hosted by Ernie Anderson.

On those occasions when a guest didn't show up — and apparently that happened a lot — Conway would come out from the booth and fill in as a guest and do an overly serious impersonation of whatever whim struck him at the moment. Anderson would play it straight and they would improvise an interview on the spot. Although Anderson played straight man for Conway, it was definitely a connecting of two similar comic minds. Anderson would later become the horror movie host Ghoulardi.

Ernie's Place quickly became a local favorite. Conway recalls, "When Ernie Anderson and I first started, we sold our show to WJW as Ernie being talent and me being the director of the show. And Ernie didn't have that much talent and I'd never directed so the show really was … awful. We couldn't get anybody to be on the show as a guest so I would be the guest every morning. Ernie would introduce me as a bullfighter or trumpet player or whatever. And it just took off because people thought we were just screwing around — which we were. We had no idea what we were doing.

"It was *live* and it was instantaneous so people were *on* to that and they were on to the fact that there was no preparation at all for this show and that whatever we did was being created right at that moment."

In 1961, actress Rose Marie was in Cleveland promoting *The Dick Van Dyke Show*, and happened to be at WJW and witnessed Conway and Anderson in action. "She thought it was hysterical," says Conway. "But we told her, 'Well, we didn't intend it to be like that. We have no guest so we're just trying to save our lives and our jobs.'"

She took a tape back to California and showed it to Steve Allen, who quickly booked Conway as a regular on his Sunday night prime time show. The recently married Conway moved out West with his wife, Mary Ann. Since there was already a 'Tom Conway' in the Screen Actors Guild, upon Allen's advice, he dotted the 'o' and became Tim Conway.

Conway was a natural fit on *The Steve Allen Show* where improvisation and wackiness were nurtured and cultivated. He came with his own material and a favorite sketch featured Doug Hereford, a character he had created back in Cleveland. Hereford was a self-styled authority on a different subject every week. One week he might be the World's Greatest Fast Draw, the next time try to pass himself off as the World's Greatest Self-Defense Fighter. In typical Conway fashion, despite Doug's serious demeanor, it would soon become apparent that he was totally incompetent.

Unfortunately, the season that Conway joined the show was the year it was cancelled and so he packed up his bags and returned to the security of Cleveland television. In the meantime, producer Edward Montagne was casting *McHale's Navy*, and remembering Conway's work on *Steve Allen*, thought he would be perfect as the bumbling Ensign Chuck Parker character.

When offered the job, Conway turned it down. He wanted to stay in Cleveland. "I didn't want it. I didn't like it out here. But when I went back home and told my boss I wasn't going to take the job, he said, 'Oh yes, you are,' and he fired me. I never really wanted to come out here. I *liked* Cleveland."[3]

Luckily Conway had an understanding boss who realized what a golden opportunity this was and so forced him to take it. Now unemployed, Conway again headed West. It's just as well. Although he insists that he would have been happy spending the rest of his life in Cleveland, local television was changing and it wouldn't have been long before the freedom he had enjoyed on *Ernie's Place* would be a thing of the past.

He would return to Cleveland during his summer breaks from *McHale's Navy* and work at WJW just for something to do, but his

Cleveland days were now behind him. In retrospect, Conway realizes that had he stayed in Ohio he wouldn't have been as creatively satisfied as he was in California. "Had I stayed in Cleveland at the TV station, would I have still had that creative freedom we had on *Ernie's Place?*" he asks rhetorically.

"No. Because eventually people got in with computers and they decided that four-letter words were much funnier than *real* humor. And then there were restrictions that 'you can't do this and you can't do that.' And ratings and numbers and all that took away a lot of the fun of television.

"Television was a *lot* of fun when we first started. I mean, you did everything yourself. You went and got the props yourself, you created your material yourself. If there was anything that was going to be done on a show that was creative, you had to create it and get the props for it. It was *live* television, there was no room for mistakes. If you didn't get a laugh, you heard the air conditioner. So it was fun time, it really was and I don't think that fun still exists in television today."

Conway may have been having fun on Cleveland television and *The Steve Allen Show* introduced him to a national audience, but it was *McHale's Navy* which made him a star. Conway's talents were well suited for the show, which featured Ernest Borgnine as the title character and a group of comedians as his undisciplined "navy." On the first day of shooting, Borgnine told the cast, "When you walk through that door, leave your inhibitions behind."[4]

That was the kind of creative environment in which Conway thrived. During script readings, ad-libs were encouraged and often made their way into the script. As well, Conway points out that unlike most shows, director-producer Montagne did not mind if the actors strayed from the script during filming. Says Conway, "He was very susceptible to being spontaneous in whatever we did."

That being the case, there was a sense of manic energy on *McHale's Navy.* On a series where scripted mayhem ruled, Conway's pratfalls and slapstick seemed all the more authentic. Set in the South Pacific during World War II, Borgnine's Captain Quinton McHale character was a bit of a renegade and a hustler. He had been captain of a tramp steamer in the area before the war and he uses his connections to turn his small island base into a personal South Seas paradise. His men wear Hawaiian shirts and run a moonshine still. They steal supplies intended for the off-island officers' club at the central naval base and use them for their own parties where they entertain the local Polynesian girls and any willing WACs or nurses. Gambling, rum-based coconut drinks, luaus and water skiing are all part of the naval experience under McHale's command.

Except for those times that they go out on patrol looking for enemy Japanese submarines and battleships, you wouldn't even know that there was a war going on.

Joe Flynn played McHale's superior officer, Captain Wallace P. Binghampton. When the series began, he had planned on using the newly transferred Ensign Charles Parker as a spy to dig up enough dirt so that he can finally court-martial McHale and run his whole outfit of thieves and con men out of the Navy.

In the series' pilot, Parker was a stiff, by-the-books navy man. However, McHale and his men realize they won't have any trouble from Parker when his own service record comes to light. It turns out that he had rammed a U.S. Navy destroyer into the docks in San Diego and once called an air strike on a U.S. Marine Corps garbage dump. By the end of that first episode, wishy-washy Parker was one of McHale's boys. He still doesn't approve of McHale's methods and seeming lack of discipline, but it's obvious that no one bothers McHale because he sinks enemy warships and subs on a regular basis. Binghampton's plans are foiled again.

Conway played the Parker character as exactly the type who would have accidentally done more damage to his own side than the enemy. He was probably thinking of his own service background involving all those misplaced troops when he told of getting hired for the show. "They needed a fumbler, a guy who can't do anything right and they thought of me right away," he told one reporter.[5]

His portrayal of inept innocence would become a Conway trademark. Parker was like a big goofy adolescent — awkward, clumsy and nervous. But he was an innocent bungler. In fact, if not for all the trouble he inadvertently causes, he would be harmless. Conway says, "The essence of Chuck Parker was that he was a bumbling ensign who had no idea that he was bumbling nor did he have any idea that his authority was really being shunned by anybody he imposed it upon. He was a funny guy — but the Army and the service was very much like that.

"As a matter of fact, while *McHale's Navy* was on the air, the enlistment for the Navy improved immensely because people actually thought, 'Gee, if you can have that much fun, why not join the Navy?'"

Parker's saving grace was that he always meant well. He's eager to please but he tries too hard and that's what gets him in trouble. "The good-natured bumbler for years has been one of the most popular of all fictional persons in the movies and in novels," Conway has said. "You remember the funny colonel played by Paul Ford in *Teahouse of the August Moon* and also in Phil Silvers' *Sergeant Bilko*? And of course there's Jim Nabors in *Gomer Pyle*."[6]

However, what those shows didn't have was Joe Flynn as the superior officer. Captain Binghampton was the nemesis of both the wheeling and dealing McHale and the incompetent Parker. In fact, Parker was the reason for Binghampton's favorite expression, "I could just scream!"

Flynn was the perfect comic foil to play off Conway. As the long-suffering and irascible Binghampton, Flynn became a master of the slow burn — which would inevitably erupt at least once an episode into a full-blown hissy-fit. He was a man completely without patience and would blow up at the slightest provocation. At just the sight of Parker or McHale, he would start ticking like a time-bomb. A bit too wound up, Binghampton seemed genuinely incapable of enjoying life as long as Parker and McHale were still in the Navy.

Flynn was to work with Conway in a number of projects after *McHale's Navy*. They would reprise their old relationship — Flynn being the blustery, fastidious type to counter Conway's out-of-control bumbling. He was a Gale Gordon to Conway's slapstick Lucy.

Conway credits Flynn as being a seasoned professional comedian who knew how to work as a team. "*McHale's Navy* was the first time I worked with Joe Flynn and we just clicked right off the bat," he says. "Joe was a very, very, very humorous guy and we understood each other. It was much like working with Harvey Korman or Don Knotts. It's a delicate situation when you run into somebody who actually knows what you're going to do, how you're going to say it and knows how to react. And most importantly, knows when to *shut up*. Joe, Harvey, Don and myself, I think we all as schooled comedians know when to shut up and get out of the picture and let whatever's funny go on without interfering with it. That's what makes funny things funny."

A testament to the chemistry between them is the fact that *McHale's* producers made two feature-length films, and when Borgnine wasn't available for the second one, *McHale's Navy Joins the Air Force*, the movie starred the two supporting actors from the series and the plot focused on Conway and Binghampton.

It was Conway's first starring role in a movie and when *McHale's Navy* was cancelled in 1966, he was offered his first TV series as the star. In *Rango*, Conway reprised his portrayal of inept innocence. Set in the old West, Conway played the title character, a Texas Ranger. Being the son of the chief Ranger, Rango was assigned to Deep Wells, the quietest post in Texas, so that he could keep out of trouble. Instead, his incompetence and naiveté makes the post a magnet for the state's criminal element and Deep Wells sees an invasion of black hats. Guy Marks played Rango's corrupt Indian assistant, Pink Cloud, and Norman Alden played the frustrated superior officer.

Rango was a mid-season replacement which never did catch on and the ABC series only ran from January to June of 1967. Of the series, Conway says, "I have never been comfortable in situations where I am the star of the show. I would much rather be the second banana."

With that in mind, although his next situation comedy was called *The Tim Conway Show,* for that project, Conway again teamed up with Joe Flynn. "I had always enjoyed working with Joe and as a matter of fact, in coming up with the new show, I really wrote it *for* Joe and myself."

In the CBS series, Conway played Timothy "Spud" Barrett, the lone pilot in a one-plane airline charter service, Triple A — "the anywhere, anytime airline." Flynn played Herbert Kenwith, the company president who hates to fly. Since Spud Barrett was an airborne variation of Chuck Parker and his plane was a flying bucket of bolts, Flynn's fear of flying was understandable. The relationship between klutzy Spud and hot-tempered Kenwith was familiar to anyone who had seen *McHale's Navy.* The show was another mid-season replacement and only ran from January to June of 1970.

Surprisingly, when the sitcom *Tim Conway Show* was cancelled, CBS announced that Conway would be back in the fall on a variety show called *The Tim Conway Comedy Hour.* "Yeah, things seem to be going in my direction and I don't understand why," he said at the time. "They cancelled the half-hour show but I'm going to be doing an hour show next year so I suppose that is twice as good. I was only out of work about an hour."[7]

Still, he lamented the loss of the sitcom because, "I think the half-hour show had some of the funnier things Joe Flynn and I had done."[8]

Not everyone else agreed. Other than dismal ratings and poor reviews, CBS decided to move Conway from the sitcom format into the variety show because of the huge success of his first TV special, *The Tim Conway Hour,* which was aired midway through the run of the airplane series. The variety special included guests Joe Flynn as well as Conway's future collaborators Harvey Korman and Carol Burnett.

Conway credits CBS board chairman William S. Paley with the change in format. "I'm told Paley saw me on the TV special and wondered why I was doing one guy in a situation comedy when I could be doing six or seven guys in a variety hour," he later said.[9]

The move made Conway a top banana but also took him back to his comic roots, where he was given the chance to let his imagination run free. However, the variety show was to be another short run and only aired from September 20 to December 28, 1970.

"I think with the variety show that we were very much ahead of our time," says Conway. "For instance, we did our Christmas show in

September; I would come down from Comedy Heaven to welcome the audience. We only had one dancer so we had solo production numbers and instead of a band we had our announcer hum the opening theme song. If anything, it was *too* clever. Some of the sketches still hold up today. Some made it and some didn't. It's difficult to say what makes a show go and what doesn't — but it all seems to work out in the end.

"It was strange times in those days. Our ratings were in the '30s— which today would be an absolute phenomenal hit. But in those days it was kind of average. Hit shows were in the '40s or high '40s so you weren't given much time to prove yourself — although I was given several 13-week runs in succession to prove myself on a number of different shows."

It was around this time, after yet another cancellation, that Conway had special license plates made for his car which said, "13 WKS."

Having so much experience at being cancelled — and there would be more to come — Conway has always been philosophical about it and refuses to take it personally. When the airline sitcom was cancelled, he said, "That a show gets cancelled doesn't necessarily mean that it wasn't a good show. Look at Red Skelton. He had been on top for 19 years and was still in the top 10 when CBS dropped him. I don't understand. They take you off if you don't get the ratings and they take you off if you do get the ratings."[10]

In 1980, on the eve of launching another destined-to-be-a-13-week series, he rationalized that "I never looked at cancellations as failures. People in failed series who are commodities are always hired again. Remaining a commodity is what this business is all about. I approach it this way: some people are the 'pet rocks' of show business — a big splash and then they disappear. Other people remain commodities."[11]

That explains Conway's longevity on television. At last count, he had starred in six series which only ran 13 weeks — or less. As he said on another occasion, it's all a matter of economics. "This business is like any other business. As long as you're valuable to somebody or are saleable to a network and can make a profit for them, you'll continue to work."[12]

He then went on to speculate on his own success on television. "I've always tried never to be restricted to one kind of character or one kind of comedy, and to be very broad. So consequently, I can fit into a lot of pigeon holes. And when those pigeons jump out of those holes, I jump in."[13]

As his license plate suggests, Conway has kept his sense of humor about the whole business of cancellation. His healthy attitude is reflected in this conversation with *TV Guide*, "I've been cancelled in all kinds of styles. Usually I find out I'm unemployed by reading the papers. Once I heard about it from a lighting man. And when I was doing *Rango*, a network executive walked into my dressing room and said, 'Don't do this anymore.' I swear those were his exact words. 'Don't do this anymore.'"[14]

Regardless of the success or failure of the first Tim Conway variety show, it was that show and his experience in performing and writing for *Hollywood Palace* in the mid-sixties that led to Conway's long association with *The Carol Burnett Show*, the longest-running of all the TV shows in which he was involved. His years on the *Burnett Show* were probably the creative highlight of his career. Since the variety series began in 1967, Conway had been a frequent guest but didn't officially join the cast until the show's seventh season in 1975.

In typically modest Conway fashion, he explains that the gig on the *Burnett Show* was just like all the other breaks in his career and came about through coincidence. "It's all been circumstance," he says. "Rose Marie coming through Cleveland was circumstance and then Steve Allen seeing the tapes; the producer of *McHale's Navy* seeing *Steve Allen;* and then Joe Hamilton, who was Carol Burnett's husband and the producer of her show, remembering some of the things I did on *Hollywood Palace* and inviting me to do *The Carol Burnett Show*—all circumstance. I started out doing three *Burnett* shows a year. Then six, then 10 a year. Then 21 a year. But it was 21 out of the 22 they did per season. I didn't want to be a regular."

Conway felt at home on the show because it was a style of comedy close to his own. "We on the *Burnett Show* were the silly gang," he says. "We never offended anybody, it was a kind show. It was just *fun* for fun's sake. We enjoyed it and so the audience enjoyed it. It was like the early Jackie Gleason years where you were really watching a funny situation with funny people."

Without the added pressure of being the star of the show, Conway could relax. As one of the show's writers, he was also given free rein to let his imagination run wild. "I had a tremendous opportunity to write on the *Carol Burnett Show* because first of all, I'm a very fast writer," he says. "With sketches, I was the fastest gun in town and could write a sketch in 20 minutes to an hour. I consider myself very lucky in that I *can* write material and most of the material I've done along the way has been written by me. I don't like to depend on somebody else and do what *they* think is funny. I have the opportunity to write my own stuff and do it in a way that *I* think is funny."

The Carol Burnett Show also gave Conway a chance to indulge himself in being spontaneous and improvising. One of his most famous sketches is one in which he went on a three-minute extended ad-lib about elephants—all from hearing the word "circus." The spontaneous bit included lines like, "They were Siamese elephants, joined at the trunk.

One sneezed and blew their heads off. They had to be buried in adjoining piano crates." Throughout, the rest of the cast tried unsuccessfully to keep a straight face.

Ad-libbing was encouraged and the cast would often expand upon the scripts they were given. But what Conway did in rehearsal wasn't necessarily what he would do when they were in front of the studio audience and one of the show's trademarks would be Harvey Korman inevitably losing control and cracking up with laughter during *any* sketch he was in with Conway. One of their classic skits is where Conway is a dentist and Korman plays his patient when much to Korman's surprise, the dentist accidentally stabs himself with a needle filled with Novocain. As Conway improvises the rest of the sketch, Korman is trapped in the dentist chair and helpless.

The creative freedom on the show and the chance to create his own characters also gave Conway an opportunity to show his range — not just the poker-faced bumbler which had always been his specialty. On the *Burnett Show,* he came up with a number of more diverse characters such as Mr. Tudball, who was the frustrated Swede businessman whose assistant was Burnett as the dim-witted Mrs. Wiggins. Another character was the little old man who did everything painfully slowly. In one skit, Conway had him fall down a flight of stairs, but using Conway-logic, the old man tumbled down the stairs in slow motion.

During his association with *The Carol Burnett Show,* Conway won three Emmy Awards for Best Supporting Actor in a Comedy Series for 1973, '77 and '78. He was also nominated for the award in 1974, '75 and '76. In his humble fashion, Conway says, "I think the reason I won most of my Emmys was because they were more interested in my acceptance speech because I never had anything to do with earning an Emmy or anything else. The first time I got one, I thanked everyone at the Tarzana Pitch n' Putt and recommended that if people wanted a nice evening it would be to go there and play some miniature golf."

Modesty aside, Conway's appearances at the Emmy Awards truly were highly anticipated. One year, both he and Korman were up for the supporting actor in a comedy award for their work on the *Burnett Show.* When Korman was announced as the winner, Conway followed him up to the dais and stood at his side, looking at him expectantly throughout Korman's acceptance speech.

Although the entertainment industry had very early on decided that Conway was indeed a star and a Top Banana, as far as he was concerned, he was a second banana — and proud of it. When once asked about his years on the *Burnett Show,* Conway embraced the label. "I really don't mind the term 'second banana.' I love it," he insisted and then added, "I would be satisfied to be Number 27 in comedy for the rest of my life."[15]

Even when he was promoting his 1983 TV series, *Ace Crawford, Private Eye,* in which he played the title character, Conway still downplayed the top billing. "My comedy works best in support, whether it's support of the show or the star. I never felt comfortable being the star."[16]

From his own experience, Conway knew the importance of the role of the second banana in creating comedy. He once explained it using a sports analogy. "With second bananas, we're like George Blandu, the quarterback. He knew the game thoroughly and just how to throw the ball to make a touchdown. A coach could tell him we need two field goals and a touchdown to win and he could go in and pull it off. That's what we're like in comedy. We know how to play the game without stepping on the star. We get off the bench and put on the frog outfit and go in and make people laugh. We give the star and the show support."[17]

Accordingly, when Conway got another variety series shortly after the end of *The Carol Burnett Show* in 1979, he surrounded himself with strong support both in front of and behind the camera. The supporting cast included comedienne Miriam Flynn, Jack Riley, his old friend from Cleveland radio, and Harvey Korman. The show was produced by Joe Hamilton from the *Burnett Show.* As such, the CBS series had a similar feel with the other show, particularly when Burnett and others from the old show made guest appearances and revived old characters.

On his first variety show from a decade earlier, Sally Struthers was the lone dancer and had to perform all the big production numbers solo. But on the new show, they had a big enough budget to hire The Don Crichton Dancers. In a Conway-like twist, however, all the dancers were kids between the ages of eight and 13.

There was also a twist in how the network judged the show's success. It was an inverse situation to that of Conway's previous variety show. In that case, he started off with *The Tim Conway Show* — the sitcom co-starring Joe Flynn in 1970. That show wasn't a big hit so the network dumped it — but gave Conway an extra 30 minutes of air time to do his variety show, *The Tim Conway Comedy Hour.* However, with his second variety series, *The Tim Conway Show* in 1980, he started off with an hour and then the next season, the network cut the show back to half an hour. At the time, Conway joked, "It's a new kind of gradual cancellation plan. Next year we'll do 15 minutes, then 7 and-a-half."[18]

The scaled-back show was obviously not a vote of confidence by the network. However, it did last longer than the 13 weeks which inspired his license plates and it ran from March 23, 1980, to August 31, 1981.

On the other hand, his next sitcom, *Ace Crawford, Private Eye*, didn't even make it to the 13-week mark. This spoof of the hard-boiled private detective genre only lasted from March 15 to April 12, 1980, before being cancelled by ABC.

A decade later, he would have similar bad luck with *Tim Conway's Funny America*. It was a *Candid Camera*–type show where Conway would use various disguises to pull jokes on unsuspecting people while a hidden camera filmed their response. It ran from July 29 to September 2, 1990, when ABC again pulled the plug.

Despite his lack of television success after *The Carol Burnett Show*, Conway had respectable box-office success in the films he made with Don Knotts. They had first teamed up in 1975 when Disney put them together as a couple of bumbling small-time crooks in *The Apple Dumpling Gang*. It was an inspired match. While promoting the movie, Conway told one reporter, "They threw us together and out came two Stan Laurels."[19]

Disney would reunite them for *Gus*, about a football-playing mule in 1976 and to reprise their roles again in *The Apple Dumpling Gang Rides Again* in 1979. The two men found their partnership so satisfying that they also teamed up for two Conway-penned films, *The Prizefighter* (1979) and *The Private Eyes* in 1980.

Both men consider their work together to be career highlights. For Conway, it was particularly rewarding. "*The Apple Dumpling Gang* was one of the best things I did I think because I had an opportunity to work with Don Knotts, who is probably the reason that I'm in this business," he says. "I used to watch him on the old *Steve Allen Show* with Louis Nye and Tom Poston doing their man-in-the-street interviews and I *liked* what those guys did on television and what they *did* to an audience. They made them genuinely laugh and crack up. They expressed themselves through facial expressions so that you knew exactly what they were thinking. They were three wonderful, marvelous unique characters and that was kind of what I was looking to do in my career."

Over his career, Conway has had three major collaborations—with Knotts, Joe Flynn and Harvey Korman. Each man brought something different to the partnership.

Of Joe Flynn, who died in 1974 at the age of 49, Conway says, "I think Joe Flynn and I probably would have gone on to do a few more things together had Joe stuck around for a little longer. I had always enjoyed working with him."

"As for Don Knotts and Harvey Korman, I think the difference between Harvey and Don is that Harvey is much more in tune with being a straight man than is Don. Don is really a first banana and I guess the others are second bananas. But all of them — Don, Harvey and Joe Flynn, are excellent comedians because they understand what comedy is all about and again — know when to shut up."

Throughout his career, Conway's approach to comedy has always been to trust his own instincts. "I am not qualified to do anything in show business," he says. "I never went to acting school or any school of that nature. I just had a funny bone and I guess I've just maintained that funny bone ever since I was born."

"The movies that I did with Don Knotts, *The Prizefighter* and *The Private Eyes*, were both written in less than two days— so as fast as I can type is as fast as I can write a movie. The only difficulty I had in writing those movies was that most of the dialogue went to Don because I've always thought that he was so funny and I knew that if I could direct the lines to Don, they would be delivered in a humorous way. Of course, then I ended up with a script that maybe only had four or five lines for myself so I'd have to go back and jot down a few for myself. I found it very easy to write those movies because I didn't spend a lot of time wondering, 'Is this funny?' I knew the characters. I knew what we could do and I knew how Don would react to certain lines that I had written."

The characters Conway wrote for himself in his movies were in the mold of his inept bumbler type. Again, it had to do with knowing what would work. "That kind of character will always win," he has said. "Those characters have always held up through comedy history, from Charlie Chaplin, Laurel and Hardy, Buster Keaton on down. They were all sympathetic characters, always the result of someone else's perpetration upon their well-being. If you have the sympathy of the audience, you're pretty much ahead. And if you don't really offend them, you can do just about anything."[20]

The trusting relationship with his audience has given Conway the freedom to work in his own unique fashion. "It's all pretty instinctual," he once explained. "I don't think I've ever spent much time trying to do something specific. Whatever I do is spontaneous because I don't like to be restricted in comedy or anything else. So whatever comes, comes."[21]

Although he's best known for playing these Ensign Parker–like bumblers, as he proved on *The Carol Burnett Show,* he's capable of creating far more diverse characters as well. That's how he came up with his Dorf character and then successfully sold a video series of comedy "how-to" tapes starring the short-legged, strange-looking Scandinavian to the direct-to-video market with titles like *Dorf on Golf, Dorf Goes Auto Racing* and *Dorf Goes Fishing.*

"With the Dorf character, that was a character who was created because people said that you can't make a tape like that, strictly for the home-consumption market, without the character having been established prior to that on television or movies *before* it was a video. So that was one of the inspirations. I love it when people say you can't do something and then you go out and do it and make it a success. But again, it was a matter of going out, having some fun and digging a couple of holes in a golf course and sticking my feet in there and acting silly."

Conway once reasoned that, "We're all 12 years old, really. We get bigger, wear different clothes but we never really get past 12. In this business we get to play dress up and do all the dumb things everyone really wants to do."[22]

Acting silly and feeling like a kid is what it is all about for Conway. He points out, "I *don't* want to do anything serious— unlike many other comics." His career has been shaped by his own childhood and when he began making movies, he chose the field of family films out of frustration that there was nothing out there that he could take his own children to see. So he made movies that he wouldn't be embarrassed to show his own children. For that matter, his TV characters, like the man-child Parker or Rango or Spud Barrett as well as his Disney-movie personas, were all the sort of goofy characters that a kid would love, and you have to wonder if he chose those roles as a way of amusing his own children.

Maintaining a childlike sense of wonder has been just as important as maintaining his sense of humor. He once told the story of making a lasting impression on one particular child. "I love playing with life. Once, a kid named Bobby wrote me a fan letter saying, 'If you're ever in St. Louis, please drop in.' It just happened I was going to St. Louis the next week. So when I got there, I drove to the kid's house, got out my suitcase and rang his doorbell. When he came to the door I said, 'Hi Bobby. You told me to drop in anytime, so I thought I'd stay for a week or so.' He was the most surprised kid you ever saw."[23]

Conway didn't have to do that. He went out of his way to give a kid a memory that would last a lifetime. It was a warm and generous gesture. It was also as inspired as his own father pulling the car over to the side of the road because he had "spotted" a dime back there.

Notes

1. *New York Daily News*; March 2, 1980; Marilyn Beck.
2. *New York Times*; June 30, 1963; "Conway Bungling for a Living"; by John P. Shanley.
3. *TV Guide*; November 1, 1980; "Who Me?"; by Robert MacKenzie.
4. *TV Guide*; May 30, 1964; "On the Set of McHale's Navy."

5. *New York Times*; June 30, 1963; "Conway Bungling for a Living"; by John Shanley.

6. *New York Daily News*; January 8, 1967.

7. TV Week; *The Houston Post*; March 21, 1970; "What Tim Conway Show?"; by Millie Budd.

8. *Ibid.*

9. *Current Biography*; "Tim Conway"; April 1981.

10. TV Week; *Houston Post*; March 21, 1970.

11. *New York Daily News*; March 2, 1980; Marilyn Beck.

12. *Cleveland Scene*; September 25, 1980; "Tim Conway Makes Cleveland Proud"; by Raj Bahadur.

13. *Cleveland Scene*; September 25, 1980.

14. *TV Guide*; November 1, 1980; "Who Me?"; by Robert MacKenzie.

15. *New York Daily News*; January 15, 1979.

16. *New York Daily News*; March 15, 1983; Kay Gardella.

17. *Ibid.*

18. *TV Guide*; November 1, 1980.

19. *New York Daily News*; July 4, 1975; Ann Guarino.

20. *Cleveland Scene*; September 25, 1980; "Tim Conway Makes Cleveland Proud"; by Raj Bahadur.

21. *Ibid.*

22. *TV Guide*; November 1, 1980; "Who Me?"; by Robert MacKenzie.

23. *Ibid.*

Tim Conway Credits

FILM CREDITS

1. *View From the Swing;* 2000; Henry
2. *O' Christmas Tree;* 1999; Squirrel
3. *Tim and Harvey in the Great Outdoors;* 1998; Himself
4. *Air Bud: Golden Receiver;* 1998; Fred Davis
5. *Speed 2: Cruise Control;* 1997; Mr. Kenter
6. *Dorf on the Diamond;* 1996; Dorf
7. *Dear God;* 1996; Herman Dooly
8. *Dorf Goes Fishing;* 1993; Dorf
9. *Dorf Goes Auto Racing;* 1990; Duessel Dorf
10. *Dorf and the First Games of Mount Olympus;* 1988; Dorf
11. *Dorf on Golf;* 1987; Dorf
12. *Dorf's Golf Bible;* 1987; Dorf
13. *The Longshot;* 1986; Dooley
14. *Cannonball Run II;* 1984; CHP Officer
15. *The Private Eyes;* 1980; Dr. Tart
16. *The Apple Dumpling Gang Rides Again;* 1979; Amos Tucker
17. *The Prize Fighter;* 1979; Bags
18. *The Billion Dollar Hobo;* 1978; Vernon Praiseworthy

19. *They Went That-A-Way and That-A-Way;* 1978; Dewey
20. *Gus;* 1976; Crankcase
21. *The Shaggy D.A.;* 1976; Tim
22. *The Apple Dumpling Gang;* 1975; Amos Tucker
23. *The World's Greatest Athlete;* 1973; Milo Jackson
24. *Star Spangled Salesman;* 1966
25. *McHale's Navy Joins the Air Force;* 1965; Lt. Charles Parker
26. *McHale's Navy;* 1964; Ensign Parker

TV CREDITS

1. *Disney's Hercules;* TV series; 1998; Griff
2. *The College of Comedy with Alan King;* TV series; 1997; Himself
3. *Tim Conway's Funny America;* TV series; 1990; Himself
4. *Walt Disney World Celebrity Circus;* TV special; 1987; Performer
5. *Circus of the Stars #9;* TV special; 1984; Himself
6. *Ace Crawford, Private Eye;* TV series; 1983; Ace Crawford
7. *The Tim Conway Show;* TV series; 1980–1981
8. *Carol Burnett and Friends;* TV series; 1977
9. *The Carol Burnett Show;* TV series; 1975–1979
10. *The Tim Conway Comedy Hour;* TV series; 1970
11. *The Tim Conway Show;* TV series; 1970; Spud Barrett
12. *Rango;* TV series; 1967; Rango
13. *McHale's Navy;* TV series; 1962–1966; Ensign Charles Parker
14. *The Steve Allen Show;* TV series; 1961; regular performer

NOTABLE TV GUEST APPEARANCES

1. *The Wild Thornberrys;* (voice) Zebra/Jackal; 11/29/1999
2. *Diagnosis Murder;* Tim Conrad; 9/23/1999
3. *Mad About You;* Clerk/Justice of the Peace; 5/24/1999
4. *Clueless;* Bob Huley; 11/24/1998
5. *Ellen;* Himself; 5/13/1998
6. *The Drew Carey Show;* Gus; 12/3/1997
7. *Suddenly Susan;* Mickey; 11/24/1997
8. *Touched By an Angel;* Freddie; 11/23/1997
9. *Cosby;* 5/12/1997
10. *The Simpsons;* Himself; 5/11/1997
11. *Diagnosis Murder;* Tim Conrad; 5/8/1997
12. *Coach;* Kenny Montague; 2/5/1997
13. *The Larry Sanders Show;* Himself; 1/8/1997
14. *Married ... With Children;* Ephraim Wanker; 5/26/1996
15. *Coach;* Kenny Montague; 2/6/1996
16. *Married ... With Children;* Ephraim Wanker; 12/10/1995
17. *Married ... With Children;* Ephraim Wanker; 12/3/1995
18. *Married ... With Children;* Ephraim Wanker; 9/17/1995
19. *Newhart;* Himself; 4/30/1990
20. *Turn-On;* Sketch Characters; 2/5/1969

Bill Daily

Roger Healey on *I Dream of Jeannie*;
Howard Borden on *The Bob Newhart Show*

71

Bill Daily is best known for his many years on television in supporting roles as fly-guys. First it was as space cadet Roger Healey on *I Dream of Jeannie* in the 1960s. During the '70s, he played Howard Borden on *The Bob Newhart Show*. There he was a navigator who always had his head in the clouds.

During the two-year lay over period between *Jeannie* and the Newhart show, Daily worked on a couple of television pilots. Both had the right stuff and if either of them had taken off, Daily might also be remembered as a very fine comic lead. Both projects were starring vehicles for Daily. One was produced by a couple of writers from *The Mary Tyler Moore Show*. The other project cast Daily as a Maxwell Smart–like secret agent. His partner was a chimp and despite how all that sounds it was actually one of the funniest shows ever captured on film.

Alas, nothing came of either project and today Daily is best known for his supporting work. On *Jeannie*, he was the somewhat goofy co-worker and best friend of fellow astronaut Tony Nelson. On *Bob Newhart*, he practically re-invented the wacky next-door neighbor role. For that contribution alone, Daily's place in television history should be assured.

Simply put, Bill Daily is a naturally funny man. Ironically, in the beginning, when he was getting his start in television, he was quite content to stay *behind* the camera. Daily began his career at the NBC-TV affiliate in Chicago in the late 1950s. He worked as a floor manager and later as news director. Singer Mike Douglas was doing a television show at the station called *Club 60* and Daily joined his staff as a writer. Douglas later recalled how Daily made the move from behind the scenes and into the limelight where he belonged. "He was always doing crazy things at meetings and finally somebody got the bright idea of putting him on the air. That was the start of it."[1]

After that, there was no stopping him. He did stand-up comedy, founded an improv group and moved with the Douglas show to Cleveland where he was discovered in 1963 by Steve Allen, who invited him to head west to Hollywood and join his show.

And so, in his early thirties, Daily began his second career. Prior to that, he had made his living as a jazz musician and had been playing professionally since he was 15. Born August 30, 1927, in Des Moines, Iowa, Daily was the only child of parents who separated while he was still a small boy. Raised by his mother, he had a lonely childhood while she was working and would usually come home from school to an empty apartment. He later reflected that the hard times contributed to his career as a comic. "You've got to be hungry to be a comedian," he said. "Ever hear of a rich kid who wanted to be a comic? We want to make people laugh so they'll love us and make up for a bad childhood — that's the story of most comics."[2]

At age 11, he and his mother moved to Chicago, where things didn't look any better. He was the only Irish kid in a lower-income Polish neighborhood and remembers being beaten up regularly on the way to school. Music became his refuge. He learned how to play the accordion and later the stand-up bass. He had been playing in strip joints since his mid-teens but while studying music at Lane Tech High School, he realized that he had what it took to go professional. After high school, he played stand-up bass in various jazz bands and eventually became a member of a trio called "Jack and the Beanstalks," which he describes as being "a little far out."[3]

He also occasionally played in big bands and it was while subbing with the Lester Lanin band as a vocalist that he learned two important things. One — he had the ability to make people laugh; and two, that no one pays attention to the lyrics while they're dancing. While he was singing "Stardust," every once is a while, he would throw in some obscene nonsense lyrics in perfect tempo with the band — and nobody noticed. Nobody that is, except for the other musicians. Says Daily, "Not a ripple from the dancers. But the guys in the band can hardly play. They're choking up with laughter. It was the first time I'd ever made people laugh. I said to myself, hey, man, how long has this been going on?"[4]

Daily's musical career continued in a somewhat informal manner when he was drafted in the early 1950s and sent to Korea. While serving in the artillery division, he teamed up with another soldier, Dick Cantino, who was a singer and accordion player. During their off-hours, the two would entertain the frontline troops, using the back of a truck for their stage.

Upon his discharge, Daily returned to Chicago. He had married his high school sweetheart, Patricia Anderson, in 1949. During the first few years of marriage, she had supported them by working as a secretary while Daily freelanced as a musician. On his return, the couple decided they wanted to have children and this meant that Daily needed a more reliable source of income. Almost on a whim he decided upon a career in the relatively new field of television. He later recalled, "I was nutty about Sid Caesar and I had some crazy idea I'd like to be a director on his show. Except I had no idea what a director did."[5]

Daily studied stage directing at the Goodman Theatre College in Chicago and got a job with the NBC television station after he graduated. Beginning as a floor manager, he worked his way up to the job of in-house director and directed everything from kids shows to the news. He also began writing for a daily talk-variety program called *Club 60* which first starred Dennis James and then singer Mike Douglas. Before long, Daily was performing on the show.

During this period, he also founded an improv comedy troupe called The Outgroup. It included actress Ann Elder and occasionally Jack Riley, who would sometimes come in as a substitute. He also began performing his own stand-up comedy act at a club called Small World. It was at this time that Daily became friends with another young Chicago comic named Bob Newhart who was also just beginning to make name for himself. "Bill and I worked very similarly and we'd lend each other material," Newhart later said. "He was just as funny then as he is now, in the same disarming way."[6]

When NBC moved *The Mike Douglas Show* to Cleveland, Daily went along as the show's director as well as a writer and performer. He had put in about 200 performances when Steve Allen appeared on the show in 1963. Allen did a quick appraisal of Daily's talents and invited him to come to California and become the announcer on his syndicated show. "He wasn't like Ed McMahon with Johnny Carson," Allen later explained. "He was always primarily a comedian with the facility to be funny extemporaneously. He doesn't need writers or a prepared routine. There was something special about Bill. It was obvious that at his creative center he had a grasp on what comedy was all about. He was funny naturally."[7]

Taking a job in Hollywood was a big challenge for Daily because he suffered from dyslexia. That's why he had gravitated to music and improvisational comedy. Throughout his career, memorizing scripts would be a problem for Daily. As the announcer on *The Steve Allen Show,* Daily also served as Allen's foil — which was fine with him because that was all ad-libbed and improvised on the spot. It was in announcing guests and performing in skits that he had to work harder.

Daily spent seven months with Allen. The exposure got him small parts on *Bewitched* and *The Farmer's Daughter*. He also did freelance work for an advertising agency, writing, performing and producing radio commercials. This work would supplement his income for a number of years.

His guest work on *Bewitched* led to an opportunity to audition for a part on another Screen Gems production, a new series called *I Dream of Jeannie*. When Daily filmed the pilot, he was just one of a group of astronauts and he only had one line of dialogue. The producers obviously liked what he did with that line because when the pilot was picked up as a series for NBC, Daily was brought back as the third banana.

However, legend has it that when Daily auditioned for the show, he played the part a bit too off-the-wall and the producers didn't think that was the right way to portray a NASA astronaut. Shortly afterwards, *Jeannie* creator-producer Sidney Sheldon met astronaut Alan Shepard — the one who played golf on the moon on the Apollo 14 mission — and he decided to give the part to Daily.

Daily was told that he had to be straight when playing Roger Healey the astronaut because he had to be taken seriously in that role if the character was to have any credibility. How he behaved away from his job was another story.

In actuality, Roger Healey is pretty well-grounded in comparison to someone like Howard Borden from *The Bob Newhart Show.* He did have a tendency to become discombobulated at times. But then, that was only natural under the circumstances. After all, Roger's predicament was that he, along with astronaut Tony Nelson (played by Larry Hagman), were the only two people who knew of the existence of Tony's own personal genie. A beautiful "Jeannie," no less. And one with a definite sense of mischief, as played by Barbara Eden.

It was often more responsibility than Roger could bear. Each episode revolved around some plot where Jeannie was about to be discovered and if that happened, both Roger and Tony would be thrown out of the space program. If Roger often seemed frazzled, it was because of all the desperation schemes they had to go through to dupe their nemesis, the ever-suspicious Dr. Bellows. The good doctor was a NASA psychiatrist who was convinced by a continuing series of Jeannie-induced bizarre, unexplainable happenings that both Roger and Tony were mentally unfit for duty.

As played by Hayden Rorke, Bellows was in the tradition of Joe Flynn from *McHale's Navy.* Like McHale's Captain Binghampton, Bellows was an officious, dour killjoy who despised the thought of anyone having any fun and that he had no control over the strange things that were going on. Midway through a typical episode of *Jeannie,* Bellows would do a double-take and say something like, "Major Nelson, why is there an elephant in your office?" Tony and Roger had to convince him that they had nothing to do with any imaginary elephants loose at NASA.

If Roger had been the master of the genie bottle, there is little doubt about how he would take advantage of the situation. In spite of his loyalty to Tony, Roger coveted his best friend's genie. Not that he wanted *her*—he was turned on by the thought of unlimited wish-fulfillment. On those rare occasions that he had access to Jeannie's powers, he impulsively wished for all manner of luxuries—expensive homes, fancy clothes, new cars and most importantly, his own harem of young nubile girls sitting poolside to wait on him hand and foot. Roger was a disciple of Hugh Hefner and Hef's philosophy of how to live The Good Life.

Roger fancied himself a swinger and surprisingly enough, he did quite well with the ladies. However, with his blatant superficiality, ordinary looks and his slightly goofy personality, most of Roger's luck with the ladies was due to his occupation as an astronaut. In the early '60s, astronauts were like rock stars today and *I Dream of Jeannie* made it clear that plenty of women were available. Unfortunately for Roger, most of them wanted Tony — the glamour boy of the space program — and so Roger was left with Tony's castoffs. Not that he minded.

On the final season of *Jeannie's* five-year run, Roger had a steady girlfriend. Tina was a sexy dumb blonde who seldom spoke and was played by a young Farrah Fawcett. What she was doing with Roger is anyone's guess. Maybe he was more of a skilled ladies' man than he is given credit. Or maybe Jeannie granted him one extra-special wish.

When *I Dream of Jeannie* ended its long run in 1970, Daily did his first feature film, *The Barefoot Executive,* a Disney family film starring Kurt Russell — and a chimp. Interestingly enough, in the film, which also featured Hayden Rorke, Daily played a navigator.

In 1971, Screen Gems, which had produced *Jeannie,* cast Daily as a secret agent in the pilot for *Inside O.U.T.,* a spy spoof. Daily played the lead and his partner was a trench coat–clad chimp. Despite how genuinely funny the show was, the show wasn't picked up to become a series. *Get Smart* had just gone off the air the year before after a long successful run and so the timing probably wasn't right for another spy parody.

It may have been just as well. The nature of situation comedies was changing. The fantasy and broad comedies of the 1960s were being replaced in the 1970s by more realistic fare played out by ensemble casts. One such show was *The Mary Tyler Moore Show.* In 1972, during the series' second season, an entire episode was written by MTM writer-producers Lorenzo Music and David Davis as a showcase for Daily as a possible spin off. It featured Daily as city councilman Pete Peterson. He was an enthusiastic, if not terribly bright rookie politician and his staff had their hands full in keeping his well-intentioned gaffes out of the news.

Although the proposed project never did become a series, things still worked out for Daily. When Music and Davis came up with the idea for *The Bob Newhart Show* for CBS, they created the character of Howard Borden specifically for him. You could say that Pete Peterson was the prototype for Howard in that both were innocent blunderers with no conception of how out of tune they were from the world around them.

Initially, the producers were concerned about having Daily back in a flight uniform just a couple of years after he had put away Roger Healey's astronaut uniform — especially since *I Dream of Jeannie* was already running in syndicated daily re-runs. However, they saw that Howard's somewhat spacey demeanor could be explained by the fact that he had a permanent case of jet lag. Howard was always either three hours behind or ahead of the rest of the world. As Davis put it, "The idea of a guy working on an airliner, always turned around by the clock, was too good to resist."[8]

The uniform and occupation were about the only things Howard Borden had in common with Roger Healey. As people, they were totally different. Roger had expensive tastes and didn't mind spending money; Howard was a freeloader. Roger considered himself a man of the world; Howard lived in his own little world. Roger was a swinging bachelor; Howard was a swinging divorced father. However, even though was popular with stewardesses, he had little luck in long-term relationships. His wife Lois had left him and even his finance, Bob Hartley's sister Ellen, moved away and never came back.

The biggest difference between the two men contains the key to how Daily played Howard. Whereas Roger was a bit of a schemer and if not a pessimist, at least a realist, Howard was an optimist who always saw the best in people and delighted in simple things. He was an innocent and in that way, he was almost like a child.

Bob Newhart had always insisted that he would never do a sitcom with kids but a big kid is exactly what he got in Howard Borden. It was unlike the kind of sitcom which Newhart detested, where the gullible father is constantly outsmarted by his kids. There was no danger of that with Howard Borden. This was one sitcom where the "child" wasn't smarter than the adults.

Howard was always next door visiting his neighbors, Bob and Emily Hartley. He was constantly showing up at dinner time, borrowing things and asking for their help. Other than navigating airliners, the only thing Howard really knew how to do for himself was iron. Not only did he do it so he would have freshly laundered uniforms for his job, but the main reason Howard ironed was because he found it therapeutic. He ironed when he was depressed. He ironed when he was happy. He took ironing seriously. Ironing and navigating is what made Howard a man.

Like a child, Howard wore his emotions on his sleeve and Daily thrived on this aspect of the character. "It's really a terrific part," he enthused at the time. "More dimensions than a casual viewer might suspect. I can go through 15 different emotions—and it all plays for me. It's no big part but it's a total gas."[9]

Daily's most obvious contributions to the character were things that Howard shared in common with Roger Healey. There was that loping "Bill Daily walk" that he used in almost every entrance. It's a carefree and jaunty stride with the arms swinging freely. There was that self-conscious, almost apologetic way of explaining things when he found himself in trouble, his hands fluttering all around his face.

His best invention for the character was how his expression perfectly conveyed the sense of jet lag. Howard had his head so up in the clouds that when someone said something that went right over his head, he didn't really notice. Daily showed this by using a blank poker face that was very slow in reacting and then combining that with impeccable timing. Like Newhart, he had always been a fan of Jack Benny and it showed in his brief scenes.

"Sometimes in one show I may have only two pages of dialogue," he explained. "I just run into the next-door apartment, do my gig, and run out again. But the words I get are key words. Crackle words. You better say them right. You can't misplace the rhythm of the words or the humor flies out the window. The rhythm, it's everything, man. Comedy is rhythm. Comedy is time."[10]

Daily's daft approach was possibly a matter of self-preservation. Howard Borden had a habit of taking things literally and quite often he would be given lines that coming from any other character would sound unbelievable and stupid. That Daily was able to carry them off is a tribute to the credibility he gave the character.

Bob Newhart's personal favorite moment on the series came in a scene where Daily gets the biggest laugh. It's a scene where Bob and Emily are being robbed in their own apartment. An armed robber has them stand with their hands up against the wall. Howard walks in, uninvited as usual, appraises the situation, yells out, "Don't worry, I'll help," and runs over and assumes the same position as the Hartleys, believing that they're trying to hold up the wall and keep it from falling down. It's an inspired moment and a perfect example how Howard's mind worked. Newhart likes the scene so much that 20 years later, he shows a film clip of it at his concert performances.

The Bob Newhart Show ended its six-year run in 1978 when Newhart decided that the show had runs its course and it was best to go out on a high note. Daily worked throughout the 1980s in supporting roles on short-lived series such as *Aloha Paradise*, a 1981 clone of *Fantasy Island*, and the 1983 detective spoof *Small & Frye*. In 1987, he joined *ALF* in the recurring role of Larry the psychiatrist. He is one of the few outsiders who know of alien ALF's existence — not unlike Daily's role on *I Dream of Jeannie*.

In 1988, Daily had his own starring role on a television series on the syndicated *Starting from Scratch*, which ran for one season. He played Dr. James Shepherd, a veterinarian whose office was in the back of his home. Again, he played a divorced father, but in this show, his ex-wife, Helen (played by Connie Stevens), who was always around, was the scatter-brained one.

Carrying his own show was a big step for Daily. He had always had problems with scripts and memorizing his lines. In sitcom director Alan Rafkin's autobiography, *Cue the Bunny on the Rainbow*, Rafkin complained that during his time on *I Dream of Jeannie*, if Daily had to perform a piece of dialogue that was more than two sentences long, it would take numerous takes before he got it right. Rafkin, who also directed Daily on *The Bob Newhart Show*, believed that Daily wasn't cut out to be an actor — although he acknowledged that the audience loved him.

On the Newhart show, Daily was famous for forgetting his lines. Newhart didn't mind. He got a kick out of standing there and watching Daily squirm as he went through the agony of trying to remember. The cast kidded him that he only knew how to pronounce seven words. Daily himself readily admits that he was a slow study and had problems memorizing his dialogue. "Words," he once complained during the show's run. "Man, sometimes I wish we could improvise, wing it."[11]

As it turns out, Daily had the last laugh. In the 1980s, he left Hollywood and moved to Albuquerque, New Mexico. He makes his living these days by directing and acting in local theatre productions. Without the luxury of having only a few lines of dialogue or being able to yell "Stop tape," he has finally been able to lick an old problem. These days, on stage, front and center, you can be sure that Daily knows his lines.

Notes

1. *TV Guide*; April 5, 1969; "I'll Never Make It as an Actor"; by Leslie Raddatz.
2. *TV Guide*; May 31, 1975; "Comedy and All That Jazz"; by Don Freeman.
3. *TV Guide*; April 5, 1969.
4. *TV Guide*; May 31, 1975.
5. *TV Guide*; May 31, 1975.
6. *TV Guide*; May 31, 1975.
7. *TV Guide*; May 31, 1975.
8. *TV Guide*; May 31, 1975.
9. *TV Guide*; May 31, 1975.
10. *TV Guide*; May 31, 1975.
11. *TV Guide*; May 31, 1975.

Bill Daily Credits

FILM CREDITS

1. *Alligator II: The Mutation*; 1991; Mayor Anderson
2. *The Barefoot Executive*; 1971; Navigator

TV CREDITS

1. *I Still Dream of Jeannie;* TV movie; 1991; Colonel Roger Healey
2. *Starting from Scratch;* TV series; 1988; Dr. James Shepherd
3. *ALF;* TV series; 1987–1990; Larry the Psychiatrist
4. *I Dream of Jeannie: 15 Years Later;* TV movie; 1985; Captain Roger Healey
5. *Small & Frye;* TV series; 1983; Dr. Hanratty
6. *Aloha Paradise;* TV series; 1981; Curtis Shea
7. *Valentine Magic on Love Island;* TV movie; 1980; Charles
8. *Rendezvous Hotel;* TV movie; 1979; Walter Grainger
9. *Murder at the Mardi Gras;* TV movie; 1977; Jack Murphy
10. *Match Game;* TV series; 1973–1979; panelist
11. *The Bob Newhart Show;* TV series; 1972–1978; Howard Borden
12. *Inside O.U.T.;* TV special; 1971
13. *In Name Only;* TV movie; 1969; Peter Garrity
14. *I Dream of Jeannie;* TV series; 1965–1970; Capt./Major Roger Healey

NOTABLE TV GUEST APPEARANCES

1. *Caroline in the City;* Doc; 12/15/1997
2. *George and Leo;* The Pilot; 11/3/1997
3. *Caroline in the City;* Doc; 5/6/1997
4. *Bob;* Vic Victor; 11/6/1992
5. *Newhart;* Sam Leary; 1/29/1990
6. *The Powers of Matthew Star;* 10/1/1982
7. *Newhart;* Howard Borden; 1982
8. *The Love Boat;* 11/17/1979
9. *The Love Boat;* 11/10/1979
10. *CHiPS;* Balford; 9/22/1979
11. *CHiPS;* Balford; 9/15/1979
12. *The Mary Tyler Moore Show;* Pete Peterson; 3/4/1972
13. *Bewitched;* Mr. Johnson; 12/23/1965

Ann B. Davis

Alice on *The Brady Bunch*;
"Schultzy" on *The Bob Cummings Show*

Here's the story of a funny lady.

Although she will always be remembered as Alice the maid on *The Brady Bunch,* before being cast on that show, Ann B. Davis had already won two Emmy Awards for her supporting role as the love-struck secretary Schultzy on *The Bob Cummings Show.* She was nominated four times during the series' five-year run during the mid–1950s.

When she was being considered for the *Cummings* show, Davis was competing against a small group of actresses which she calls "the funny ladies." They included Kathleen Freeman, Rose Marie and Nancy Kulp.

"We were always up for the same parts," says Davis. "They would never bring us in together for interviews but we ran into each other all the time. We were all great friends."

They would have to be. Although Davis got the job as Schultzy, the other "funny ladies" all ended up as semi-regulars on the series. Rose Marie played the brassy man-hungry type she later perfected on *The Dick Van Dyke Show.* Freeman, best known for her appearances as the bossy type in Jerry Lewis movies, played Schultzy's best friend and confidante, and Kulp, who played Bob's bird-watching friend on the show, was later cast by the series' writer-producer Paul Henning to play the bird-watching secretary Miss Jane Hathaway on another of his series, *The Beverly Hillbillies.*

At the time, when there was a shortage of comediennes, or actresses who *wanted* to be funny, all of these women were at the top in their field. But on *The Bob Cummings Show,* for female second bananas, Davis was the best of the bunch.

Davis was 29 when she was cast for the *Cummings* show and although it was her first television job, she had done hundreds of roles before then in various regional theatres after graduating from college.

But to hear her tell it, Davis—who shares the same droll, self-deprecating wit as her two most famous characters—says that her future in show business was assured when she was a child. At the age of six, she earned $2 from putting on a puppet show for friends and family and she says, "I was impossible to live with for weeks."

Ann Bradford Davis was born May 5, 1926, in Schenectady, New York. Shortly afterwards, the family moved to Erie, Pennsylvania, where her father was employed as an electrical engineer.

Davis came from a family background where there was some show business in their blood. Her mother performed regularly in supporting roles at the Erie Playhouse. Her elder brother Evans was a professional dancer in New York. After graduating from Strong Vincent High School, Ann and her twin sister, Harriet, enrolled in the University of Michigan. Harriet studied speech and drama and had plans of working in the theatre. Ann, however, who was a natural cut-up, enrolled in pre-med, intent on becoming a doctor. In their junior year, she abandoned her dreams of working in the surgical amphitheater for dreams of working on the legitimate stage.

The change in plans came about from a trip the two girls had made to visit their brother Evans, who was then in Chicago as the lead dancer in a touring production of *Oklahoma!* They spent time backstage and going out with the cast after the show. With this insiders' look at the glamour of show business, Davis was smitten. "I thought this was just marvelous, isn't this exciting!" she recalls. "But my sister Harriet, who had been studying drama, had a different reaction. She thought she couldn't keep up the pace and couldn't do it." The result of that eye-opening trip was that Harriet abandoned her thespian aspirations and Ann switched her own major to speech and drama.

Upon graduating in 1948, Davis began her apprenticeship years. She made her professional debut in *Too Many Girls* at the Cain Park Theatre in Cleveland, Ohio, where she spent the summer of '48.

The following year was spent as an apprentice at the Erie Playhouse in Erie, Pa. Here she received a solid grounding in theatre, learning every aspect of production and playing a wide variety of roles— from teenagers to 60-year-old grandmothers.

However, the most valuable lesson she would learn about her chosen profession literally came while out in a field working for a tent repertory company in the summer of 1949. Based out of Plateau, Pa., the Manhattan Players ("so called because they had inherited some stationery already printed," says Davis), they played one-week stands in small towns throughout the area.

"We did eight different shows a week. Six different shows a night and two musical after-pieces. One was a roaring '20s musical and the other was a minstrel show, which is something nobody ever does anymore. The tent show was a unique experience. It was one of the last tent repertory theatres— or 'tent-reps' that survived radio and movies. I dined out on those stories for years.

"I learned an awful lot about the theatre that summer. But not a whole lot about acting. We did a different show every night with two weeks of rehearsal and so one week was opening night *every* night and it was *pressure!* I got $20 a week and I used to help them put the tent up and down so they gave me a raise to $25 a week."

Although she played in all the shows and recalls that her big role was as Peg in *Peg O' My Heart*, Davis says that she learned the key to being a good support player while with the tent-rep. It was a lesson she learned off-stage while helping with the set-up for each performance. "I helped them set up the tent, unload the props and prepare the stage — all of which I knew nothing," she explains.

"The light comedian in our show was in charge of all that and I was assigned to help him. While he was putting things up, I watched him like a hawk so I got so I could *anticipate* what he needed next — what tool to hand him, what to go and get, that kind of thing. So it was very good training in how to play support."

Davis continues, "In Psalm 123, verse 2, it says, 'Eyes of servants look to the hands of their masters; eyes of the maid to the hand of the mistress and so our eyes should look to the Lord, our God until He shows us His mercy.' I came across that passage recently. It's one of those lessons that one learns along the way and then you look back on some 40 or 50 years later.

"But as an actor, over the years, I'd say 99 percent of my career, I played supporting roles and you get to know what it takes to hand the laugh to somebody else or how to time the approach because you were working in *support* of somebody else.

"Nowadays I don't think anyone considers dreaming about being anything but a star and that's *not* very good practice for supporting somebody else because what you end up with is competition instead of support. It doesn't work out at all."

After that summer of tent-rep, Davis took whatever money she had managed to put away and with her retired parents picked up and headed out West. Naturally they went to California but instead of Hollywood, they ended up in the San Joaquin Valley where Davis began an apprenticeship at the Barn Theatre, a semi-professional company in Porterville.

"It was community theatre and you worked for room and board," Davis explains. "That's what you did in those days. You wrote the publicity, you did the props, you handled the costumes, you collected the tickets, you played your part on stage and then afterwards you swept the stage and cleaned the johns. You did whatever you had to do."

Davis remembers that time as three of the most wonderful years of her life. She formed lifelong friendships with fellow apprentice Richard Deacon, who became another well-known character actor and is best known as Mel Cooley on *The Dick Van Dyke Show*. She also later worked with the Barn's director, Peter Tewksbury, who went on to direct TV's *Father Knows Best* and *My Three Sons* and to write a sitcom pilot specifically for Davis after *The Bob Cummings Show* ended.

As the head of the Porterville theatre company, Tewksbury assembled a core group of actors and recruited additional players from the community.

"I was in what Pete called 'the nucleus,'" says Davis. "It was a few actors, most of us just out of college, and a technical director. Everyone else came from the community. We did some very good work there. I was very blessed because I had two very good directors in a row when I first got out of college. I had Newell Tarrant at the Erie Playhouse and Pete Tewksbury at the Barn Theatre. So I had very good directors at a very formative time in my life and I've always been grateful for that."

After three years at Porterville, including a couple of summers with the troupe at Yosemite, Davis left to work briefly at the Wharf Theatre in Monterey before taking her life savings and heading for Hollywood.

Arriving in 1953, she moved into The Studio Club, an all-woman's residence, and shortly afterwards began performing at a Sunset Boulevard nightclub called Cabaret Concert. "We did sketch comedy and takeoffs and some original material that a friend of mine, Jim Layton, had written. He was a writer and put together these variety shows. It was great fun. I *loved* it. I played six or seven different characters and it was very funny."

About a year after arriving in town, Davis got her big break and was "discovered" at Cabaret Concert and subsequently cast in the new *Bob Cummings Show*. Says Davis, "A friend of mine was dating Robert Walker, who was doing casting for another show in town, and he asked what she wanted to do for her birthday and she said, 'I want to go see Ann at Cabaret Concert.' So after the show, he told me that they were looking for a supporting character for *The Bob Cummings Show* and to get my agent to call them, so I did and he set up an interview. I walked into a room with the show's producers — Freddie DeCordava, George Burns and Bob Cummings. I was nearly scared to death — but I read for the part and got it."

That's surprising considering that prior to this, her only television experience had been a guest on the *Eddie Cantor Show* doing one of her characters from Cabaret Concert. Landing a regular role on a network sitcom only a year after arriving in town is the kind of Hollywood fairytale that still makes young hopefuls flock to La-la-land. Remarkably enough, in this case, the story is actually true. "The once-in-a-hundred chance happened," says Davis. "Good fortune claimed me for its own."

As mentioned earlier, she was competing against all the other "funny ladies" in town including former child star Jane Withers, who was the best known of all the candidates. "I remember Jane Withers was mostly in the running for the part of Schultzy, but she, being a 'name', wanted more money — and I would have done it for scale."

That's a typically modest Davis remark and she's shortchanging herself here. The truth is, she got the part on the strength of her own personality. Davis is naturally quick-witted and has an irrepressible upbeat personality which contrasts well with her droll, dry wit and self-depre-cating sense of humor. She was *exactly* what the producers were looking for in a secretary who has a huge crush on her boss but no hope of ever getting him — and she knows it.

"A lot of funny ladies were up for the part but they weren't what they wanted," says Davis. "They wanted whatever I was. As I later learned, in this business, most of the casting is done between the door and the desk and if you're what they're looking for, that's it."

On *The Bob Cummings Show,* the star played a photographer whose line of work meant a non-stop parade of glamorous models coming through his studio. Bachelor Bob Collins was forever trying to bed them — well, as much as that could be implied in a sitcom that debuted in January 1955. Two years later, Hugh Hefner invented *Playboy* magazine for guys just like Bob. Despite his superficial suave charm and the fact that he was on the make 24 hours a day, Bob's success rate with the ladies was about what you would expect on a show that ran in the '50s and had to go through network censors.

Amidst this weekly parade of female cheesecake were Davis and the other funny ladies. Nancy Kulp played Bob's bird-watching friend, Pamela Livingstone. Kathleen Freeman was Schultzy's best friend and Rosemary DeCamp played Bob's disapproving sister. Actually, the only one who did-n't disapprove of Bob was his nephew Chuck, played by Dwayne Hickman, himself getting invaluable experience for when he later played girl-crazy *Dobie Gillis* in his own series. There wasn't much difference between ado-lescent Dobie and middle-aged Bob.

Like the rest of the women, Charmaine Shultz, better known as Schultzy, was disapproving as well — but she remained loyal to him in the hope that one day her boss might mature enough to see past the surface beauty of the lovelies and finally take notice of the secretary he had been taking for granted all those years. In the meantime, she condescended to him with frustrated and eyeball-rolling line-readings of "Right, boss."

Of course, Bob and Schultzy never did get together and that's what kept the show going for five years. "Bob played a womanizing photogra-pher — actually a pretty tame one compared to today," says Davis. "But he would have all these beautiful models around. Schultzy had a secret crush on him which was no secret to anybody but him. He just didn't see it. He saw us as pals. There were a couple of dream sequences where he was smit-ten by Schultzy but that was as close as it would come.

"The show was about sex only in that they called him a wolf and he was always looking at women and always making come-on remarks. They were terribly tame and it wouldn't play now because comedy has changed so much. It's laughable in the sense of how risqué it was considered at the time and when compared to today's standards. Geez! There were a lot of double-entendres. Today on television, nobody knows what they are. There's only single-entendres.

"I think the success of the show was a combination of the fact that Paul Henning had an idea of a relationship and a very clear idea of that relationship. George Burns was also very involved in it because he owned half the show. So winning those two Emmys was all that combined with whatever I brought to the show—whether I knew it or not. They were constantly giving me good things to do and I was constantly trying to do my best with what they gave me. Paul Henning gave me wonderful things to do and Bob Cummings let me do them and the directors didn't fool around with what was working."

Davis credits Cummings for her share of laughs on the show. "Bob was very generous and in script readings he would say things like, 'You know, Bob would never say that—Schultzy would say that,' and so I'd get the line and I'd get the laugh. He was very conscious of the importance of support players. So occasionally, as a supporting player you would get some really good lines and you'd bring them home and somebody *else* works harder.

"Most of the big stars are *very* generous and know *exactly* what they need. They realize that's what will make their show better too. You'd better believe it! Nobody works alone.

"As a light comedian, Bob is a very honest actor. He's a good actor and he's a believable actor and the exaggeration that you have to do in comedy can only be based on that reality, on the honest acting. Like that saying goes, 'dying is easy, comedy is hard'—it's because you have to walk an edge between believable and being funny.

"Before the *Cummings* show, I had done a take-off on *A Streetcar Named Desire* for Cabaret Concert. I played the Blanche DuBois part. It was about a seven-minute sketch and we rehearsed it for weeks and they wouldn't let me play it for comedy at all. No matter what the lines said, I had to play it absolutely dead seriously and by the time we got it on stage, it was a big hit. But it had to be done straight and based on believability because if you start comedic, what you get is just ham and exhibitionism—which is a lot of what you see on TV these days."

All of this brings us to the obligatory question—was there much of Ann B. Davis in her characterization of Schultzy? "Oh sure," she readily admits. "Whatever it was. Whatever people saw of it. At the time I was younger than people thought I was. But I was *born* a character actor. I've had a character woman's face since I was a kid.

"You have so little rehearsal time in television that it's best to keep as much of yourself *there* as you can. You'll provide background from your own life, subtext and stuff which doesn't affect anything that's going on but it just gives you a little more to work with."

As the producers and writers got to know Davis better on the set, they also began writing more for her own personality. "That's the great thing about them getting to know you," she says. "They found out I could do that loud whistle where you put your fingers in your mouth and so they began to write that into the scripts. They found out that I never stopped acting as long as the cameras were still running and so occasionally they would extend the scene for when I was reacting or listening or whatever. They find out what you do—that just makes sense. They find out what you do well and they write to it."

With a wealth of other characters on the set, Davis says she was in a good position to learn just through observation and working with the other funny ladies. "You watch people work and if you're paying any attention at all, you don't steal, you just pick up things. Years ago, I saw a production of *Everybody Loves Opal* starring Eileen Heckart on Broadway which only ran a couple of weeks—but I picked up things from her that I've used in every production after that. It's just learning from the best, that's all."

For the young actress, the experience of her first TV series was an invigorating experience and one that never got boring. "It was different every week," she says. "It's like good summer stock or good stage work. Your character is the same. Well, your character develops but it's basically the same. But the plots and the words change so it's fresh every week. That part's fine. I love that."

On top of all that were her Emmy nominations and wins for 1957 and 1958, and all of that extra exposure resulted in Davis becoming the first television supporting player to play the lead in summer stock theatre during the *Cummings* show's summer hiatus. This is one of her most proud accomplishments.

"I was the first person who played support on television who went out and played leads in summer stock," she brags. "Nobody knew at that point if anybody would *pay* money to come see what they were getting for free on television. And I did it a year before Vivian Vance.

"I did *The Matchmaker* with Lyle Talbot. We played four or five places and every place we went we broke the house record. Lyle was a movie name of course, but I was an untried television supporting player. I was being recognized all over the country but nobody knew whether or not I could sell tickets—but I did. After that, a lot of supporting players went out and did it. The audience accepted the fact that I could play a leading role. Somebody had to do it first."

The Bob Cummings Show was cancelled in 1960 after a five-year run. Davis followed it up by going back to theatre in a big way. The same year, she was the personal choice of producer George Abbott to replace Carol Burnett in her Broadway hit, *Once Upon a Mattress*. Later that year she also starred as Agnes Gooch in the lead role of *Auntie Mame* on the summer stock circuit.

In the early 1960s, Davis appeared on television as the lead in an episode of *Wagon Train* titled "The Countess Baranoff Story." She also played supporting roles in the feature films *Pepe, All Hands on Deck* and *Lover Come Back.*

In 1962, her old friends—producer Pete Tewskbury and writer Jim Layton wrote a sitcom pilot specifically for her, *R.B. and Myrnalene.* "Aldo Ray played R.B. and I was Myrnalene," Davis recalls. "We meet when we separately walk up to a boarding house door and each wants to rent the only available room. And the landlady assumes we're a married couple. It was a 'midwesterner,' as Jim called it—or Unwed Mother with No Children. We had wonderful ideas for plots so when it didn't sell, we were all terribly, terribly heartbroken."

In 1965, Davis was signed to play support on *The John Forsythe Show* which also had been created by her friend Tewksbury. After the first season, Tewksbury quit and the show, which had been a gentle comedy about a lifelong bachelor now running an all-girls school, changed its focus in its second season and turned into a spy series. There wasn't a third season.

In 1969, Davis was working in theatre and nightclubs when producer Sherwood Schwartz was casting for his new TV series, *The Brady Bunch.* The situation comedy would be about the antics and hijinks that ensue when two young widowed parents marry and bring their families together. The father, Mike Brady, had three sons; his new wife, Carol, already had three girls, all roughly the same age as the Brady boys.

As the glue that would hold these two disparate families together, Schwartz thought of a neutral character, a maid who wouldn't take sides in the inevitable disagreements between the two sexes. Not that anything too earth-shattering ever happened on *The Brady Bunch.* The show was the last of a vanishing breed of domestic sitcoms about the family life of unnaturally wholesome middle-class white people.

For the part of the maid, Schwartz had originally envisioned Davis' old friend, Kathleen Freeman from the *Bob Cummings Show.* At this point, for the role of Carol, he had been considering Joyce Bulifant (best known as

Murray Slaughter's wife Marie on *The Mary Tyler Moore Show*). Bulifant was a known actress with a nice comic touch and pairing her with the stern and matronly Freeman would be a good team-up.

However, Schwartz ended up giving the part to Florence Henderson, who was then best known as a singer. Since the two characters would be sharing a lot of scenes, he felt that Henderson and Freeman together would seem too much like two straight women and wouldn't work as a comedy team.

Schwartz knew he needed a comedy actress to play off Henderson and he immediately thought of Davis. "It had to be someone with a comic talent to add to the humor and, at the same time, an acting ability to add to the reality of the Brady family life," Schwartz has said. "Certain roles cry out for certain actors, and this one screamed out for Ann B. Davis."[1]

Davis had a quality which Schwartz would refer to as being "genuinely, immediately and automatically funny."[2]

"They flew me in from Seattle where I was doing a nightclub act," Davis remembers about how she got the part. "They ran me out to the studio in the Valley and introduced me to Sherwood Schwartz and then rushed me back to the plane and I went back onstage that night with my nightclub act. The next day I got in my car, drove down to Los Angeles, shot the pilot and that was the end of my nightclub days. I had to buy my way out of my contract with the club. It took me the first 13 weeks of the show for me to pay them off."

Although it had been a decade since *The Bob Cummings Show*, Davis knew within the first season of *The Brady Bunch* that she wouldn't be stopped on the street and called "Shultzy" anymore. She tells the story of realizing that she now had a new generation of fans when she ran into a friend and her young daughter one time. "My friend said, 'You remember Schultzy.' And her daughter said indignantly, 'That's not Schultzy, that's Alice!'"

Ever since first putting on the maid uniform in 1969, thanks to the continuous reruns in syndication, Davis has been known as Alice to every subsequent generation.

Davis acknowledges being typecast but in her case, she doesn't mind because it has worked to her benefit in getting her work instead of losing jobs. "When you're typed for what you do best, that's not bad," she says.

Indeed. In her post–*Brady* years, she even became a spokesperson for Wisk and as such did commercials and personal appearances for them as "the world's best house-keeper"—a label she personally finds amusing.

But she didn't get to be known as a whiz in the housekeeping department just on the basis of that blue uniform alone. Davis takes her job seriously and even on a show aimed at kids, she took a method approach to the role in order to look authentic. She recalls, "I see myself trying to find little bits of business to make me look occupied and legitimate and maid-like, even though they usually had to be stationary and small, not calling for any extra props. Like feeling a coffee pot with the back of my hand before Carol carries it away—making sure it's hot enough. Or I would mop with minimal movement so as to not interfere with camera placement or cause any of the kids present to move out of position. I made sure that Alice was always busy, always in a bit of a hurry, but not too busy to listen."[3]

When an episode called for a scene to be shot in Alice's room of the Brady manse, Davis brought in a suitcase full of her own photos and knick-knacks to give it a more Alice-looking feel than the usual generic servants' quarters.

Still, even with those personal touches, the room was in marked contrast to the way she decorated her own dressing room at the studio. Boxes of the dime-store snack Screaming Yellow Zonkers hung on a wire from the ceiling and she would read the jokes on the back of the boxes to visitors. On one wall hung a poster of *Laugh-In* regular Henry Gibson, naked with a strategically-placed daisy and stretched out like Burt Reynolds in his infamous *Playgirl* centerfold. Other than the many examples of her needlepoint that decorated the walls, the room itself was probably a bit too wild for prime time.

By all accounts, Davis was the quiet professional on the set. Always prepared. Always knew her lines. To kill time during the long delays of television production, she took up the very Alice-like pastime of needlepoint. It's easy to imagine Alice similarly occupied—alone in her room after the supper dishes had been done, stitching away while relishing the peace and quiet and half-watching her portable television. Or quietly sitting in the Brady kitchen while the kids were at school, hooking a rug while keeping a watchful eye on a simmering pot of stew on the stove. By the time the series ended, Davis had half the cast doing needlepoint and she herself even made it into a book called *Celebrity Needlepoint.*

Just as Alice was the support of the Brady clan, Davis knew that like the other adults in the cast, she was basically playing support to a group of kids. Not that playing second banana to a bunch of kids bothered her. "The kids were very good kids and they were *nice* kids and they were good professional actors and that's the way they were treated and so that's the way they responded. When they weren't working they were kids. When they were working, they were pros. Whatever the plot called for, that's what you did. I never sat down and asked myself, 'Well, am I supporting a seven-year-old kid?' No, I would be thinking, 'I want to be in the right position on camera for Bobby to say something to me.'"

On this particular series, as the comic support, Davis was in the enviable position of also getting all the good lines. Neither Mike nor Carol was known for spontaneous wit and so Alice got most of the laughs. As she recalls, "Watching the show ... I'm reminded of how nice it is to play a supporting role. The leads have to work so hard and carry most of the load, then I stick my head in and get the laugh line! I got some very good lines, too!"[4]

Still, gratifying as that was, unlike her Emmy-winning years on *The Bob Cummings Show,* her stint on *The Brady Bunch* didn't yield any Emmy awards. There are a number of reasons for the show's lack of Emmy wins but the most obvious reason in Davis' case was that she was nominated in the wrong category. She remembers being nominated by the show's producers in the Best Actress category instead of the more logical Best Supporting Actress in a Comedy Series grouping.

"I actually called the Emmy people and said, 'I'm honored of course, but is there any way to change the category you have me in because I'm not actually starring on the show.' And they said, 'You know, nobody's ever asked us that before.'"

Although she's justifiably proud of her Emmys from the *Cummings* show, she's also proud of her work as Alice and doesn't like to favor or compare the two characters because the two shows were so vastly different — one being a situation comedy for adults and the other a domestic show aimed at kids.

Davis credits the family aspect of *The Brady Bunch* for being part of the reason for the show's popularity in syndication. "My feeling is that the show came out just about the time that television began to get so sexy," she says. "There was *Three's Company* and that kind of stuff, where you began to have a lot of unpalatable situations. Also, at the same time, we suddenly began to have a lot more television stations available. We had all that hardware and no software, so when they started to rerun things like *Three's Company* and some of the less tasteful shows, a lot of parents complained to their local stations and said, 'Don't put that on at 3:30 in the afternoon when my children come home from school,' and so it was either us or *Gilligan's Island* — both owned by Sherwood Schwartz."

She continues, "Plus there was the fact that it was a children's show and based on kids' relationships and so every year of syndication we picked up a new generation of kids who hadn't seen it. You've no idea how many letters I get from people saying that they watched it growing up and now they're watching it again with their own kids and I think we all wanted to live in that sort of world."

It's true that nostalgia and camp can be credited for the show's long-lasting appeal to successive generations. But many were surprised that it lasted as long as it did in its original run. Even as a show aimed at kids, it didn't bear much resemblance to the lives of many kids growing up in the early 1970s. Still, it lasted five years and Davis points out that even at the time, nobody on the show realized how popular they were.

"We always got terrible reviews, right from the start, and we were often used as an example of how bad a situation comedy could be. After 20 years it's easy to laugh at this, but at the time we all held our breath every six or seven episodes waiting to see if we were going to be picked up to go on. I don't think anybody took us seriously until they realized that we had knocked off some 13 series that were our competition."[5]

Regarding the Bradys' ultra-idealized home life, Davis says, "I remember one time in an interview, someone made some sort of snide remark about how unrealistic *The Brady Bunch* was—and Florence Henderson lit into them like a tiger. She talked about the fact that when she was a kid, her family was very poor and she was the youngest of 10 children and the only joy they had was to go to the movies and see all those wonderful worlds that didn't exist—'*And that's what we're doing!*' She's a very feisty lady."

When *The Brady Bunch* was cancelled in 1974, it was a different world on television for sitcoms. Compared with the then-new concept of in-your-face, issue-oriented programs like *Maude, All in the Family,* even *The Jeffersons,* well, *The Brady Bunch* seemed stuck in another time or even from another planet no matter how "with it" the writers tried to make the family.

But the cancellation notice in '74 was hardly the end of the Bradys. Now affectionately known as "the TV show that won't go away," the cast has been reunited for a number of Brady TV series and TV movies throughout the years.

Davis has appeared in all the various incarnations beginning with the variety show *The Brady Bunch Hour* in 1977, the TV movie *The Brady Girls Get Married* and its short-lived series, *The Brady Brides* in 1981. When the 1988 TV movie *A Very Brady Christmas* pulled in such high ratings that the network wanted another series, a one-hour drama series, *The Bradys,* again reunited the cast in 1990 but it only lasted a few episodes.

Maybe after all this time, TV audiences have realized that although they obviously like to see how the characters are getting on with their lives (and see how the actors have aged), a little bit goes a long way and maybe the characters are best remembered in 30-minute reruns.

Still, they are such an undeniable pop-culture phenomenon that two feature-length parodies came out in the late 1990s. In 1995's *The Brady Bunch Movie*, Davis had a cameo as a truck driver, cleverly named Schultzy, who gives some badly needed advice to middle-child Jan who is running away from home. The movie is an affectionate spoof but Davis wouldn't agree to do a cameo in it until she knew that the project had the blessing of Sherwood Schwartz.

She has mixed feelings about the results—a movie that manages to make fun of the show and celebrate it at the same time. "It was made for the new audience—it wasn't made for me," she explains. "I went to see it to see how it went over with the audience it was made for and they loved it. I even found myself tearing up every once in a while, it was such fun."

When *The Brady Bunch* folded (the first time) in 1974, Davis made some life-changing decisions. At the age of 47, she became a born-again Christian and took an indefinite voluntary retirement from show business to work with the homeless. "Around the time the show ended, I was going through a spiritual renewal which had started out with Bible study and I became more and more interested and more and more involved," she says.

She had met Reverend William C. Frey, an Episcopalian bishop who worked with the homeless with his wife Barbara and a group of volunteers. "I had just finished doing some theatre in Canada and I was on my way back to L.A. and the Freys had just bought a big Victorian house in downtown Denver so I stopped by to see what it was like," she says. "I called my agents and told them that I was in Denver and if you need me I can be in L.A. in a few hours—and I didn't hear back from them for five months and then I got five job offers within three days and I realized that I didn't want to leave. I realized that *this* was my home and that I lived here in this community. I sold my house in Studio City, gave up my Porsche 914 and I've been with the Freys ever since—later in Pennsylvania and now in Texas."

She says that at the time she felt she was missing something in her life. "I had everything the world had to offer and it wasn't enough. I felt kind of guilty—what do I think I don't have?"

Davis had never married and had always put her career before a personal life. Now she found herself in a different sort of family. "To live with people who are that much in touch with the Lord was wonderful," she says. "I was born again. It changed my whole life for the better."

Other than the occasional *Brady* project, her life was devoted to the work she did with the Freys for the next 15 years. It was inevitable, though, that she would eventually miss show business. "But in the meantime, what I would do to sort of scratch that itch was to go and give my Christian testimony to any group that would buy me a plane ticket and I did that for a number of years."

In 1990, she received an offer to do dinner theatre ("I call it 'digestive theatre,'" she says) in Canada and she anguished for days over the decision and finally consulted her friend Barbara Frey, who told her, "Oh, I've been praying forever for you to go back to work!" So she performed in *Cemetery Club* for several months.

Then she was asked to join the Broadway road company tour of a revival of the Gershwin musical *Crazy For You*. She played the starchy 1930s New York matron who sends her son to Deadrock, Nevada, to foreclose on a theatre.

"I did that for about 18 months and then they asked me to come to New York and finish up six months of the Broadway version which closed in January of 1996," she says. "So I had a wonderful time. I loved that. The epitome of my dreams was to end up on Broadway. I'd been on Broadway before—briefly—but this time I played six months on Broadway in the Shubert Theatre and so as far as I was concerned, I went out with a *flash*."

It's only fitting that Davis end her career on a high note like a Broadway musical. She has loved the theatre throughout her career, performing literally in hundreds of plays and productions. From her tent-rep days to summer stock to dinner theatre and then closing on Broadway, the theatre has always been her first love as an actress.

Still, it will be from her work on television that she will be best remembered. In her roles as a secretary and a maid, she was a throwback to prefeminist days in the way her character doted on her male boss or selflessly served another employer's family. Ironically, in reality, Ann B. Davis was a feminist pioneer. Back in the 1950s and '60s, not many women worked outside the home. But Davis, by her own account, sacrificed the chance for home and domestic happiness for her career.

When she became a born-again Christian and left her career in show business, she found the sense of family that she had set aside for so long. Instead of serving the likes of photographer Bob Collins or the Bradys, she began serving her Lord by serving others who didn't have it as nice as she had for all those years. Her legacy is as one who has served others—onscreen and off.

Throughout it all, her spirit has remained the same. That deadpan sense of humor which has endeared her to audiences as Shultzy and Alice is inseparable from Ann B. Davis. When asked about her greatest strength as an actress she speaks with a mock ego which nonetheless couldn't be more true. "I think I'm loveable. That's the gift God gave me. I don't do anything but be loveable. I can't help it."

Notes

1. *Alice's Brady Bunch Cookbook*; by Ann B. Davis; Rutledge Hill Press; 1994; page 7.

2. *Growing Up Brady*; by Barry Williams; Harper-Collins; 1992; page 40.

3. *Alice's Brady Bunch Cookbook*; by Ann B. Davis; page 63.

4. *Alice's Brady Bunch Cookbook*; by Ann B. Davis; page 182.

5. *Alice's Brady Bunch Cookbook*; Ann B. Davis; page 203.

Ann B. Davis Credits

FILM CREDITS

1. *The Brady Bunch Movie; 1995;* Schultzy
2. *Naked Gun 33⅓ — The Final Insult*; 1994; Herself
3. *Lover Come Back*; 1961; Millie
4. *All Hands on Deck*; 1961; Nobby
5. *Pepe*; 1960; Cameo appearance
6. *A Man Called Peter*; 1955; Ruby Coleman

TV CREDITS

1. *The Brady Bunch Movies*; TV special; 1995; Alice Nelson
2. *The Bradys*; TV series; 1990; Alice Nelson
3. *A Very Brady Christmas*; TV movie; 1988; Alice Nelson
4. *The Brady Brides*; TV series; 1981; Alice Nelson
5. *The Brady Girls Get Married*; TV movie; 1981; Alice Nelson Franklin
6. *The Brady Bunch Hour*; TV series; 1977; Alice
7. *The Brady Bunch*; TV series; 1969–1974; Alice Nelson
8. *The John Forsythe Show*; TV series; 1965–1967; Miss Wilson
9. *The Bob Cummings Show*; TV series; 1955–1959; Charmaine "Schultzy" Shultz

NOTABLE TV GUEST APPEARANCES

1. *Something So Right*; Maxine; 4/29/1997
2. *Hi Honey, I'm Home*; Alice Nelson; 1991
3. *Day by Day*; Alice Nelson; 1989
4. *Wagon Train*; Countess Baranof; 5/11/1960

Jamie Farr

Corporal Max Klinger on M*A*S*H

Some actors look good in a dress. Jack Lemmon and Tony Curtis in *Some Like it Hot*. Dustin Hoffman in *Tootsie*. Jaleel White as Steve Urkel's cousin, Myrtle Urkel on *Family Matters*. And of course the cast of *Monty Python* in just about every project they ever did. Some actors can pull it off.

Jamie Farr isn't one of them. As reasonably good-looking as he is, and as fine an actor as he is, there is just no way that Farr can look convincingly feminine in a dress. As Corporal Max Klinger on *M*A*S*H*, he usually sported a five o'clock shadow. On high heels, he walked like a man and coupled with his six-foot-plus frame, his steps weren't exactly dainty or lady-like. His forearms and legs were unshaved and hairy. Thankfully, the show's wardrobe department spared us the sight of Klinger in a halter top. Although dressed like a woman, Klinger carried himself like a man and the sight was hilarious. In the process, Farr became one of the most famous cross-dressers in television history. The world may be full of drag queens but for the most part they are anonymous and forgettable. But the memory of Farr in one of his Carmen Miranda outfits is an image that stays burned in your mind.

Interestingly, although it was the woman's clothing that established Klinger on *M*A*S*H* and was his most identifiable feature for a number of years, Farr did so much more with the character that when the dress-shtick was finally dropped in the eighth season and he began to wear normal army fatigues—no one really cared. The character retained his popularity and Farr was free to further explore and exploit other aspects of Klinger's personality.

"The only thing that made that stuff work was that wearing the dress was secondary," explains Farr. "If that was all the character was about, then the character wouldn't have lived. So he had other areas they could explore. The dress was only part of it. It was like the uniform of the day. It was his *desire* to get out of the war and by *what* means he was going to get out, that was important to him."

M*A*S*H was a situation comedy set in a mobile army surgical hospital near the front lines of the Korean War. For a sitcom, it was unusual in that it dealt with life and death and the insanity of war on a weekly basis. As such, Farr's Corporal Max Klinger, whether in or out of a dress, was a much needed and reliable bit of comic relief.

Ironically, Farr, who played the character who was the most desperate to get out of Korea, was actually the only member of the cast to have served in the Korean War as a member of the U.S. Army. When *M*A*S*H* first began, in the emotional aftermath of the war in Vietnam, it was criticized by some as being anti-war. "What does that mean?" asks Farr. "I don't know anybody who is *for* war. As a civilian and a soldier who was in Korea, I was against the war — but you serve your country. It's like the characters on the show — they were doctors and nurses trying to *save* lives. They didn't like war, but they did what they had to do."

Klinger's reasoning behind his wardrobe choices was that eventually someone would finally decide he was crazy and mentally unfit for duty and send him home. For Klinger, home was Toledo, Ohio. Home for Jamie Farr was also Toledo. He was born there on July 1, 1934, to Lebanese parents who named him Jameel Farah. He kept the name through the beginning of his acting days in Hollywood and only changed it to Jamie Farr after his career was interrupted by his stint in the Korean War. Upon his return, he felt like he was having to start all over again and so changed his name.

Farr attended Woodward High School while growing up in Toledo. It was the alma mater of fellow Lebanese comic Danny Thomas. In high school, in addition to drama productions, Farr was busy as the student body president, editor of the school newspaper and manager of the football and basketball teams.

Upon graduating, he headed out West in 1954 and began an apprenticeship at the Pasadena Playhouse. While there he made his first big screen appearance as a juvenile delinquent in *The Blackboard Jungle* in 1955.

In the mid–1950s Farr hooked up with Red Skelton, who took him under his wing and taught him the basics of comedy — including the importance of being a second banana. Farr worked on Skelton's CBS variety hour, *The Red Skelton Show*, until he was drafted in 1957. Skelton's style of comedy was broad but with small moments of pathos and warmth — not unlike what Farr would experience years later on *M*A*S*H*.

Farr worked with Skelton for a number of years, as a personal assistant and second banana both on television and while he was doing concerts and nightclubs on the road. "A second banana is very, very important," says Farr. "I know about comedy. Red Skelton was my mentor and I worked with all the greats. On *The Danny Kaye Show* in the early sixties, I did sketch comedy with Harvey Korman on the show and you did what the second banana does on a show like that — you play a number of different supporting characters."

"But the expression 'second banana' comes from the burlesque days. There was the Top Banana and the second banana was the guy who worked with him. So if you're a second banana, that's important because that's what makes the Top Banana work. The function of the second banana is to make the Top Banana really solid and give him something to play off of. A lot of people don't know what the credibility of a second banana is — it's often the straight man. You had Abbott *and* Costello, Martin *and* Lewis.

"It's the reversal of that situation on TV. There, it's the funny one who plays second banana to the straight man. But it's for the same reason — to give credibility to the star, to the Top Banana of the show. But whether it's on the stage or TV, the second banana plays a very important part in the success of any show by giving the Top Banana credibility."

When he was drafted in 1957, after basic training, Farr was initially sent to work in New York to help make training films for the Signal Corps. Then he was shipped to Korea where he furthered his education in the art of being a second banana while touring with the USO.

After returning from Korea, Farr traveled with Skelton on the nightclub circuit in 1959 and 1960. Returning to Hollywood, he began getting frequent work on sitcoms and small parts in feature films. This was good because in 1963, he married his wife, Joy, while he was filming *The Greatest Story Ever Told.*

Throughout the 1960s, Farr guest-starred on most of the classic sitcoms. He was often cast as ethnic characters on shows like *The Andy Griffith Show, I Dream of Jeannie, F Troop* and *My Favorite Martian.* On *My Three Sons,* he played a beatnik named Itchy and on *Family Affair* he was cast as "Hippie."

On *The Dick Van Dyke Show* in 1961, he had a recurring role as "Delivery Boy," who would bring up sandwiches from the deli for Rob and Buddy and Sally in the writers' office. From his experience working with all the great second bananas on that show, Farr realized one main thing: "I'm not a comedian. I'm a comedy actor."

Near the end of the decade, however, acting jobs became fewer and he found himself doing all manner of other work. Over the years when work was slow he paid the rent by working as a delivery boy, postal clerk and even on a chinchilla farm. He had also teamed up with a friend to write scripts and produce pilots for a couple of game shows.

In 1971, he had been signed as a supporting player in the CBS situation comedy *The Chicago Teddy Bears.* Set in the underworld of 1920s Chicago, Farr was cast as the bodyguard of Dean Jones' character, a mobster who owned a popular speakeasy. Other bodyguards included veteran second bananas Mickey Shaughnessy, Mike Mazurki and former Bowery Boy Huntz Hall. Unfortunately, the show was cancelled after three months.

Coupled with the disappointment from the show's cancellation and the lack of work in general, Farr was seriously considering getting out of the business in 1972 when he received a call for a one-shot appearance on a new series called *M*A*S*H.* What was supposed to be just one day's work ended up being an 11-year job.

The series had already begun filming but had not yet gone on the air when Farr was called in and he had no idea what he was getting into. Upon arriving on the set, the situation was explained to him and he was put into a WAC uniform and pair of high heels and told to camp it up. The next day, he was called back to re-shoot the scene. This time he decided to play it straight and that was when he found the handle by which to play the character. "If I had played it swish again that second time, it would have only been a one-day job. I would have been in and out of there."

It was a good insight into the character. Klinger was conceived of as a guy who wants out of the Army so badly that he dresses up as a woman in the hope that he will be classified as being mentally unfit for duty and sent home. He reasoned that if you wear a dress and act normal, people will think you are crazy. But if you put on a dress and camp it up, people will just think that you like to wear women's clothing.

With his ludicrous schemes to get out of Korea and his outlandish outfits, Klinger could have been the living embodiment of the idea that war is crazy. Unfortunately for the character, he wasn't crazy—other than in the sense that he was crazy like a fox. Certainly no one in the 4077th Mobile Army Surgical Hospital base to which he was assigned thought he was crazy. The truth was that he was a good soldier. He was reliable and could be depended upon for guard duty and working as an aide to the doctors and nurses in the surgery tents. When the helicopters flew in carrying new batches of wounded soldiers, Klinger was usually one of the first there to meet them.

Farr explains that no one thought Klinger was crazy. "The character had an objectivity. Everyone on the show had an objective and his objective was to get out. If you had an objective as a performer, that's the key. For Klinger, his objectivity was in his desire to get out. The women's clothing was just the means to fulfilling that objective. So the fact that he wore those clothes was really secondary.

"One thing you have to understand is that *M*A*S*H* was not a sitcom in the normal sense. It wasn't like *Happy Days* or *The Honeymooners* or *Gilligan's Island*. It had a very serious side to it, an element that hadn't been seen on a half-hour sitcom before and so they had to give it a new name and called it a 'dramedy.'

"I handled my situation with Klinger wearing women's clothes the same way the other actors on the show handled it. If you recall, the other characters— Hawkeye, Trapper, B.J.— they *all* did really outlandish things which made it real crazy and so to bring my character on was really just an extension of that. It was our firm belief that if *you*, the actor believe it, the audience is going to believe it. So you have to go with that depiction.

No matter how outrageous something may be that the character does, you're going to accept it because you're in a minefield in Korea somewhere.

"Nobody really believed Klinger was crazy. If you watch the show, the other characters didn't really pay any attention to how he was dressed — except for the occasional flip comment. On the MASH compound that was all acceptable. He wasn't a threat to them. He was a good soldier. They found him extremely amusing. And I think that's the whole secret. I think it was the attitude of the show itself. Trapper and Hawkeye would get gorilla suits and put them on and wear them around — I mean, what sane people would be doing something like that? Especially doctors!

"So if you want to analyze the whole show, Klinger was just an extension of the insanity that was going on at a MASH unit near the front lines of the war in Korea."

Farr's first episode ran after the series had been on a couple of months but was such a hit that he was brought back as a recurring character throughout the rest of the season. He appeared more often in the second season but still not in every episode. When the third season came, he says it finally began to feel like a real job. "In the third year they gave me a full-time contract. It was partly on my insistence because I wanted to know if I was part of the team or not. I didn't want to sit at home wondering if I was going to get a phone call to report for work that week or not. They could have written me out of the show, but I felt they wanted to bring me back. And I knew my importance to the show based on the public reaction everywhere I went."

Undoubtedly, Klinger was one of the most popular characters on the series. As the show went on, his outfits became increasingly elaborate and outrageous. Most women Stateside during the war would have been happy to afford some of the outfits Klinger was able to find in the middle of a war zone in Korea. Farr and the *M*A*S*H* producers were able to raid the wardrobe departments of 20th Century–Fox and some of the gowns Klinger wore had originally been designed years before for the likes of Alice Faye, Betty Grable and Carmen Miranda.

No longer content to just wear a WAC uniform or a simple black cocktail dress with matching purse and pumps, as the series went on, the character was likely to show up for guard duty dressed up like Cleopatra or Scarlett O'Hara. Klinger would have been the envy of any drag queen working the Vegas strip.

The gimmick was beginning to get tiresome when the producers decided to take the character in a different direction in the eighth season. When Gary Burghoff, who played company clerk Radar O'Reilly, left the show in 1979, instead of bringing in someone new, the producers moved

Klinger to the vacated position. With the promotion came a new uniform: a real uniform of regulation army fatigues with a standard issue cap instead of the series of multi-colored babushkas which Klinger had been fond of wearing. The new position carried more responsibility. Not only was he company clerk but he was also the personal assistant of Harry Morgan's Colonel Potter character. The credibility of his new position would have been undermined if he was still showing up for work dressed like Marie Antoinette or Mata Hari.

Although he had lost his colorful wardrobe, Klinger still held on to his dreams for getting out of the Army on a mentally unfit classification. New schemes involved floating back to the States on an inflatable raft; going AWOL in a hang-glider; sitting on a flagpole, and eating the Colonel's Jeep piece by piece. Probably his most inspired ruse to convince the powers-that-be that he was losing his mind was when he put on civilian clothes, pretended he was back home in Toledo and went tent to tent selling aluminum siding.

Obviously, the show's writers took great delight in writing for Klinger. "They *loved* it," laughs Farr. "He was like a cartoon character. They could do anything they wanted with him — fly over the base in a hang-glider, set fire to himself, eat a Jeep. You name the situation and Klinger probably did it. I don't think there ever was a character in the history of television who had that kind of bizarre characterization."

Farr says that he wasn't hesitant about losing the women's clothing, even though it had been Klinger's most identifiable feature. "At that point, my character was so established that the dress wasn't important anymore. Besides, you're an actor, you go in and do what's necessary to make the show work. So it's another challenge and you just keep going. If you're in your eighth year, you know that the show is a bona fide hit and when you're a part of something special and you trust the decisions that are made and go along with them, it's an adventure.

"In making Klinger the company clerk, that gave us a new storyline and direction for the character. Rather than bring in someone new, if you take somebody who's already there, that person has to go through a period of incompetency and that gave us more stories. So I thought it was brilliant."

One of the other aspects of Klinger's character that came out when he became company clerk was his abilities as a hustler and a procurer. He was able to swap medical supplies and food for the base that normally wouldn't have been so readily at their disposal. Judging by his past achievements, it was no surprise to learn that Klinger was a natural-born con artist and scammer. He was a fast operator who would have been right at home in Bilko's unit on *The Phil Silvers Show*.

Farr says the show's creators had an intuitive feel for knowing what to do with all the various characters in the ensemble cast. "They knew how to allot the humor and dole it out. That's what made *M*A*S*H* so special, it was the handling of the show. Knowing exactly what to do with it. It's like playing a wonderful symphony — you know what to do to make it all come together. With Klinger's dresses, the guest stars were only allowed one double-take. On other sitcoms, something like that would have been indulged in and they would just ride that horse to death. But on *M*A*S*H,* they didn't do that. You just got a sampling of this, a sampling of that. You just did what was necessary and moved on to what was the main theme — 'War is Hell and let's continue on.'"

Farr credits *M*A*S*H's* producers for successfully balancing the comedy and the tragedy. He says it was done by taking advantage of small, brief moments. There would be a short scene full of emotion but they wouldn't dwell on it to the point where it became saccharine and lost its poignancy. As an example, he cites the interplay between himself and actor David Ogden Stiers, who played the stuffed shirt Major Charles Winchester. "What makes good comedy?" he asks rhetorically. "Two opposites. Klinger and Winchester were opposites but I think our styles of acting were opposites too. David is a really wonderful high-polished actor — as opposed to myself which is more the personality kind of actor, and I think that the combination of our styles is what made our brief scenes together work.

"The two characters were really antagonists and there was a scene in an episode where I had found the cap he wore as a little boy and so I gave it to him for Christmas and he calls me 'Max' and I say, 'Merry Christmas to you, Charles.' It was just a little moment. But that's what made the show special. There were tiny little moments like that. They knew how to use brevity. They knew how not to indulge in something — just take it, take the moment, it's there, use it and move on. But just that one moment, it's like finding a huge gold mine."

Amid all the comedy — the one-liners, the deadpan gallows humor and sight gags — was also the reality that there was an unseen war going on a few miles away. Occasionally, that reality would take its toll on the characters — most of whom had been drafted and didn't want to be there.

"There are moments of insanity that happened to all the characters because of the war going on," says Farr. "How many times did Hawkeye break down? Even Colonel Potter broke down at times. There are low moments that every character has — all of which makes the character well-rounded, so it's not just one note that you're playing. That's part of the fun of being an actor. It's in stretching things. A wonderful Shakespeare teacher at the Pasadena Playhouse once told me that the greatest tragedians are the comedians."

In 1983, the show's producers pulled the plug on M*A*S*H, believing that after 11 years on the air, they had explored all the possibilities for the members of the 4077th MASH unit. In the final two-and-a-half hour episode, with the war finally over, everyone is sent home — all except Klinger. Ironically, the guy who had always been the most desperate to get out of there had fallen in love with a Korean woman, married her and decided to stay in Korea to help his wife find her family.

Farr reflects on that episode and says, "I think it goes to show how important the character was, that there was a fulfillment to it, it was good storytelling. There's irony to that ending and that's what makes for good drama. Was Klinger just a dress or a character? Well, he was a full character and that ending emphasized that."

Klinger was back on TV the next season, however, in AfterM*A*S*H, a series which reunited him with Harry Morgan as Colonel Potter and William Christopher, who played Father Mulcahy on the original series. The new series was set Stateside after the war. Potter was chief of staff of a veterans' hospital and chose Klinger to be his administrative assistant. Mulcahy was the hospital chaplain. The series only lasted one season and Farr doesn't like to talk about it. However, he doesn't disagree with the suggestion that a show needs something more than three supporting players in order to work.

Farr experienced the usual typecasting problems after playing Klinger for over a decade. "Ten years seems to be the usual length of time before they'll let you come back on television," he says and then jokes, "But mine seems to have been a bit longer than that. Maybe my character was a bit more indelible than the others and so I have to suffer a little more."

He hasn't suffered too much though — being associated with a successful television series has its perks and has opened many doors into doing theatre. "M*A*S*H is still played all over the world and that's one of the reasons I keep getting offers for work in the theatre," he says. "The theatre is where I make my living these days."

Throughout his years on M*A*S*H, he performed in dinner theatre during his summer breaks. He continued with theatre after the series ended and the highlight of his career on stage was playing Nathan Detroit in *Guys and Dolls* on Broadway in 1992. "It was my Broadway debut and I wound up as part of the longest-running musical revival in the history of Broadway. Not bad."

These days he is a popular performer at The New Theatre in Kansas City where he has appeared in a number of different plays. "I've been offered all kinds of roles. The world is your oyster in the theatre. It's whatever they think you might be right for."

Ironically, most of the people who come to see him are the same audiences who watched him on *M*A*S*H*. But after the show, television casting agents told Farr that the television audience wouldn't accept him in any other roles because of Klinger. Yet, those same conservative middle-aged audiences aren't narrow-minded at all and in fact are willing to pay to see him on stage. The attitude seems to be, "Yes, we've seen you on *M*A*S*H*, we know you can act. Now, let's see what other characters you can do."

"Exactly!" agrees Farr. "And that's why I get invited back and they come see me again. They come see you in one thing and because they enjoyed it they come back to see you again even though the plays you are doing aren't even remotely reminiscent of anything you had done with the TV series."

Big-time success came relatively late in Farr's career and that is probably why he has been able to maintain a healthy attitude about the industry. He was 38 when he was cast in *M*A*S*H* and he played Klinger for the last time when he was 50. Before then were years as a struggling actor. Farr had certainly paid his dues and from that perspective he was better able to appreciate his success and not take it for granted. All those years of training prepared him not only as an actor on a long-running series but also for how to keep working in show business once that series ended.

In his autobiography, *Just Farr Fun*, he sums up his career this way— "I say simply that I'm an entertainer. I may not be a great actor. I may not be a tragedian. I'm certainly not a standup comic. I am not a good-looking guy. (I am not a bad-looking guy either.) I only know one thing. I give people something they need. They need laughter. So I give them comedy. They love it. And they love me. Why would I want to do anything else?"[1]

Note

1. *Just Farr Fun*; by Jamie Farr, Eubanks/Donizetti Inc.; Clearwater, Florida; 1994; page 342.

Jamie Farr Credits

FILM CREDITS

1. *You Snooze, You Lose*; 1995; Dr. Hanley
2. *Speed Zone!*; 1989; Cannonballer #2
3. *Curse II: The Bite*; 1988; Harry Morton

4. *Scrooged;* 1988; Himself (TV Jacob Marley)
5. *Happy Hour;* 1987; Crummy Fred
6. *Cannonball Run II;* 1981; The Shiek
7. *The Gong Show Movie;* 1980; Himself
8. *Arnold;* 1973; Dybbi
9. *Heavy Traffic;* 1973
10. *With Six You Get Eggroll;* 1968; Jo Jo
11. *Who's Minding the Mint?;* 1967; Mario
12. *Ride Beyond Vengeance;* 1966; Pete
13. *Out of Sight;* 1966
14. *The Loved One;* 1965; (uncredited) Waiter at English Club
15. *The Greatest Story Ever Told;* 1965; Thaddaeus
16. *No Time for Sergeants;* 1958; (uncredited) Lieutenant Gardella, co-pilot
17. *Three Violent People;* 1956; Pedro Ortega
18. *Kismet;* 1955; (uncredited) Orange Merchant
19. *Blackboard Jungle;* 1955; Santini

TV CREDITS

1. *Port Charles;* TV series; 1999; Ernie the angel
2. *Memories of M*A*S*H;* TV special; 1991; Himself
3. *Run Till You Fall;* TV movie; 1988; Michael Reuben
4. *A Masterpiece of Murder;* TV movie; 1986; Himself
5. *Wordplay;* TV series; 1986; Sub-Announcer
6. *Combat High;* TV movie; 1986; Colonel Frierick
7. *Circus of the Stars #9;* TV special; 1984; Ringmaster
8. *For Love or Money;* TV movie; 1984; Larry Melody
9. *Circus of the Stars #8;* TV special; 1983; Performer
10. *AfterM*A*S*H;* TV series; 1983; Max Klinger
11. *Circus of the Stars #6;* TV special; 1981
12. *Return of the Rebels;* TV movie; 1981; Mickey Fine
13. *Murder Can Hurt You;* TV movie; 1980; Studsky
14. *Kraft Salutes Disneyland's 25th Anniversary;* TV special; 1980; Himself
15. *Circus of the Stars #4;* TV special; 1979
16. *Circus of the Stars #3;* TV special; 1979
17. *Amateur Night at the Dixie Bar and Grill;* TV movie; 1979; Snuffy McCann
18. *The $1.98 Beauty Show;* TV series; 1978; Panelist
19. *The Gong Show;* TV series; 1976; Panelist
20. *Joys;* TV special; 1976
21. *The Blue Knight;* TV movie; 1973; Yasser Hafiz
22. *M*A*S*H;* TV series; 1973–1983; Max Klinger
23. *The Chicago Teddy Bears;* TV series; 1971; Lefty

NOTABLE TV GUEST APPEARANCES

1. *Just Shoot Me;* Himself; 5/9/2000
2. *Diagnosis Murder;* Doug Hanson; 1/22/1998
3. *Hey Arnold!;* (voice) Mr. Wacko; 1997
4. *Men Behaving Badly;* Himself; 11/20/1996
5. *Women of the House;* Himself; 1/9/1995
6. *Reading Rainbow;* Himself; 1995
7. *Mad About You;* Dry Cleaner; 1992
8. *Murder, She Wrote;* Theo Wexler; 10/30/1988
9. *New Love, American Style;* 1985
10. *The Fall Guy;* Himself; 12/16/1982
11. *The Love Boat;* 1977
12. *Barnaby Jones;* Marty Paris; 3/11/1975
13. *Kolchak: The Night Stalker;* Jack Burton; 1/17/1975
14. *The Streets of San Francisco;* Ernie Walker; 1973
15. *Emergency!;* Alan Austen; 12/16/1972
16. *Family Affair;* Hippie; 4/7/1969
17. *Get Smart;* Musician; 9/21/1968
18. *Garrison's Gorillas;* Tony; 2/13/1968
19. *Gomer Pyle, U.S.M.C.;* Effects Man; 1/22/1968
20. *Garrison's Gorillas;* Pablo; 11/27/1967
21. *F Troop;* Standup Bull; 3/29/1966
22. *The Andy Griffith Show;* Grecos; 2/21/1966
23. *I Dream of Jeannie;* Achmed; 1/8/1966
24. *Gomer Pyle, U.S.M.C.;* Sergeant; 12/24/1965
25. *My Favorite Martian;* Benny; 11/28/1965
26. *My Three Sons;* Itchie; 11/19/1964
27. *The Dick Van Dyke Show;* Delivery Boy; 12/19/1961
28. *The Dick Van Dyke Show;* Delivery Boy; 11/14/1961
29. *The Dick Van Dyke Show;* Delivery Boy; 10/24/1961
30. *The Dick Van Dyke Show;* Delivery Boy; 10/ 17/1961
31. *The Rebel;* 3/26/1961

William Frawley

Fred Mertz on *I Love Lucy*;
Bud O'Casey on *My Three Sons*

William Frawley was the W.C. Fields of the small screen.

He's best remembered as the irascible, acid-tongued neighbor Fred Mertz on *I Love Lucy*. On *My Three Sons*, his character, Bub O'Casey, was a bit more laid back, but he was still a gruff—but loveable—old curmudgeon. In real life, Frawley was not unlike his TV persona. He came from an era when men were men and women were dames and for most of his years, he lived the bachelor's life—hanging out in his favorite bars, playing cards, going to the ball game and talking sports with his pals. In the first episode of *I Love Lucy*, his character wanted to go to the fights instead of take his wife out on the town for their 18th wedding anniversary. Frawley was also just that kind of guy.

Frawley was an aging rebel, known for saying exactly what was on his mind. He didn't care who he insulted. He once told his boss, Lucille Ball, that her singing voice was like "a shovel of shit on a baked Alaska." He was anti-establishment and couldn't hold himself back in the presence of authority figures. On *My Three Sons*, he and the cast were contractually obligated to do commercials for the show's sponsors. But while filming spots in front of a room full of visiting executives from Heinz or Quaker Oats, Frawley would deliberately grimace while tasting the product, spit it out and then let loose with a slew of profanities to describe the taste.

Like Fields, he had little use for the institution of marriage or authority of any kind, and after half a century in his chosen profession, he had no patience with pretentious actors. Like Fields, he also liked his booze.

Unlike Fields, he wasn't anti-*everything*. He had a fine singing voice and loved barbershop quartets. It was just that he had no interest in matters that didn't directly concern Bill Frawley. Many people reach a point in their later years where they feel they can finally get away with saying whatever they want. Not Frawley. He had been that way all his life. Of all the character actors in Hollywood, Frawley was one of the few who truly was a "character."

William Frawley was born on February 26, 1887, in Burlington, Iowa. In his youth he had sung with the St. Paul's Catholic Church Choir and also at the Burlington Opera House. He had worked briefly as a railroad clerk for the Union Pacific Railroad in Omaha but after appearing in the chorus of a musical, *The Flirting Princess* in Chicago, his future was set. His mother didn't approve and sent his brother Paul to Chicago to bring him home. But once home, the two of them wrote a show called *Fun in a Vaudeville Agency* and put it on in an unused theatre. They made a nice profit and after that left town and toured the vaudeville circuit as The Frawley Brothers. The partnership was a brief one, but both brothers eventually made their own separate ways to Broadway.

In 1910, Frawley landed a year-long solo gig at the Rex Café in Denver. After that he hooked up with piano player Franz Rath and they toured west of the Rockies with a show they called, "A Man, A Piano and a Nut." In 1912, with Rath, Frawley was the first person to perform the sentimental standard "Melancholy Baby." He also claimed to be the first to do "Carolina in the Morning."

In 1914, he picked up a new touring partner — his wife, Edna Louise Broedt. They did a husband and wife act with Louise playing straight woman to him. As "Frawley and Louise," they played the Orpheum circuit, which was the better class theatres on the vaudeville circuit. In 1915, that led to a gig at The Palace in New York, which was the pinnacle of success back then. They separated in 1921 and Frawley remained single for the rest of his life. "I never married again," he later said. "Once was sufficient."[1]

By the 1920s, Frawley was based in New York and performing regularly on Broadway in musical revues and musical comedies. Now in his mid-thirties, he had lost much of his hair and had a middle-aged spread. He looked like he always would for the rest of his life. In 1933, he was cast in *Twentieth Century,* a farce written for Broadway by the team of Ben Hecht and Charles MacArthur, who had earlier made it big with *The Front Page.* His character, Owen O'Malley, was a Broadway press agent and was the quintessential Bill Frawley character. He was an arrogant cynic who said what was on his mind. In a review in the *New York Herald Tribune,* critic Percy Hammond summed up the character this way — "A profane and humorous two-bottle chap who, when assisted by a couple of drinks, thumbs his nose wittily at Art and the universe."[2]

Frawley made such an impression in the part that he was offered a seven-year contract with Paramount as a studio player. He moved to Hollywood in 1934. Upon his arrival, he was called in to meet the studio executives who wanted to know what he had done in the past. After he named off a string of credits, one of them made the mistake of saying they had been hoping for someone with more hair. In typical Frawley fashion, he jumped up and told them, "If it's hair you want, hire a fucking lion!" and stormed out.[3]

That incident did not affect his job and for the next few years he was cast in all kinds of movies — musicals, westerns, war dramas and comedies. After his contract with Paramount ended in 1940, he freelanced and got work from all the other studios in town. He did his share of B-movies but was also cast in big movies like Bing Crosby's *Going My Way* in 1944 and in 1947 was in both *Miracle on 34th Street* and Charlie Chaplin's *Monsieur Verdoux.* "I must have made seven or eight pictures a year," Frawley later said of his movie days. "Once I was working in two pictures at the same time — played a doorknob in one and a bathmat in the other."[4]

In total, Frawley had over 100 movie credits to his name. However, by the end of the 1940s, even small roles were starting to dwindle. His career was going nowhere when *I Love Lucy* came along in 1951 and at the age of 64 he called up the show's producers and stars, Lucille Ball and Desi Arnaz, and offered his services because he had heard they were looking for a "type."

Frawley wasn't in the pilot for *I Love Lucy*. Neither was Vivian Vance, who was to be his co-star. After the pilot had been filmed, Lucy and Desi realized they needed something else and taking their cue from Lucy's previous radio series, *My Favorite Husband,* they decided they should have an older couple be their neighbors on the show. In that way, they could generate more storylines by pitting the men against the women. In other episodes the conflict could be between the younger couple and the older couple. They also decided to have the older couple be the landlords of the small Manhattan apartment building where Lucy and her musician husband, Ricky Ricardo, lived.

Frawley was the right age to play the ex-vaudevillian-turned-landlord Fred Mertz. But as his wife, Ethel, they chose Vivian Vance, an actress who was 22 years younger than Frawley. To play Ethel, Vance had to look like a frumpy housewife, someone who would look like a logical match for the rumpled Frawley. She was less than flattered to think that people would assume she was old enough to marry someone who was really old enough to be her father. Not only that but she was horrified that some people might actually think that they *were* married. Vance didn't endear herself to Frawley when he overheard her voice these complaints and refer to him as an "old coot."

In addition to all that, there was also the difference of their backgrounds. Frawley was from vaudeville; Vance was from the theatre. She was interested in the new "method" approach to acting where everything about the character was analyzed by the actor. Frawley was from the old school, where the only "motivation" he needed in a scene was the promise of a paycheck. Vance liked to rehearse. Frawley, however, only memorized his own lines of dialogue and seldom had any interest in how they affected the plot and the other characters. In fact, he would have been happier with fewer lines. To his credit, he was always prepared and knew his lines and after half a century in the business, his comic timing was impeccable after years of honing before live audiences. *I Love Lucy* was filmed before a live studio audience and Frawley was right at home working in front of an audience.

Fortunately, the natural dislike Vance and Frawley felt for each other is what made them so convincing as the long-married and long-suffering couple. Although the fat and bald jokes flew between them, the hen-pecked husband often called his wife "honey-bunch" and those insults and the petty bickering seemed to come more out of habit than from any genuine hate.

The pair kept up the act off-screen as well. If the public believed they were just like Fred and Ethel, it was because Frawley and Vance didn't pretend to like each other. After the show ended, an oft-quoted remark by Frawley was, "As for Vivian, I don't know where she is now and she doesn't know where I am and that's exactly the way I like it."[5]

If anything, their real-life squabbles were just as much out of habit as the ones between Fred and Ethel. Stanley Livingston, who played "Chip" on Frawley's next job, *My Three Sons,* believes that to a large extent, Frawley and Vance were just keeping up with the public's expectations in continuing their so-called feud.

"Whatever sparked it was still going on when we doing *My Three Sons,*" says Livingston. "On the third season of our show, lo and behold, Lucy decided to do *The Lucy Show* and they were on the next stage over from ours. She probably picked that stage knowing Bill and Vivian would have to pass each other. When Bill saw Vivian, he'd yell some sort of obscenity at her. He got me to participate in a couple of his pranks. When she was doing a scene, he'd get us kids on the show to sneak in and knock over a stack of empty film cans or throw them in like a frisbee to make a big racket and ruin her scene so she'd have to do it again.

"But by then, I think they both thought, 'This is kinda fun.' You know, the media always blows things out of proportion. I don't really think they felt any anger at each other at that point. It was just sort of like that was expected of them. That's my feeling and it just got to be fun pranks to keep the 'feud' going, because that's what people expected of them because they thought they hated each other's guts. So that was how they greeted each other on the studio lot — he'd yell out horrible things and she'd yell back."

When *I Love Lucy* ended its eight-year run in 1959, Frawley was immediately cast in three different pilots for Desilu before signing on with *My Three Sons* in 1960. He was the first one signed for the show — even before Fred MacMurray. On the show, 73-year-old Frawley wasn't a supporting character, he was a co-star and the main comic lead. As Bub O'Casey, he was the father-in-law of MacMurray's character, Steve Douglas, a widower raising three boys. Bub was the family's housekeeper and den-mother and the regular sight of gruff and no-nonsense Frawley in the kitchen wearing an apron and baking a chocolate cake or a pot of Mulligan's stew was a sight gag in itself.

If anything, Bub O'Casey was a kinder and gentler version of Fred Mertz. Frawley was noticeably more relaxed on *My Three Sons*. Livingston jokes, "The explanation for that is because we didn't have Vivian Vance working on the show. That's probably what gave a little edge to his work on *I Love Lucy*."

When the producers cast Frawley, they knew what they were getting. On *I Love Lucy*, he played himself and they expected he would take the same approach on *My Three Sons*. "He was obviously intelligent enough to know that 'This is what's working for me and this is what people expect from me,' and I think after a while you sort of become that," says Livingston.

"I don't know if that was truly acting for him or if it was just a matter of doing the lines and reacting naturally. I didn't see too much difference in his off-stage persona than I did when we were actually filming. Obviously when the cameras stopped, he was a lot more profane.

"He was a pretty profane guy. He was always yelling, 'Who wrote this crap?!' Another frequent Frawleyism was, 'That guy's a double-barreled asshole!' The most fun for us on the set would be if he blew his lines or couldn't remember a line. When he got to that point, he would go crazy and profanity would fly out of his mouth like machine-gun fire. He had a colorful way with words."

Livingston is doubtful of the notion that Frawley was the type who gets to his senior years and realizes he can get away with saying anything he wants because of his age. "No, I think he was probably one of those guys who shot his mouth off his whole life. You can imagine him as a kid, he would be the one making noises in class. Even on the set, if there was the presence of anyone of authority around, Bill would be the guy who would say the things that probably shouldn't be said. Or else, he'd sit there quietly and when something was said, he'd make some rude, inappropriate noises. He just liked being cranky. I don't think he was as cranky as he appeared to be — but that was part of the persona people expected of him."

Given all that, Livingston wasn't afraid of Frawley. In fact, he was his favorite character on the show and his best friend on the set. Livingston was nine years old when he was cast as the youngest son on *My Three Sons*. The other two sons, Tim Considine and Don Grady, were in their teens and had their own interests and teenage concerns. But the youngest and the oldest members of the cast bonded and Livingston has a unique perspective on Frawley.

"I never knew my own grandfathers and that was my connection with Bill. I kind of became like a grandson to him because he never had any children of his own. Before working together, I had seen him on *I Love*

Lucy and I would always see him in old movies on TV from the 1930s and '40s and he looked *exactly* the same as he did on *My Three Sons*. He probably looked like that ever since he was 10 years old.

"I had heard that he wasn't really fond of children but for whatever reason, maybe because of the scenes we had together and rehearsing, we sort of bonded. He took a liking to me and you could feel it. When you're a kid, you can tell if somebody really likes you or not.

"So we would hang out and I'd go to his dressing room and play cards and checkers with him. And almost every day I would go to lunch with him at Nickodells, a famous restaurant across the street from the studio. He'd have a three-martini lunch and it became my unofficial job to shepherd Bill back from lunch everyday. I went to that restaurant for years after the show was over and part of the fun for me was that I'd walk in there and you almost felt like that was where Bill Frawley's ghost was, especially in the back where he had his own booth. I'd go to that same booth and sit in the spot where Bill had sat and it was still sunken in from the weight of him. There was always the aura of him around whenever I went back and sat at that table."

Livingston says it wasn't until years later that he realized how special Frawley had considered their friendship. "For my 13th birthday he got me a surfboard. At the time I just thought, 'Wow, what a neat gift.' But when I think back on it now, I realize that he had to really be in tune with what my interests were. He picked me out a nine-foot Dewey Martin surfboard which was like top of the line. So he must have gone somewhere, found about good boards and that would have been a lot of trouble for him because this was a guy who didn't even drive. I don't know how he got it back to the studio. But that made a big impression on me years later when I realized how much trouble he had gone to for me."

Besides getting an insight into a warm and thoughtful side of the man which few people saw, the memory also left Livingston with a lasting humorous image — the incongruous sight of Frawley at a surf shop on the beach. "He must have looked out of place walking into that shop to buy a surfboard — and knowing him, he probably acted cranky and gave them a hard time too."

In the fifth year of *My Three Sons,* the producers were forced to write the 78-year-old actor out of the show because of his poor health. He had suffered a small heart attack a couple of years before and throughout the 1964–65 season, he had trouble remembering his lines and would often fall asleep during the middle of filming a scene. When he didn't pass the annual insurance company physical, they had no choice but to let him go. "The doctor told them, 'This guy should be dead by now,'" says Livingston. Years of drinking and late-night card games had finally taken their toll.

On March 3, 1966, Frawley had a heart attack and died on Hollywood Boulevard while walking home from a movie.

His last television appearance had been filmed a few months earlier. It was a surprise cameo on *The Lucy Show* in October 1965. In the episode, he and Lucy momentarily bump into each other and when they part, Lucy says, "You know, he reminds me of someone I used to know."

Notes

1. *TV Guide*; August 5, 1961; "Bill Frawley Calls 'Em as He Sees 'Em."
2. *Meet the Mertzes*; by Rob Edelman and Audrey Kupferberg; Renaissance Books; Los Angeles; 1999.
3. *Meet the Mertzes*; by Rob Edelman and Audrey Kupferberg; page 65.
4. *TV Guide*; "Bill Frawley Calls 'Em as He Sees 'Em"; August 5, 1961.
5. *TV Guide*; "Bill Frawley Calls 'Em as He Sees 'Em"; August 5, 1961.

William Frawley Credits

FILM CREDITS

1. *Safe at Home;* 1962; Bill Turner
2. *Rancho Notorious;* 1952; Baldy Gunder
3. *Rhubarb;* 1951; Len Sickles
4. *The Lemon Drop Kid;* 1951; Gloomy Willie
5. *Abbott and Costello Meet the Invisible Man;* 1951; Detective Roberts
6. *Blondie's Hero;* 1950; Marty Greer
7. *Kill the Umpire;* 1950; Jimmy O'Brien
8. *Pretty Baby;* 1950; Corcoran
9. *Kiss Tomorrow Goodbye;* 1950; Byers
10. *East Side, West Side;* 1949; Bill the Bartender
11. *Home in San Antone;* 1949
12. *The Lady Takes a Sailor;* 1949; Oliver Harker
13. *The Lone Wolf and His Lady;* 1949; Inspector Crane
14. *Red Light;* 1949; Hotel Clerk
15. *Chicken Every Sunday;* 1948; George Kirby
16. *The Girl from Manhattan;* 1948; Mr. Bernouti
17. *Texas, Brooklyn and Heaven;* 1948; Agent
18. *Joe Palooka in Winner Take All;* 1948; Knobby Walsh
19. *The Babe Ruth Story;* 1948; Jack Dunn
20. *Good Sam;* 1948; Tom Moore
21. *Blondie's Anniversary;* 1947; Sharkey the loan shark
22. *Hit Parade of 1947;* 1947; Harry Holmes
23. *I Wonder Who's Kissing Her Now;* 1947; Jim Mason

24. *My Wild Irish Rose;* 1947; William Scanlon
25. *Monsieur Verdoux;* 1947; Jean LaSalle
26. *Down to Earth;* 1947; Police Lieutenant
27. *Mother Wore Tights;* 1947; Mr. Schneider
28. *Miracle on 34th Street;* 1947; Charles Halloran
29. *Crime Doctor's Man Hunt;* 1946; Inspector Harry B. Manning
30. *The Inner Circle;* 1946; Det. Lt. Webb
31. *Rendezvous with Annie;* 1946; General Trent
32. *The Virginian;* 1946; Honey Wiggen
33. *Ziegfeld Follies;* 1946; Mr. Martin
34. *Hitchhike to Happiness;* 1945; Sandy Hill
35. *Lady on a Train;* 1945; Police Sergeant
36. *The Flame of the Barbary Coast;* 1945; Wolf Wylie
37. *Lake Placid Serenade;* 1944; Jiggers
38. *Minstrel Man;* 1944
39. *Going My Way;* 1944; Max
40. *The Fighting Seebees;* 1944; Eddie Powers
41. *Whistling in Brooklyn;* 1943; Detective Ramsey
42. *Larceny with Music;* 1943; Mike Simms
43. *We've Never Been Licked;* 1943; Traveling Salesman
44. *Moonlight in Havana;* 1942; Barney Crane
45. *Wildcat;* 1942; Oliver Westbrook
46. *Gentleman Jim;* 1942; Billy Delaney
47. *Roxie Hart;* 1942; O'Malley
48. *Give Out, Sisters;* 1942; Harrison
49. *It Happened in Flatbush;* 1942; Sam Sloan
50. *Treat 'Em Rough;* 1942; Hotfoot
51. *Cracked Nuts;* 1941; Mitchell
52. *Public Enemies;* 1941; Bang
53. *Footsteps in the Dark;* 1941; Hopkins
54. *The Bride Came C.O.D.;* 1941; Sheriff McGee
55. *Blondie in Society;* 1941; Walter Pincus
56. *Six Lessons From Madame LaZonga;* 1941; Beheegan
57. *Dancing on a Dime;* 1940; Mac
58. *The Farmer's Daughter;* 1940; Scoop Trimble
59. *The Quarterback;* 1940; Coach
60. *Rhythm on the River;* 1940; Mr. Westlake
61. *Sandy Gets Her Man;* 1940; Police Chief O'Hara
62. *Untamed;* 1940; Les Woodbury
63. *One Night in the Tropics;* 1940; Roscoe
64. *Opened By Mistake;* 1940; Matt Kingsley
65. *Those Were the Days;* 1940; (uncredited) Prisoner
66. *Ambush;* 1939; Inspector J.L. Weber
67. *Ex-Champ;* 1939; Mushy Harrington
68. *Grand Jury Secrets;* 1939; Bright Eyes
69. *Night Work;* 1939; Bruiser Brown
70. *Stop, Look and Love;* 1939; Joe Haller

71. *St. Louis Blues;* 1939; Maj. Martingale
72. *Rose of Washington Square;* 1939; Harry Long
73. *Persons in Hiding;* 1939; Alec Inglis
74. *The Adventures of Huckleberry Finn;* 1939; Bilgewater, the "Duke"
75. *Sons of the Legion;* 1938; Uncle Willie Lee
76. *Touchdown Army;* 1938; Jack Heffernan
77. *Professor Beware;* 1938; Snoop Donlan
78. *Mad About Music;* 1938; Dusty Turner
79. *Blossoms on Broadway;* 1937; Frances X. Rush
80. *Double or Nothing;* 1937; Pederson
81. *High, Wide and Handsome;* 1937; Mac
82. *Something to Sing About;* 1937; Hank Meyers
83. *F-Man;* 1936; Hogan
84. *It's a Great Life;* 1936; Lt. McNulty
85. *The Princess Comes Across;* 1936; Benton
86. *Rose Bowl;* 1936; Soapy Moreland
87. *Three Married Men;* 1936; Bill Mullins
88. *The General Died at Dawn;* 1936; Brighton
89. *Three Cheers for Love;* 1936; Milton Shakespeare
90. *Desire;* 1936; Mr. Gibson
91. *Strike Me Pink;* 1936; Mr. Copple
92. *Alibi Ike;* 1935; Cap
93. *College Scandal;* 1935; Chief of Police Magoun
94. *Hold 'Em Yale;* 1935; Sunshine Joe
95. *Ship Café;* 1935; Briney O'Brien
96. *Harmony Lane;* 1935; Ed Christy
97. *Welcome Home;* 1935; Painless
98. *Car 99;* 1935; Sergeant Barrel
99. *Roberta;* 1935; (uncredited) Bartender
100. *The Crime Doctor;* 1934; Fraser
101. *The Lemon Drop Kid;* 1934; The Professor
102. *Shoot the Works;* 1934; Larry Hale
103. *Here Is My Heart;* 1934; James Smith
104. *Bolero;* 1934; Mike DeBaere
105. *The Witching Hour;* 1934; Jury Foreman
106. *Hell and High Water;* 1933; Milton J. Bunsey
107. *Miss Fane's Baby Is Stolen;* 1933; Captain Murphy
108. *Moonlight and Pretzels;* 1933; Mack
109. *Fancy That;* 1929
110. *Lord Loveland Discovers America;* 1916; Tony Kidd

TV CREDITS

1. *My Three Sons;* TV series; 1960–1965; "Bub" O'Casey
2. *I Love Lucy;* TV series; 1951–1959; Fred Mertz

NOTABLE TV GUEST APPEARANCES

1. *The Lucy Show;* 1965
2. *Bronco;* 4/16/1962
3. *Westinghouse Desilu Playhouse;* 12/11/1959
4. *The Gale Storm Show;* Jim Comstock; 10/8/1959
5. *Westinghouse Desilu Playhouse;* 2/4/1959
6. *The Silver Theatre;* 5/1/1950
7. *The Silver Theatre;* 1/9/1950
8. *Your Show Time;* 4/15/1949

Gale Gordon

Theodore J. Mooney on *Here's Lucy*;
Osgood Conklin on *Our Miss Brooks*

Gale Gordon once described his character, Osgood Conklin, the school principal on *Our Miss Brooks*, this way: "There's nothing subtle about Osgood. No nuances. Just a lot of very satisfying acid, bluster and bellowing, with an occasional weak moment of cordiality thrown in for leavening. It is practically impossible to overplay him. Even when he's being cordial, he's like an elephant trying to waltz."[1]

He could just as easily been talking about his later, more famous, role — that of banker Mr. Mooney on *The Lucy Show*. Interestingly enough, as the hot-tempered dictatorial principal on *Our Miss Brooks*, Gordon was a model of restraint in comparison to the blustery stuffed shirt he played opposite Lucille Ball. There was no such thing as playing a role too broad or extreme on the slapstick *Lucy* shows. In fact, in playing Lucy's long-suffering foil, that was often a prerequisite. Gordon matched her high energy with over-the-top bluster and bellowing. In playing support to Ball, Gordon was able to show off his expertise at reaction shots — the double-take, the spit-take, and his specialty — the slow burn, letting things build up until he would finally explode with a booming "Lucille!!!"

By the time he first appeared on *Here's Lucy* in the early 1960s, Gordon's TV persona had long been established with television audiences. He had spent four years perfecting his character-type on *Our Miss Brooks*. Before that, he had done the radio version of the show with the rest of the original cast from 1948 until they made the jump to television in 1952. When it ended, he was in a few short-lived series — *The Brothers, Sally, Pete and Gladys* — and then spent a couple of seasons on *Dennis the Menace* as crotchety Mr. Wilson. His television resume is full of long-suffering, ill-tempered characters. It's no coincidence that his character in Ozzie and Harriet Nelson's feature film, *Here Come the Nelsons*, was actually named "Mr. Bellows."

His legacy however, is his work with Lucille Ball. Their professional relationship goes back to the late 1940s when he and Bea Benaderet ("Kate" from *Petticoat Junction*) played the upstairs neighbors on her radio show, *My Favorite Husband*. When Ball and real-life husband Desi Arnaz were creating *I Love Lucy*, Gordon and Benaderet were their first choices to play their television neighbors, The Mertzes. Gordon, however, was contractually tied up with the radio show *Our Miss Brooks*. Nonetheless, he was soon working for the Arnazes. Their production company, Desilu, produced the television version of *Our Miss Brooks*. He also guest-starred in a couple of episodes of *I Love Lucy*. In fact, his very first appearance on television was a guest shot on *I Love Lucy* in May 1952. Desilu also produced the sitcom *The Brothers*, which starred Gordon in 1956. After working with Gordon on her own programs and specials throughout the 1960s and '70s, when Ball made her TV comeback as a 72-year-old Lucy in 1986 in *Life With Lucy,* she insisted that the 80-year-old Gordon be by her side.

On one episode of *Here's Lucy,* when Lucy worries that she's about to be fired by Mr. Mooney, a friend reassures her by pointing out, "I know you two have your differences, but Mr. Mooney is loyal. If he wasn't, he'd have hired a good secretary long ago." Gale Gordon felt the same kind of loyalty for Lucille Ball. Over the years, many books have been written about how difficult she was to work with and yet in all those pages you won't find one quote where Gordon says anything bad about her — or about anybody else for that matter.

Gordon lasted so long with Ball for two reasons. First off, she genuinely thought he was one of the funniest men in the world. Secondly, like her, he prided himself on being a professional and always came to set prepared and ready to work. Ball, who owned her shows, would not tolerate anything less in her employees.

By the time he was hired for *The Lucy Show,* Gordon was in his late fifties and had decades of credits to his name. Right from birth there was little doubt that he would find a career in the entertainment field. He was born Charles T. Aldrich Junior in New York on February 2, 1906, to show business parents. His father, Charles T. Aldrich, was a vaudeville performer. His mother, Gloria Gordon, was an actress who was later best known to radio audiences as Mrs. O'Reilly on *My Friend Irma.*

Although he was born in New York City, Gordon spent his first eight years in England. When his family returned in 1914, he found out the hard way that on this side of the Atlantic, boys don't wear short pants to grade school. Getting beaten up that first day of classes not only set the tone for his remaining nine years of school but also shaped the embittered attitude of his future character of principal Osgood Conklin, who seemed to despise teachers and students alike. At the time of *Our Miss Brooks,* Gordon revealed, "The character of Osgood Conklin was not only born but pickled in vinegar during those nine years. I hated school, from the principal on down."[2]

In 1924, at the age of 18, Gordon returned to England and began to work in the theatre. It was there that he perfected his celebrated voice with its flawless diction and slight hint of British refinement. Legendary actor John Barrymore once noted that Gordon's diction was the best of anyone in the business.

Being a master of enunciation was his job ticket when he returned to the States and began working regularly in radio in the early 1930s. However, his beginnings in radio were certainly inauspicious enough — in one of his first roles he didn't even have a speaking part, he played the footsteps of The Unknown Soldier. By 1933 he was making $15 a week playing in *English Coronets*. His big break in radio came two years later when he was cast as the leading man opposite the star on *The Mary Pickford Show* and began making $100 a week. At the time, that made him the highest-paid radio actor in Hollywood.

Over the next two decades, Gordon's cultured tones and deep bass voice could be heard on any number of radio programs. He was the father on *Junior Miss*. For seven years he was the leading man opposite Irene Rich on *Dear John*. On the popular long-running *Fibber McGee and Molly*, he played Mayor LaTrivia for 12 years. On that show's spin-off, *The Great Gildersleeve*, he was Mr. Bullard from 1941 to '53. Along the way, he also did a stint as *Flash Gordon*, played a Texas millionaire on the *Burns and Allen Show* and worked opposite Basil Rathbone on *Sherlock Holmes*. He once claimed to be so adaptable that on one episode of *Gangbusters*, he played a killer, the cop that arrested him and "the siren that presaged the advent of the cop."[3]

Also in the late 1940s, on Lucille Ball's radio series with Richard Denning, *My Favorite Husband*, Gordon and Bea Benaderet played their neighbors, the Atterburys. Mr. Atterbury was also the boss of Dennings' character. He was a bank president.

In 1948, Osgood Conklin was heard for the first time on the radio on Eve Arden's CBS comedy series, *Our Miss Brooks*. The show made the jump to the CBS television network in 1952 while still continuing with the same cast on the radio.

The program was about schoolteacher Connie Brooks who takes a job teaching English at Madison High. Plots revolved around her work life and love life — or rather, the lack of one. When *Our Miss Brooks* began on radio, Eve Arden was already well-known to audiences for her movie roles, where she generally played the caustically witty best friend of the star. Her innate gift for cracking wise made her perfect for the high school setting whether she was working off of her students, Principal Conklin or her love interest, biology teacher Mr. Boynton, a dullard who wasn't worthy of her attention. Brooks was so sharp-witted that most of her throwaway lines went soaring over the heads of most at whom they were directed.

That wasn't the case in her scenes with Principal Conklin. If Miss Brooks had an occasional tendency to use sarcasm, it was because she was upset about getting something done for her students. But with Conklin, sarcasm flowed from him so easily simply because he was naturally mean-spirited. As a former military officer, he ran his school as a strict disciplinarian. Of course that clashed with Miss Brooks' more free-spirited approach to teaching. On *Our Miss Brooks*, Osgood Conklin provided most of the conflict.

Gordon's acting differed on *Our Miss Brooks* from what he would do later on *Here's Lucy* because *Miss Brooks* was a character comedy and *Lucy* was situation comedy. On *Miss Brooks*, nothing momentous ever happened, it was largely about the small daily events that involved the single school-teacher and her regular circle of friends and co-workers. In addition to the reliably crusty principal, there was also the hormonally charged, squeaky-voiced student Walter Denning, played by an ever-aging Richard Crenna, and Miss Brooks' scatterbrained landlady, Mrs. Davis.

Arden was sexy and sassy and the comedy came from her reactions to the different people she encountered in her daily rounds. She made Connie Brooks warm and vulnerable and that humanity was extended to the other characters. Osgood may have been an intemperate crank, able to blow his stack at the slightest provocation, but Arden's character was so rooted in reality that all of Gordon's ranting and raving were entirely believable. When he ranted and raved on *The Lucy Show*, it was usually as the punch line to a bit of slapstick set in motion by Ball. Since that style of comedy was broad in the first place, it wasn't necessary to take Mr. Mooney's reactions too seriously. He was reacting as anyone would have in dealing with that walking disaster known as Lucille Carmichael. Gordon was nominated in 1955 as Best Supporting Actor in a Comedy Series for his role on *Our Miss Brooks*. There would be no such nominations for all his years with Lucy.

In 1955, the producers changed the setting of *Our Miss Brooks*—not just because Walter Denning had been in high school since the series began on radio seven years earlier, or because after all that time her romance with Mr. Boynton was still going nowhere, but rather because the ratings were starting to fall. Madison High was demolished to make way for a new highway and Miss Brooks began a new job at Mrs. Nestor's Private Elementary School. Upon arriving for her first day on her new job, just her luck, she discovered that the school was being run by Principal Osgood Conklin. This should have been a foreshadowing of bad things to come. In its new format, the new show only lasted one season before being cancelled in 1956.

The same year, *Our Miss Brooks*, a big screen version of the TV show, was released with all the original actors. It chronicles Miss Brooks' arrival and her problems with the principal, and gives a more optimistic look at her romance with Mr. Boynton.

When school finally let out for good on *Our Miss Brooks*, Gordon was immediately back on TV starring in the Desilu production of *The Brothers* for CBS in 1956. The series ran for two years and was about two brothers who owned a photography studio. Gordon played Harvey Box. Bob

Sweeney, a comic actor who had worked on *Our Miss Brooks* and later went on to direct *The Andy Griffith Show,* played his brother, Gilmore.

Plots revolved around the relationship between the two vastly different brothers and their equally different girlfriends. As can be expected, the older brother Harvey was bossy and full of bluster and brother Gilmore was shy and quiet and inclined to let his brother take charge.

Before *The Brothers* went off the air at the end of summer reruns in September 1958, Gordon had also been co-starring for a few weeks on *Sally,* an NBC sitcom starring Joan Caulfield as Sally Truesdale. The series had begun the previous fall with episodes being about Sally's adventures in working as a companion to an eccentric wealthy widow, Mrs. Myrtle Banford, played by eccentric character actress Marion Lorne, who is best known as the constantly befuddled Aunt Clara from *Bewitched.* However, in February 1958, they ended their world travels and returned home where Mrs. Banford had inherited half of the Banford-Bleacher Department Store which her husband had co-owned with Gordon's character, Bascomb Bleacher. It was exactly the same premise used 30 years later for Gordon and Lucille Ball on their last sitcom, *Life with Lucy.*

Considering what he was up against in the well-meaning but blundering Mrs. Bascomb and her trouble-shooting assistant Sally, it's not hard to imagine Gordon flexing his well-exercised lungs and doing a lot of yelling. Not helping matters was his incompetent son, Bascomb Bleacher Jr., who was played by a young Arte Johnson. However, like *Our Miss Brooks,* the change in setting did not bring higher ratings and *Sally* was off the air by April 1958.

In 1960, Gordon was cast in *Pete and Gladys.* The series was a spinoff of *December Bride,* in which Harry Morgan played Pete Porter, a next-door neighbor who was always complaining about his wife, Gladys. On the original series, Gladys was never seen but on the new show she was played by Cara Williams. Gordon played Uncle Paul Porter for the show's two-year run. During the last half of the final season of *Pete and Gladys,* Gordon again found himself in the position of doing double duty by working on two shows at the same time. He was called in by the producers of *Dennis the Menace* to fill in as Mr. Wilson's brother, John, when Joseph Kearns, the actor who played George Wilson, died in May 1962 before filming was completed for the season. Gordon was introduced as Wilson's brother who was just visiting his sister-in-law. When the next season began, Gordon was installed as the new Mr. Wilson.

Gordon's patented short-tempered TV persona made him a perfect foil to play opposite the troublesome Dennis, played by Jay North. Dennis, while not a deliberately mischievous or evil kid, was probably one of the more annoying brats to have an entire prime time show devoted to his antics. If Mr. Wilson was carefully nurturing some potential prize-winning roses, the day before the competition, Dennis was likely to show up at the door with a handful of Wilson's roses, saying that he picked them to cheer up Mrs. Wilson. He meant well, but that didn't make him any the less aggravating.

Gordon had worked with actor Joe Kearns on *Our Miss Brooks* where Kerns played Osgood Conklin's boss, the superintendent of the school board who disapproved of Conklin's dictatorial style. The difference in the two actors' styles as Mr. Wilson is noteworthy. As the original Mr. Wilson, Kearns was an understandably frustrated but essentially kind-hearted old soul who simply wanted to enjoy his retirement in peace. But Gordon, as Wilson, was his usual bellowing, impatient self and it was good to see Dennis being yelled at by a true master. However, maybe Gordon was *too* intimidating as the new Mr. Wilson. The show was cancelled after the 1962–'63 season. Or maybe it was because Jay North was now almost 12 years old and no longer looked cute in the red and white striped shirt, overalls and that ingratiating grin.

When Lucille Ball decided to return to television in 1962 with *The Lucy Show,* she enlisted the help of her old sidekick Vivian Vance as well as Gordon. Set in Danfield, Connecticut, Ball played Lucy Carmichael, a widow with two children. She shared a house with divorcee Vivian Bagley (Vance) who also had a child. Gordon played Theodore J. Mooney, the president of the Danfield First National Bank.

Vance's involvement gradually wound down as she tired of commuting to Los Angeles from her home in Connecticut where she was living with a new husband. In turn, the show, which originally centered around the "kooky capers" of Lucy and Viv, began to revolve around the workplace and Lucy's almost weekly attempts to save her job and not be fired because of whatever misunderstanding would have put her job in jeopardy that week. Mr. Mooney was the threat that inspired most of the action.

In 1965, the setting was changed to San Francisco where Lucy worked for Mooney as his secretary at the Westland Bank. At the bank, Mooney was only a vice-president and so not only was Lucy's job in constant uncertainty but her all-encompassing incompetence meant that even Mooney's job wasn't safe.

In 1968, Ball changed the format once again and came up with a new setting and premise. The new show was called *Here's Lucy* and she brought in her own teenaged children, Lucie and Desi Junior. Now located in Los Angeles, her character was a widower named Lucille Carter. Gordon's character was her brother-in-law, Harrison Carter — or "Uncle Harry." He felt sorry for her and hired her as his secretary at the business he owned, The

Unique Employment Agency. Of course Lucy was just as inept here as she was in the bank but Harry couldn't fire her because of guilt and a sense of family.

The employment agency was the perfect set-up to bring in guest stars as well as putting Lucy in a different situation every week where she could perform her schtick and have things get out of control. Often the plots were just excuses to set up the centerpiece of the episode, which was always a few minutes of slapstick and mayhem, usually culminating with Gordon going from slow burn to an all-out blow-up at finding himself in some humiliating and embarrassing situation. Yet somehow, no matter how degrading the circumstances, he always managed to retain a bit of dignity.

Gordon once acknowledged of his work on the show that "We had some scripts that were very weak. Lucy never tried to be funny. We played everything we did perfectly straight."[4]

But audiences never tired of Lucy's brand of comedy and Gordon credited her sense of perfection and professionalism for the show's success. "In my humble opinion, she knows more about show business than anybody alive today," he once said. "I've always loved *working* with her and I've always loved and admired *her*. She works harder than anyone on the set, always has. *Everything* has to be perfect because the play is the important thing, as far as she is concerned. Work and concentration and perfection are the key words to describe Lucille Ball."[5]

But Gordon himself lasted for the entire run of the series by sharing Ball's work ethic. Like her, he came prepared and ready to work. His professionalism was rewarded. Lucille Ball made him a rich man. Between his first appearance on television with a guest shot on *I Love Lucy* in 1952 and his last episode of *Here's Lucy* in 1974, he had over two decades of straight employment on TV as a regular on various series. From 1952 onwards and throughout the 1960s and the early part of the '70s, there was never a time when he didn't have a full time job on TV. Of those 22 years, there were only five years when he wasn't working either with Lucy or as an employee of her company. Twelve years after *Here's Lucy* went off the air in 1974, Ball was lured back to episodic television again for *Life With Lucy* in 1986. One of the conditions she insisted upon was being reunited with Gale Gordon, who was then 80 years old. He was paid $25,000 an episode. But tastes in television comedy had changed and the show only lasted a handful of episodes. But it's the thought that counts.

By all accounts, Gordon was not anything like his television persona. Interviews show him to be a reflective, quiet man with a dry sense of humor who liked to relax by painting, gardening and spending time away from Hollywood with his wife and their many dogs at their desert home in Borrego Springs.

Lucie Arnaz, who knew him both as a family friend and then later as a co-worker on *Here's Lucy*, remembers him this way: "I adored Gale and worshipped his comedic talent and his kind and gentle soul and his enormous wit both offstage and on. I called him Gale and I am sure I wished he were my real uncle. He acted as though he were. Always watched over Desi and I in a paternal type fashion. What an extraordinary man.

"Since I had known him through all of the years that he played Mr. Mooney on *The Lucy Show*, he certainly was a family friend who became a co-worker but that didn't change the relationship, it only broadened it. Our respect for each other as performers and professionals deepened. I got to see *how* he rehearsed and prepared and behaved around a set and around other people who weren't always as professional as the rest of us."

She continues, "He was, by example, a phenomenal teacher and a real inspiration to me — of not only how to be good, but how to be *nice* and professional and be able to work and get along with people. Since then, I have met quite a few actors who could have benefited from working with someone like Gale Gordon for a few years."

When Gale Gordon died at the age of 89 on June 30, 1995, Arnaz was asked by *TV Guide* to share her thoughts about the man. Her first comment says it all and captures the feeling of anyone who had ever seen him perform on one of the *Lucy* shows. "What a sport!" said Arnaz. "There was always some closet full of tin cans that had to fall on his head, but he took it like a gentleman. He was refined and relaxed — almost the opposite of the characters he played."[6]

Notes

1. *TV Guide*; March 26, 1955; "Danger! Gale (Gordon) Blowing Up!"
2. *TV Guide*; March 26, 1955; "Danger! Gale (Gordon) Blowing Up!"
3. *TV Guide*; March 26, 1955; "Danger! Gale (Gordon) Blowing Up!"
4. *Desilu: The Story of Lucille Ball and Desi Arnaz*; by Coyne Steven Sanders and Tom Gilbert; William Morrow and Company; New York; 1993; page 274.
5. *Photoplay Magazine*; June 1974; "Gale Gordon's Love Affair with Lucille Ball"; by Will Tusher.
6. *TV Guide*; December 30, 1995; Obituaries.

Gale Gordon Credits

FILM CREDITS

1. *The 'Burbs*; 1989; Walter
2. *Speedway*; 1968; R.W. Hepworth

3. *Sergeant Deadhead;* 1965; Captain Weiskopf
4. *Dondi;* 1961; Colonel
5. *All Hands on Deck;* 1961; Commander Bintle
6. *All in a Night's Work;* 1961; Oliver Dunning
7. *Visit to a Small Planet;* 1960; Bob Mayberry
8. *Don't Give Up the Ship;* 1959; Congressman Mandeville
9. *The 30-Foot Bride of Candy Rock;* 1959; Raven
10. *Rally Round the Flag, Boys!;* 1958; Colonel Thorwald
11. *Our Miss Brooks;* 1956; Osgood Conklin
12. *Francis Covers the Big Town;* 1953; District Attorney Evans
13. *Here Come the Nelsons;* 1952; H.J. Bellows
14. *A Woman of Distinction;* 1950; Station Clerk
15. *Here We Go Again;* 1942; Cadwalader

TV CREDITS

1. *Life with Lucy;* TV series; 1986; Curtis McGibbon
2. *Bungle Abbey;* TV movie; 1981; The Abbot
3. *Lucy Calls the President;* TV special; 1977
4. *CBS Salutes Lucy; The First 25 Years;* TV special; 1976; Himself
5. *Here's Lucy;* TV series; 1968–1974; Harrison Carter
6. *The Lucy Show;* TV series; 1963–1968; Theodore J. Mooney
7. *Dennis the Menace;* TV series; 1962–1963; John Wilson
8. *Pete and Gladys;* TV series; 1960–1962; Uncle Paul Porter
9. *Sally;* TV series; 1958; Bascomb Bleacher Sr.
10. *The Brothers;* TV series; 1956–1957; Harvey Box
11. *Our Miss Brooks;* TV series; 1952–1956; Osgood Conklin

NOTABLE TV GUEST APPEARANCES

1. *Hi Honey, I'm Home;* Theodore J. Mooney; 1991
2. *Harrigan and Son;* Merril Davis; 9/22/1961
3. *The Lucy-Desi Comedy Hour;* The Judge; 1957
4. *The Real McCoys;* P.T. Kirkland; 1957
5. *I Love Lucy;* Mr. Littlefield; 6/9/1952
6. *I Love Lucy;* Mr. Littlefield; 5/26/1952

James Gregory

Inspector Luger on *Barney Miller*

James Gregory isn't one to suffer fools gladly. In conversation, he's likely to lose his patience and in turn, his temper. But that's allowed in someone who is 90 years old and has survived three strokes. Yet, it's also uncannily close to the sort of characters he has played over the years—somewhat abrasive, no-nonsense authority types.

Although he has created memorable characterizations on the stage and the big screen, Gregory is best known to television audiences as the gruff but loveable Inspector Frank Luger from ABC-TV's *Barney Miller* in the 1970s. It was also a character close to his own personality. In an interview, although he is prone to a temper outburst or two, he immediately realizes he's gone too far and makes light of it. *Barney Miller* producer Danny Arnold once described both Luger and Gregory this way — "Luger is a kind of Ebenezer Scrooge who has within him another person entirely. He's tough and crabby, but he's also a sentimental guy who cries at the drop of a hat. Outside, Jim's a very flinty old curmudgeon, but inside he's soft as mush."[1]

That's as true today as it was 20 years ago and probably 20 years before that. He still mails out autographed photos to anyone who takes the trouble to write and for someone who could accurately be called a cranky old cuss, he's also a very likeable guy. And he knows it.

If there are similarities between himself and Inspector Luger, Gregory doesn't like to over-analyze them, knowing that the root of "analysis" is "anal." Still, there are similarities. Both have fine singing voices. Luger had a tendency to warble a chorus or two of some old sentimental favorite if the mood struck and Gregory used to sing with a barbershop quartet in his spare time. As that may suggest, both are representatives of a different era. Luger would often bend Barney's ear when talking about the good old days when he was walking a beat on the police force with his long-gone friends, Foster, Klein and Brown. Gregory is just as likely to reminisce about "the good ol' days and nights" in New York in the 1940s and '50s when he was working on Broadway and appearing on live dramatic productions in the early days of television.

It was in The Golden Age of television that Gregory established his reputation as a reliable, hard-working actor and he never lacked for work as a result. To hear him describe it though, it's all just work. Just a job. He's being modest. It's true that he takes a working man's approach to his profession. But in his hands, it's not just a trade. He takes his craft and turns it into art. Gregory would deny that of course, but you only have to look at his performances in films like *The Manchurian Candidate* and *The Sons of Katie Elder* to see how he gives substance and a humanity to what could have easily been one-dimensional characters if left in the hands of someone less gifted. Even in *Beneath the Planet of the Apes*, in which he played Ursus, the war-mongering gorilla, Gregory's talent shines through all the fur and latex of that 200-pound monkey suit.

He is both an actor's actor and a journeyman actor — always prepared and professional and that combination has meant that he was always in demand. Simply put, before retiring in the mid–1980s, James Gregory was probably the most successful freelance actor in television. Although he has starred in a couple of TV series, his work on *Barney Miller* was in a recurring role and the bulk of his paychecks over the years came from a steady stream of guest appearances on television and character parts in movies. By the time *Barney Miller* came along in 1975, *TV Guide* estimated that he had been "the face of more than 1000 different supporting characters."[2]

That figure is a bit of an exaggeration but he certainly had more credits than any of his peers. Having played all those different roles might explain why he isn't overly attached to any particular character. For that matter, Gregory says he doesn't even have a preference to doing guest work or work as a regular on a series. "I like a *job*. For an actor, the most important thing is the next job. You don't go into it expecting to *like* anything. You may like some jobs more than others. But the thing is the job. The work. That's what you do."

That kind of work ethic has governed his entire working history and comes from entering the job market shortly before the Depression. Before becoming an actor, Gregory worked a variety of jobs. He was a busboy and waiter for the New York Athletic Club, a Wall Street runner, worked in retail sales and sold real estate. It was while working as a private secretary for a Wall Street firm that he decided to go into acting full time after he was yelled at for being late. "It was the happiest thing I ever did," he says.

Gregory was born December 23, 1911, in the borough of the Bronx in New York. He spent most of his youth in the suburb of New Rochelle. As a teenager he first became interested in acting and was elected president of the drama club at New Rochelle High School. He recalls that his first role was in a comedy, *The Showoff*. At the time, he didn't have any show business aspirations. "I liked acting but I didn't think I would take it on as a profession," he recalls.

He was also captain of the golf team and it was his interest in golf that led to his first full-time job after high school. "I had been a caddy for a member of the firm Hayden Stone and Company in New York and he told me that if I wanted, he could get me a job as a runner on Wall Street. The stock market crash of 1929 came along and men were selling apples on the street just to feed their families. And then I went from being a runner to private secretary for a member of the firm. I quit one morning because the guy I was working for bawled me out for being a little bit late."

During the five years he was working on Wall Street he had also been involved in community theatre at home in Westchester County. "I was affiliated with an amateur acting company and I liked it," he says. Shortly after quitting his job on Wall Street, he turned pro. One of the directors he had worked with in Little Theatre got a job directing summer stock in Deer Lake, Pennsylvania, and took Gregory along in 1935.

"And that's when I joined Actors Equity which made me a professional actor," he says. The following year he worked in a travelling repertory company, earning $25 a week. "We worked what was called the Chataqua Circuit based out of Ohio. We played one-night stands for three months. We traveled with a trailer full of all our props and a curtain for our stage. There was five of us and we set everything up ourselves and played in school gymnasiums, church basements and civic auditoriums in all the small towns."

His first job on Broadway came only three years later in *Key Largo* with Paul Muni. Gregory says that before his big break, he was just another struggling actor looking for work during the Depression. "An actor's life is hard and it was hard back then. I trouped around all over Broadway like many other young actors before I landed my first big professional job in *Key Largo*."

He worked regularly on Broadway for the next 17 years, with the exception of three years of military service during World War II, and appeared in 25 plays. They included *Dream Girl, In Time to Come, All My Sons, Dead Pigeon* and *Fragile Fox*. He played Biff in *Death of a Salesman* and over the course of its long run, he worked with five different "Willy Lomans"—Lee J. Cobb, Gene Lockhart, Thomas Mitchell, Albert Dekker and Robert F. Simon. His last play on Broadway was in 1956 with Paul Newman and Karl Malden in *The Desperate Hours*.

In the early 1950s, Gregory became involved in the new medium of television and was a busy participant in the live televised dramas now known as TV's Golden Age. It was a natural career move for a young stage actor. New York was the center of live television production and the new medium married the excitement and feeling of spontaneity of live theatre with many of the production techniques of movies. At the time however, many Broadway actors were snobbish about television, putting it down for its often cheap, primitive look. The real reason had to do with not wanting to make their mistakes in front of an entire nation of viewers. If they made a mistake in the theatre, the only people to see would be that night's audience of a few hundred people.

Gregory, however, says that the real true snobs about television back then lived in Hollywood. "The people who were snobs were the Hollywood movie actors because they couldn't learn all their lines or be able to sustain a scene or an act. You should have experience in the theatre before doing live television because it was real acting. The Hollywood actors didn't do it because they couldn't memorize that many lines."

Gregory's first work on television was in 1951 on a live installment of *The Web*, an anthology series of plays adapted from stories written by members of The Mystery Writers of America. The episode was called "All the Way to the Moon," and co-starred Henry Jones and Elenor Wilson. Throughout the 1950s, he appeared on all the various "TV theatre" shows and appeared 11 times alone on *Kraft TV Theatre*. He was also invited back in different roles to the anthology series *Love Story, Danger* and *Alfred Hitchcock Presents*. Many of the shows he did were melodramas, and others like *The Men Behind the Badge* or *The Big Story* were docu-dramas based on real stories.

At the peak of his busiest period Gregory set a record for the number of live performances. "I once appeared live in five different productions in a ten-day period," he says. "And I was running back and forth like a jackrabbit, I tell you."

During this time in the 1950s, he was also working regularly in New York theatre and starring on the radio drama *21st Precinct* as Captain Vincent Cronin. That was just one of many police officers Gregory would play over the years. His first starring lead role on a TV series came in 1959 on *The Lawless Years*, on NBC where he played New York City detective Barney Ruditsky, the head of the rackets squad back in the prohibition days of the 1920s. The NBC series was based on actual cases and the real Ruditsky served as technical director.

"We had an element of truth to that show because Barney was right there on the set," says Gregory. "A few months after we were on they came out with *The Untouchables*, which was set at the same time in Chicago. They tried to copy us. In real life, Elliot Ness was a clerk in an office, he wasn't a detective working in the field. We also had a different criminal each week and that's what made it more authentic." However, *The Untouchables* had a regular villain in the form of Frank Nitti, someone for the audience to hate on a weekly basis and so *The Lawless Years* only enjoyed a two-year run and was cancelled in 1961.

Gregory and his wife, Anne, a singer he had married in 1944, had moved to California in the late 1950s and he began appearing in "A" movies starting with *The Manchurian Candidate* in 1962. He played a right wing communist witch-hunting megalomaniac, Senator Johnny Iselin, who is being set up for the presidency, ironically through a Communist plot. The Cold War thriller starred Laurence Harvey, Frank Sinatra and Angela Lansbury as the Senator's evil, manipulative wife. "But if you think about it," suggests Gregory, "my character was actually the title character. He was the one that Angela Lansbury and the Communists from Manchuria were promoting to be president."

That was followed by *The Great Escape* in 1963. In 1965, he had a major role in the John Wayne western *The Sons of Katie Elder,* in which he played the black-hearted, greedy landowner who kills his own son when his plans are challenged.

Of course no discussion of his film career would be complete without mentioning his work in Don Knotts' 1969 parody of Hugh Hefner, *The Love God?* Gregory had a brief but commanding courtroom scene as Knotts' hypocritical defense attorney. He's a blustery windbag and Gregory chews up the scenery with great comic flair. He also worked with Andy Griffith in O*nionhead* in 1958 as "The Skipper," in a naval version of Griffith's military comedy from the year before *No Time for Sergeants.*

Although he was often cast in dramas as cops and military officers, his work in comedies has been just as strongly represented throughout his television career. Before *Barney Miller* came along, he had also been a regular on *The Paul Lynde Show* in 1972 and also played the temporary "den mother" named "Cappy Engstrom" on *My Three Sons* when that show was in the process of replacing William Frawley with William Demarest. Over the years, he has also done guest shots on the sitcoms *Hogan's Heroes, F Troop, Sanford and Son, All in the Family* and *The Partridge Family.* While working on those shows, he had also been on just about every TV series that involved horses and cowboy hats and every show where you carried a badge and a gun.

In fact, Gregory had played a cop so many times that when *Barney Miller* producer Danny Arnold came up with the idea of Inspector Frank Luger in 1975, he didn't even consider anyone else for the part. "After I did the first episode, I remember that they immediately came to me and told me that Luger would be written in for the next week as well," Gregory recalls. "There was nobody else up for the part to the best of my knowledge." Arnold had known both Gregory and the real life detective Barney Ruditsky from *The Lawless Years.* According to Gregory, Arnold named his show's title character Barney Miller, the same first name as Ruditsky, as a tribute.

Arnold may have taken other elements of Ruditsky and applied them to Luger when he created the character. The one thing the two men had in common was that they were each cops from a distinct era. With Luger, one way that was conveyed was through his wardrobe. The Inspector was a dapper dresser but by the late 1970s, his gray flannel suit topped off with a matching fedora and a little bow tie was about 20 years out of style. In fact, the outfit is indistinguishable from what Gregory wore in *The Manchurian Candidate* in 1962.

Gregory sees no real connection between Luger and Barney Ruditsky. "No, the real Barney Ruditsky was a very down-to-earth New York detective and there was no shilly-shallying with him. He had a sense of humor but he was not a comedian or a comic and nor was Luger."

As for establishing the character through wardrobe, he takes credit for coming up with the bow tie but says there was nothing significant about the rest of it. "I wouldn't delve into that too much," he advises. "I see nothing there. A lot of men wear fedora hats and a lot of men are cops."

In his job of inspector, Frank Luger is like a roving goodwill ambassador. He is a combination morale booster and nuisance the police department didn't really know what to do with — so they made him an inspector. On his visits to the 12th Precinct in Greenwich Village, where the show was set, most of the time he holes up in Barney's office talking about the good old days and his now-dead friends on the force. You can easily imagine Luger pounding a beat in the 1940s in any old movie with The Dead End Kids. In the 1950s, you can picture him as one of the plainclothes cops you would see in the detective room on TV's *Naked City*. In fact, Gregory's first movie was an uncredited performance as a patrolman in the 1948 feature film *Naked City*. For that matter, Luger came from an era when it was natural to get a bottle of scotch from the merchants on his beat at Christmas time and it was often easier to deal out some back-alley justice to a punk. It's not too much of a stretch to imagine Luger working in that world.

To the younger detectives under Captain Barney Miller's command, Luger was a bit of a curiosity, an antique. They smiled politely and condescendingly. They were respectful but looked at him as you would a favorite uncle in the early stages of senility. As Barney, Hal Linden was sympathetic and too polite to do anything but tolerate him. Barney was the link between the two generations. Instead of Luger's zero-tolerance approach, Barney preached compassion. Although the colorful Luger always brightened the squad room with his visits, if you thought about him, it was a bit sad. By the 1970s, the police force had changed. Society had changed. But Frank Luger remained exactly the same.

Barney Miller was a breed apart from other sitcoms of the time because of the quality of its writing. The high number of one-liners consistently delivered laughs while also getting to the heart of the individual characters.

Even the crooks were portrayed with dignity and given a measure of humanity. In the character of Frank Luger, the writers had their work cut out for them. For someone who was nearing retirement, Luger was very much a big kid and wore his heart on his sleeve. He could pout and be stubborn. He was a troublemaker — he deliberately called Ron Carey's "Officer Levitt" character by the wrong name whenever they met. And as befitting a person of his years, there was an honesty to the character in that he would say whatever was on his mind and hold nothing back.

However, even the best written characters need to be fleshed out by the actor to be brought to life. Gregory brought an old pro's talents to the chore of creating the character. He invented little bits of business that were true to his personality and helped further the idea that he was of another time. Often when he came out of Barney's office after a talk, his whole body would loosen up and he would bang his fists together while softly singing some old sentimental standard to himself. When he was in a really good mood, he would occasionally do a bit of soft-shoe dancing as he said his good-byes while exiting the squad room.

Gregory acknowledges his contributions but downplays them as all just being part of the job. "That's *acting*. You *think* about the character. You have to know and care about the character. You get to learn the character and then you invent things that the character would do. A lot of it is just to make him interesting and so you aren't just standing there like a post. That's *acting*. It's all part of the contribution you make as an *actor*. You come up with things for your character that are inventive and suggestive and you react to the other characters the way he would. You bounce off one another. Somebody sets up something for you and you do it or you set up a gimmick for them and they get the punch-line. But the bottom line is that you *know* your character and then you can embellish it; enlarge upon it. You polish it. You hone it."

In 1979, Gregory was offered the starring role in the ABC sitcom *Detective School*, in which he played an irascible Luger-like retired detective named Nick Hannigan who ran a school for aspiring private eyes. The show only lasted four months and Gregory returned to *Barney Miller*. When that show went off the air after seven seasons in 1982, Gregory himself retired shortly afterwards and eventually settled in Arizona with his wife, Anne.

In reflecting on his long career, Gregory is surprisingly unsentimental regarding his various characters and professes to have no particular favorites. "My favorite job is the next job," he says. "Even though I'm retired, I have fond memories of many, many shows, too many to enumerate. I've worked with a lot of nice people and it's quite a lot." As for Inspector Luger, he simply says, "Luger was a nice part and I enjoyed it."

However, he does point out that he enjoyed the style of comedy that was used on *Barney Miller*. "Comedy is a very subtle thing. If you are playing *for* comedy, if you have to knock people over the head to tell them, 'Oh boy, this is going to be funny,' and you have to do it with a grimace or overacting, well, that's not funny to me. That's just slapstick.

"On *Barney Miller*, the style of comedy we did was what I would call 'humorous' or 'amusing.' What they call funny on television today makes me want to regurgitate." As for whether he prefers comedy to drama, he won't commit himself despite being proficient in both worlds. Instead, Mr. Practical — television's most successful freelancer — goes back to his old refrain. But it's notable that he delivers the statement with the timing of a veteran comic. "I like *a* job. When you decide to take a job, you read the script. And if you like it, you do it. And if you don't like it, you say 'no' — or ask for more money."

Spoken like a true comic master.

Notes

1. *TV Guide*; October 25, 1980; "James Gregory of Barney Miller"; by William K. Knoedelseder, Jr.
2. *TV Guide*; October 25, 1980.

James Gregory Credits

FILM CREDITS

1. *The Flight of the Dragons;* 1982; Smrgol
2. *The Main Event;* 1979; Gough
3. *The Strongest Man in the World;* 1975; Chief Blair
4. *The Late Liz;* 1971; Sam Burns
5. *$1,000,000 Duck;* 1971; Rutledge
6. *Shootout;* 1971; Sam Foley
7. *The Hawaiians;* 1970; Dr. Whipple Sr.
8. *Beneath the Planet of the Apes;* 1970; Ursus
9. *The Love God?;* 1969; Hughes
10. *The Secret War of Harry Frigg;* 1968; General Prentiss
11. *The Ambushers;* 1967; MacDonald
12. *Clambake;* 1967; Duster Hayward
13. *Murderers' Row;* 1966; MacDonald
14. *The Silencers;* 1966; MacDonald
15. *Our Man Flint;* 1965; Eagle handler
16. *A Rage to Live;* 1965; Doctor O'Brien

17. *The Sons of Katie Elder;* 1965; Morgan Hastings
18. *Quick Before It Melts;* 1964; Vice Admiral
19. *A Distant Trumpet;* 1964; General Quint
20. *Twilight of Honor;* 1963; Norris Bixby
21. *Captain Newman, M.D.;* 1963; Colonel Edgar Pyser
22. *PT 109;* 1963; Commander C.R. Ritchie
23. *Two Weeks in Another Town;* 1962; Brad Byrd
24. *The Manchurian Candidate;* 1962; Senator John Iselin
25. *X-15;* 1961; Tom Deparma
26. *Hey Boy! Hey Girl!;* 1959; Father Burton
27. *Al Capone;* 1959; Sergeant, Captain, Inspector Schaefler/Narrator
28. *Onionhead;* 1958; The Skipper
29. *Underwater Warrior;* 1958; Doctor (Lieutenant) William Arnold
30. *The Big Caper;* 1957; Flood
31. *Gun Glory;* 1957; Grimsell
32. *The Young Stranger;* 1957
33. *Nightfall;* 1956; Ben Fraser
34. *The Scarlet Hour;* 1956
35. *The Frogmen;* 1951; (uncredited) Chief Petty Officer Lane
36. *The Naked City;* 1948; (uncredited) Patrolman Albert Hicks

TV CREDITS

1. *Wait Till Your Mother Gets Home!;* TV movie; 1983; Dan Peters
2. *Goldie and the Boxer Go to Hollywood;* TV movie; 1981; Leo Hackett
3. *Gridlock;* TV movie; 1980; General
4. *The Comeback Kid;* TV movie; 1980; Scotty
5. *Detective School;* TV series; 1979; Nick Hannigan
6. *The Bastard;* TV miniseries; 1978; Will Campbell
7. *Francis Gary Powers: The True Story of the U-2 Spy Incident;* TV movie; 1976; James Donovan
8. *Barney Miller;* TV series; 1976–1982; Inspector Frank Luger
9. *The Abduction of Saint Anne;* TV movie; 1975; Pete Haggerty
10. *Miracle on 34th Street;* TV movie; 1973; District Attorney
11. *The Paul Lynde Show;* TV series; 1972–1973; T.R. Scott
12. *The Weekend Nun;* TV movie; 1972; Sid Richardson
13. *Columbo: The Most Crucial Game;* TV movie; 1972; Coach Rizzo
14. *A Very Missing Person;* TV movie; 1972; Oscar Piper
15. *Columbo: Short Fuse;* TV movie; 1972; David L. Buckner
16. *Hawaii Five-O: Cocoon;* TV movie; 1968; Jonathan Kaye
17. *The Wild, Wild West;* TV series; 1965–1970; Ulysses S. Grant
18. *The Lawless Years;* TV series; 1959–1961; Barney Ruditsky

NOTABLE TV GUEST APPEARANCES

1. *The Love Boat;* 1980
2. *Cannon;* Ed Madigan; 10/15/1975

3. *Barney Miller;* 5/1/1975
4. *Emergency!;* 1/25/1975
5. *Police Story;* 10/8/1974
6. *M*A*S*H;* General Iron Guts Kelly; 10/1/1974
7. *Kolchak: The Night Stalker;* Captain Quill; 9/27/1974
8. *The Partridge Family;* Claude Tubbles; 1/26/1974
9. *The Streets of San Francisco;* Joe Shay; 1973
10. *All in the Family;* William R. Kirkwood; 10/21/1972
11. *Night Gallery;* Sgt. Stanley Beverlow; 2/9/1972
12. *Mission: Impossible;* Joe Corvin; 1/1/1972
13. *Sanford and Son;* Commander; 1972
14. *Sanford and Son;* Commander; 1972
15. *Cade's County;* 10/10/1971
16. *The Virginian;* Sheriff; 12/9/1970
17. *Hawaii Five-O;* Mike Finney; 11/26/1969
18. *The Big Valley;* Harry Bodine; 3/31/1969
19. *The Virginian;* 2/12/1969
20. *Bonanza;* Sgt. Russell; 2/2/1969
21. *Lancer;* Marshall Barker; 10/22/1968
22. *The Outcasts;* 10/7/1968
23. *The Big Valley;* Senator Bannard; 3/28/1968
24. *The High Chaparral;* 3/10/1968
25. *Gunsmoke;* Wes Martin; 1/1/1968
26. *Cowboy in Africa;* 10/30/1967
27. *Cimarron Strip;* 10/5/1967
28. *The Big Valley;* Simon Carter; 9/18/1967
29. *Ironside;* Herb Jarman; 9/14/1967
30. *My Three Sons;* Cappy Engstrom; 4/27/1967
31. *F Troop;* 3/16/1967
32. *The Virginian;* 2/15/1967
33. *Bonanza;* 1967
34. *Star Trek;* Dr. Tristan Adams; 11/3/1966
35. *The Fugitive;* Pete Crandell; 11/1/1966
36. *The Big Valley;* Simon Carter; 10/10/1966
37. *F Troop;* 4/26/1966
38. *The Loner;* 1/29/1966
39. *A Man Called Shenandoah;* 1/24/1966
40. *Gunsmoke;* Judge Calvin Storm; 12/18/1965
41. *The F.B.I.;* 10/24/1965
42. *Rawhide;* 9/28/1965
43. *Gunsmoke;* John Scanlon; 5/22/1965
44. *Hogan's Heroes;* General Biedenbender; 1965
45. *The Rogues;* 9/20/1964
46. *Rawhide;* 5/14/1964
47. *Bonanza;* 1964
48. *Rawhide;* 2/1/1963
49. *Empire;* 12/18/1962

50. *The Virginian;* 12/12/1962
51. *The Twilight Zone;* The Sergeant; 10/6/1961
52. *Frontier Circus;* 10/5/1961
53. *Wagon Train;* Ricky Bell; 2/24/1960
54. *Laramie;* 12/1/1959
55. *The Twilight Zone;* Air Force General; 10/2/1959
56. *Westinghouse Desilu Playhouse;* 9/1/1959
57. *Alfred Hitchcock Presents;* Mr. Wescott; 5/18/1958
58. *Alfred Hitchcock Presents;* John Gregory; 10/20/1957
59. *Alfred Hitchcock Presents;* Wayne Campbell; 3/10/1957
60. *Star Tonight;* 12/8/1955
61. *The Alcoa Hour;* 11/27/1955
62. *Appointment with Adventure;* Roy; 4/10/1955
63. *You Are There;* 1/16/1955
64. *The Philco Television Playhouse,* "A Young Lady of Property"; 4/5/1953
65. *The Philco Television Playhouse,* "Marcia Akers"; 10/21/1951
66. *The Web,* "All the Way to the Moon"; 10/3/1951

Pat Harrington

Dwayne Schneider on *One Day at a Time*

There was never any doubt that Dwayne Schneider, the cocky, self-assured apartment building superintendent on *One Day at a Time*, was master of his domain. Known as the "super" super, he was celebrated as much for his skills with a Phillips screwdriver as for his abilities in tending to the needs of his lonely female tenants.

Pat Harrington, who played Schneider, wasn't always as sure of himself in his own career choices. After a stint in the Air Force and time spent as a salesman, it wasn't until he finally left the 9-to-5 world for the more precarious prospects of a career in show business that Harrington felt comfortable with his chosen path in life. After that, he was as happy as Schneider would be with the challenge of a backed-up sink or a new divorcee in his building.

That all said, it was only inevitable that Harrington would end up in show business.

As the son of entertainer Pat Harrington, young Pat grew up in that world. Pat Harrington Sr. was a well-known New York–based song and dance man who appeared in 19 Broadway productions, worked the nightclubs and also toured the vaudeville circuit. However, it was a vocation that he didn't want for his children and he did his best not to encourage it. Pat Junior, who was born in New York on August 13, 1929, explains that as a young child, he and his brother Terry often toured the country during the Depression years with their parents as their father cobbled a living together by going town to town, singing on radio programs, and playing at Rotary Clubs in the small towns and nightclubs in the bigger cities. Undoubtedly it was an adventure but it wasn't the sort of future a parent hopes for their own children.

"My parents wanted us kids to get an education," Harrington says today. "Growing up, I didn't know anything about what a career in show business would be like except for the career my father had — and my father had plenty of hard times. Until I was school age, we traveled around the country in a Hupmobile and Dad worked week to week, hand to mouth by singing and playing drums and entertaining. He didn't want that for his kids because he knew it was a very hard life."

Harrington grew up in New York and during the times when his mother accompanied Pat Senior on the road, the two kids would be sent to boarding school and then later when they were old enough, to military school.

Although both St. Claire's Academy in Hayden, N.Y., and LaSalle Military Academy in Oakdale had drama departments which put on annual school shows, Harrington didn't get involved. It wasn't until he was at Fordham University in the Bronx working towards a bachelor's degree and then his master's in political studies that Harrington made his first tentative steps towards the dramatic arts by doing a bit of work with the school's Mimes and Mummers Club. But it was just for fun, a diversion from his studies. Despite his background there were no epiphanies or life-changing moments of affirmation when he first trod the boards.

"I wasn't struck by any bolt of lightning," explains Harrington. "I was used to that world. Performing was something that I had grown up next to. My father would come home in the morning after working as an entertainer in the cafes of New York City and he'd bring Pat O'Brien or Jimmy Dunn or Bing Crosby with him and they'd sit down for eggs as I'd be going off to parochial school.

"So no, I was just gravitating towards show business. It was a long, slow process. I was doing what my parents wanted me to do, which was to get an education. But at the same time, my subconscious was guiding me towards something that I really wanted to do."

Yet it was an urge he kept resisting even after college. After graduating in 1952, Harrington spent two years in the U.S. Air Force and became a First Lieutenant. Back in the civilian world, he got a job in the mailroom of NBC and shortly was promoted to time-salesman in the sales department. Harrington agrees that it was no small accident that he chose a white-collar career at the head office of a broadcasting empire in the heart of one of the entertainment capitals of the world. It was a way to be in show business without being in show business. It was also the first step to being noticed.

"At the time, I didn't really understand the process that was going on. I wasn't that in tune with my psyche so I did what everybody else was doing. I bought the Brooks Brothers suits with the striped shirts and regimented tie. I became a Madison Avenue clone and took the 8:26 train into the city in the morning and went back home on the 6:15.

"In the meantime, I didn't know it but I was honing certain aspects of my sense of humor and I was beginning to step out a little bit at entertaining people." As a way of getting noticed, Harrington would pull practical jokes. His proudest effort came about after meeting a little fellow in the Lambs Club who looked exactly like General David Sarnoff, then the head of RCA, the parent company of NBC, Harrington's employer. The lookalike was given $20 and told to show up at the sales office of NBC the next day for the weekly sales meeting. On cue he came in and walked up to Harrington and asked, "How are sales?" The junior salesman responded, "Why don't you just get back upstairs and tend to your electrons and I'll take care of the sales."

As rehearsed, the "General" patted Harrington on the shoulder and said, "Good for you young man. That's the spirit!" and then left. As everyone sat there in slack-jawed disbelief, Harrington strode over to the head of the sales department and said, "Look, I'll be out for the rest of the day," and walked out as well.

As classic as that practical joke is, it was another practical joke in which he imitated an Italian survivor of the *Andrea Doria* naval disaster that got Harrington onto television in 1956 and on his way to a career in show business. Harrington and fellow salesman Lynn Phillips used to spend their lunch hours at the bar of Toots Shors' restaurant and show-biz hangout. For laughs they would put people on by introducing Harrington as a fictional Italian celebrity or Irish advance man for the Abbey Players.

The sinking of the *Andrea Doria* Italian luxury liner after colliding with a Swedish ship was big news at the time and on the spur of the moment, Phillips introduced Harrington to a CBS newsman at the bar as a survivor of the disaster and that he had been on the bridge when it happened.

Harrington — who doesn't speak any Italian — gave an account of the accident in both fractured English and Italian accompanied by a thick accent. "It was a-dark. Verra dark. But we knew we were a close when-a Captain Calamai ask a question an' somebody answer in Swidish."

After that, Phillips took him to Rose's, an Italian restaurant, and introduced him as a junior officer from the *Andrea Doria*. "I couldn't talk Italian, I could only fake it — but when we were able to fool the waiters at Rose's, we realized we had something."

Harrington gave the character the name of Guido Panzini (partly named after his golf buddy, Luigi Panzini) and Guido began to show up at parties and being introduced as a junior officer from the Italian navy or head of the Italian Dairy Association. "But even before he had a name, he had his own identity," says Harrington. "He was an evolution within me of sound and attitude that I had appropriated. I knew Italian words but I didn't know what they meant. But all my life I hung out with Italians. I played on an Italian baseball team and in college my two best friends were Italian so over the years I had heard a lot of Italian."

As for Guido, it was explained that he learned his English when he was a submarine officer in the Italian Navy during the war. His vessel would sneak up on American ships at night and watch the movie they were playing. He and the rest of his crew were eventually captured when the Americans put on a double-feature and the Italians followed them into port.

Not long after the birth of the Guido Panzini character, Jonathan Winters was guest-hosting NBC's late night talk show, *The Jack Paar Show*, and one day in Toots Shors' he was introduced to Guido. "Johnny believed it 100 percent. He bit hook, line and sinker. He believed that I was Italian and when he found out that I wasn't, he loved it. He absolutely adored it."

In fact, Winters was so impressed that he asked Harrington to do Guido that night when he hosted the *Paar* show. And so, in 1957, with next to no performing experience, Pat Harrington made his television debut in front of millions of viewers. His convincing blend of Italian dialect and broken English bafflegab not only fooled the studio audience and viewers at home but also the United States Immigration Service, which contacted NBC and officially requested a date and port of entry for Guido because they had no record of him.

Winters asked Harrington back for four more appearances as the little Italian and when Paar returned to work, Guido became a frequent guest and showed up 85 times during the next two years. The character became an overnight sensation and as a result, Harrington was named Most Talented Male Newcomer of 1959 by *Radio-TV Daily*. Over time, Guido evolved into an Italian golf pro but Harrington himself kept his day job and only golfed on weekends.

"I remained a time salesman for NBC for the first 18 months of doing Guido," he says. Harrington had met his wife Marge while he was still in the Air Force and they were married in 1955. The first of their four children was born in 1956. At the time, he saw his salesman job as a security blanket.

As popular as Guido Panzini had become, Harrington had second thoughts about jumping into show business based on a few appearances on a late night talk show as a novelty character. Just the same, performing was in his blood and it was only a matter of time before he would be following in his father's footsteps. "I didn't decide to go into show business," he says today in retrospect. "I simply gravitated towards it almost on a parallel but converging track and so when I did make the move into show business, it was only a four-foot jump to my ride."

Harrington concedes that the put-ons and practical jokes he pulled at NBC were all attempts to get himself noticed within the industry. When he was hired to join *The Steve Allen Show* on NBC in 1958, that was all behind him. In fact it wasn't until the *Steve Allen Show* moved to California the next year that things looked good enough for him to quit his salesman's job at NBC and move West with the rest of the cast. Until then, he was prone to saying, "Some guys play golf as a hobby. Me — I do *The Steve Allen Show* as a hobby."

Harrington remembers that both he and his wife thought the timing was right to make the move into entertainment full time. "We made that decision together," he says. "I was still doing the *Paar Show* and had been very successful with Guido. Sheldon Leonard had come East and offered me a job on *The Danny Thomas Show* as Danny's son-in-law and at the same time, Steve Allen decided to move back to California and he was going to pay the tab for all his people to move with him and so it was perfect."

It was around this time that Guido Panzini made his last appearance on the *Paar* program. "It was around 1959 and Paar revealed who I was and after Guido was revealed, there seemed no point in doing him anymore on there. I put him aside because I went on to do other things. It wasn't because I was tired of him. And the thought of being typed as him never entered my mind and never became a problem."

Although Harrington explained that Guido was going back to Italy, he still brought him out occasionally on *The Steve Allen Show* and in the next few years he made appearances in Harrington's nightclub comedy act, on *The Man from U.N.C.L.E.* and many years later on *One Day at a Time.*

In the meantime, Harrington found himself in a comedian's nirvana as a regular on *The Steve Allen Show,* the prime time weekly variety show which was considered to be the hippest comedy program of the time.

Due to his success with Guido, Harrington was hired for the show because of his improvisational skills and being able to submerge himself into a character. His gift for mimicry and doing dialects was an added bonus and during his time on the show, his most popular characterizations included an Italian busboy, a Scottish laird, a horse jockey, a former boxing champ and of course Guido Panzini on the show's popular Man in the Street interview segment.

But as much as he had to offer, Harrington felt a bit intimidated in joining Allen's already fabled core group of second bananas— Tom Poston, Don Knotts and Louis Nye. "They were all wonderful and supportive," he says. "But it was still intimidating because I'd been watching those guys every week for a couple of years. It was not a competitive cast. What would happen was we'd come in and the writers would write to our individual strengths. We liked each other and got along well. We were all professionals.

"That show was a great education for me. It was like matriculating and getting a master's degree in comedy. Steve had one of the best writing staffs in the business. There were 10 writers and the writers were as funny as we were and of course Steve was the ringleader. Steve was a mentor without acting like a mentor. He'd suggest this or that but it was always 'live and let live.' He was always there like a rock. He was funny and he was also a great straight man. He *loved* to laugh! Anything at all that had a little bit of fun in it, he'd respond."

The person that Harrington was closest to on the show was Bill Dana, the head writer who also appeared as the shy Spaniard, Jose Jimenez. Together they collaborated on Harrington's first comedy album, *Pat Harrington as Guido Panzini and Bill Dana as Kooky as Ever*. It's an album of two-person dialogue bits in a variety of settings—a barroom, a ball park, a foreign hotel lobby. Although Harrington had done the Guido routines before, they always changed with each performance and so on the record they have an improvised feel. Other sketches were ad-libbed from spontaneous suggestions made by the small crowd at the recording session.

"It was Steve's idea for the two of us to sit down and do our characters and Bill was the straight man for Guido. In fact, he was the best straight man I ever had. And later when he had his success with Jose Jimenez, I straighted for him."

With the move to California in the fall of 1959 came a schedule change for *The Steve Allen Show*. It was moved from its long-held spot on Sunday nights to Monday night. In 1961, it was moved to Wednesday night. All that schedule-flipping didn't help keep the show's established following and it was cancelled by the end of 1961.

Harrington's luck with *The Danny Thomas Show* was no better. During the 1959–61 season, he made 14 appearances on the show as Pat Hannigan, a nightclub performer who becomes Danny's son-in-law after marrying his daughter Terry, played by Penney Parker. Thomas had planned on spinning off the newlywed couple into their own series but it never happened and they were written out of the show.

Now, suddenly and unexpectedly out of the two full-time jobs that brought him out to Hollywood, Harrington did what he could to make a living. With a couple of former *Steve Allen* writers, he created a nightclub act and took it on the road, playing in rooms like The Hungry I in San Francisco; Mr. Kelly's in Chicago and the Blue Angel in New York. His act was also recorded live and released as his second album, *Some Like it Hip*. In 1962, he hosted a celebrity game show entitled *Stump the Stars* for three months. Most importantly, he began taking acting lessons.

"I've been in acting workshops all throughout my career once I got into the business," Harrington points out. "I started with Eric Morris back in the early '60s in Los Angeles and later with Justin Smith and Curt Conway's Circle Theatre in L.A. and recently with Milton Katselas' Master Workshop."

The acting classes were a good investment because they showed that he was not just a comic who specialized in dialects but was an actor of considerable range. It all led to a number of theatre jobs during the sixties—off–Broadway in *The Golden Fleecing* in 1960, *Catch Me If You Can* at the

Players Ring in Los Angeles in 1963 and on Broadway in 1968 in *Happiness is a Rolls-Royce.*

Although he once described his career in the early '60s as lean years, his resume is full of appearances on all the pop-culture favorites of the time — *The Munsters, F Troop, Beverly Hillbillies, Captain Nice* and two guest shots on *The Man from U.N.C.L.E.* There was also work playing corporate-executive types in feature films like Disney's *The Computer Wore Tennis Shoes; Move Over Darling* — a remake of Marilyn Monroe's abandoned last vehicle, *Something's Got to Give*; the Elvis Presley flick *Easy Come, Easy Go*; and an acclaimed turn as a smoothly oiled telephone company spokesman in 1967's *The President's Analyst* with James Coburn.

He may have been busy but for a family man, freelance work didn't come with the same advantages as working on a series — both in terms of the security of a guaranteed income as well as time with his family. "There's a big difference between working on episodic television and a series," says Harrington. "I also worked a lot of nightclubs and cafes outside of Los Angeles. I was on my own on the road, living alone in hotels in Pittsburgh and St. Louis and Chicago and it wasn't that easy.

"With episodic TV, you're only talking about three or five days' work. It's not like doing a series. They aren't hiring anyone to do 10 freelance episodes a year on a series. You're lucky if you get to do two or three. There are 52 weeks in a year and even two guest shots in *The Man From U.N.C.L.E.* only represents two weeks' work. I had children who had to be fed. Thank God for the game shows. I did a lot of game shows."

Another series eventually came along in 1969 in the form of the short-lived sitcom *Mr. Deeds Goes to Town* starring Monte Markham as the naïve Longfellow Deeds. Harrington played Tony Lawrence, his big-city best friend and a slick public relations man. It only ran for 17 episodes.

Things picked up in 1971 with Arthur Hill's legal drama, *Owen Marshall, Counselor at Law.* Throughout its three-year run, Harrington appeared in 27 episodes as the hot-tempered prosecutor, Charlie Gianetta. The role became one of his personal favorites. It also marked the first time he was doing drama instead of comedy on a TV series.

When *Owen Marshall* came to an end in 1974, Harrington was quickly back on TV in what was to become the signature role of the second half of his TV career. If his own generation knew him best as Guido Panzini from the first part of his career, to another generation he is best known as Dwayne Schneider, the macho superintendent on *One Day at a Time,* which ran from 1975 to '84.

One Day at a Time starred Bonnie Franklin as Ann Romano, a recently divorced middle-aged woman trying to earn a living and raise her two teenage daughters and hopefully find a little romance. She is never without a lack of advice in how to cope with her new life because of the frequent presence of her building superintendent, Dwayne Schneider. He was a longtime single man who was never at a loss when it came to offering an opinion on subjects he knew nothing about — like raising children, meeting a compatible mate and being a career woman in a man's world. In an apartment of three strong females, Schneider's 1950s-era morality and male chauvinist attitudes were a source of constant eye-rolling frustration for Ann Romano and her two young feminists-in-training. But they loved him in spite of himself and he was like a member of the family. In fact, in many ways, he was the father figure on *One Day at a Time*.

However, he wasn't exactly a role model in what to look for in an ideal husband. Dwayne Schneider considered himself to be a consummate ladies' man. And with his old-world pencil-thin mustache and swarthy good looks, he did cut an impressive figure — until he spoke. Schneider had a blunt, no-nonsense way of talking that seemed to make almost anything he said seem like, — well, nonsense.

Also undercutting the Casanova image he wanted to project was his janitor's uniform. The slick Latin-lover grooming doesn't go very far when Ed Norton from *The Honeymooners* seems to be your fashion guide. Schneider wore a Nortonesque denim vest and T-shirt look which he accessorized with a jangling tool belt and obligatory pack of smokes rolled up in the shoulder of his T-shirt sleeve. Or was it a deck of cards?

But those were just his working clothes. On Saturday nights when he dressed up in deference to his reputation as Indianapolis' Lothario-at-large, Schneider was capable of looking a lot snazzier. It would be an open shirt with some jewelry at the neck and a loud sports coat or suit, all of which would have been acceptable because everyone dressed that way in the 1970s, except Schneider was still wearing them in the '80s.

Hard as it is to believe, whatever Schneider was doing worked and his reputation as a swinging single was well earned. "I think that in his social circle, he was a very successful male," offers Harrington. "I think he was an attractive guy who knew how to be charming to the people in his circle. But he was also a bit of a braggart. You never knew how much of it was true or just in his mind."

Originally, the character was more sleazy in his sexual ambitions. In the pilot episode, after Schneider had been hitting on his new tenant Ann Romano, it turned out that he was married and had a wife downstairs. "That never got beyond the pilot," says Harrington. "It was my objection." Harrington was bothered that as initially conceived, the character was an adulterer and a blatant letch. He was an unattractive character on a show full of attractive characters. The producers, probably realizing that this was not the image they wanted to project with their new show, agreed and the character was modified.

"Anyone doing episodic comedy must be terribly proprietary about his character," Harrington has said. "The writers have creative control, but an actor can come up with a variety of excuses, while being as diplomatic as possible, until there's a mutually agreeable alternative."[1]

As an example, he cited the fact that "Schneider still brags about his abilities as a lover. They're considerable. The women in the laundry room don't call him 'super' for nothing. But he no longer makes passes at Ann Romano."[2]

In an effort to broaden the character, Harrington spent considerable time rewriting his lines and also wrote 12 episodes for the series. It all came out of his frustration in how the character was used. Harrington resented the fact that most of the time, Schneider would walk into the Romanos' apartment, do the equivalent of a comedy monologue and then leave. But over the course of a season there would be a few episodes in which Schneider was the focus of the story.

"We do three or four of that kind a year, just to show that the character has depth and isn't strictly a cartoon," he has said. "The problem is I'm doing farce while the rest of the cast is doing dramatic comedy. That's like oil and water, but the writers try to blend them."[3]

Harrington may have been frustrated that the writers didn't make better use of what he had to offer but in retrospect he's both pragmatic and accepting about it. "The series was about a divorced middle-aged woman supporting herself and raising two daughters," he says. "*That's* what the series was about.

"Of most of the episodes we did, Schneider had to come in for five pages in the first act and five pages in the second act and guarantee some laughs so they could deal with some serious themes. I knew that it wasn't a series about a middle-aged man who was lonesome. That's why they didn't use the character to the fullest. They had to use Bonnie and the girls. My function was not that of leading man."

For the actors on the series, *One Day at a Time* was an aptly named show. Characters came and went on a yearly basis. Each season seemed to bring in a new supporting cast. But the one constant throughout its nine-year history is Harrington, in the role of support and Schneider, became an audience favorite. They weren't the only ones to respond favorably to the character. During the show's run, Harrington received two Emmy and four Golden Globe nominations as Best Supporting Actor in a Comedy Series. In 1981 he won the Golden Globe Award and in 1984 won the Emmy for his work on *One Day at a Time*.

Originally, Schneider would pop into the Romanos' apartment under the guise of having to fix something. For the most part it was really because he was nosy. And lonely. Despite his claims of a busy love life, Schneider's life revolved around his tenants, drinking beer with his cronies at the Lodge and picking up floozies at the bowling alley on Saturday nights. It's no wonder that he began hanging around the Romanos' apartment. They became his surrogate family.

TV audiences responded to the character because despite his gruff exterior and knack for saying the wrong thing, somehow Harrington successfully conveyed the unspoken truth about the character — that he genuinely cared about this family. Over the course of the series, it got to the point where it seemed that Schneider was at their apartment all the time. "Well, the character grew and became part of the family and began to participate in the rest of their problems," reflects Harrington.

One of the last episodes of the series was one in which Schneider contemplates moving down to Miami to raise his brother's orphaned children. It was meant to be a pilot for a spinoff series about Schneider but it wasn't picked up. Harrington has mixed feelings about the project and its fate. "I didn't really like the premise they had come up with," he admits. "But I didn't mind the idea of a spinoff. I wouldn't have minded doing another series about the Schneider character."

Of course, another series in a role he had done for almost a decade would have further exacerbated the inevitable typecasting problems. Harrington admits that during the show's run, typecasting was something he worried about but instead of being bitter, he's now philosophical about it. "Sure, typecasting was a concern at the time. But you have to make exchanges in life. I mean, I got 10 years work out of this series and if I was penalized by typecasting, then that's the price you have to pay."

Typecasting did have an effect and although he still does occasional guest shots on television, it has been the theatre which has provided the majority of his work as an actor in the years since *One Day at a Time* went off the air in 1984. "After *One Day at a Time*, I did a lot of theatre because that's what was available to me," he says. "But I would much rather do a play than three guest shots on episodic television. With a play, you sign up and you do it. But with episodic television, you go in and you read and you usually don't get the part. That's the way it is."

Although he doesn't mention it, the theatre can also be more rewarding. Since 1985, he has worked in theatre on an annual basis and has performed in a broad range of roles and productions — from the gangster black-comedy *Breaking Legs* to the Stephen Sondheim musical *Into the Woods*. In 1990, he won the L.A. Dramalogue Critics Award for Best

Performance for his work in John Guarre's *House of Blue Leaves*. He also played Cap'n Andy in the North American Broadway touring production of *Show Boat* in 1997 and '98.

Perhaps most personally rewarding of all is the realization that when he's on the road, living out of hotels and performing in touring productions of Broadway musicals, he has reached a point in his career where he is living his father's life. Despite his father's initial discouragement about a show business career for his son, he probably also realized that it was in his blood.

From Pat Harrington Sr. to Pat Harrington Jr., it almost seems like a life which has come full circle.

"Well, certainly, I think about my father when I'm on the road. When I'm waiting to go on and standing in the wings, I think of Dad because Dad had a terrific career on Broadway and I'm quite proud of the fact that I'm doing this kind of work now."

Notes

1. *Philadelphia Inquirer*; TV Week; "Schneider Now, Panzini Again?"; by Harry Harris' March 12, 1978.
2. *Ibid.*
3. *Ibid.*

Pat Harrington Credits

FILM CREDITS

1. *Ablaze;* 2000
2. *Round Trip to Heaven;* 1992; George
3. *The Nine Lives of Fritz the Cat;* 1974; (voice)
4. *Every Little Crook and Nanny;* 1972; Willie Shakespeare
5. *The Candidate;* 1972; Dinner emcee
6. *2000 Years Later;* 1969; Franchot
7. *The Computer Wore Tennis Shoes;* 1969; Moderator
8. *The President's Analyst;* 1967; Arlington Hewes, President of TPC
9. *Easy Come, Easy Go;* 1967; Judd Whitman
10. *Move Over, Darling;* 1963; District Attorney
11. *The Wheeler Dealers;* 1963; Buddy Zack
12. *Stage Struck;* 1958; Benny

TV CREDITS

1. *These Old Broads;* TV movie; 2001; Tony
2. *Spring Fling!;* TV movie; 1995; Guido Mazzolini

3. *I Yabba-Dabba Do!;* TV movie; 1993; (voice)
4. *Between Two Brothers;* TV movie; 1982; Russ Frazer
5. *Circus of the Stars #6;* TV special; 1981
6. *The Last Convertible;* Mini-series; 1979; Major Fred Goodman
7. *The Critical List;* TV movie; 1978; Jimmy Regosi
8. *The New Love Boat;* TV movie; 1977; Ernie Klopman
9. *Benny and Barney: Las Vegas Undercover;* TV movie; 1977; Joey Gallion
10. *One Day at a Time;* TV series; 1975–1984; Dwayne F. Schneider
11. *Columbo: An Exercise in Fatality;* TV movie; 1975; Buddy Castle
12. *Let's Switch!;* TV movie; 1975; Randy Colbert
13. *The Healers;* TV movie; 1974; Joe Tate
14. *The Affair;* TV movie; 1973; Frank
15. *Match Game;* TV series; 1973–1980; Panelist
16. *Savage;* TV movie; 1973; Russell
17. *The Pink Panther Show;* TV series; 1969; various voices
18. *Mr. Deeds Goes to Town;* TV series; 1969; Tony Lawrence
19. *Journey to the Center of the Earth;* TV series; 1967; (voice) Alec McEwan
20. *The Superman/Aquaman Hour of Adventure;* TV series; 1967; various voices
21. *The Jack Paar Show;* TV series; 1959–1962; Guido Panzini
22. *The Tonight Show;* TV series; 1959–1962; Guido Panzini
23. *Make Room for Daddy;* TV series; 1959–1960; Pat Hannigan
24. *The Steve Allen Show;* TV series; 1958–1961

NOTABLE TV GUEST APPEARANCES

1. *Diagnosis Murder;* Mr. Reese; 4/29/1999
2. *Fantasy Island;* 1/23/1999
3. *The Wayans Bros.;* Mr. Neidermeyer; 5/1/1996
4. *Roseanne;* Stomp; 10/10/1995
5. *Burke's Law;* 3/28/1995
6. *Empty Nest;* "Toronado" Mulvaney; 1/14/1995
7. *Kirk;* Stan Lee; 1995
8. *Silk Stalkings;* Benny Lorenzo; 11/20/1994
9. *Duckman;* (voice); 4/16/1994
10. *The George Carlin Show;* 1994
11. *The Golden Girls;* John; 11/2/1991
12. *Murder, She Wrote;* Nick Cullhane; 5/12/1991
13. *Street Justice;* Felker; 1991
14. *Sydney;* Priest; 1990
15. *Murder, She Wrote;* Lt. Lou Brickman; 10/29/89
16. *The Ray Bradbury Theatre;* Robert; 7/14/1989
17. *Murder, She Wrote;* Gunnar Globle; 1/18/1987
18. *Crazy Like a Fox;* 10/6/1985
19. *Murder, She Wrote;* Mel Comstock; 3/10/1985
20. *Who's the Boss?;* Dominic Battaglia; 1/29/1985
21. *The Love Boat;* 1977

22. *The Invisible Man;* Warden; 11/3/1975
23. *Ellery Queen;* Mitchell McCully; 10/9/1975
24. *McMillan and Wife;* 9/28/1975
25. *Kolchak: The Night Stalker;* Thomas Kitzmiller; 1/17/1975
26. *McMillan and Wife;* 12/8/1974
27. *Banacek;* Phil Ross; 3/12/1974
28. *The Partridge Family;* Roger Harper; 11/3/1973
29. *Cade's County;* 10/24/1971
30. *Marcus Welby, M.D.;* 3/16/1971
31. *The Partridge Family;* Harry; 11/6/1970
32. *Captain Nice;* Arthur; 4/3/1967
33. *The Man from U.N.C.L.E.;* Peter Sweet; 2/17/1967
34. *The Beverly Hillbillies;* Phil Gordon; 4/20/1966
35. *F Troop;* 2/15/1966
36. *The Munsters;* Thatcher; 4/29/1965
37. *The Man from U.N.C.L.E.;* Guido Panzini; 2/15/1965
38. *Alfred Hitchcock Presents;* Insurance Man; 5/15/1960

Ted Knight

Ted Baxter on *The Mary Tyler Moore Show*

It all started in a small 500-watt radio station in Hartford, Connecticut.

The weekend newscaster job at WCCC for young Tad Konopka while he studied acting in town at the Randall School of Dramatic Arts was the first of many positions in small radio and television stations across New England in the late 1940s and early '50s.

One night, after introducing the news, the then–Tadeus Wladzui Konopka was informed by the station manager that by the time he had finished announcing his own name, there was little time for the actual news. "Change your name," he was advised. Overnight, after consulting his wife and the local phone directory, Ted Knight was born.

In working at those small stations in small-town eastern America, Knight served in a number of roles—announcer, movie show host and even kiddie show host. But it was his own occasional work as a newscaster and his close proximity to the other professionals of local news that through the process of osmosis, Ted Knight's greatest characterization would be born some twenty years later—that of the pompous, self-absorbed small-market TV anchorman Ted Baxter on *The Mary Tyler Moore Show*.

Changing his name was not a move young Tad—now Ted—took lightly. Born on December 7, 1923, he was the youngest son of Polish immigrants. He grew up in the Polish neighborhood of Terryville, Conn., a factory town 20 miles west of Hartford. It was a close-knit community and as a child, Tad Konopka spoke only Polish until he entered grade school. Although his great-grandfather was a Polish lord and a town in Poland bears the family name, in America, Tad grew up in near-poverty during the Depression. His father, a bartender, died while Tad was very young. His mother remarried two times and owned a small candy shop. Neighbors helped each other out and that was something he never forgot, and he always remained proud of his Polish heritage because of that strong sense of community and family.

Tad Konopka graduated from Terryville High School in 1943 and enlisted in the Army. During World War II, he served overseas as a radio reconnaissance operator. As one of the first American troops to enter Berlin, he was awarded five Bronze Stars. "I didn't do anything heroic," he recalled years later. "I just happened to be in the right place at the right time."[1]

Returning to the States and his hometown after the war, Konopka decided to try show business as a career. Although he had shown no interest in student productions or drama during high school, he always had show business in the back of his mind from the times as a kid when he and his cousin would put on backyard shows. "I always had a little ham in me," he later admitted. "Even at an early age I had the ability to make people laugh. You might say the seed was planted then."[2]

Also influencing his decision was a sense of self-confidence so strong that like many people, he often looked up on the screen in his local motion picture theatre and realized, "Hey, I could do that!" "I felt I had the ability to achieve greatness," Ted Knight once modestly reflected in Ted Baxter–like fashion during his *Mary Tyler Moore Show* years. "I looked at myself objectively and felt I could do as good as what I had seen in the movies. I could mimic accurately."[3]

Fans of *The Mary Tyler Moore Show* know of Knight's gift for impersonations from the rare occasions when the producers would let him do his James Cagney or Clark Gable. Knight, as Baxter, took such giddy delight in them that it's not hard to imagine him doing them more frequently at cast parties. Knight once claimed that if he had worked at it, he probably could have equaled Rich Little. Who knows? His favorite subjects for impersonation were the character actors he saw in the movies as a kid. It's doubtful that Knight would have had much competition from Little when he pulled out his specialty act — imitations of now-forgotten actors like Thurston Hall, Eugene Pallette or Edgar Kennedy.

According to Knight's relatives, even as a child he had a knack for imitating the people around him. "I think all good actors must be able to mimic. It reflects humanity," he has said. "I have always been a mimic even in those little tent shows I used to put on."[4]

After the war, with his education subsidized by the government through the G.I. Bill, in 1946, Knight enrolled in the Randall School of Dramatic Arts in nearby Hartford and also began working weekends at the town's radio station, WCCC.

On one episode of *The Mary Tyler Moore Show,* when asked why he went into television, a straight-faced Ted Baxter matter-of-factly replied, "Because God told me I was too good looking for radio." You can almost imagine Ted Knight — not quite so seriously answering a similar question on why he decided upon a career in the entertainment industry. Likely in his best Baxter baritone, Knight once told a reporter that it was almost a foregone conclusion — "I didn't feel a good-looking young stud like myself should be an 8 to 5 working slug. It was a life of booze and broads for me."[5] A Baxter-like self-conscious giggle undoubtedly followed that statement.

He was only kidding of course, because by the time he left Hartford, he was a happily married man. On September 23, 1948, he married his life's companion, Dorothy Clark from nearby Niantic, Conn. They would have three children, the first, Ted Jr., being born in 1955.

Knight had put in a couple of years at Hartford and then was hired by WFFY in Greensboro, North Carolina, where he worked as a disc jockey on radio and also did his first work on television as an announcer.

After a year he moved to New York to continue his education and trained at the American Theatre Wing. While still in school, he did various big-time network radio and television shows such as *Big Town, Suspense* and *Lux Video Theatre*. He also had his first taste of live theatre and later recalled, "My positively biggest thrill — not only there but anywhere — was when I shared a lead with Betty Field and Melvyn Douglas at a Purim Festival show in Madison Square Garden before 10,000 people. You know, even though there may be a million people watching you on TV, it's not like standing up before 10,000 real, live people. It's a tremendous feeling, really."[6]

When an old friend became station manager at WJAR-TV in Providence, Rhode Island, he offered Knight a job in 1953. It was here that he began to develop the skills and characterizations that he would later pull out of his bag of tricks as Ted Baxter. He was an on-air jack of all trades, an all-purpose station "personality" — he hosted a kiddies' show, did the news and was also hosted a late-night movie show as Teddy the Milkman. As Teddy, he would do little skits and puppet shows during the intermission and commercial breaks.

"I did the news, naturally, on this Providence station," he later noted. "After the 11 P.M. news, the Charlie Chan movie began and so I inserted myself in the movie from time to time. I thought I was an asset — giving the history of the performers and the movies' early days. But too many complained that I was interfering with the movie, and that ended that."[7]

Far more popular was the first kids' show he created, *Children's Theatre*, in which he used his ventriloquism skills in working with two puppets — Bernard, an impish boy, and Duncan, a hoity-toity dog. They would banter back and forth with Knight playing the straight man in the middle. In addition, he was also the Ringmaster on *Tip Top Circus*, a kids' talent show.

"I became a really good puppeteer at WJAR," Knight has said.[8] Fans of *The Mary Tyler Moore Show* who remember the couple of occasions in which Ted Baxter did a bit of puppetry with Flopsy the dog will agree that Knight's claim is true. He would do more puppetry in the next decade on *Too Close for Comfort*. As a hobby, Knight would later collect ventriloquist memorabilia and put on skits for friends and neighborhood kids.

The skills Knight picked up in Providence were put to greater use when he took a similar all-utility position at TV station WTEN in Albany, New York. In addition to introducing morning movies on *The Early Show,* later in the day he would don a policeman's uniform as Officer Ted for the afternoon kids' show. Still later, as Windy Knight he would host that evening's screening of a cowboy movie. Wearing a false beard, 10-gallon hat and ranch-hand duds, he would introduce that night's western from the front porch of his cabin.

Knight worked at WTEN in Albany from 1955 to '57. He left when a better-paying job as a disc jockey came from a radio station in town. The return to radio didn't last long. In this case it wasn't a matter of realizing that he was too good looking for radio, but he soon left for more practical reasons— problems with the station management.

As Ted Baxter might say, it was Fate. But as Knight himself once put it, "After an argument, I got a little ticked, so I put my little chickee in the car and drove out to California."[9] Ted Baxter couldn't have put it better.

Upon arriving in Hollywood in 1957, it didn't take Knight long to get established. He found an agent and began doing theatre. Gavin McLeod, who would later play newswriter Murray Slaughter on *The Mary Tyler Moore Show*, once recalled for *TV Guide* how he first met Knight in 1957. "He was playing the Mencken character in *Inherit the Wind*. And I've never seen it done as well before or since. It turned out we had the same agent and we've been close ever since."[10]

Theatre kept Knight busy in Los Angeles between bit parts in television and the movies. During the next 15 years he played lead roles in over 20 plays at The Players Ring in West Hollywood and the Pasadena Playhouse. However, starring roles in film and television initially eluded him. Not that he wasn't working— bit parts on television, voice-over work on cartoons and commercials all enabled him to support his family of now three children and buy a comfortable house in the San Fernando Valley. Including commercials, he claimed to have played 300 roles on television. "They were just jobs," is how he later assessed his early work on television.[11]

There was also the occasional movie. Although his first film work was an uncredited performance as a prison guard at the end of Alfred Hitchcock's *Psycho* in 1960, the majority of his films were B-grade westerns and war movies.

Knight's first regular gig on a network TV series was in 1960 on *Clear Horizon*, a CBS soap opera set at the Cape Canaveral Space Center in Florida. With stories centered about the first astronauts and their "lonely" wives, it was a timely series which should have had the right stuff to survive, but lasted only a few months.

In films and TV guest roles, he seemed to specialize in authority figures— army officers, prison wardens, judges, even a priest. With his proud Aryan looks, the Allied vet once bragged that he played "a great Nazi" and so he was cast a number of times as a Nazi officer on various shows and films. On *Combat* alone, he made four appearances as different German officers. Knight later told a reporter, "When you go in for war show casting, they ask you, 'Can you speak any German?' And I would give them this..." and then he rattled off a string of foreign-sounding words using a German accent. "They were very impressed. Know what it means? It means 'I'm very tired, I have a headache and I want to go to bed,' in German."[12]

From the time of his arrival up to the mid–1960s, Knight was a busy man. In addition to pop-culture faves like *The Wild, Wild West, The Twilight Zone, T.H.E. Cat, The Outer Limits* and *Alfred Hitchcock Presents,* Knight also put in a couple of appearances apiece on *Bonanza, The F.B.I., The Fugitive* and *Get Smart*—where of course, he played a KAOS agent.

"I was a good working-slug actor before this came along," he once said of his break on *The Mary Tyler Moore Show.* "I was quite successful and did a lot of voice-over work and cartoons."[13] By the end of the sixties, the majority of his work was coming from commercials and Saturday morning cartoons. On *Superfriends* and *The Batman-Superman Hour,* he was the narrator, very likely summing up the previous episode in Ted Baxter's voice of doom.

But other guest shots on TV were becoming less frequent. In the book *Love is All Around: The Making of The Mary Tyler Moore Show* by Robert S. Alley and Irby B. Brown, *Mary Tyler Moore Show* casting director Ethel Winant appraised the state of Knight's career just prior to his big break on the series as being that of a bit player and often out of work. "As an actor he had really come upon hard times and was doing one-or-two line parts, or, if you had a bunch of Army officers, he was the colonel or a distinguished looking judge who would say, 'Guilty.' That was the sort of thing that he was doing."

Knight himself saw things differently. "I may have been anonymous to the public, but I was highly regarded by the film community. I never lacked for employment," he said.[14] He even claimed that in taking the *Mary Tyler Moore Show* job to have lost money from potential voice-over income during his first couple of years on the show.

All of that contradicts Winant's assessment of his career at that time, but more importantly, it emphasizes the one constant throughout his career—Ted Knight was a proud man.

Nonetheless, in 1970, all those years of an unpredictable work schedule would be behind him. That year, he went from supplying uncredited off-camera dialogue on *M*A*S*H* to his starring role on *The Mary Tyler Moore Show.*

Of all the characters on that show, Ted Baxter was the one who evolved the most and yet fundamentally stayed the same. In press reports from the first couple of seasons he had been described as "egocentric newsman," or "pompous newscaster"—even as a "strutting bubble-head." When the series ended in 1977, he was still an egocentric pompous bubble-head but now he was a loveable one. From being a cartoonish caricature, he developed into a fully-rounded, three-dimensional character full of insecurities, vulnerability and goofiness.

It wasn't an overnight change. Before the show was even cast, the producers didn't know what they wanted in Ted Baxter. But Ted Knight knew instinctively how to play that character—and how to convince the producers of that fact. He remembers his audition this way: "When I first read that script, I wanted that role more than anything. They didn't know if they wanted a young romantic type or an older man or what type; so I asked if I could take the script home. They said fine, so over the weekend I bought a blazer with an insignia on it and some gray flannel trousers. I lay in the sun and got a terrific tan and memorized the role. When I came in Monday morning, I was Ted Baxter and they loved it."[15]

Knight had his work cut out for him in creating the prissy anchorman. All those years in small New England TV stations gave him plenty of source material to draw upon and he often admitted that Ted Baxter was a lot of different styles and mannerisms he had observed in local broadcasters during his early days in the business. He also had another source to draw upon—himself. He once said, "I've had lots of experience doing regional TV and that's why I identified so much right off with Ted Baxter. I was this guy when younger—I dreamed of money, fame, and broads. I had talent, too, but it was very thin. When I read the character of Baxter in the original script for the series, I marveled at the insight the writers had.

"Every guy who'd ever held a mike to his face got auditioned for Baxter," Knight continued. "But from the moment I read the script, I knew who this guy was—there's one like him in every station—and I guess I was a Baxter myself at various times."[16]

It wasn't just the style and mannerisms of the small-market big egos that he imitated. He told *TV Guide* that he also studied some of the more flamboyant TV news personalities in the Los Angeles market. In fact, his homage was so dead-on that one night at a banquet, well-known L.A. news commentator George Putnam shouted out to him, "Hey Ted, why don't you get your own act?"[17]

"The character may be somewhat exaggerated," he admitted. "But I've bumped into people with an ego almost as big as his."[18] In fleshing out Baxter's persona and way of speaking, Knight took pains not to make the character too extreme while giving him some defining characteristics. "It's easy for me to play Baxter and it's fun. But there's a fine line in the portrayal. You can't make it too boffo. You've got to give him dignity. He's not a total idiot. I've tried to make him into a distinctive character. I gave him that Penguin-type walk that I put on when I know the camera's on me. You'll never see Baxter walk in the door the same way twice. I also gave him that George Sanders tilt that he has."[19]

Knight also borrowed from a more surprising source for inspiration. His natural gift for mimicry was put to use, this time incorporating his idol, William Powell, the 1930s and '40s film star whom Knight called "the best light comedian who ever lived."[20] "I studied every move he made, every inflection," he told *TV Guide*. "I combined him with a few more vulnerable types, the kind that weren't above groveling."

Groveling, unwarranted self-confidence and being oblivious to others' opinions of him all became part of Knight's stock in trade as Baxter. However, after the first two seasons, Knight had serious misgivings about how the character was being written and perceived by the public.

Eventually, he would be able to say, "It used to bother me playing a national dummy on television. But I've got enough self-confidence to overcome that now."[21] Part of his concern was due to his children. "I used to worry about what effect that would have on my children, being the butt of all the jokes. But it didn't have any effect."[22]

Not helping matters was that in the beginning, Knight wasn't sure that even his own co-workers were aware of the differences between himself and the dim, pompous character he played. He told one reporter how, early on, during rehearsals, directors would often ask him to stay in character between rehearsal scenes just to break the monotony. The rest of the cast picked up on it and would do put-down jokes just like on the show. "I started getting paranoid about it," he said. "They began laughing at me when I was trying to be serious. The first two years it was touch and go whether I was a Jekyll or Hyde character."[23]

However, it was a long time before Knight was able to come to terms with the nature of his character — and then appreciate just how well-loved was this creation he had made. His misgivings reached the point where he approached the show's producers and told them that he couldn't do it anymore.

In the book *Love Is All Around*, producer Allan Burns tells the story of how a visibly upset Knight came to see him during the show's third year and told him, "I can't do this, I can't play this character, this stupid, arrogant, ignorant man who is a laughing stock. It's just gotten into my soul, and I can't, it's just so difficult for me. I'm identified with this person. And I just don't want to do it anymore."[24]

Burns and his co-producer, Jim Brooks, managed to calm Knight and point out that the character was much loved by the audience. They pointed out that Jack Benny's public persona was also cheap and difficult and conceited and yet surely Benny didn't feel that way about himself.

A direct result of that meeting was that it was the beginning of the humanization of Ted Baxter. The audience came to accept Ted's huge ego and pettiness because scripts were written so that they could understand his insecurities. They gave him a girlfriend, Georgette, played by Georgia Engel. She would become his wife. Georgette was as aware as anyone of Ted's failings and yet loved him in spite of them. A partner enabled the writers to show the softer side of Ted Baxter and just how unfamiliar he was with close relationships. It went a long way in explaining his boorishness and complete lack of people skills in general.

As producer Burns told the *Love Is All Around* authors, "We did work with the writers to find the humanity in the character. We tried to get a little deeper, understand Ted's fears. Some of that is evident in the shows with Georgette where Ted has trouble saying 'I love you.' All of this occurred as a result of our anxiety to make Knight feel more comfortable with the role. He would have his problems from time to time, but I think he got more comfortable after we started that process. Gradually I think, he realized that people really loved the character."[25]

The audience had no trouble in responding to the "new" Ted Baxter — probably because the character himself didn't change, only the way in which the writers approached him. Despite making the character more sympathetic, he remained essentially the same. Still a boob, but now a loveable boob.

Knight can take most of the credit for this. Mary Tyler Moore herself once noted, "He made an essentially unlikable character loveable."[26] Certainly the writers gave him his share of good lines but Knight supplied the voice that gave them that extra spin.

Baxter could be an uncomprehending dolt or an opinionated ignoramus and Knight would alter his vocal delivery to suit Baxter's mood of the moment. His deep newscaster's voice was for when he wanted to be taken seriously. That high-giggly voice was for when he was feeling as giddy as an excited child. The dismissive couldn't-care-less tone was his normal speaking voice for all matters that didn't affect Ted Baxter.

Regardless of the subject, all of these different vocal tones were used on topics where Ted didn't have any idea what he was talking about. No matter what was coming out of his mouth, be it an on-air news report about foreign policy or off-air expounding on his theories about women — or "chicks," as Ted would put it — Baxter was consistently an uncomprehending clueless buffoon and totally oblivious to all the rolled eyes and smirks that greeted his every utterance.

With all his stock of different vocal styles and facial expressions—no one could convey more with a single raised arched eyebrow—and his near emotional meltdown whenever pleading for something, "Pleeese, pleeeaasssee..."—Knight became one of the show's biggest drawing cards. He was one of the main reasons to make a weekly habit of tuning in on Saturday nights.

Like many second bananas, he often had to play his character like a child. No one could do it better. He was a natural scene-stealer. As Mary Tyler Moore once acknowledged, "Never try to top children, dog acts or Ted."[27]

His efforts paid off. Unlike his character, who all but once went home empty-handed from The Teddy Awards, Knight's work was recognized by his peers and critics. He won two Emmy Awards, both for Outstanding Continuing Performance by a Supporting Actor in a Comedy Series, in 1973 and '76. With the exception of the first season, he was nominated for an Emmy every year during the show's seven-year run. He also received two Golden Globe nominations for Best Supporting Actor in Television for 1973 and '76.

In trying to appease Knight by more fully rounding out the character, the producers knew they were also building on one of the show's biggest strengths. They knew from the start that they had struck gold in this pompous figure that everyone could make fun of—yet also loved.

In one episode, newsroom head-honcho Lou Grant summed up Ted Baxter's appeal. "I guess he's not the world's worst anchorman. I mean he's no Walter Cronkite, no John Chancellor, no Harry Reasoner. But he's got something that they don't have —*unpredictability*. Oh sure, you know when you watch him that he's going to put his foot in his mouth. But the thing you can never figure out is, how is he going to get the *other* one in there with it."

In another episode, Murray Slaughter rationalized his constant jokes by pointing out that Ted made a natural target because he was such a preposterous figure. He was vainglorious, yet what a glorious pain he was.

All of this is why we like to laugh at Ted. But why we like him is because of Ted Knight. Ted Baxter wasn't the first resident dummy on a sitcom but Knight carried it all off with such elan that he was able to legitimately claim that "Ted Baxter has become a classic. An original."[28]

About his TV character, Knight himself once noted, "Ted Baxter is the butt of all the jokes. They all bounce off him. But it's been rewarding where the public is concerned. Viewers all love Ted and sense his innocence and vulnerability. Ted has escaped into a bubble of unreality. And a lot of people in this country would like to find a bubble like that."[29]

Early on he may have had concerns about the character. In 1973 he realized, "I didn't think people could have as much pomposity, vanity and bigotry as Ted Baxter. When you think about it, I'm the only one in the series who doesn't play a hero."[30]

Only a couple of years later, even he was able to admit he liked the anchorman and that, "To me, Ted Baxter reveals the frivolities of man. It gives the producers the opportunity to expose the weaknesses of man and maybe that's why people laugh at him."[31]

After the series had ended, Knight reflected back and summed up Baxter's appeal far more succinctly, "Ted Baxter gave the whole world a superiority complex."[32] And a lot of laughs, he might have added.

After the sixth season in 1976, Mary Tyler Moore decided to pull the plug on the show and the next season would be its last. Her reasoning was that the show was at its creative peak and it was better to go out while they were on top. In the final episode, a new owner buys the station and appalled at the low ratings of the newscast, he fires the whole newsroom team — except for Ted, the resident incompetent and likely the cause of those low ratings.

All the regulars quickly moved on to other projects— Mary to movies and Broadway, Gavin McLeod to captain *The Love Boat* and Ed Asner to put a dramatic spin on his character on *Lou Grant.*

Knight's first foray on his own was to the short-lived sitcom *The Ted Knight Show* in 1978. Knight played Roger Dennis, owner of a New York escort agency. It was cancelled after only six episodes. He later referred to the show as "the lamented failure," yet he didn't regret its cancellation. "I was glad. It was too soon after Mary. I felt uncomfortable with it from the beginning. The premise of an escort service smacked of an offensive lifestyle."[33] Knight admitted that the character and show wasn't in keeping with the image he wanted to project.

It would be a couple of years before he would be given a second chance to headline a show. As with most second bananas, Knight discovered that he had been typecast as Baxter. "No one seems to remember anything I did before *The Mary Tyler Moore Show* and a lot of people didn't seem to think I could do anything else," he complained.[34]

In the meantime, he had a lot of time on his hands because he didn't like doing talk or game shows or doing guest shots just to keep his name out there. He joked to *TV Guide*, "Sometimes when I got a little lonely or depressed I would go down to the supermarket in hopes of being recognized. I would squeeze a few melons and look around surreptitiously. Raise my voice if I had to: [in full Baxter cry] 'Are these fresh?'"[35]

In 1980, ABC cast Knight for the lead in the sitcom *Too Close for Comfort*. It was a concept "borrowed" from a popular British sitcom, *Keep It in the Family*. Knight played work-at-home cartoonist Henry Rush, creator of a kiddies' cartoon called "Cosmic Cow." He was a married, overprotective father of two college-aged daughters who move out of the family home and into the vacant downstairs apartment of their San Francisco townhouse.

Unlike *The Ted Knight Show*, this was a project closer to home for family man Knight and a setting in which he could feel more comfortable. His wife Muriel was played by Nancy Dussault. It was a family show with stories revolving around the parents and their two young girls and their need for independence.

To give Knight a sounding board to complain about his domestic troubles, Henry Rush would talk to his Cosmic Cow puppet — which of course gave Knight a chance to show off his considerable puppetry skills.

Although there may have been a few superficial similarities between Ted Baxter and the new character, Henry Rush was his own man. Knight once said that one of the reasons he took the part on *Too Close for Comfort* was that it was a chance to shed the Ted Baxter image. "I would have an opportunity to do something more than the one-dimensional character that Ted was. He was limited in that he could never display any intelligence."[36]

At the same time, he and the producers realized that audiences expected to see a bit of Baxter in the new character and so they put in some Baxterisms. In the pilot episode, when the daughters move into the downstairs apartment — which was just vacated by a transvestite — the first big laugh came when Knight walks into the all-mirrored bathroom and suddenly stops to smooth down his hair. It was a bit of déjà vu for *Mary Tyler Moore Show* fans who remembered a similar scene set in Sue Ann (The Happy Homemaker) Nivens' bedroom when Ted Baxter entered and did the exact same thing when he noticed the mirrored ceiling over her bed.

"At least during the early episodes, I resorted to some Baxteresque stuff," Knight later admitted — "if only to wean myself from Baxter. But I'm also giving Henry Rush some bits of business that are entirely his own. I'm 51, I'm as old as Donald Duck.[37]

"I never really wanted to shake Ted Baxter. People want to see that character. Playing Ted Baxter was an asset. I'll be able to reach back into my memory banks and modify little bits of things. Ted's a very adaptable character.[38]

"There are little moments when Ted Baxter seeps through. His voice sinks down ... there's a momentary expression. Ted Baxter is an extension of

Ted Knight. I'll never completely divorce myself from that guy. But Baxter was limited, he only reacted, he couldn't resolve a critical situation. In *Too Close*, I retain little things I developed as Baxter but in more subtle ways."[39]

Perhaps the greatest proof that he had moved on was the fact that on *Too Close for Comfort*, he was the *star*, he was the Top Banana and not a stooge. In fact, almost as if to mollify Knight, the producers gave him his own second banana and in the character of Monroe Ficus, and actor Jim J. Bullock came up with someone who was even dumber and more annoying than Ted Baxter.

Too Close for Comfort ran for three seasons until it was cancelled by ABC in 1983. However, the producers sold the show to first-run syndication where it ran from January 1984 to September '85. At that point, the show was revamped as *The Ted Knight Show*. In the new format, Henry Rush became publisher of a weekly newspaper and he and his wife moved out of the old townhouse, leaving the girls behind. Second-banana Monroe, however, made the move with them.

The new *Ted Knight Show* was about to go into production for its second season in the fall of 1986. It would have meant another successful seven-year run on prime time for Knight.

But it wasn't to be.

The year before, Knight had been hospitalized for removal of a cancerous growth from his urinary tract. In August of 1986, he was back again in the hospital due to complications from the previous surgery. On August 26, at the age of 62, he died from cancer at his Pacific Palisades home with his wife Dorothy and their three children at his side.

He remained a proud and optimistic man till death. "I'm not going to die from this," he told his brother three weeks before the end. "He was in a lot of pain but he always kept his spirits up," said one relative who added, "It was the best act of his life."[40]

Despite starring in a long-running series as cartoonist Henry Rush at the time of his death, all of the obituaries concentrated on his memorable characterization as the pompous, self-centered and egotistical Ted Baxter on *The Mary Tyler Moore Show*. Although he will forever be remembered that way, Ted Knight was nothing like that aspect of his character. The producers could not have "humanized" Baxter if Knight hadn't supplied the base material to build upon. Baxter became likeable because Knight already was.

Yet, there was a lot of Ted Knight in Ted Baxter and vice versa. But it was the loveable aspects of Baxter that Knight possessed. In 1976, a year before *The Mary Tyler Moore Show* went off the air, Knight was honored in his home town with a banquet. It was a scene like an evening at the

Teddy Awards on *Mary Tyler Moore*. After a series of speeches and accolades by old friends and family, Knight took the stage but after the familiar Baxteresque greeting of "Hi guys," he was so overwhelmed with emotion that he broke down in sobs and was unable to finish. The writers on his old show couldn't have captured a more Baxter-like moment.

Not long after, on another visit home he told a reporter, "I wish every kid could grow up where there were traditional values, the kind we had that were brought over by the immigrants. We don't have them anymore, but over the years, those values have been my sustenance."[41]

To the end he remained a proud but humble man who remembered his heritage and where he came from. His grave at Forest Lawn Cemetery in Glendale, California, consists of a simple flat slab of marble. In big, bold letters is the name Tadeus C. Konopka. Directly below it, in smaller script and quotation marks, reads, "Ted Knight." Below that are the comedy and tragedy masks signifying his craft.

Notes

1. *The Bristol Press*; October 5, 1978; "Ted Knight Back to Reminisce"; by Mike Bazinet.

2. *Ibid.*

3. *Ibid.*

4. *Waterbury Republican*; May 25, 1975; "Terryville's Favorite Knight"; by John Gentile.

5. *Ibid.*

6. *The Providence Journal*; February 23, 1955; "WJAR-TV's Ted Knight"; by Kenneth W. Parker.

7. TV Time; *The Philadelphia Bulletin*; April 29, 1973; "One Like Him in Every Station"; by Rex Polier.

8. *Waterbury Republican*; May 25, 1975; "Terryville's Favorite Knight"; by John Gentile.

9. TV Time; *The Philadelphia Bulletin*; April 29, 1973; "One Like Him in Every Station"; by Rex Polier.

10. *TV Guide*; January 3, 1981; "Ted Knight"; by Bill O'Hallaren.

11. *Waterbury Republican*; May 25, 1975; "Terryville's Favorite Knight"; by John Gentile.

12. *The Hartford Courant*; June 12, 1976; "Ted Knight Comes Home"; by Ken Crvickshank.

13. *Ibid.*

14. Associated Press; November 8, 1989; "He's Still Ted Baxter"; by Jerry Buck.

15. *The Bristol Press*; April 16, 1973; "Star's Surprise Visit"; by Paula Miller.

16. TV Time; *Philadelphia Bulletin*; April 29, 1973; "One Like Him in Every Station"; by Rex Polier.

17. *TV Guide*; January 3, 1981; "Ted Knight"; by Bill O'Hallaren.

18. United Press International (UPI); February 3, 1973; "TV Dummy Lives Down Real Name."

19. TV Time; *Philadelphia Bulletin*; April 29, 1973; "One Like Him in Every Station"; by Rex Polier.

20. *TV Guide*; January 3, 1981; "Ted Knight"; by Bill O'Hallaren.

21. UPI; February 3, 1973; "TV Dummy Lives Down Real Name."

22. *Waterbury Republican*; August 27, 1986; "Actor Ted Knight Dies."

23. UPI; February 3, 1973; "TV Dummy Lives Down Real Name."

24. *Love Is All Around: The Making of the Mary Tyler Moore Show*; by Robert Alley and Irby Brown; Delta Books; 1989; page 118.

25. *Love Is All Around*; page 118.

26. *Plymouth Herald Press*; August 31, 1997; "A Good Knight for Comedy"; by Eve Sullivan.

27. *Family Weekly*; March 22, 1981; "Hear Now Ted Knight"; by Mark Goodman.

28. UPI; February 3, 1973; "TV Dummy Lives Down Real Name."

29. *Ibid.*

30. *Ibid.*

31. *Waterbury Republican*; May 25, 1975; "Terryville's Favorite Knight"; by John Gentile.

32. Associated Press; November 8, 1980; "He's Still Baxter"; by Jerry Buck.

33. *TV Guide*; January 3, 1981; "Ted Knight"; by Bill O'Hallaren.

34. *Ibid.*

35. *Ibid.*

36. *Waterbury Republican*; August 27, 1986; "Actor Ted Knight Dies."

37. *Family Weekly*; March 22, 1981; "Hear Now Ted Knight"; by Mark Goodman.

38. Associated Press; November 8, 1980; "He's Still Ted Baxter"; by Jerry Buck.

39. *TV Guide*; January 3, 1981; "Ted Knight"; by Bill O'Hallaran.

40. *The Bristol Press*; August 28, 1986; "Ted Knight's Final Act Said Best Ever"; by John Paradis.

41. *The Bristol Press*; October 5, 1978; "Ted Knight Back to Reminisce"; by Mike Bazinet.

Ted Knight Credits

FILM CREDITS

1. *Caddyshack;* 1980; Judge Smails
2. *M*A*S*H;* 1970; (voice) (uncredited), Offstage Dialog
3. *Anatomy of a Crime;* 1969
4. *Countdown;* 1968; Walter Larson
5. *The Katherine Reed Story;* 1965; Narrator
6. *Young Dillinger;* 1965; Johnsyn

7. *Blindfold;* 1965; (uncredited); Dr. Bob Bereford
8. *The Candidate;* 1964; Frank Carlton
9. *The Final Hour;* 1962
10. *Hitler;* 1962; Major Buch
11. *13 West Street;* 1962; Baldwin
12. *Two Rode Together;* 1961; Lieutenant Upton
13. *Swingin' Along;* 1961; Priest
14. *Cry for Happy;* 1961; Lt. Glick
15. *13 Fighting Men;* 1960; Samuel
16. *Cage of Evil;* 1960; (uncredited), Lt. Dan Ivers, S.F. Police
17. *Twelve Hours to Kill;* 1960; Denton
18. *Psycho;* 1960; (uncredited), Prison Guard

TV CREDITS

1. *Circus of the Stars #9;* TV special; 1984
2. *Too Close for Comfort;* TV series; 1980–1986; Henry Rush
3. *The Ted Knight Show;* TV series; 1978; Roger Dennis
4. *Sandy in Disneyland;* TV special; 1974; Himself
5. *Lassie's Rescue Rangers;* TV series; 1973–1975; (voice) Narrator, Ben Turner
6. *Super Friends;* TV series; 1973; (voice)
7. *The Mary Tyler Moore Show;* TV series; 1970–1977; Ted Baxter
8. *The Batman/Superman Hour;* TV series; 1968; (voice) Narrator, Commissioner Gordon, Penguin, Riddler
9. *Fantastic Voyage;* TV series; 1968 (voice) Jonathan Kidd, Professor Carter
10. *Journey to the Center of the Earth;* TV series; 1967; (voice) Prof. Lindenbrook, Count Saccunson
11. *The Superman/Aquaman Hour of Adventure;* TV series; 1967; (voice) Narrator
12. *The New Adventures of Superman;* TV series; 1966; (voice) Narrator, Perry White
13. *The Young Marrieds;* TV series; 1965; Phil Sterling
14. *Nightmare in Chicago;* TV movie; 1964
15. *The Clear Horizon;* TV series; 1960

NOTABLE TV GUEST APPEARANCES

1. *The Love Boat;* 1983
2. *Rhoda;* Ted Baxter; 10/28/1974
3. *Star Trek;* Carter Winston (voice); 10/13/1973
4. *Bonanza;* Sgt. Brown; 3/19/1972
5. *The Flip Wilson Show;* Himself; 1970
6. *The Wild, Wild West;* General Lassiter; 11/10/1969
7. *The Outsider;* Nick Ames; 12/4/1968
8. *The Wild, Wild West;* Daniel; 11/1/1968
9. *Garrison's Gorillas;* Werner; 3/5/1968

10. *The Invaders;* Air Force Major/Invader Assistant; 9/26/1967
11. *Get Smart;* KAOS Agent; 4/1/1967
12. *The Fugitive;* Dr. Rains; 10/25/1966
13. *The F.B.I.;* 10/9/1966
14. *T.H.E. Cat;* Hardman; 10/7/1966
15. *Combat!;* 10/4/1966
16. *Gomer Pyle, U.S.M.C.;* Don Mills; 4/15/1966
17. *The Fugitive;* Lieutenant Mooney; 3/22/1966
18. *Get Smart;* KAOS Agent; 3/5/1966
19. *The F.B.I.;* 12/5/1965
20. *Twelve O'Clock High;* Lt. Col. Rogers; 11/22/1965
21. *Combat!;* German Sergeant; 3/17/1964
22. *The Outer Limits;* Mr. Jerome; 2/3/1964
23. *The Virginian;* 5/1/1963
24. *Combat!;* Kurt; 1/22/1963
25. *Combat!;* German Captain; 12/4/1962
26. *The Virginian;* 10/3/1962
27. *McHale's Navy;* 1962
28. *McHale's Navy;* (voice); 1962
29. *Bonanza;* Halloran; 5/27/1961
30. *Mr. Lucky;* Dr. Furst; 6/4/1960
31. *Alfred Hitchcock Presents;* Mr. Maynard; 5/29/1960
32. *The Twilight Zone;* Adams; 11/13/1959
33. *Peter Gunn;* Poole; 9/28/1959
34. *Gunsmoke;* Jay Rabb; 5/23/1959

Don Knotts

Barney Fife on *The Andy Griffith Show*;
Ralph Furley on *Three's Company*

> *"That's what I get for crash-landing into a civilization that worships Don Knotts. You don't? Well, you should. The man's a genius."*
>
> — ALF, from *ALF*, 1986

That's right ALF, and people are finally realizing that fact. It's not just the writers of sitcoms about furry aliens but big-name Hollywood has also recognized the Don Knotts legacy. Kitsch director John Waters has long talked about his dream project — making The Don Knotts Story. That "funny-looking guy" Steve Buscemi from the Coen Brothers movies would be a natural for the part and the brotherly director-producer team have even commented on Buscemi's resemblance to Knotts. When the producers of *Pleasantville* wanted an instantly recognizable pop-culture icon from the good old days of television, they chose Knotts to play the magical, God-like TV repairman in the film. Hollywood's current reigning king of comedy, Jim Carrey, had planned on paying tribute to Knotts by mounting and starring in a remake of Knotts' animated movie, *The Incredible Mr. Limpet,* which was to feature a cameo by the original star.

But Knotts' genius has never been in doubt. As Deputy Barney Fife on *The Andy Griffith Show,* Knotts won five Emmy Awards before packing up the old salt-and-pepper suit to wear in movies like *The Ghost and Mr. Chicken* and *The Love God?* before ending up as senior swinger Ralph Furley on *Three's Company* and eventually reuniting with Andy Griffith as a Barney Fife–like semi-regular on *Matlock.*

Since the early 1960s, Barney Fife has never left the world's television screens and new generations have discovered him either through the show's syndicated reruns or Knotts' occasional guest appearances as Deputy Barney on the cartoon *Scooby-Doo.*

Despite his five years on *Three's Company* and twenty some movies, it's his legacy as Barney Fife which has resulted in Knotts' being universally acknowledged as television's greatest second banana. He's even a mythic figure among second bananas. "He's my favorite and I think he's the best there ever was," gushes Tom Lester, who played Eb the handyman on *Green Acres.* Ron Palillo, who was Arnold Horshack on *Welcome Back, Kotter,* agrees—"I think Don Knotts is brilliant." Even no less an authority than Tom Poston — Knotts' old colleague from *The Steve Allen Show* and no slouch in the second-banana department himself — while in character as George Utley on a typically absurd episode of *Newhart,* raved about Knotts being the ultimate TV stooge. Of course the episode was capped by a quick cameo by the man himself.

Now in his mid-seventies, Knotts handles all the high praise in a very unBarney–like fashion — humbly and gracefully. When asked how it feels to be a bona fide genuine pop-culture icon for his work as Barney on *The Andy Griffith Show,* Knotts aw-shucks his way through a response. "Well, I'm proud of it, of course. But I must say that it was so much fun to do that show and the memory is the main thing. The most important thing for me is the memory of the good time we had doing that show."

The writers on the old *Griffith* show loved to write for Barney because he was so wonderfully transparent that he was a comic treasure. Knotts himself admits, "Barney was like a child and that's exactly how I played it." Like a kid, when he was happy, he couldn't help but show it. When he was mad, he was furious and when he felt slighted, he pouted. Armed with just one bullet (which Sheriff Andy made him keep in his pocket) and a repertoire of distinct facial expressions, Knotts made Barney Fife into such a rich unique character that he almost defies impersonation.

With his string-bean build, Knotts became the physical model for the majority of second bananas to come. But unlike many of those one-dimensional cardboard cut-outs, Knotts' creation was a full-blown three-dimensional 138-pound bundle of insecurity and over-confidence. He put his own stamp on the character so indelibly that you simply cannot imagine anyone else in the role.

Although it may be a stretch to imagine someone of Knotts' build as a lawman, Barney made up for it with his exaggerated sense of self. Naturally vain and dangerously close to pomposity on occasion, whenever Barney was feeling full of himself, Knotts employed a series of gestures which perfectly captured Barney's feelings of self-importance. When he was bragging, Knotts would clear his sinuses just to punctuate the moment and give a little extra emphasis to his self-conscious bravado. He'd usually top it off with a smug, self-satisfied smirk. Whenever Barney was letting the boys know about his luck with the ladies, Knotts would give an almost lewd open-mouthed grin as if he'd just told a hot one. On other occasions, as a cocky blowhard, Knotts would deepen his voice and speak in the commanding authoritative tone of a Mr. Know-it-All, strutting around like a peacock.

Knotts' physical mannerisms were not used just to convey the immensity of Barney's big ego. As a lawman, Barney was a well-meaning incompetent, which was the ideal vehicle for showcasing the bug-eyed look and jittery, easily rattled mannerisms Knotts had perfected during four years on *The Steve Allen Show* as the little meek and nervous Man on the Street.

As second banana on *The Andy Griffith Show,* Barney's purpose was to regularly get into some sort of predicament so that Andy Taylor could get him out of it — and thoughtfully do it in a way that did as little damage as possible to Barney's fragile ego. The nature of the trouble was not necessarily confined to plots involving the law-and-order game where Barney's ineptness and gung-ho enthusiasm would contribute to his being overwhelmed by circumstances.

Although he was a spry, albeit small-boned, lawman full of gumption, the greatest danger Barney faced was not from a bigger, more intimidating lawbreaker but from his own incompetence leading to the inevitable blow to his ego. Barney was very sensitive. His mother was like that too. For that reason, some of the best episodes are ones where Andy had to get Barney out of an emotional jam or repair some psychic damage done to his easily wounded deputy and best friend. He may have thought of himself as fearless in the face of danger but he was far more vulnerable to hurt feelings. No one could wring more pathos out of a scene than Knotts as a fallen, humiliated Barney. Knotts would build the high-spirited deputy up so high that any fall was bound to be a hard one.

Often scripts found Andy restoring Barney's self-esteem after some messy skirmish in the battle of the sexes. In his white wide-brim hat and salt-and-pepper tweed suit (it hung just right for doing the dip while dancing), Barney fancied himself a ladies' man. He kept a photo of Rock Hudson taped to his mirror as a guide for when combing his hair and getting slicked up. He was the kind of guy who would sing along to Frank Sinatra on the radio and think he was just as smooth. No one in Mayberry was quite so blind in their self-delusions as Barney. But his over-confidence obviously worked — although he went steady with Thelma Lou, the thin-lipped loverboy was also getting a little side attention from Juanita, the waitress down at the all-night diner on the outskirts of town.

Barney Fife became such a beloved character because although he was a bit of a joke in his own home town, Barney always took himself very seriously. The character became so memorable because in bringing him to life, Don Knotts took him just as seriously. His greatest accomplishment with the role is in not turning the character into a cartoon. He walked a fine balancing act: it was obvious that Barney was something of a nut and yet Knotts never overdid it or crossed that line to the point where the character wouldn't be believable enough for the audience to care about him.

"I was aware that I had to be believable as that person, otherwise it wouldn't have worked," Knotts explains. "Any time we tried anything sketchy or unbelievable, we wound up throwing it out because it just didn't work. These people had to be real, even if they were a little bizarre."

Knotts says that in a second-banana role, although you get to be funnier than the star, you cannot be *too* extreme — because if Barney was unbelievable, then the Andy-Barney relationship wouldn't have any credibility. "That's certainly the way it was on *The Andy Griffith Show*," he says. "But we tried to make the entire show as real as we could — but with slight exaggerations, sure. And people seemed to identify with the characters and the way they felt and talked and so on."

As for that fine balancing act, Knotts says it wasn't hard. "I don't remember it as feeling difficult. I had done a lot of acting before I did *The Andy Griffith Show* and luckily I had some experience by the time I hit the show."

Actually, he had been working towards that character for about twenty years before becoming Griffith's deputy. Knotts had always known he was going to be in show business.

Jesse Donald Knotts was born in Morgantown, West Virginia, on July 21, 1924. He grew up in a somewhat unusual family situation. Before Don was born, his father had suffered a severe nervous breakdown and physical collapse and was mostly bedridden until his death from pneumonia when Don was 16. To support them, Knotts' mother leased a large house near the town's university and rented out rooms to students. Don had three much older brothers, Bill, Sid and William Earl — whom everyone called "Shadow" because of his frail physique.

Knotts says it was his mother who sparked his interest in show business. "Ever since I can remember, I knew that I wanted to be in show business," he says. "And I don't think I ever veered from that from the time I was five or six years old. I think it came from my mother being a big movie fan and she took me to all the movies when I was real young. When you start leaning that way it's hard to remember why, but I guess it was because I was exposed to a lot of show business just as a member of the audience.

"But although it was my mother who turned me on to show business because she was such a big movie and radio fan, I think it was my brother Shadow who really got me started in comedy because he was a real clown and naturally funny. I remember one time, he was sick in bed and I asked him what was wrong and he said, 'Everything I eat goes to my stomach.'"

As a child, Knotts loved radio comedy and Jack Benny, with his impeccable timing, was one of his idols. Another favorite was Edgar Bergen with Charlie McCarthy, who inspired Knotts to launch his own career at the age of 13 with a ventriloquist act which he admits was largely "borrowed" from Bergen. Throughout high school, Knotts would perform his ventriloquist act with a professionally made dummy named Danny at various civic functions and school events.

High school was a turning point for Knotts and he really began to blossom into his own person. His father had died in Knotts' last year of junior high and this was almost a relief to those at home. "When I started high school, it was with a whole new bunch of friends and my home life had changed somewhat with the death of my father. I just seemed to open up somehow. It's hard to tell what all goes into that but I started becoming active in everything I could think of."

During his high school years, the popular Knotts was elected vice-president of his junior class and president of the senior class. He was nick-named "Spider" because of his wiry build and was on the basketball and wrestling teams. He performed in high school drama productions, wrote sketches for shows and emceed at assemblies.

He also wrote the humor column for the school newspaper. He sense of humor can be seen in the 1941 edition of his school yearbook, *The Mohi-gan*. Under his photo, he lists his ambition in life as "To become a mechanic." Knotts chuckles at the memory today — "That was just for fun. Anybody who knows me, knows that I'm not in the least bit mechanically inclined."

After high school, Knotts enrolled as a speech major at West Virginia University expecting to come out as a teacher. However, shortly after starting classes, he enlisted in the Army to serve in World War II. His entrance papers had him listed as a "ventriloquist" and so after basic training, he was assigned to Special Services and spent two years in the South Pacific in *Stars and Gripes* entertaining the troops.

It was while performing in that military revue show that Knotts became more interested in comedy and began doing more skits and less ventriloquism. In his autobiography, *Barney Fife and Other Characters I Have Known*, he recalls how fellow comic Red Ford taught him the ropes. "One night at the base, I was having a coke with some of the guys and I looked up and noticed that Red, who was sitting at a nearby table was staring at me and laughing. Finally, he walked over and said, 'You know something? You're a funny little son of a bitch'."[1]

He adds that shortly after that, Ford wrote him into his act, gave him a few jokes and coached him on how to play a deadpan comic and walk on stage to interrupt him. It was Knotts' first experience and training as a second banana.

Midway through his military hitch in *Stars and Gripes*, Knotts' ventriloquist dummy, Danny, "disappeared." "I used to tell people that I threw him overboard," Knotts jokes. "But actually I left him behind on the beach on one of the islands. I just didn't want to do ventriloquism anymore so I reported him missing.

"The truth was that by then I was doing a double act with Mickey Shaughnessy, the top comic of our troupe and they were occasionally letting me do a monologue I had written and I just wanted to do more comedy. I think I was just enjoying the straight comedy more than I was the ventriloquism. I never really saw myself as becoming a great ventriloquist. It was just something to get me into show business."

After that he never picked up a ventriloquist dummy again. However, he reports that years later, after his success on *The Andy Griffith Show* and in feature films, his mother would tell him that the folks back home always want to know why he didn't do his ventriloquism act anymore.

When his time in the Army was up he returned home and finished his university education. But the show business bug had bitten him good and with his mother's blessing he headed for New York. "My mother was certainly the most influential person in my life," says Knotts. "My interest in show business came from her but she also gave me the idea that I could do *anything* I wanted to do—*and I believed her.*"

In New York in the early 1950s, Knotts made the rounds of radio stations and nightclubs looking for work. His first big break came in 1950 on the radio western series *The Bobby Benson Show,* set on a ranch called the B-Bar-B. Bobby Benson was a 12-year-old kid who owned the ranch and 26-year-old Knotts played a Gabby Hayes–like old-timer ranch hand named Windy Wales. "Pete Dixon put that show together," recalls Knotts. "I had met him on another radio program at WOR and he just asked me one day, 'Do you think you can play an old-timer?' I said 'Sure.' After all, it was for radio and he hired me on faith, with no audition or anything and I just went in and did it with a creaky voice. I had never done that kind of character before, but actors will say anything if it means a job."

His first regular job on television was on *Howdy Doody* in 1954 as the wonderfully named Tim Tremble. At the same time, he also had a recurring role on the soap opera *Search for Tomorrow,* in which he played Wilbur Peterson, an almost catatonic character who could only relate to his sister and wouldn't speak to anyone else. A silent Don Knotts is a bit of a waste, but he was with the show off and on for the next four years.

In 1955, Knotts met Andy Griffith when they were both appearing in the Broadway hit *No Time for Sergeants.* It was Griffith's big break as hillbilly Army draftee Will Stockdale. Knotts wasn't cast as a Barney Fife–type but as the staff psychologist at the recruiting center. His character was a highly nervous individual.

During the run of *No Time for Sergeants,* Knotts began creating his own stand-up comedy material and had literally dreamed up the character of the nervous little man based on an after-dinner speaker he had seen many years ago back in his home town. The man shook with bad nerves, spilled from his water glass, rattled and lost the pages to his speech. Knotts debuted the character during a stand-up bit on Gary Moore's afternoon talk and variety TV show. It was such a hit that it led to a regular gig on *The Steve Allen Show* in 1956.

"Steve Allen discovered me when I did some monologues on his late-night show. He then hired me to do sketch comedy on his popular Sunday night variety show. I was a regular and did the nervous little man for four years."

Knotts worked with Louis Nye and Tom Poston on *The Steve Allen Show* and together they became the classic triumvirate of TV stooges. They set the standard for all second bananas to come and many bananas cite these three as being their inspiration for getting into show business for the work they did on *The Steve Allen Show* — particularly the Man-on-the-Street interviews.

Of his two cohorts, Knotts says, "There was no competition between us on that show because we all had our own styles but the goal was always to put on the funniest show we could. Louis Nye had a knack for improvising and his ad-libs would break us all up, especially Steve. Tom Poston is a very funny guy, but he can be both funny and serious. Tom's a helluva actor. He's just a good fine actor and whatever you give him he does well."

Knotts went with the show when it moved from New York to Hollywood in 1959. Unfortunately, it was cancelled after that season. He wasn't out of work for long and what came next proved to be the highlight of his career. Knotts recalls, "When I was finishing up the last season of *Steve Allen*, I got wind of the fact that Andy Griffith was going to do a TV series about a sheriff. So I called him up and suggested that he needed a deputy. He said, 'Okay,' and that's how I got on *The Andy Griffith Show*."

Knotts and Griffith had been friends since working together in *No Time for Sergeants* — first on Broadway in 1955 and then in the feature film version in 1958, and their real-life friendship came through on *The Andy Griffith Show*. If they sounded comfortable in their roles as small-town best friends it's only natural. According to Knotts, much of the series' humor came from their own lives. "Andy and I found out on *The Andy Griffith Show* that we had a lot in common. Our backgrounds were similar — he's from a small town in North Carolina and I'm from a small town in West Virginia and we shared a lot of experiences that cracked us up and they found their way into the scripts."

Griffith's personal favorite moments from the series were those leisurely scenes set on the Taylors' front porch or the bench outside the courthouse where Ange and Barn would lounge around, watching the world go by and raising the art of small talk to new heights of the mundane. Comfortable in each other's thoughts, they were just passing time but would occasionally muster up the energy to suggest going downtown for a bottle of pop or to the drug store and getting some ice cream for "later."

Knotts recalls how those slow-moving front porch scenes came from their childhoods. "We both grew up in rural areas and we used to talk about our experiences and how people behaved in those days. I'd always talk about my relatives on the farm just outside of Morgantown and I'd overheard parts of conversations that we ended up using on the show. I remember standing around at our relatives' one Sunday afternoon. And farmers don't say much you know, but finally one of them would say, 'You wanna go down to the gas station and get a bottle of pop?' And they'd keep talking about it but never get around to doing it. We worked that into a little comedy routine on the show and did it every once in a while."

Although Griffith owned the show, Knotts says that he never acted like a boss or treated the other actors as subordinates or employees. "Our friendship prevailed through the series," he says. "We hung out together a lot and we worked together on the stuff that we would do, some of the bits we would do. So there's no question that we continued to be close friends as well as two people working together. I still bowed to his decisions because he was the boss and he got involved in every aspect of the show. You knew he was the boss and that he was doing things but somehow you never saw him doing it and he never acted like a boss."

They worked well on the show for five years, but in the fall of 1964, Griffith decided that he would leave the show at the end of its fifth season. It's inevitable that any second banana will want to play a starring lead role but when Knotts left the show at the end of the 1964–65 season, although he went on to bigger things, starring in his own films for Universal, he didn't leave because he was tired of Mayberry or the character. He thought Griffith was pulling the plug on the show and so he made his own plans.

"I thoroughly enjoyed working on *The Andy Griffith Show*," explains Knotts. "The reason I actually left the show to go into the motion picture business with Universal was because I thought Andy was going to leave after the fifth year himself. And then I got an offer to do pictures and I'd always wanted to do movies so I took it. And then he changed his mind and decided to stay on."

To put Knotts' importance to *The Andy Griffith Show* in perspective, all you have to do is look at the first five seasons with Barney Fife and compare them to the last three seasons. In a word, the Knotts-less episodes are boring. Although the series made the jump from black and white to color when Knotts left, Mayberry was a far less colorful place without

Barney. Even Griffith seems tired and Andy Taylor clearly isn't having as much fun. Griffith himself has commented about Knotts: "He made our show what it was and it was never as good after Don left."[2]

Ever the diplomat, Knotts says, "I know the show took on a different hue after I left. And it was very nice of Andy to say that, but I wouldn't know what to say about it because I don't agree with it. I think he missed the relationship that we had as Andy and Barney which did work so well and made us a funny team. But the show continued to do well in the ratings."

Maybe so, but it wasn't the same show — except for those infrequent occasions which highlighted each season with one or two episodes featuring a visit from Barney Fife. Knotts won Emmy Awards for his guest appearances on the show in episodes titled "The Return of Barney Fife" and "The Legend of Barney Fife." However, it should be noted that in all of his return visits, each episode is tinged with a bittersweet you-can't-go-home-again feeling.

As proof of Knotts' popularity at the time, it's important to remember that he's the only second banana to make the leap from supporting role on television to starring in his own movies as the sole lead.

Prior to leaving the show, in 1964, he starred in the live-action and animated feature *The Incredible Mr. Limpet*. True, it was a kids' movie, but it proved his bankability. His five-year contract with Universal called for him to do a movie a year starting with *The Ghost and Mr. Chicken* in 1966, followed by *The Reluctant Astronaut*, *The Shakiest Gun in the West*, *The Love God?* and *How to Frame a Figg*.

Knotts returned to television in 1970 in the short-lived variety hour *The Don Knotts Show*. In one regular segment called "The Front Porch," Knotts and his guest that week would sit in rocking chairs and chew the fat in a scenario reminiscent of those scenes on the old *Griffith Show*.

Another weekly feature was one about the grind and headaches involved in putting on a weekly television show. It was a theme which Knotts could identify with and he says he didn't really enjoy the variety show experience. "I just wasn't comfortable doing that kind of show and being the star of the show. I did tons of variety shows as a guest star doing sketches and stuff, but to come out and introduce the acts and have it be focused on me was something I wasn't comfortable with in being in that role. I don't know why — I've never been too comfortable on stage by myself when I was just being myself and not being a character. I guess I'm more of an actor than a star. And that show was a huge responsibility. I didn't realize how big a responsibility it would be — to be out there every week for a full hour and to have to approve and okay all the sketches and all the material that goes into the show. Being with the writers and going through an hour's worth of material was just overwhelming. Some guys take to it and like it but it just never suited me."

In the mid-seventies, Knotts teamed up with fellow comic and former second banana Tim Conway for a series of family films for Disney — *The Apple Dumpling Gang* (1975), *Gus* (1976) and *The Apple Dumpling Gang Rides Again* (1979). They reunited for their own starring vehicles, both written by Conway, *The Prize Fighter* in 1979 and *The Private Eyes* in 1980. The pair's comic timing reminded some of the classic comedy teams like Laurel and Hardy. For fans of Knotts, his characterizations were like very broad versions of Barney Fife.

That broad acting style — seemingly devoid of subtlety and nuance — was what TV audiences saw when Knotts returned to situation comedy on the mindless and mindlessly popular *Three's Company* in 1979.

Wearing loud leisure suits and scarves — the gaudier the better — Knotts played senior swinger Ralph Furley for the series' last five seasons. Knotts admits that the deluded ladies' man had a bit of Barney Fife in him but also owed a lot to Abner Peacock, his character from *The Love God?*, in which he played a parody of Hugh Hefner.

Fans of *The Andy Griffith Show* who remember how absolutely "on" Knotts was as Barney Fife prefer not to think about *Three's Company*. But the show bears mentioning, if only because for Knotts it was another five-year gig as a second banana on a Top 10–rated sitcom. However, there were no Emmys this time around. Mayberry purists dismiss *Three's Company* as an empty-headed jiggle-fest of one-dimensional characters where all the humor was in the form of sexual innuendo, double entendres and one-liners. They criticize Knotts' performance on the show as being an unseemly exaggeration of all the extreme parts of Barney Fife — the sinus-clearing when playing a braggart, the lewd grin when in lover-boy mode.

But when you look at *Three's Company* as a whole, Knotts' acting style and approach to his character was in keeping with the rest of the show — *everybody* acted like that. Considering the nature of the show, broad was the only way to play it.

Knotts himself explains that the difference in his acting styles is due to the fundamental difference between the two shows. "Well, you see, a show like *Three's Company* is altogether different from *The Andy Griffith Show*. It's farce comedy really, so you really just go and get real wild and crazy — whereas the old *Griffith* show was character humor. There's really a world of difference between the two shows. On *The Andy Griffith Show*, we tried to keep in fairly real or give the illusion of being real. And, we didn't do jokes. Andy said, 'If it sounds like a joke, throw it out,' because we were doing character comedy.

"But on *Three's Company,* you were really doing jokes, because the object there was to make the studio audience laugh. On *The Andy Griffith Show,* we had no studio audience of course. So we weren't striving to get a laugh every two minutes and that makes it a totally different show. And when you do a show like *Three's Company,* you really have to play it much broader. It was really farce, that's what it was."

As a comedian and an actor, Knotts prefers to work and create as they did on the *Griffith* show. "Well, the *Griffith* show was done on film," he elaborates. "We filmed it like a movie with no audience there to worry about and I prefer that kind of work.

"But when you put a studio audience *and* three cameras on you at the same time as was the case with *Three's Company,* it's a lot of pressure. You're doing a brand new show each week and so you have to not only know the lines but figure out if they're going to be funny or how to make them funny and so forth."

If nothing else, the aging Knotts' tenure on *Three's Company* prepared TV audiences for his reunion with Andy Griffith, first as Barney Fife on the TV movie *Return to Mayberry* in 1986, and then as a semi-regular on Griffith's popular lawyer-drama, *Matlock.* This time around it was Griffith who called up Knotts and asked if his services were available. It couldn't have happened at a better time. The call came in the summer of 1988 when Knotts was feeling depressed and recovering from an eye disease which could have left him blind. "That was typical of Andy," recalls Knotts. "To get involved and help somebody however he could. He helped me a great deal."

It turns out that Griffith had been feeling nostalgic for some of those old front porch scenes and thought they might provide some comic relief on *Matlock.* "It was all Andy's idea," says Knotts. "As a matter of fact, I couldn't have imagined how I could fit into that show since it's not a comedy. Andy sort of got the whole thing started and he knows as much about me as I do so he figured out what the character would be and it wasn't that different, I guess you could say he's a little older Barney Fife."

Widower and retired businessman Les ("Call me Ace") Calhoun may not have been as spry as Barney once was but he had the same old mannerisms. The old salt-and-pepper suit had been exchanged for some equally tacky patterned sweaters and he was still trying to set Griffith's character up with girls—"I stopped off at this bar the other day and there were a coupla dames in there, couldn't of been a day over 48...."

During his stint on *Matlock,* Knotts wasn't concerned about any similarities and comparisons between Les and Barney. "No, it didn't bother me much. When you get to be my age, you don't worry about these things anymore." It should be pointed out that Knotts was all of 63 when he made that statement. He went on to add that Barney was the character of which he was the most proud. "I try not to do Barney anywhere else. I will of course in *Matlock*. But not entirely, I won't do him entirely the same because I'm too old to behave that way.

"I've been typecast, sure. But I haven't minded that. It's kept me working," Knotts says. It was also responsible for his jump to feature films. After his Universal films of the late sixties, Knotts' feature film career was comprised of supporting roles in family films, mostly for Disney. *Gus* was about a football-kicking mule on an NFL team. *Herbie Goes to Monte Carlo* was about a talking Volkswagon. His character in these films was usually the nervous, high-strung type.

However, nearing the end of the millenium, Knotts movies were also being given a reappraisal. An episode of Bob Newhart's short-lived sitcom *Bob* pointed out that women go crazy for Don Knotts movies. In that 1992 episode, Newhart's character revealed that his wife proposed to *him* after they saw *The Ghost and Mr. Chicken* and that their daughter was conceived after a matinee screening of *The Love God?*

The capstone of his later films was certainly 1998's *Pleasantville*, in which he had the small but pivotal role of the mystical God-like TV repairman who sent the two main characters into a world which was a 1950s–era black-and-white situation comedy. Director Gary Ross wanted a recognizable actor from that Golden Age of television. Knotts was flattered by the gesture. His performance is not as broad and extreme as some of his movies have been. If anything, he seems more restrained and focused. He says that Ross reined him in for the role: "What the director was trying to do was to put an edge on this guy because you find out that he wasn't an easygoing Barney Fife. Underneath he was nasty."

Of his film career, Knotts says he has three personal favorites. "I've made about thirty movies and my favorite is *The Ghost and Mr. Chicken*, which was the first feature I did on my own after I left *The Andy Griffith Show* and I had a lot of control over the writing and everything. And then another picture I liked was the one that Tim Conway and I got together on later at Disney, *The Apple Dumpling Gang*. And the other picture I'm proud of is *The Incredible Mr. Limpet*."

In *Limpet*, Knotts played a nebbish accountant who falls into the ocean and becomes a fish through "reverse evolution" and then goes on to affect the outcome of World War II. The film is important for two reasons. Made in 1964, the same year as *Mary Poppins*, it also married animation and live action in a feature film. The second reason was that for the first time in a movie — Don Knotts *sings!*

Although the animation is crude by today's standards, the animators got Knotts' look and mannerisms down so well that you immediately forget about him as a cartoon fish and just accept him as the same Don Knotts–character he usually plays. If anything, it's harder to get used to seeing him wearing glasses than looking like a cartoon fish.

Knotts' work on the big screen has remained popular largely because of the character he created on the small screen as TV's ultimate second banana. Audiences identified with that character. Although Knotts once worried about typecasting as much as any actor, he also knew what audiences wanted. You only have to look at *The Ghost and Mr. Chicken* for proof.

Made in 1966, *Mr. Chicken* was the first of his Universal films and his first post–Mayberry film. It also represents the first time he made a conscious decision to exploit and parlay that typecast image into a career move. His contract gave him creative control and so he surrounded himself with colleagues who understood what made Don Knotts funny.

He hired the writing team of Jim Fritzell and Everett Greenbaum, who would also write his next two pictures for Universal — *The Reluctant Astronaut* and *The Shakiest Gun in the West,* as well as supply the story idea for *The Love God?.* They were also old friends and frequent contributors to *The Andy Griffith Show,* having written many of the classic Barney episodes including "Barney's Sidecar," "Man in a Hurry," "Convicts at Large" and "Up in Barney's Room."

Alan Rafkin, who had directed episodes of the *Griffith* show, was hired to direct the film. Knotts also surrounded himself with recognizable faces from Mayberry in bit parts. In fact, the movie opens with a familiar shouting match between Knotts and Hal Smith, who played Mayberry's town drunk, Otis Campbell, and here played the town drunk Calvert Weems.

The result is that *The Ghost and Mr. Chicken* is like a two-hour Barney Fife–fest. His character may be called Luther Heggs, but he's really Barney Fife in all but name only. The writers feel free to steal from themselves and throw in classic Barney lines lifted directly from the TV show, like, "I've been studying karate by mail for years. My whole body is a weapon."

And just to make sure the audience makes the identification in the jump from small screen to big screen, Knotts wears the exact same wardrobe as when he was in his civvies on a night off from fighting crime in Mayberry. It was the same ol' salt-and-pepper suit with the little bowtie and wide-brimmed white hat.

The movie's haunted house gimmick is the perfect vehicle to show-case Knotts' various gifts. He gets to do his nervous-nellie routine while spending the night alone in a haunted house and later even gets to resurrect his nervous little man character from *The Steve Allen Show* doing an after-dinner speech. When Luther emerges from the haunted house as a hero, Knotts turns into a cocky, strutting Mr. Hotshot before everybody finds out he's a fake and turns on him. And as every visitor to Mayberry knows, there's nothing more poignant than a downcast, humiliated Barney Fife.

That's basically what happens in all Knotts' Universal movies. He's a meek, mild guy who inadvertently becomes a hero, is revealed as a fake and then has to redeem himself and does it by forcing himself to overcome his fears. In his next film, *The Reluctant Astronaut*, his dad gets him a job at NASA even though his character has a fear of heights.

Sure, it's all formula movie-making, but it works. Do we really want to see Don Knotts in a serious dramatic departure? Of course not. And Knotts knows it too. When he deliberately chose to put on that old salt-and-pepper suit for his first movie away from Mayberry, he knew that we really wanted to see Barney Fife. He was right and it's no coincidence that he wore it in his next movie too.

Notes

1. *Barney Fife and Other Characters I Have Known*; by Don Knotts with Robert Metz; Berkley Boulevard Books; New York; 1999, page 38.
2. *Entertainment Weekly*; "The Last Don"; by Chris Nashawaty; October 23, 1998.

Don Knotts Credits

FILM CREDITS

1. *Tom Sawyer*; 2000; (voice) Muff Potter
2. *Pleasantville*; 1998; TV Repairman
3. *Cats Don't Dance*; 1997; (voice) T.W. Turtle
4. *Big Bully*; 1996; Principal Kokelar
5. *Pinocchio and the Emperor of the Night*; 1987; (voice) Gee Willikers
6. *Cannonball Run II*; 1984; CHP Officer
7. *The Private Eyes*; 1980; Inspector Winship
8. *The Apple Dumpling Gang Rides Again*; 1979; Theodore
9. *The Prizefighter*; 1979; Shake

10. *Hot Lead and Cold Feet;* 1978; Denver Kid
11. *Herbie Goes to Monte Carlo;* 1977; Wheely Applegate
12. *Gus;* 1976; Coach Venner
13. *No Deposit, No Return;* 1976; Bert
14. *The Apple Dumpling Gang;* 1975; Theodore Ogelvie
15. *How to Frame a Figg;* 1971; Hollis Figg
16. *The Love God?;* 1969; Abner Peacock
17. *Rowan and Martin at the Movies;* 1968; Himself
18. *The Shakiest Gun in the West;* 1968; Jesse W. Heywood
19. *The Reluctant Astronaut;* 1967; Roy Fleming
20. *The Ghost and Mr. Chicken;* 1966; Luther Heggs
21. *The Incredible Mr. Limpet;* 1965; Henry Limpet
22. *It's a Mad, Mad, Mad, Mad World;* 1963; Nervous Man
23. *Move Over, Darling;* 1963; Shoe Clerk
24. *The Last Time I Saw Archie;* 1961; Captain Little
25. *Wake Me When It's Over;* 1960; Sergeant Warren
26. *No Time for Sergeants;* 1958; Corporal Brown

TV CREDITS

1. *Quints;* TV movie; 2000; Mayor
2. *Doug;* TV series; 1991–1993; (voice) Vice Principal Bone
3. *Matlock;* TV series; 1989–1991; Les Calhoun
4. *What a Country;* TV series; 1986–1987; Principal F. Jerry "Bud" McPherson
5. *Return to Mayberry;* TV movie; 1986; Barney Fife
6. *Three's Company;* TV series; 1979–1984; Ralph Furley
7. *Joys;* TV movie; 1976
8. *I Love a Mystery;* TV movie; 1973; Alexander Archer
9. *The Don Knotts Show;* TV series; 1970–1971
10. *The Andy Griffith Show;* TV series; 1960–1965; Barney Fife
11. *The Steve Allen Show;* TV series; 1956–1960; various characters
12. *Search for Tomorrow;* TV series; 1953–1955; Wilbur Peterson

NOTABLE TV GUEST APPEARANCES

1. *Burke's Law;* 4/15/1994
2. *Step by Step;* Police Sergeant; 1994
3. *Newhart;* Iron; 1990
4. *George Burns Comedy Week;* Himself; 1985
5. *The Muppet Show;* Himself; 1977
6. *The Love Boat;* 1977
7. *The Late Summer-Early Fall Bert Convy Show;* 8/25/1976
8. *Here's Lucy;* Ben Fletcher; 1/8/1973
9. *The Andy Williams Show;* 10/18/1969
10. *Mayberry R.F.D.;* Barney Fife; 9/23/1968
11. *The Andy Williams Show;* 1/15/1967
12. *The Andy Williams Show;* 12/10/1963
13. *The Joey Bishop Show;* Barney Fife; 1961
14. *The Many Loves of Dobie Gillis;* 3/16/1960

Tom Lester

Eb Dawson on *Green Acres*

Eb Dawson. Was he a dim-witted hayseed or a role model for minimum-wage earning slackers everywhere?

As the tall, lanky hired hand on the Douglas farm on *Green Acres,* no one was quite as ingenious and hard-working in their laziness and schemes to get out of work as Eb. Outwardly he was full of gung-ho enthusiasm, inside he was really a crafty layabout. Although Mr. Douglas had his suspicions, none of the other residents of Hooterville ever realized how sharp Eb actually was—as he pointed out in one episode after being caught saying something that actually made sense. "Oh, I'm sorry," he explained. "I get so used to playing the court jester for Mr. Douglas, I guess I forget that I have a serious side."

The serious side of Eb Dawson. Now, there's a scary thought. This is also the guy who studied barbering through correspondence school, actually got excited about Mrs. Douglas's hot-water soup and had a pig for a best friend.

"I played that stuff straight and read those lines for real," says Tom Lester of his earnest portrayal of the deceptively dim Eb. "I mean, Eb really *believed* her hot-water soup was great so I played it straight, just like everybody on the show," Lester continues in a soft Southern drawl. "You watch *Green Acres* and everybody played their stupidity straight or it wouldn't have worked."

The result was a hybrid of rural weirdness which today is regarded as a timeless classic. Produced by Paul Henning, creator of *The Beverly Hillbillies* and *Petticoat Junction, Green Acres* was a situation comedy set in the country but was one with elements of the absurd and the surreal. Its humor had less in common with *The Beverly Hillbillies* than it did with *The Rocky and Bullwinkle Show.*

Long before director David Lynch created a cast of oddball characters to populate the small town of *Twin Peaks,* the residents of Hooterville had eccentricity down to an art form. In Hooterville, everyone was odd (with the exception of Eddie Albert as the transplanted New Yorker, Oliver Douglas—he was just puzzled) and Lynch's Log Lady would have fit right in. In fact, it's not unreasonable to suspect that *Green Acres* was Lynch's inspiration to create *Twin Peaks.* Even the names of the two towns are similar.

Lester credits the writing of the late co-producers Jay Sommers and Dick Chevillat for the show's original success from 1965 to '71 and its continuing popularity in syndicated reruns. "The show was very much ahead of its time and I don't think a lot of people realized just how innovative the show really was," he said.

Green Acres was Lester's first job in television. He was born in Jackson, Mississippi, on September 23, 1938. Eb Dawson comes by his aversion to farm work honestly because Lester's youth was spent on his grandfather's farm where he picked cotton. He would have preferred to be out hunting and fishing.

The farmboy also dreamed of going to Hollywood. During his years at George S. Gardner High School in his home town of Laurel, Miss., he had no interest in drama classes or school theatrical productions but knew in the back of his mind where his future lay. But when he graduated in 1955 — standing six-foot-four and weighing only 118 pounds — Lester says that his friends told him that he was too ugly to make it in the movies and so he enrolled in the University of Mississippi and graduated with a degree in chemistry and biology.

After graduating in 1960, he taught general science and biology at a school in Purcell, Oklahoma, for a year. However, he knew that it wasn't for him and so in 1963 he decided to follow his dream and headed for California. But when he headed West, he wasn't just hearing the siren call of Hollywood. Lester says that he was answering another call. "From the time I was 10 years old, that's when I came to Christ and I began to understand that God had a purpose for my life — as he does for everyone — and I felt very certain that he wanted me to go to Hollywood and be an actor.

"All along, in my heart, I had wanted to go to Hollywood, but all my friends all told me that I would never make it because I was too tall and too thin and didn't look like Rock Hudson. See, we're a very negative society and so I taught school for a year and teaching is a wonderful profession, but I knew that it wasn't what God wanted me to do and so I came home and told my parents that I was going out to Hollywood and give it a try and if it didn't work out, I'd come back home — but I was going to at least give it a try. I'd rather go out and try and fail than never have gone out at all. So I got in my little car, left Mother and Dad crying in the driveway and drove off to Hollywood, California."

Once there, he put his chemistry degree to use and worked in a film lab during the days and spent his evenings studying acting and working in Little Theatre. "Through my church out there, I met a wonderful drama coach named Laureen Tuttle. She got me into Little Theatre."

Within two years of his arrival, he was discovered by Paul Henning, who encouraged him to audition for the role of Eb on his new 1965 series, *Green Acres.* "When I was doing Little Theatre, Linda Kaye Henning was in each of our presentations. Paul Henning was her daddy and came to see her and liked me and told me to come and try out for Eb," says Lester.

"I think they read over 400 guys and screen-tested about 30 people for the part of Eb and of course all of them had more experience than I had. Originally they were looking for an older guy, but Mrs. Henning, wife of the producer, called me the night before and said, 'If you try out for this part, don't get your hopes up, they want an older man, but Mr. Henning thinks it will be good experience for you to audition.'

"So I went over there knowing there was only the slight possibility of getting a screen test. So when I got through my reading — which I didn't too well because I had no experience — I looked over at our producers, Mr. Chevillat and Mr. Sommers and I said, 'Okay, when's my screen-test?' Well, they both started laughing because only Eb would have done such a sorry job of reading and yet think he's good enough to get a screen test. Eb was the kind of guy who would put on a horrible suit and think he looked really cool. So the only difference between me and Eb is that I'm not as stupid as Eb."

That misguided spunky attempt at bravado earned Lester a screen test and in turn, a job. "That was on a Saturday. I screen-tested with Eddie Albert on Monday, they called me on Thursday to say I had the job and I went to work the next Monday."

When asked if he realized at the time how lucky he was, Lester interrupts and says, "Not lucky — *blessed*. It was just wonderful and terrific for me because I hadn't done anything at all before this — I had just gotten to Hollywood two years before. I felt like it was part of God's plan for my life."

Lester explains that although he was following his dream, he didn't move out to Hollywood with any delusion of becoming a movie star. "I was very happy playing Eb and if I could have gotten on another show as a character actor that would have been fine with me because I don't need the lead role at all. I couldn't care less about playing a lead role. When I went out there to Hollywood, California, I went knowing that I was a character actor and would always be a character actor so I never had the desire for the lead roles. If I had, I never would have made it in the industry. You have to be honest with yourself and know what your abilities and talents are. If you're honest with yourself, you can take the gifts that God gave you and use them."

Lester points out that when he was doing Little Theatre after arriving in Los Angeles, lots of agents and casting scouts would show up, "But they never came and talked to me afterwards. They only talked to the good-looking guys and gals. They signed lots of them to contracts and not one of them got a lasting job in the industry. They didn't know how to find a real character or know what to do with someone who was different. They didn't know how to pick up on that special thing that makes it work for a person in this industry whereas Paul Henning did. *That's* why he was such a great producer in casting all those shows. He saw something in me that none of the others could see."

That kind of humble attitude means that Lester is comfortable and not offended by the term "second banana." "Well, that's exactly what we were," he points out, and adds that Henning cast his entire show with unique character actors and well-respected comics and second bananas. The large supporting cast alone was largely responsible for *Green Acres'* success.

"The key is that in comedy, you have to have a straight man. On *Green Acres,* Eddie Albert was the straight man and everyone else, including Eva Gabor as his wife, we were all the comic relief. *We* said the goofy things and he would react. Basically, his reaction is what the audience is feeling and so the audience is with him. If you read through one of our scripts you can see the number of times Eddie Albert had to say, 'Oh, for the love of Mike!' or 'What the … !' It may not seem like much on paper, but on film, that's great writing.

"The reason the comedy worked so great was because we all played our comedy *straight*. Whenever I ate Mrs. Douglas' hot-water soup, I *loved* her hot-water soup. I thought it was great. I believed she made the best hot-water soup in the whole valley. Now see, that's funny because we know her soup was just hot water. But because Eb thought it was the best, that makes the joke funny. But if I was to play it tongue-in-cheek, then it's not funny at all. The writing was so great that all we had to do was deliver the lines *truthfully*. If a producer or a director says to me, 'You've got to make this funny,' well *forget* that, because if I've got to make something funny that's not funny, well, I've got a disaster on my hands."

As Lester admits, initially there wasn't a lot of difference between himself and Eb. The writers kept this in mind when developing the character. "In the beginning, I had a lot to learn about my craft. It being my first job, I was real up and high but after about three weeks I began to work with the writers on the character to make it more real. I had no experience at all and so I had a lot of work to do real fast on Eb.

"What happens with any part is that the character begins to grow and the producers and writers add some of the actor's idiosyncrasies and Eb's character grew in a wonderful sort of way from the original. The character became more natural and smarter. They began to write him as being a little shiftier for getting out of work and knowing what's going on. Eb was never as stupid as say, Jethro on *The Beverly Hillbillies,* but he was very naïve. I'm a very naïve person in real life anyway and I'll believe almost anything anybody tells me.

"I'm also a very *up* person and naturally when I got this part I was very excited and Eb was written as a character who had a *lot* of energy. As they came to know me and see my energy in real life and my little idiosyncrasies—for instance, in real life I'd say, 'Gollee!'—and they'd work that into the scripts. They would find other little things I would do and write them into the character. After about the second year it became so easy to learn my lines because they were almost what I'd say in real life."

After six years, in 1971, CBS cancelled *Green Acres* when they callously dropped all their rural comedies including Top 10 shows like *The Beverly Hillbillies* and *Mayberry R.F.D.* in an attempt to win viewers in the big cities. The purge was bad news for Lester. "The last year of the show, just before we went into production, Mr. Sommers called me in and told me that CBS wanted to do a spinoff with me and Arnold Ziffel, the pig in our series—which was terrific news until CBS cancelled all their country shows."

Although Lester was briefly reunited with Arnold in 1990's *Return to Green Acres* TV reunion movie, after the cancellation, for the next 20 years, Lester's fortunes still remained inextricably bound to those of the pig.

"When *Green Acres* ended, a friend of mine took the little dog from *Petticoat Junction* and decided he wanted to make a movie with it. Everybody laughed at him and said it would never happen. He raised the money in Dallas, cast me in it as one of the crooks and we made a little movie called *Benji* which grossed $42 million. So I went to my old producers Jay Sommers and Dick Chevillat and said, 'You guys ought to make a movie with Arnold the pig.' It was the last thing they wrote before they passed away and it was incredible!"

With Eb-like enthusiasm, Lester launches into a description of the script—"If you think *Green Acres* was surreal and wild, you've got to read this script. This pig has a paper route, swims into a lake and saves a kid from drowning, becomes an international hero, goes to work for a billionaire by starring in commercials for a big sausage company, and then inherits the company and *that's* just the first part of the story. It's just the wildest stuff you've ever seen. It's incredible!"

Lester spent almost two decades trying to raise the money to make the film. Initially he worked with the late Alvy Moore, who played the brain-addled county agent Hank Kimball on *Green Acres*. Even though Moore had produced the sci-fi cult film *A Boy and His Dog* starring a young Don Johnson and a talking pooch, there wasn't sufficient interest in a pig movie and Moore dropped out.

"I worked on it for 17 years trying to put it together," says Lester. "I went all over America trying to raise the money. I had the option on the script and kept it until I ran out of money and couldn't pick up the option anymore."

The movie was eventually made as *Gordy* in 1995—with Lester as a co-star but not as a producer. The film's executive producer—new to the movie business—wanted to make a good old-fashioned family movie.

"The first thing she did was hire a writer to put in a country and western theme and rewrite the original script. Sommers and Chevillat's script had dialogue that was just magnificent, every line was a laugh line. It was written for adults as well as children just like *Green Acres*. But the new writer for *Gordy* didn't use one bit of dialogue from the original script. It was not the same movie at all," laments Lester.

"Alvy Moore told me, 'You know, she doesn't have any idea what she has and it's real sad.' It's too bad, what a great opportunity she missed." Judging by what those two fertile minds created on *Green Acres,* we have no reason to doubt him.

Although his connection with *Green Acres* also meant guest appearances on Henning's other shows, *The Beverly Hillbillies* and *Petticoat Junction*—they were in the character of Eb Dawson. After the show was cancelled, Lester found himself typecast after his first job in the business. "Several times I'd try to get auditions and they'd tell my agent, 'Yeah, we liked him as Eb, but he's not right for this.' Well, how did they know unless they read me for it? So yeah, it hurt me but that didn't bother me because I loved Eb so much."

Lester still maintains his membership in the Screen Actors Guild for the occasional job. "The new casting people they've got out there, they've never even heard of *Green Acres*, it was so long ago, so some jobs do come up," he says.

A devoted Christian, he now often puts his trademark high-energy and enthusiasm to work with public-speaking appearances to youth groups and has also appeared with Billy Graham on stage three times.

These days he mostly tends to the family business back in rural Mississippi. It is a business you can almost imagine Eb Dawson dreaming about—a 235-acre timber farm where you only harvest the trees every few years. But unlike Eb, Lester works at it. "I've planted pine trees and developed the natural habitat for game. I built two ponds which are full of fish and I'm trying to really improve the farm since we don't do farming anymore like we did back when I was picking cotton on my grandfather's farm. So what you do is plant trees."

His efforts have been recognized. In 1999, he was named Mississippi's Wildlife Farmer of the Year.

Tom Lester Credits

FILM CREDITS

1. *Gordy;* 1995; Cousin Jake
2. *Pistol: The Birth of a Legend;* 1991; Pete as adult

3. *Intruder;* 1988; Officer Matthews
4. *Benji;* 1974; Riley

TV CREDITS

1. *Return to Green Acres;* (1990); TV movie; Eb Dawson
2. *Petticoat Junction;* TV series; Eb Dawson; 1966–1970
3. *Green Acres;* TV series; Eb Dawson; 1965–1971

NOTABLE TV GUEST APPEARANCES

1. *Little House on the Prairie;* Mr. Wilder; 12/21/1981
2. *The Beverly Hillbillies;* Eb Dawson; 12/25/1968
3. *The Beverly Hillbillies;* Eb Dawson; 11/27/1968
4. *The Beverly Hillbillies;* Eb Dawson; 1968

George Lindsey

Goober Pyle on *The Andy Griffith Show*

When a reporter from *People* magazine visited the set of *Return to Mayberry*, a 1986 TV reunion movie of *The Andy Griffith Show*, George Lindsey told her, "I couldn't remember how to do Goober at first."[1]

Huh?

After arriving in Mayberry in 1964 to join the cast of *The Andy Griffith Show* as town mechanic Goober Pyle, Lindsey hung around after Griffith left in 1968 and the show became *Mayberry R.F.D.* When that show was cancelled in 1971, Lindsey took Goober's grease pit monkey beanie and headed straight to *Hee Haw* where he played an all-but-in-name-only Goober-like character for the next 20 years.

"I couldn't remember how to do Goober at first."

Say what?!

If ever there was an actor who has made a lifelong career out of playing one character, it's Lindsey. During the *Hee Haw* years and after its last canned laugh in 1992, Lindsey has built a lucrative living out of the Goober character. With his Goober beanie firmly in place, he works regularly on the convention and personal appearance circuit and has also been the national spokesman at the core of the advertising campaigns for the Liberty Trouser Company and Getty Oil and Truckstops.

Although it was often to his chagrin that he would see himself billed on Las Vegas marquees as George "Goober" Lindsey, during the white tie and tails stand-up comedy days of his post–*Mayberry* years, he also knows that the recognition factor has opened a lot of doors and he has learned to embrace the character. Who says you can't go home again?

According to Lindsey, playing Goober was something he was put on this Earth to do. "Really and truly and I don't know why and I still can't explain this but for some reason or other, the universe ordained that I was supposed to be on *The Andy Griffith Show*," he insists.

It almost didn't happen.

Originally, Lindsey had auditioned for the part of dim fillin' station attendant Gomer Pyle when the character was created in 1962. As a Southerner, Lindsey thought he was a natural for the role. Like Gomer, he had worked part-time in a garage during his teenage years. Lindsey had played a number of dull-witted and naïve Gomer–like roles in the past. When the struggling actor who had only recently arrived in Hollywood did his audition, he felt that he had nailed the part and the casting people told him that he had the part.

However, in the meantime, one night Andy Griffith had gone to a nightclub called The Horn in Santa Monica and had seen a young comic and singer named Jim Nabors. He was so impressed that after a quickly arranged screen test, Nabors was signed as Gomer.

Nabors' first appearance as Gomer was on the highly acclaimed "Man in a Hurry" episode in which a travelling businessman passing through town has car problems and is forced to spend an entire Sunday in Mayberry. The episode has become a classic and it was a perfect introduction to the Gomer character. But when Lindsey saw the episode on the night it first ran and saw Nabors in the role that had been promised to him, his reaction was to jump out of his chair in a rage and kick in the picture tube of his TV set.

"I guess that's why I'm no longer married," Lindsey sheepishly says today, adding that he probably wasn't the easiest person to live with at that time. Goober was the sort of character whose emotions were always close to the surface and the anecdote sounds like something the childlike mechanic would do.

Lindsey, however, disagrees with that assessment. "I don't think Goober would do that. I don't think he had that kind of a temper." Well, he's the one who would know.

Before donning the Goober beanie, Lindsey had done a number of A-list projects both on TV and in the theatre — often cast as a heavy and playing a less kind and gentle rural Southerner, often with a dark side.

It was a back story he knew well because much of it was like his own. He grew up in poverty during the Depression with alcoholic, argumentative parents who Lindsey says could only aspire to be white trash.

Lindsey was born in Jasper, Alabama, sometime around 1933. Like many actors, he refuses to give out his actual birthdate. "I just figure it's nobody's business," he explains. "I always tell people that I'm too old to be drafted but I'm young enough to enlist."

Growing up in the Depression made for a hard childhood. There was no running water in the house, an outhouse was out back and there was no electricity until Lindsey was in junior high school. His parents were divorced when he was in grade eight and he saw little of his father after that. Due to his mother's drinking, Lindsey was basically raised by his better-off maternal grandparents and an older aunt. She happened to run an automobile garage and body shop where Lindsey worked after school and on summer vacations. It proved to be an invaluable experience for when he eventually became Mayberry's sole mechanic and would need to know the difference between a carburetor and an alternator.

Lindsey always had a feeling that he would go into show business because he admittedly enjoyed being the center of attention. A class clown in school, the resultant poor marks made him ineligible to take part in high school drama club productions.

However, it was while attending Florence State Teachers College on a football scholarship that he first became involved in showbiz by appearing in the Florence Little Theatre's production of *Oklahoma!* He also began entering college talent shows and eventually won first prize for his imitation of President Franklin Delano Roosevelt. When interviewed by the school newspaper, *The Florola*, about what he was going to do in the future, the teachers' college student didn't mention teaching as a career goal. Instead, "I'm either going to be a coach or an actor."[2]

That decision was postponed, however, when he joined the U.S. Air Force immediately after graduation. While stationed in Florida, during his spare time he did a bit of drama at Rollins College in nearby Water Park. He also began doing stand-up comedy in small clubs and military service sponsored talent shows.

Lindsey met his future wife, Joyanne, at Rollins College in Florida and they were married in 1954 while he was stationed in Puerto Rico. Instead of re-enlisting, the newly married Lindsey decided that the military life wasn't for him and he spent 1955 teaching history and coaching at a rural school back in Alabama at a small crossroads near Huntsville.

After a year he also realized that teaching wasn't his calling and funded by the G.I. Bill, he spent the next two years in New York studying at the American Theatre Wing. In his second year, he began getting work as an extra in various TV productions and did a short tour of military bases in *Broadway U.S.A.*, a revue of current samplings from the Great White Way.

In 1960, Lindsey finally got his big break when he was spotted by a William Morris agent doing a stand-up comedy act in a Greenwich Village coffeehouse and promptly signed to the well-known talent agency. Within months, he was cast opposite Ray Bolger in *All-American*, a Broadway comedy directed by Josh Logan. His character was named Moose and had attended the Southern Baptist Institute of Technology for 17 years. To reinforce the idea that Moose wasn't the brightest Baptist in the congregation, the producers had him wear a football jersey with the number "0" on it.

For a Broadway newcomer it was a surprisingly large part and the story revolved around Lindsey's character. If Ray Bolger's Professor Fodorski character could teach Moose to think, then he could do the same with the engineering students. This would somehow save the school, which was up for a funding review.

The show lasted three months.

However, before it closed, Lindsey got his first taste of being typecast. He was signed to be in the touring Broadway production of *Wonderful Town*, a musical version of *My Sister Eileen*. He was offered the comedy lead without an audition just based on his work in *All-American*. Again, he played a college football player. This time he was named The Wreck.

When the show finished its tour in San Francisco after a six-week run on the road, Lindsey headed south to Hollywood and on the strength of his William Morris connections, he began making the rounds of television studios looking for work.

One of his first jobs after arriving in Hollywood in 1962 was on *The Rifleman*, playing a maniacal killer. That was an indication of things to come. On his first of five appearances in different roles on *Gunsmoke*, he played Orville Hack in an episode called "Pa Hack's Brood."

"When I first got out there, they cast me as a heavy in westerns," says Lindsey. "I always played the sort of character where the retarded family comes to town and kills everybody."

In the ten years between his arrival in Los Angeles and being cast in *The Andy Griffith Show* in 1964, he did sporadic work in episodic television. Although *Gunsmoke* was his most regular employer, as an actor, Lindsey is most proud of the work he did on *The Twilight Zone* and *Alfred Hitchcock Presents*.

"If you look at my body of work before Goober, you'll see that I'm better than just that," he says. "I did a lot of really fine acting before the *Griffith Show* came along."

He says his best work was an *Alfred Hitchcock* installment called "The Jar," which was based on a Ray Bradbury story. The episode was directed by Norman Lloyd, the father of Josie Lloyd, who would later play Goober's wet-blanket girlfriend, Lydia Crosswaithe. In "The Jar," Lindsey played Jukie Marmer, a mouth-breathing simpleton in the dirt-poor rural South. For the audition, he didn't comb his hair, hadn't shaved for a few days and showed up in dirty overalls. Although the role had already been cast, Lindsey got the part.

The emotional core of the episode came in a five-minute monologue in which Lindsey's character reminisced about being a child and told by his father to drown a litter of newborn kittens in a large jar of water. In his autobiography, *Goober in a Nutshell*, Lindsey recalls, "I really got into this character, Jukie, and I stayed in him." A bit of Jukie may have still been in Lindsey when he shortly afterwards auditioned for the part of Gomer Pyle on *The Andy Griffith Show*, lost out to Jim Nabors and then kicked in his TV set.

When another role opened up on the *Griffith* series, Lindsey turned it down. It was for the role of Dud Walsh, the new husband of Charlene Darling from the family of pickin' an' strummin' hillbillies who made occasional visits to Mayberry. "I turned that role down even though I needed the money. I just felt that if I had played that role, I'd never be on the show again," says Lindsey. His instincts proved correct. "As it turned out, the actor who took the part was only on two times."

As Fate would have it, Jim Nabors proved to be so popular as Gomer that he was given his own series in the Mayberry spinoff, *Gomer Pyle*, and Lindsey was brought in to play his mechanic cousin, Goober Pyle. "I think when they decided that Jim should have his own show, they thought of replacing him with the guy who did next best in the original auditions and that was me. Although it was about a year and a half later, during all that time, they often referred to Goober. But Goober was never seen. So I had a built-in identity." Lindsey then pauses and then continues, laughing, "And the one thing that I always say is that I played Goober better than anybody!"

As Lindsey says, he believes it was destiny that he play Goober. "The universe ordained that I was supposed to have been on *The Andy Griffith Show*," he says. "Now, maybe I wasn't supposed to have been *Gomer*. I always thought that was the place for me. But I've always believed this—if I hadn't gotten the *Griffith* show, I would have gotten on some other series because I was good enough and back then, just about every show had a 'Goober' somewhere." Lindsey's first appearance as Goober was in an episode called "The Fun Girls." Coincidentally, it was also Nabors' last appearance as Gomer. The show is a fan favorite not just because it's the only teaming of Lindsey and Nabors but also because of the Fun Girls, a couple of "wild" women who start off the episode with Andy and Barney and end up with Gomer and Goober.

Lindsey says that to this day, people will come up to him and ask him to perform something from the bag of tricks he used in the episode as a way to showcase Goober as a charmingly untalented extrovert. He imitates Edward G. Robinson and Cary Grant with machine-gun styled delivery. He hops around like Chester on *Gunsmoke*. His grand finale is a piece of pantomime where he pretends to sew his fingers together.

Although Barney and Andy roll their eyes at the tricks, the Fun Girls think he's a hoot and Gomer himself is in a state of awe while watching his cousin. In fact, the episode shows the differences between the two slack-jawed cousins. Goober, after all, is an accomplished mechanic. He once hopped up an old V-8 engine and put it in his boat so that it could do 80 miles an hour. Gomer, on the other hand, works at the garage but he's only allowed to pump gas and check the oil.

The difference between the two similarly-named characters is this— Gomer is naïve and not too bright and just doesn't know any better. But Goober is a naïve and not too bright but *thinks* he's quite sharp and on the ball. In one episode, in order to impress his date, he takes her to a fancy restaurant and orders a bottle of champagne. When the waiter brings the bottle and says, "Here is your wine, sir," Goober indignantly pipes up, "Hey, I ordered champagne!"

Lindsey himself credits Andy Griffith for explaining the Goober character to him in a nutshell shortly after he began on the series. "All I needed to know about the character, I got from Andy when he told me that Goober was the kind of guy that would go into a restaurant and say, 'Hey, that's great salt!'

"I don't believe in breaking down and analyzing a character," says Lindsey. "You can analyze yourself out of the acting business and you don't mess with Babe Ruth's swing."

Originally, Lindsey wasn't too happy with how the character was being written. At first, Goober was too much like the simpleton that was Gomer Pyle. "I felt that in the first year of Goober being on the show, they wrote my part as too stupid. Like he was a moron. They didn't give him any heart. They didn't make him a real person. They wrote him as a 'duh' guy — and I think that was the easiest way to write him."

Over time though, the character eventually came into his own. "They were still writing for Jim in the beginning, but I think as they went along, he evolved because there were some little nuances that I would put in and Goober was such a different character than Gomer."

His main contribution to the character was wardrobe. Originally, the only wardrobe the producers gave Goober was the beanie and a white shirt. Having worked in a garage himself, Lindsey cut a few holes in the hat like he had seen the mechanics back home do for ventilation so that they wouldn't be so hot. He also tucked a white rag into the back pocket of his jeans and carried a tire gauge in his front shirt pocket. "I was just trying to do anything I could that wouldn't look like Jim's character," he recalls.

Although it would be two seasons before Lindsey would muster up the nerve to make suggestions during the weekly script readings, he says that he was able to contribute in other ways. All those novelty tricks he did in the Fun Girls episode were old bits from his stand-up comedy act. In an episode called "Goober and the Art of Love," another fan favorite, Barney Fife, being the experienced ladies' man that he is, tutors Goober in how to seduce a woman. Lindsey says that he was able to add a lot of his own business which was not in the written script. "I think some of the best things I ever did was in that episode where I'm standing at the door waiting to ring the doorbell and go into Lydia's house. All that stuff I did at the door checking my notes and later with her hand on the couch, all of that's pure *me*, that's not direction. And I think that's what makes the Goober character."

Part of the character's growth came from the producers getting to know Lindsey. "The evolution came about so gradually that you didn't see it happen. They are aware of what you are like and start writing more for you. But I always hated saying, 'Yo.' I never was comfortable with that.

"Anyways, I got real comfortable with the character and started living with it and started really *liking* him. And that made it much easier to play." It got to the point that Lindsey says he could pick up a script and know how Goober would act in any situation. He was so comfortable with the character — or perhaps put so much of himself into the character that he says, "I came home one time and I was telling my wife about the new script and that 'Goober says ...' and she looked at me and said, 'But you *are* Goober.'"

So just how much of Lindsey is Goober and vice-versa? "This is what I always say to people," he says of that question he's been asked a thousand times. "*We* thought we were those people and *you* thought we were those people — and when we were acting, we *were* those people."

When Andy Griffith decided to pull the plug on *The Andy Griffith Show* in 1968, the producers kept the series going as *Mayberry R.F.D.* and replaced Griffith's character with Ken Berry as newcomer Sam Jones. All the old *Griffith Show* characters remained and Lindsey found that his role had increased to co-star billing and he was involved in more storylines. With the increased status on the show came added opportunities. "Well, the more they pay you, the more you can experiment and the more strength you have. It was a different atmosphere on that show." Goober, though, remained essentially the same until *Mayberry R.F.D.* was cancelled in 1971, when CBS made its purge of all rural shows despite the fact that the show was rated 15th at the time in the Neilsens.

With the cancellation, Lindsey went directly to *Hee Haw* and spent the next 20 years wearing the familiar beanie. However, it was only on special occasions that he was referred to as Goober. "When we did an occasional sketch called Goober's Service Station, *Hee Haw* bought the rights to do that. But the rest of the time, it was against the rules to use the Goober name and no one was allowed to call me that on the show."

In the late 1970s, Lindsey filmed a pilot for a proposed series called *Goober and the Paradise Truck Stop.* By his own admission, Lindsey, who also served as producer, says the series didn't sell because it wasn't any good. "That show's failure was totally my mistake," he reflects. "I thought I knew how to produce a show and I didn't know and ruined it. We shot a half-hour television show and it took 14 hours to film it. I should have just stuck with the acting part of it. I had a cell phone and didn't even know how to do 'Hold my calls,' because I didn't have any calls."

Another opportunity that got away was a proposed variety series with Loretta Lynn for CBS called *The Orange Blossom Special.* "I'm not sure that I ever got to ride the A-train and a lot of it's my fault," Lindsey says wistfully in a reflective moment.

Not that he's complaining. Over the years, he has put out two recordings of stand-up comedy. Although it bothered him that he would often be booked into Las Vegas casinos as George "Goober" Lindsey, he points out, "Up until a few years ago, I would not work in the Goober suit. I only worked in white tie and tails or a tuxedo— and I'm just as funny either way."

Today though, when he makes personal appearances it is in the familiar Goober outfit. "I call what I do— Gooberizing America."

Of being too strongly identified with one character, Lindsey has come to terms with that. And after all, it was *his* choice. "I saw Jason Alexander from *Seinfeld* on a talk show recently and they said to him, 'You're going to be George Costanza forever.' And he answered that he had been talking to William Shatner from *Star Trek* about that and Shatner told him that it's rare that an actor gets to play a part that he can *define* himself and that he should be remembered for. So I feel good about what I did because I brought life and George Lindsey to Goober."

Another more practical reason for his lack of resentment can be seen in the closing lines to a poem he wrote, "What Mayberry Means to Me," which he uses to close his stand-up comedy shows and convention appearances.

"It's everything and everybody, and when you talk about it
You get that very, very special itch.
But the thing that I like about Mayberry most of all,
It's made ol' Goober rich!"[3]

Notes

1. *People;* "Going Home to Mayberry"; by Jane Hall; April 7, 1986.
2. *Goober in a Nutshell;* by George Lindsey, Ken Beck and Jim Clark; Avon Books, 1995; page 55.
3. *Goober in a Nutshell;* by George Lindsey, Ken Beck and Jim Clark; Avon Books; 1995; page 208.

George Lindsey Credits

FILM CREDITS

1. *Cannonball Run II;* 1984; Cal
2. *Take This Job and Shove It;* 1981

3. *The Rescuers;* 1977; (voice) Deadeye
4. *Treasure of Matecumbe;* 1976; Coahoma Sheriff
5. *Robin Hood;* 1973; (voice) Trigger
6. *Charley and the Angel;* 1973; Pete
7. *Snowball Express;* 1972; Double L. Dingman
8. *The Aristocats;* 1970; (voice) Lafayette
9. *Ensign Parker;* 1964; Lindstrom

TV Credits

1. *Return to Mayberry;* 1986; TV movie; Goober Pyle
2. *Hee Haw;* TV series; 1969–1993; Himself
3. *Mayberry R.F.D.;* TV series; 1968–1971; Goober Pyle
4. *The Andy Griffith Show;* TV series; 1965–1968; Goober Pyle
5. *The Tycoon;* TV series; 1964; Tom Keane

Notable TV Guest Appearances

1. *Dr. Quinn, Medicine Woman;* Mr. Simpkin; 2/15/1997
2. *Newsradio;* Himself; 2/5/1997
3. *CHiPS;* Wayne Cato; 1/17/1982
4. *M*A*S*H;* Capt. Roy Dupree; 2/13/78
5. *Banacek;* Lt. Bradshaw; 1/10/1973
6. *Gunsmoke;* Pinto Watson; 1/14/1967
7. *Gunsmoke;* Skeeter; 3/19/1966
8. *Gunsmoke;* Billy Yager; 5/8/1965
9. *Voyage to the Bottom of the Sea;* Collins; 11/16/1964
10. *Gunsmoke;* Bud; 11/14/1964
11. *Daniel Boone;* 9/24/1964
12. *Twilight Zone;* Pierce in "I Am the Night, Color Me Black"; 3/27/1964
13. *The Alfred Hitchcock Hour;* Jukie Marmer in "The Jar"; 1964
14. *Gunsmoke;* Orville Hack; 12/28/1963

Dave Madden

Reuben Kincaid on *The Partridge Family*;
Earl Hicks on *Alice*

"For the longest time I thought I had been on *The Brady Bunch*," offers Dave Madden. "Over the years, about 500 people must have walked up to me on the street and said, 'Loved ya on *The Brady Bunch*' and I figured, well, those 500 people can't be wrong."

Madden is joking of course, but it's hard to tell when he tells the story in his trademark deadpan style.

Of course, it was another family sitcom, *The Partridge Family*, where Madden spent the early years of the 1970s. He played the singing group's somewhat ineffectual and often rattled manager, Reuben Kincaid.

Like many of his other roles—and to an extent, like Madden himself—Reuben was a bit of an outsider. In the Partridge Family nest, although he was treated like one of the family, Reuben was the lone non–Partridge on the show. Being an outsider is something Madden can relate to—and he admits that for much of the early part of his career he was a bit of an introvert. That could pose a bit of a challenge when you're trying to make your living as a stand-up comic.

"I've always been fairly introverted," admits Madden. "I escaped that to some degree when I started doing TV series. But I don't think I escaped it while I was doing nightclubs. I would get up and I'd do my performance and then I would go off and sit by myself somewhere. I couldn't really mix with a lot of people.

"I don't really know if that's commonplace or not, I mean introversion being relative to performing. I often think that maybe the reason I got up onstage was because that way I wouldn't have to sit in the audience—because sitting in a group of people was something I didn't like. So I had a problem apparently. I don't seem to have that problem anymore, but I did back then."

Madden elaborates that he thinks it's a peculiar mental state common among nightclub performers. "There is an illness I think that is inherent in anybody who does stand-up. Everybody in the world wants the acceptance of their peers, their friends and family. Everybody looks for acceptance in that area—but not everybody looks to be accepted by *everyone*.

"Now, if you have a *need* to be accepted by everybody, then why in God's name would get up on a stage and in a sense, give everybody a chance to throw rocks at you? There's no logic to that. It's like a form of mental illness. It certainly doesn't require being put into institution but it certainly requires observation, I think."

Well, on the basis of that statement alone, it's obvious that even if he's no longer an introvert, he certainly is introspective.

He always has been. During high school, as the editor of the joke column in the school newspaper, instead of taking jokes out of a joke book or stealing them off the radio, young Madden wrote humorous personal observations. "I still have some of those joke columns and I didn't realize it at the time, but I was writing monologues. Now, who in the world in high school back in the 1940s wrote monologues rather than just putting in jokes? So in terms of humor, I was already thinking in the monologist vein rather than the tell-a-joke vein. I used to do material about the teachers and what happened in school. So, a lot of stuff in the joke column was what you would call current comedy."

Even back then in his teens, Madden employed the same wry, sardonic sense of humor that is familiar to anyone who remembers his deadpan style on *The Partridge Family*. "Based on those old columns, I'd say that it was pretty much the same voice back then," he says. "I don't know how I put those things together but the tone of the humor in the column was sardonic more than anything else."

Madden's ambivalent approach to life goes back to his childhood. Born in Sarnia, Ontario, in Canada on December 17, 1931, Madden was sent to Terre Haute, Indiana, to be raised by his aunt and uncle at the age of two when his father died. "My aunt was a Catholic and my uncle was a 32nd degree Mason, which may account for a certain amount of confusion I grew up with," Madden has said.[1]

The area that Madden grew up in was out in the country, seven miles north of Terre Haute. He was close enough to Terre Haute but not enough to be a "townie" and although they lived out in the country it wasn't on a farm. "I went to Otter Creek High School which was a country school and the biggest thing you could be in that school would be one of The Future Farmers of America or in the 4-H Club."

So what did Madden choose to do to help him fit into this community? He became a magician.

A bicycle accident at the age of 12 had put him out of commission with a long healing process ahead of him so he sent away for a book on magic. "I'd never seen a magician. What magician ever came to Terre Haute? And if one ever did, he'd quickly make himself disappear," Madden has said.[2]

Magic was to be his ticket out of Terre Haute. He did magic shows in town and at school and eventually he began to work comedy into the act. Although in his high school yearbook, Madden is named as the class clown, it's hard to imagine him as the stereotypical extroverted cut-up who would do anything for a laugh. Maybe in comparison to his other classmates, his dry sense of humor did make him the only comedian of note in the schoolyard but Madden says that he probably got the nod as class clown just for writing the joke column. "I was still pretty introverted," he says.

Upon graduating from high school, he attended Indiana State Teachers College in Terre Haute for one semester and then worked in a bakery for a short time. In 1951, he joined the Air Force and was assigned to the entertainment unit of Special Forces because of his magic background. Stationed in Libya in North Africa, Madden began to introduce more comedy into his act by virtue of necessity. "Magic got me into the entertainment unit but while I was in the service, I also did some emceeing that was kind of forced upon me and so I had to write monologues. By the time I got out of the service I was doing a kind of comedy-magic act."

When his tour of duty was up in 1955, Madden was unsure of what he wanted to do with his life but once he discovered the then-new world of television, he enrolled in the communications course at the University of Miami. "When I got out of the service, after four years I had seen practically no television and hadn't seen an entire television program all the way through. I had spent two years in North Africa and two years in Big Springs, Texas—which was kind of like North Africa only without the Arabs. And as a result, my knowledge of television was practically nil.

"When I got out of the service, I went to Florida and sat down in front of my folks' TV set and saw an entire television show for the first time without snow. And I thought this might be something I'd like to do. Not as a performer; I thought I'd like to direct television.

"I checked around and ended up signing on as a radio, television and film major at the University of Miami. That's what I wanted to do. I just wanted to graduate and go to some small station somewhere and get a job as a TV director.

"In my final two years, I did a lot of student directing and we also did student directing at local television stations because there were no unions down there. I directed variety shows, live documentaries, drama and all kinds of different kinds of shows during my final two years of college and when I got out of school, I felt competent enough to go into any local station and direct anything they could throw at me.

"But what I found out—and that no one bothers to tell you when you enroll—was that you just can't go out and get a job as a director, whether you can do it or not. You start off as a prop man and maybe helping with the lighting and five or 10 years after you had been there, after you had been there long enough and enough people had died, because nobody ever quit in those days—then you *might* get a job as a part-time director and you'd be directing the news and weather and *Popeye's Playhouse* and that would be it.

"Now, that was a very depressing revelation to me."

Luckily, during his college years, Madden was earning a part-time income as a comic at frat houses and small local clubs. During that time, he began concentrating on the comedy and phasing the magic out of his act.

"Magic, unlike today, was not terribly popular back then in the mid–1950s and so there was not a lot of people doing it. I think one of the things that hurt magic back in those days was that there were an awful lot of people performing magic who shouldn't have been — and I very possibly was one of them. To go into an agent's office back then and say that you're a magician would be like cutting your own throat. They just didn't really want you. Combining comedy with magic was certainly better than just being a magician. But as the years in college went by I did less and less magic and more and more comedy. By the time I got out of college I had a pretty solid stand-up act."

After graduating in 1959, the reality of the unlikely prospect of being handed a directing job in television hit home and Madden focused on doing stand-up comedy in Miami Beach nightclubs. Again, he didn't exactly fit in and was like a walking incongruity. "Most of the places I ended up working were with an older Jewish crowd that didn't speak that much English — and I was doing monologues. So you can imagine the problem I had. Being a tall blond Gentile comedian-magician working Miami Beach was not an easy row to hoe but it helped pay the rent and that's when I got into the union, The American Guild of Variety Artists.

"I won a talent contest at one of the hotels and the prize they used to lure contestants was a paid membership into the union and a six-month contract with the Gold Coast Theatrical Agency."

That was the start of a two-year stint on the Southern nightclub circuit. "I don't think the Gold Coast Agency ever got me a job during that six-month contract," he recalls. "All the jobs I got were ones I solicited myself. I would go from hotel to hotel and motel to motel with my glossy photos and faked resume trying to get work. I had a number of set pieces in my act that would work anywhere. For example, I had a routine about All-State Insurance because a routine like that I could do for two or three years and so that's the style of comedy I geared myself towards."

By his own admission, the places he worked on the Southern circuit weren't exactly the best clubs and Madden refers to many of them as "toilets." He later looked back on those days and summed them up as, "Two years of rejection and loneliness. I'd open as a comedian and due to audience demand, I'd finish as a folk-singer. I'd give what I assumed was a witty monologue. All they wanted was dirty jokes. What they wanted even more was for me to shut up and bring on the stripper."[3]

In 1961, he took his life savings of $400 and headed for Hollywood. Madden is quick to point out that he didn't make the move with the intention of becoming an actor. "I didn't go to Hollywood because I wanted to act," he says. "I went to the West Coast because I wanted to work better class clubs. I was really working the toilets in the South. I wanted to get into better rooms and I just assumed that either New York or L.A. was the place to go. New York kind of scared me at the time. It was a little too big and too fast for a kid from Indiana so I went to the West Coast as an alternative. But the idea of acting never entered my mind to be honest with you."

Even in high school and college, Madden had no interest in acting. No high school plays, no membership in the drama club. Incredibly enough, the first time he actually acted was his first day of work when he was signed as a regular to the sitcom *Camp Runamuck* in 1965.

After meeting with the series' producer, Madden got the role of camp counselor Stanley Pruett on the show. No audition was involved. No network approval needed. Madden points out that such a situation would never happen today.

He explains that he was working in a nightclub in Beverly Hills called Ye Olde Little Club which was owned by his manager. Sitcom writer Jerry Davis later approached him, said he liked his act and asked if he was interested in doing pilots. "I said sure, because I was interested in doing anything."

An interview was set up with the head of casting at Screen Gems and he was told that there were two series in development that he might be suitable for—*The Wackiest Ship in the Navy* and *Camp Runamuck*. Madden decided to first check into *Camp Runamuck*, figuring that he would probably be lost in the crowd in a big cast like *Wackiest Ship*.

"So I was sent over to see David Swift who wrote the pilot and was going to produce *Camp Runamuck*. I went over and talked to him in his office for about 20 minutes and we talked about everything except the reason I was there—namely, the show.

"We talked about writing and humor and things like that and the interview ended and I thought well, that's that and chalked it up to good experience in looking for work. Three days later I got a copy of the pilot script and was informed that I had the role of Stanley Pruett in the series.

"As it turns out, Swift was the kind of person who did things like that—he gave people breaks and hired them just on his own intuition. He did because he was in a position where he could. But today that would all have to go through the network and you wouldn't have a chance. Just because a producer wanted you, wouldn't mean anything today.

"So I got the job — my first as an actor and first attempt as an actor and the whole year that we did that show it was school. It was a learning experience. I had no idea what I was doing."

It should be pointed out that David Swift first made his mark in television as the writer-creator of *Mr. Peepers* starring Wally Cox in 1952. Like much of that show, *Camp Runamuck* was full of Swift's love of slapstick and broad comedy.

"*Camp Runamuck* was even broader than *Gilligan's Island* if you can imagine," says Madden. "It was a very slapstick kind of humor. I didn't need a lot of subtle dramatic skills on a show like that."

One of Madden's co-stars was big, goofy Dave Ketchum, probably best known as the undercover agent on *Get Smart* who was always hiding in couches or grandfather clocks. "Dave Ketchum was a naturally funny guy," recalls Madden. "Dave more or less idolized Danny Kaye in Danny's earlier days and so an awful lot of the physical things he did in terms of takes and things were very Danny Kayeish in their style.

"My character, Pruett, was just a gullible guy who could be led or taken in any direction by anybody. I guess in some ways, he was much like the way Gilligan was. There was an all-girls camp across the lake and he had a crush on one of the girl-counselors and Pruett would go into a panic every time she came around and he'd start vibrating like crazy."

The show lasted one season before being cancelled. "We were on opposite *The Flintstones* and a new series called *The Wild, Wild West* and so we were caught between the two and the two age groups which both shows attracted and so our ratings were never that good."

As fate would have it, later in his career, Madden played a role on *The Wild, Wild West* reunion movie in 1980 and also spent a decade doing voice-over work in commercials for Flintstones Vitamins.

The three years before landing the part on *Camp Runamuck* were spent honing his stand-up comedy act on the West Coast and gradually getting booked into better rooms. In the audience at one Palm Springs show, sitting ring-side was Frank Sinatra. "It was eerie," Madden later said. "The audience ignored me and stared at Sinatra. If he laughed, they laughed."[4]

Sinatra recommended Madden to Ed Sullivan who booked him for three appearances on his influential Sunday night TV variety show.

After *Camp Runamuck* ended, Madden's new-found TV profile brought him guest shots on *Bewitched*, *Hogan's Heroes* and a couple of episodes of *Love, American Style* and on-camera commercial work. The *Sullivan* gigs led to greater demand for his stand-up work and it was while working in this capacity that he was spotted by Dan Rowan and Dick Martin and asked to join their new show, *Laugh-In*, in 1968.

Like everyone else in the huge cast of that psychedelic variety show, Madden had a couple of regular characters which were seen every week. One was the morose weather man. Another was the guy with the martini glass full of milk who would say his bit and then throw confetti into the air during the show's cocktail party scenes. The character perfectly sums up Dave Madden at that stage of his stand-up career — a lonely guy standing off to the side in a roomful of swinging hedonists, trying to fit in and look happy despite that basset-hound face and quietly wondering if the martini glass of milk was half-empty or half-full. There was a warm, trusting look on his face but one with just a bit of doubt to it — as if he was unsure he really wanted to be there — capped off with an "Oh, what the heck" expression of abandon as he tossed a fistful of confetti.

The character mirrors a lot of Madden's own ambivalent feelings to his place in show business. He never really felt comfortable in a nightclub full of people unless he was up on stage. He was making a living in the entertainment industry — but he was doing it from a variety of jobs. He was a nightclub comedian who also acted in situation comedies on television.

He was a performer who didn't consider himself exclusively as either an actor or a comedian. "It didn't matter to me — as long as I could work," Madden says of that stage of his career. "Ultimately, I was happy that I was getting enough work in Hollywood that I didn't have to go out on the road anymore because I was sick of the road. Not that I didn't like performing stand-up. It was just that I didn't like the lifestyle that went along with it. Living in hotels and out of suitcases."

Laugh-In was an opportunity to be on the most popular television program at the time. From the moment it debuted in January 1968, the show was a national phenomenon and was the Must-See TV show of the late '60s.

Proof of its impact as a pop-culture fad was the fact that among other merchandising spinoffs was the introduction of *Laugh-In* bubblegum cards. "Next to *Batman*, it was probably the most heavily merchandised show at that time," says Madden, who elaborates on the financial rewards of being on such a popular TV show.

"At the end of the *Laugh-In* run, we had done an enormous amount of merchandising including two record albums. At the end of all that I got a check for my share of all that merchandising as well as a sheet of paper that broke down and explained why this was my fair share of the merchandising money.

"I still have the check and it is made out for $0.02. That's right, zero dollars and two cents. I had the check laminated and took it on several talk shows. I didn't want to cash it because of course my agent would then want his ten percent. Besides, it was more valuable to me as a prop to take on the talk-show circuit."

However, despite the lucrative side benefits of being on the show, Madden decided to leave after two seasons. "I had fun, I liked the people but the *Laugh-In* experience was frustrating," Madden has said.[5]

He elaborates, "*Laugh-In* was an editors' show. It was put together to look like an hour of pandemonium. But they tended to have us do the same things over and over, week after week. So by the time you've spent a year on a show like that, you've done everything they'll let you do and have gotten all the exposure you could possibly get from doing the same thing. To do another few years of that seemed like it would just be spinning your wheels creatively.

"So I got out mainly just because I wanted to do other things. I thought I had gotten as much as I could out of that show and I felt it was time to move on.

"People have wondered if it took a lot of nerve to leave a top-rated show at its peak or if it was the smartest decision, but even though it was still highly rated, what does that mean? I mean if you're just going to come out and throw confetti at cocktail parties and do the weather report again week after week, what are you gaining? You're not gaining anything.

"I could see that I would be locked into doing the same thing and I worried a bit about being stereotyped. I know that Ruth Buzzi and Arte Johnson stayed for the whole five years and I think that the people who stayed the course had the toughest time with their careers afterwards. They were so locked in to an image that they just couldn't escape it. Hollywood loves to stereotype. And for years afterwards, Arte would pop up saying 'Verrrry interesting,' and Ruth would be in the hairnet as Gladys. They had to do reprises on their characters and often couldn't get work that was not related to their *Laugh-In* characters.

"Now, if you compare that with *Saturday Night Live* where easily 75 percent of the people on that show became movie stars and *big* stars after leaving, that just did not happen with our show. Goldie Hawn was the only one with a big career after *Laugh-In* and even won an Academy Award for her first movie, which was pretty amazing."

Immediately after *Laugh-In,* Madden found work on *The Partridge Family* in 1970. He says he didn't leave *Laugh-In* because he already had a job lined up on the new ABC-TV series about a family rock band. In fact, before landing his third job as a regular on a TV-series, for the first time, he actually had to audition for the role.

"The first time I auditioned for *The Partridge Family* was with about 60 other guys. For the second audition they had cut it down to 25 people. The last time they had cut it down to three. Oddly enough, Dave Ketchum from *Camp Runamuck* was also one of the three."

It's not hard to imagine either Ketchum or Madden in the part of the rock group's manager, Reuben Kincaid. But at the time, the producers were casting against type. Prior to that, most agent-manager roles were cast as somewhat sleazy, fast-talking, cigar-chomping sharks. "Bernie Slade, the creator of the show, told me he was casting against type," says Madden. "I told him that I know what agents looked like, I used to be with the William Morris agency. I knew what the stereotype was and I certainly don't fit that image. He said, 'No, you don't but when I wrote the character, I had in mind a friend of mine who looks very much like you.'"

However, Slade's other original ideas about the character also puzzled Madden. The description of Reuben Kincaid in the script for the pilot episode read, "He is part off–Beverly Hills and Oscar Levant with a body built for child-bearing. Hates dogs and children, though not necessarily in that order."

Madden read that and didn't know what to do.

"What does it mean — 'off–Beverly Hills'?" he later asked. "It confused me. I figured they wanted someone who's sardonic, like Oscar Levant, witty in a low-pressure way, maybe negative and neurotic and sarcastic."[6]

Since the rest of the characters were a close family unit that not only sang together but rocked together, originally Reuben Kincaid was created as a way of counter-balancing the saccharine tendencies of the rest of the group. Once again, Madden was cast as the outsider. Compared to the covey of lovey-dovey Partridges, manager Reuben Kincaid had little in common with his clients. He was a bachelor who lived in a swinging singles apartment building, had a little black book full of possibilities and read *Playpen* magazine. As such, the word "commitment" seldom came up in the same sentence as "relationship."

However, he was undeniably committed to the success of his clients, The Partridge Family. He was also secretly envious of the mother, Shirley, and the love she shared with her brood of five kids which ranged in age from grade-schoolers to the eldest in their late teens. After all, it wasn't just any mother who could inspire her kids in 1970 to do something as uncool as insisting that their mother join their rock band. As the title song says, "It all came together when Mom sang along."

The character of Reuben Kincaid was initially conceived as a natural antidote to all that family togetherness. But the original idea for the character as a W.C. Fields type who didn't like kids didn't last long. Partly it was Madden's way of delivering a line of nasty dialogue and leaving the viewer unsure whether he actually meant it.

"The character emerged as well, softer," Madden has said. "He doesn't actively dislike the kids, he's just frustrated and confused by them and not quite able to cope."[7]

In fact, all that child-bashing was really just a front. In one episode, Reuben becomes engaged to one of Shirley's friends but he calls it off when he finds out she doesn't want to have kids. As well, for someone who supposedly hates kids, he was *always* around. He's forever sitting around the kitchen table or living room drinking coffee or dropping by ostensibly to get Shirley to sign some papers and ending up being invited to stay for dinner.

Script-wise there were more practical reasons for Reuben's frequent visits that have nothing to do with his vicarious love-hate relationship with children. "Well, if I wasn't over there drinking coffee, how the hell could I be in the show?" asks Madden. "They even talked at one point of having Reuben rent a room upstairs but they decided that in the early 1970s, that would not sit well with the families of middle America to have this bachelor living in the same house as Shirley. And they also talked about Shirley and Reuben getting married but they negated that and I think they were right because that would have killed the adversarial relationship between Danny Partridge and I if I were to suddenly be his stepfather."

When Reuben was around the kids, Madden often wore a slightly-bemused expression on his face. But the kid who surely fascinated him was 11-year-old Danny, a red-haired precocious financial wizard who was himself something of an anomaly in his own family.

If Reuben was intrigued by Danny Partridge, Madden was equally fond of child actor Danny Bonaduce, who many years later still thought that Madden was the one of the funniest guys in the world. "Yes, we got along very well," says Madden. "During the *Partridge Family* years, Danny probably spent more time at my house out in Malibu than he did in his own home. There were lots of problems at home with his father and many times his mother would ask me to take him for the weekend."

The comic chemistry between the two is apparent on the screen as Danny usually gets the best of Reuben in their ongoing battle of wits. However, he didn't always fare so well in their real-life rivalry. Madden admits to often subtly changing Bonaduce's appearance so that the editors wouldn't be able to use the young actor's close-up for a reaction shot and would have to use Madden's close-up instead.

"I used to do awful things," Madden gleefully confesses. "I would discreetly change Danny's physical appearance in a scene so that they couldn't match his close-up with the master shot. I'd ruffle his hair or unbutton a shirt button so that it wouldn't match shot to shot. I got away with that for a long time. Actually it's just the sort of thing that Danny Bonaduce would probably try to do to me if we were working today. But he wasn't that bright back then."

If Madden had the need to worry about Bonaduce and practical jokes, Reuben Kincaid had far more serious cause to worry about Danny Partridge. He was probably worried that his protégé was after his job. Danny, who daily read *Variety*, was constantly second-guessing Reuben's judgement in how he was managing the Partridges' career and in retrospect he may have had good reason for all those doubts.

Looking over the series' entire four-year run, the band's level of success was baffling at the best of times. It's true that at Danny's insistence and persistence, Reuben became the then-unknown band's manager and took them out of the garage and got them a recording contract. By the end of the first season, they even had a hit record with *I Think I Love You*.

So how did Reuben parlay all that success into concert dates? Keith Partridge (played by David Cassidy) was a teen idol in his own hometown. He was constantly being chased by young girls wanting an autograph. Under the guidance of anyone else, the band should have been playing live concerts to thousands of screaming teenyboppers. Instead, the usual gig that Reuben lined up for them was in a supper club against a backdrop of velvet curtains and playing for a room full of about 30 of Shirley's contemporaries.

Of course in reality the TV show's producers couldn't afford to shoot any huge concerts on a regular basis and they wanted the band to still live a normal middle class lifestyle so the audience could relate. So the band couldn't be *too* successful.

And under Reuben's guidance, they weren't.

He had them playing an Indian reservation one week, starting a European tour another week, he had them accidentally booked into a black ghetto for another gig and in between, an endless succession of generic Holiday Inn–type lounges.

All of the prestige gigs that accompany a series of hit records seemed to elude the Partridge Family. Madden is the first to question Reuben's abilities as a manager. "Reuben failed as a manager," he admits. "Let's face it—at the end of the final year of the series, they were still working toilets. I never understood that—they had all these hits and kids wanted their autographs wherever they went and they were still working these dumb little folk rooms in front of audiences of about 30 people. And these were older people too, not young fans. There was a lot of illogic and inconsistencies with *The Partridge Family* and that was just one of them."

Madden points out that Reuben also wasn't the swinging bachelor he pretended to be. It's true that his little black book contained names like Candy, Daisy and Lola, and he once dated a burlesque showgirl named Bubbles LaRue, but his only reliable date was a stewardess named Bonnie Kleinschmitt. He picked her up with the line, "You don't want to go through your whole life with the name Kleinschmitt, do you?"

"Reuben was pretty much a bumbler with the ladies," Madden surmises. "He tried to create the image of being a hip guy who went after the girls but he always failed. He had one girl, Bonnie Kleinschmitt, that he tried to make out with and was never able to do it for one reason or other — mostly Danny. Danny would screw up every opportunity Reuben ever had with Bonnie. On-screen, he was a miserable failure as a lover."

Regardless of Reuben's failings as a manager, the show was a hit and became a pop-culture icon for baby boomers and nostalgia buffs in the years to follow. Madden even got to see other actors playing "Dave Madden" in two different TV movies, which aired in 2000 — *The David Cassidy Story* and *Come On, Get Happy: The Partridge Family Story.*

He wasn't too impressed with either effort. "The one about David Cassidy was at least fairly accurate," he says. "But the other one which focused on Danny Bonaduce did not have one accurate piece of information in it from beginning to end. I couldn't believe it, I kept waiting for something to come up which was true and *nothing* was true."

When *The Partridge Family* ended in 1974, Madden returned to voice-over commercial work, toured Canada in the play *A Thousand Clowns* and did guest shots on television series like *Happy Days* and *Barney Miller.*

It was while doing a one-time guest appearance on *Alice* that Madden ended up with his longest-running job on television. Although he's universally remembered as Reuben on *The Partridge Family*, many are surprised to learn that he spent seven years on Linda Lavin's series, *Alice*, as Mel's Diner gadfly Earl Hicks.

He was first introduced in a 1978 episode simply as "Soccer Coach." "It was just supposed to be a one-timer. Alice was left in the place by herself and I was a soccer coach and the whole team was in the bus outside and so I had to order 22 hamburgers and they all wanted them different ways. So it was a trick memory job more than anything else.

"I had to rattle off all these different ways the guys wanted their hamburgers and Linda Lavin would stand there with her pad and then she'd say, 'Well, that's only 21.' And then I'd have to do a reprise of the whole thing. What was funny about all that was that I had to memorize it all but

Linda had it all pre-written on her pad and so when I finished the second time, she said, 'Ok, let me see if I have this straight,' and she read off everything I had said, *and she got the applause!*

"The studio audience actually thought that she had managed to copy all that down as fast as I was saying it — or they thought she was repeating everything I had said as a memory trick. But she got a big round of applause and I thought, 'Boy, oh, boy — if they ever knew all the work I went through to learn all that.'"

In the long run, all that hard work paid off. "The producers liked what I did in the performance of that guest shot and so they brought me back as Flo's boyfriend. Then when Polly Holliday left the show for her own series, *Flo,* they said, 'Well, he's a coach so let's have him be the baseball coach of Alice's son, Tommy. Then Tommy went off to college so they had me be Mel's poker buddy who would talk him into getting into all kinds of trouble. They kept switching the focus of who Earl Hicks was so that I lasted right up to the final episode and was on there for seven of their nine years on the air."

At one point, Madden's character was even engaged to Mel's mother, played by veteran actress Martha Raye, who would have been at least 20 years older than Earl Hicks. When asked if the difference in their ages seemed unusual, Madden points out how the very broad humor of *Alice* differed from all other visual art forms in the early 1980s. "Well, producers don't pay any attention to things like that!" he laughs.

"You know, we're not only talking about a *sitcom,* but when you're talking about *Alice,* you're talking about a *Neanderthal* sitcom. The style of comedy and writing and even the way it was shot was very similar to *I Love Lucy.* And that's easy to understand when you consider that the two people who wrote *I Love Lucy,* Bob Carroll and Madeleine Pugh Davis, were now the producers of *Alice.* You look at everything else that was on TV in the late '70s to 1985 and we were nothing like that. We were a throwback to a style of comedy from 25 years earlier."

But on a show as broad as *Alice,* Madden's work stands out for its subtlety in comparison to the rest of the cast. On a show which starred such acclaimed dramatic actors as Vic Taybeck, Holliday and star Lavin, it is Madden who is the most low-key and restrained actor of the bunch.

While the others are doing recycled riffs from Lucille Ball's body of work, Madden is quietly sitting on a stool at the counter and tossing off dry, droll observations punctuated with the way he raises his coffee cup or arches an eyebrow, or the way he has of smiling out the corner of his mouth. It's a wistful look and those kindly, expressive eyes convey a look of resignation and hopefulness at the same time. Even back in his *Partridge*

Family days, one writer noted that Madden's usual expression "is a hand-maiden to his dry, flat prairie tone of voice and seems to reflect the inner mulling of some long-cherished private joke."[8]

For someone with such an expressive face, it's a pity it wasn't seen more often on TV after *Alice* ended in 1985. Madden continued to do occasional guest work on television but by the 1990s, it was in parts such as "The Manager" on *Boy Meets World* or as "Reuben Kincaid" on *The Ben Stiller Show*—you can't get much more typecast than that.

Although viewers did not see his face, they certainly heard that recognizable voice as the lack of on-camera roles meant more voice-over work. Madden doesn't mind the switch in focus in his career—largely because the voice-over field is far more lucrative. He points out that in the five years alone after *Alice,* he earned more money doing voice-overs than he had in his entire TV career of regular roles on four TV series spanning the 20 years from 1965 to 1985.

Now semi-retired and living in Las Vegas, Madden says that he is no longer actively pursuing work but doesn't turn it down when it comes his way. Voice-over work was a nice way of rounding out a varied career, he says. Not only did it provide a good income and keep him working but it was also a convenient escape route from the current state of television.

Ever the iconoclast, he concludes, "Voice-over work was a good way of phasing out of a business which frankly, I don't really understand anymore."

Notes

1. *TV Guide*; December 18, 1971; "Television's Blond Babysitter."
2. *TV Guide,* December 18, 1971; "Television's Blond Babysitter."
3. *TV Guide,* December 18, 1971; "Television's Blond Babysitter."
4. *TV Guide*; December 18, 1971; "Television's Blond Babysitter."
5. *TV Guide*; December 18, 1971; "Television's Blond Babysitter."
6. *TV Guide,* December 18, 1971; "Television's Blond Babysitter."
7. *TV Guide*; December 18, 1971; "Television's Blond Babysitter."
8. *TV Guide*; December 18, 1971; "Television's Blond Babysitter."

Dave Madden Credits

FILM CREDITS

1. *The Curse of Monkey Island;* 1997; (voice) Dinghy Dog
2. *Eat My Dust!;* 1976; Big Bubba Jones
3. *Charlotte's Web;* 1973; (voice) Ram/others

TV CREDITS

1. *Marvin: Baby of the Year;* TV movie; 1989; (voice) Dad
2. *More Wild Wild West;* TV movie; 1980; German Ambassador
3. *The Stableboy's Christmas;* TV movie; 1978; Roman Centurion
4. *Alice;* TV series; 1978–1985; Earl Hicks
5. *The Partridge Family, 2200 A.D.;* TV series; 1974–1975(voice) Reuben Kincaid
6. *The Partridge Family;* TV series; 1970–1974; Reuben Kincaid
7. *Rowan and Martin's Laugh-In;* TV series; 1968–1969; Regular Performer
8. *Camp Runamuck;* TV series; 1965–1966; Counselor Pruett

NOTABLE TV GUEST APPEARANCES

1. *Sabrina, the Teenage Witch;* Dr. Egglehoffer; 10/30/1998
2. *Boy Meets World;* The Manager; 11/17/1995
3. *Married ... With Children;* Manager; 2/6/1994
4. *CBS Storybreak;* Arnold's Dad; 10/11/1992
5. *The Ben Stiller Show;* Reuben Kincaid; 9/27/1992
6. *Fantasy Island;* 10/27/1979
7. *Barney Miller;* Clayton Walsh; 2/9/1978
8. *Barney Miller;* Clayton Walsh; 2/2/1978
9. *The Love Boat;* 1978
10. *Starsky and Hutch;* 9/17/1977
11. *ABC Afterschool Special — Mighty Moose and the Quarterback Kid;* Coach Puckett; 10/1976
12. *Happy Days;* Jack Whippett; 11/26/1974
13. *Bewitched;* Fred; 4/17/1969
14. *Love, American Style;* 1969
15. *Love, American Style;* 1969
16. *The Hollywood Palace;* 1968
17. *Bewitched;* Joe; 1967

Whitman Mayo

Grady Wilson on *Sanford and Son*

223

When Whitman Mayo reluctantly agreed to do a one-shot guest appearance on *Sanford and Son* as family friend Grady Wilson, he thought that his acting days were behind him. But he was asked back to do another episode. Then another. Grady became a recurring character on the NBC comedy starring Redd Foxx and Demond Wilson as the battling father and son Sanfords—Fred and Lamont.

The Grady character became so popular that when Foxx walked out in a contract dispute near the end of Mayo's first season on the show, the producers asked him to fill in as the comic lead for the remainder of the season. That was in the 1973–74 season. In 1975, Mayo was rewarded with his own spinoff, *Grady*. It only lasted four months and Mayo was welcomed back to *Sanford and Son*, and when further problems with the two title characters ended the series in 1977, Mayo immediately returned as Grady for a featured part in its replacement series, *The Sanford Arms*.

A four-year run on three different series as the same character is quite a coup for a talent agent who originally didn't even want to audition for the role because he had come to Hollywood in search of acting jobs for his clients. Although he had been an actor earlier, in the early 1970s Mayo was focusing his energies on his job as president of Nasaba Artists Management based in New York.

In 1973, he was in Los Angeles looking for work for his clients. Shortly after arriving in town, the casting director for *Sanford and Son* wanted *him* for a part. Mayo only agreed to audition for the show because Redd Foxx had been a friend of the black actor-producer Frank Silvera. "I tried that first episode because the late Frank Silvera, whom I idolized, spoke so highly of Redd Foxx, the star of *Sanford*," Mayo later said.[1]

Silvera had been Mayo's mentor and acting teacher earlier in his career. In fact, Mayo's first major experience as an actor was in the Silvera stage production of James Baldwin's *The Amen Corner* which ran on Broadway in 1965. Mayo was 35 years old at the time. Although he had toyed with the idea of becoming an actor since he was a kid of 13, he didn't give it a serious shot as a career until the early 1960s.

Whitman Mayo was born November 15, 1930, in New York City and grew up in Harlem and Queens. At the age of 17, he moved with his family to Fontana, California, a small town 60 miles east of Los Angeles.

In his new high school, Mayo took acting classes and in his last two years of school, he became involved in the drama and speech clubs. Upon graduating in 1949, he spent a year at Chaffey College before being drafted into the Army in 1951 for a two-year hitch. On his release, he spent three years in college, studying at Los Angeles City College and UCLA.

In need of a full-time job after graduating in 1956, Mayo worked as a counselor at an institution for delinquent boys. In 1963, after seven years at that job, he quit to pursue his first love, acting.

He became involved in Los Angeles theatre groups and that's how he came into contact with actor/producer/director/teacher Frank Silvera. The black show business veteran had been part of the Harlem Renaissance in his New York days during the 1950s and also had a long list of credits on Broadway and other New York stage productions. He was also an early and strong voice in the civil rights movement. Silvera became a mentor of Mayo's when he cast him in the first professional production of *The Amen Corner* in 1965. Silvera co-produced the show with Maria Cole, the wife of Nat King Cole. He also directed and starred in the show.

For Mayo, the experience was a career highlight. "I've done quite a bit of theatre," he has said. "But the one production that stands out was *The Amen Corner,* written by the late James Baldwin. We opened in a 78-seat house in Los Angeles and ended up on Broadway, New York City."[2] The play opened in New York on April 15, 1965, and was the Broadway debut of the rest of the cast, which included Isabel (*The Jeffersons*) Sanford and Beah Richards, who was a regular on *Sanford and Son* the season before Mayo arrived. Unfortunately, the show only ran for a few weeks before it was forced to close from lack of sales.

Following *The Amen Corner,* in 1966, Mayo appeared in his first film, an exploitation flick called *The Black Klansman.* The two race-themed projects had an affect on Mayo and he retired from acting for a while to do community work. "It was right after the Watts riots. I helped kids get interested in drama," he later explained.[3]

In 1969 Mayo moved back to New York and joined the New Lafayette Theatre. The company was located in Harlem and its mandate was to give both black and white audiences a non-stereotypical look at black culture. One production, *What If It Had Turned Heads,* teamed him up with Carol Cole, the daughter of Nat King Cole who would later play Mayo's daughter on his TV series, *Grady.*

In the early 1970s, Mayo started up his talent agency, Nasaba Artists Management. When a New York friend offered him a free ride to Los Angeles in 1973, Mayo thought it would be a good opportunity to visit the studios and pitch his clients for work. Shortly after arriving, he was contacted by the casting director of *Sanford and Son.* One of Mayo's New York friends, Ilunga Adell, was a writer and story editor for the series and had suggested Mayo for a part in an upcoming episode. Mayo protested that he was only out there looking for jobs for his clients, not himself. "I had given up acting, myself," he said. "Actors seem inevitably to end up in Hollywood where people had always been cold and cruel." But knowing of Foxx's reputation from Silvera, Mayo decided to audition. "Then, after I saw how warm the cast and crew were, I decided that TV is not so bad." [4]

His part was written for one show only but producer Aaron Ruben liked Mayo's performance and asked him to stay for the next episode. Mayo reasoned that the extra money would allow him to stay in town longer and scout for jobs for his talent agency. Besides, his partner Karen Baxter could handle things back East.

Mayo, however, never did end up going back to New York. He did find work for Nasaba clients like screenwriters Sonny Jim Gaines and Richard Wesley, who had written the Sidney Poitier movies *Uptown Saturday Night* and *Let's Do it Again*. Knowing how unpredictable an acting career could be, he also opened a Whitman Mayo Travel Agency in Inglewood, California. Not that he had much to worry about when it came to Grady. That one episode turned into four years of employment — not bad for someone who had no prior television experience.

In retrospect, it's easy to imagine Mayo protesting to the *Sanford* producers: "I don't understand this," he actually told producer Ruben, "I came to get parts for clients. I have given up acting."[5] After all, that's just the sort of thing that would happen to Grady.

Grady Wilson was Fred Sanford's best friend. Of the two, Fred was the type of old man who was cantankerous and ornery. Grady was laid back and relaxed. If anything, too relaxed. He often gave the impression of having no energy at all. His hangdog expression was that of a man who stumbles through life and every day is pleasantly surprised to find himself still alive. He takes delight in simple things— visiting friends for checkers, watching television, the occasional adult movie. He's a well-dressed man — always in a vest and tie and takes obvious pride in his appearance. A bachelor at the time of the show, he still has luck with the ladies but although he's delighted to know he's still got it, he's simultaneously puzzled and has a hard time remembering what to do with *it*.

Lamont's puritanical Aunt Esther would characterize Grady as "an old fool." Superficially, he may seem like a simpleton but he's a wily old fool in spite of himself. In any confrontation, be it with Fred, Lamont or Esther — it's usually Grady who had the last laugh.

In playing the part of senior citizen Grady, Mayo came up with a number of his own contributions to convey the character's age and personality. He invented a Grady walk, in which the stoop-shouldered old man literally dragged his feet across the room, seemingly never even lifting them once off the floor. Although the character originally had a stuttering problem, Mayo gave him a lyrical tone in the delivery of some of his lines.

When he was puttering around and talking to himself, his voice had a sing-song quality — such as his oft-repeated line, "Yes sir, I think I'll go watch me a little tell-y-vision." As for Grady's catchphrase, "Good gobbily goop," used as an all-purpose expression of joy, astonishment or horror, Mayo put everything he could into the line.

With his graying Brillo-pad hair and scruffy beard, Mayo did such an effective job of handling the physical aspects of the 65-year-old Grady, that it is surprising to realize that Mayo himself was only 42 years old when he first played the character.

It was not the first time he had been cast in a role much older than himself. He once said, "I've always played older parts. When I was 19, I played 60. When I was a kid, I got pleasure out of studying old people. I took joy in their idiosyncrasies. Older folk are like children. They can do and say what they want and get away with it."[6]

Certainly there was an undeniable childlike quality to Grady. He could be stubborn, superstitious and was surely a man of simple interests. However, audiences responded to his uncomplicated nature. When Redd Foxx walked off the show near the end of the second season, the producers expanded Mayo's role by moving him into the Sanford household for the last six episodes of the season. Despite being in the unenviable position of having to fill in for Foxx, Mayo brought a new tone to the series. Viewers appreciated the fact that Grady wasn't mean-spirited, unlike Fred who would call his son "Dummy" and insult him at every opportunity. Grady was just too good-natured to seriously insult anyone. Ratings for the Foxxless episodes remained high and when Foxx balked at returning on time for the start of the next season, Mayo was again promoted to co-star.

In response to the popularity of the Grady character, the producers created a spinoff series for Mayo called *Grady*. The series put the character in a domestic setting with his grown married daughter inviting him to leave Watts and live with her family in a racially mixed middle-class neighborhood. Carol Cole, whom he had worked with at the New Lafayette Theatre in New York, played his daughter Ellie.

The series lasted four months and when it was cancelled, Grady returned to Watts and Mayo to *Sanford and Son*. On that series, Redd Foxx left in the fall of 1977 to do a variety show on ABC. As well, Demond Wilson's contract demands were not being met by NBC and so he also wasn't returning. Without its two title characters, the producers renamed the show *The Sanford Arms* and expanded the roles of the supporting players, particularly those of Mayo and LaWanda Page who played Aunt Esther. Grady was married in the new show but the series lasted less than a month.

Although he had been nominated for a Golden Globe Award for Best Supporting Actor in a Television Series in 1975 and had established himself as a reliable comic actor, much of Mayo's subsequent TV appearances were serious roles on episodic television dramas such as *Hill Street Blues, Lou Grant, Trapper John M.D., In the Heat of the Night* and *ER.* In his post–*Sanford* years he also found work as a regular on four TV series but none of them lasted longer than a season. He played Howlin' Joe on the high school drama *The Best of Times* in 1983. In 1985, he played Robert Blake's assistant in *Hell Town,* an inner-city drama which had Blake playing a hard-boiled priest of all things. Mayo returned to situation comedy in *The Van Dyke Show,* a sitcom starring Dick Van Dyke in 1988. Set in a small regional theatre, Mayo played Doc Sterling, the longtime stage manager of the theatre. *The Cape* was a syndicated drama in 1996 that was about the space program at Cape Canaveral and shot on location. Mayo's light comic touch was called for in his scenes as the owner of the Moonshot Bar and Grill, the after-work hangout of all the astronauts-in-training, the instructors and all their girlfriends.

He also worked in a number of films after his *Sanford and Son* years. His favorites were *The Main Event* with Barbra Streisand; the 1981 TV movie *Of Mice and Men,* which reunited him with Robert Blake, whom he had first worked with in an two-part episode of *Baretta* in 1975; and a cameo in *Boyz N the Hood* in 1991.

In 1994, Mayo and his wife Gail (whom he had married in 1973 and raised three children with) moved to a small town in Georgia near Atlanta. In 1996, he became an adjunct professor at Clark Atlanta University where he taught drama to the film and theatre classes. He also began hosting a weekly TV series, *Liars and Legends* on the Turner South Network. In 2001, he had a part in *Boycott,* a TV movie filmed and set in the South. It was about the civil rights movement in Alabama in the 1950s after Rosa Parks refused to give up her seat on a bus. It was the type of film that would have made Mayo's mentor, Frank Silvera, proud.

In March 2001, Mayo was hospitalized due to hernia problems. On May 22, he died of a heart attack while being transferred to another hospital. He was 70 years old.

Although he claimed that the theatre was his first love, Mayo will always be best remembered as Grady on *Sanford and Son.* In 1996, NBC's *Late Night with Conan O'Brien* wanted to use Mayo in a sketch for their variety-talk show. However, he had left Los Angeles by then and the producers weren't able to locate him. So O'Brien went on the air and launched a "Where's Grady?" search. They milked the gag for over a month before he was actually found. There were nightly updates and a hotline number where people could phone in and report sightings. They even recruited Robert Stack, host of NBC's *Unsolved Mysteries*, to narrate a dramatic "re-enactment" of the days leading up to Mayo's "disappearance."

Of course Mayo hadn't actually disappeared, he had just relocated and not being a *Late Night* viewer was totally oblivious to the nationwide search going on for him. When he was finally found he was brought to *Late Night* with great fanfare. O'Brien and the producers built up the anticipation by showing live reports of his plane landing at New York's LaGuardia airport and then made periodic checks on the progress of his limousine en route to the NBC studios. When he arrived during the final segment of the show, the studio lights were cut as he walked across the stage. As he reached center stage, a large lighted sign which simply said "GRADY" was lowered behind him as the audience gave him a raucous standing ovation.

Wearing a vest and tie, Mayo raised his hand triumphantly, yet looked out at it all with an expression of bemused appreciation. It was an attitude that acknowledged that to most people, he will always be remembered as Grady. But most importantly, it also showed that Whitman Mayo was a great sport.

Notes

1. TV Book; *The Detroit Free Press*; June 9, 1974; "Whitman Mayo"; by John Alexander.
2. www.the-cape.com/Biography of Whitman Mayo.
3. TV Book; *Detroit Free Press*; June 9, 1974.
4. Jet Magazine; December 25, 1975; "Grady Bids for TV Stardom on His Show"; by Bob Lucas.
5. TV Book; *Detroit Free Press*; June 9, 1974.
6. TV Book; *Detroit Free Press*; June 9, 1974.

Whitman Mayo Credits

FILM CREDITS

1. *Waterproof;* 1999
2. *The Seventh Coin;* 1992; Coin Shop Owner
3. *Boyz N the Hood;* 1991; The Old Man
4. *D.C. Cab;* 1983; Mr. Rhythm
5. *The Main Event;* 1979; Perry
6. *The Black Klansman;* 1966; Alex

TV Credits

1. *Boycott;* TV movie; 2001; Rev. Banyon
2. *The Cape;* TV series; 1996; Sweets (owner of the Moonshot Bar and Grill)
3. *The Cape;* TV movie; 1996; Sweets
4. *You Must Remember This;* TV movie; 1992; Jesse
5. *Final Shot: The Hank Gathers Story;* TV movie; 1992; Nick
6. *The Van Dyke Show;* TV series; 1988; Doc Sterling
7. *The Grand Baby;* TV movie; 1985
8. *Hell Town;* TV series; 1985; One Ball
9. *The Best of Times;* TV series; 1983; Howlin' Joe
10. *Of Mice and Men;* TV movie; 1981; Crooks
11. *The Sanford Arms;* TV series; 1977; Grady Wilson
12. *Grady;* TV series; 1975; Grady Wilson
13. *Sanford and Son;* TV series; 1973–1977; Grady Wilson

Notable TV Guest Appearances

1. *ER;* 2/25/1999
2. *Martin;* Mr. Mackay; 2/16/1995
3. *Full House;* Eddie Johnson; 10/29/1991
4. *Good Grief;* 10/29/1990
5. *In the Heat of the Night;* Winston Tyler; 1/30/1990
6. *Family Matters;* Fletcher; 1989
7. *227;* Henry, Mary's Father; 2/27/1988
8. *227;* Henry; 3/8/1987
9. *Hill Street Blues;* Vagrant; 10/2/1986
10. *227;* Henry; 2/15/1986
11. *Trapper John M.D.;* 11/29/1985
12. *Whiz Kids;* Teddy; 2/25/1984
13. *Trapper John M.D.;* 10/28/1983
14. *Hill Street Blues;* Barney; 2/17/1983
15. *Lou Grant;* Fred Jenkins; 1/26/1981
16. *Diff'rent Strokes;* Jethro Simpson; 1979
17. *Starsky and Hutch;* Jeeter; 1/14/1978
18. *Baretta;* 1975

Don Most

Ralph Malph on *Happy Days*

When the independent feature film *The Last Best Sunday* was released in 1999, one review praised its "surprisingly sophisticated direction by *Happy Days*' Ralph Malph."[1]

Don Most, also known as "*Happy Days*' Ralph Malph" takes it all in stride. After all, he's been closely identified with the outgoing, carrot-topped, class cut-up Ralph ever since voluntarily leaving the series in 1980, four years before it went off the air.

Still, he's a bit confused that a film he *directed* and did not appear in would be mentioned in the same breath as Ralph Malph. "I'm not an extrovert and this film is a far cry from Ralph," says Most. "In fact, it's diametrically opposed to anything like Ralph. But I guess, sometimes people don't realize that it's directed by *me*, not Ralph. I'm not much like the character I was playing back then. For me, Ralph was a stretch; I'm more introspective."

Spoken like a natural-born artist. His low-budget drama has earned reviews noting Most's attention to detail, creating mood and even for the influence of his background in television. The Internet magazine Nitrate Online pointed out, "*The Last Best Sunday* is something special, a familiar story given new life by a director who has clearly embraced television's often misunderstood and underused knack for combining drama and comedy."[2]

Small wonder then that people are surprised that such a subtle intimate film could be the product of the man who gave life to Ralph Malph, the big doofus with the goofy grin. Around Arnold's Drive-In, the burger joint on *Happy Days*, Ralph was the resident king of the one-liners. A stand-up comic-in-training, attention grabbing Ralph would reel off more jokes than you could shake a Morey Amersterdam joke book at and then crow, "I've got it, I've still got it!"

Despite Most's protestations of the dissimilarities between the souls of himself and Ralph, his background does contain one nugget that is close to that of his alter ego. During the 1960s, as a teenager, he spent some time playing resorts in the famous Borscht Belt of the Catskills, the working circuit of every second-rate comic and many a top banana during the 1940s and '50s. For Ralph, it would have been a dream come true. At that point in his career, Most was living Ralph Malph's fantasy life.

"When I was 14, I was in a group of kid performers called The Broadway Show-offs. Charlie Rowe was an old vaudeville performer who ran an acting school with his wife and that was the world he came from and he set us up with an act for a nightclub revue which we appropriately played one summer at resorts in the Catskills," says Most.

Just like Ralph, Most discovered his show business aspirations early. Born on August 8, 1953, Most grew up in the Flatbush section of Brooklyn,

New York, the son of an accountant and a homemaker. A normal child in every other regard, when he was in grade three, he became obsessed with one particular movie and watched it so many times that he knew all the dialogue by memory. While other nine-year-olds in the early 1960s were caught up with Davy Crockett and Abbot and Costello on TV, young Donny Most was completely captivated by *The Al Jolson Story*.

"There was a station in New York that would play the same movie two times a day and then again four times a day on weekends. I became obsessed with that movie and must have seen it 30 times over a two-year period."

However, it was while in high school, Erasmus Hall, that he decided to change his focus from singing to acting and even though he was studying drama at school, he began taking outside acting classes as well. Although his high school gave us Barbra Streisand and Eli Wallach, Most says that the school's theatre department wasn't much different than other high schools. While at the school, he was involved in the annual student productions.

"I began taking acting lessons in New York and doing workshops," he says. "At this time, I met Selma Rosen, who became my manager for the next 15 years. I got my Screen Actors Guild card and started going to auditions and doing commercials." His TV debut came when he was 16 years old and cast in a Rice Chex cereal commercial. He also remembers later doing a Reese's Peanut Butter Cup commercial with another unknown aspiring actor, Robbie Benson.

In 1970, Most graduated high school and started classes at Lehigh University in Bethlehem, Pennsylvania. Although he maintained his showbiz aspirations, he enrolled as an engineering major and then transferred into business school. It was a way to keep his parents happy so that he would have something to fall back on if he needed it. "But I was only really interested in acting," he admits. "I was spending a lot of time in their drama department, The Mustard and Cheese Dramatic Club and probably spent more time in the drama department than my classes. In the meantime, I was travelling back to New York for auditions."

Everything changed, however, in 1973. Most decided to spend the summer before his senior year of college in Los Angeles. Unlike most others, he didn't just head out West armed with only a dream. "I had done well in commercials in New York and so through my agent I had connections in the business and I followed up on them when I got to L.A."

More importantly, in those few short months before school started again in September, he also got cameo shots on television on *Emergency* and *Room 222*. His agents suggested that now that the ball was rolling, why not take six months off school and stay in California and if things didn't work out he could always come back and finish college. "When they suggested that I take time off and see how it goes in L.A., I remember that I didn't even have to think about it. It seemed such a natural and foregone conclusion. I know that was what I wanted to do—I had an immediate visceral response."

Now based in L.A., more commercials and TV cameos followed and within a year he had landed a full-time job on *Happy Days*. Following the success of George Lucas' film *American Graffiti*, *Happy Days* was an attempt to cash in on the wave of 1950s nostalgia created by that film. Starring *American Graffiti* lead Ron Howard as clean-cut, all–American high school student Ritchie Cunningham, the series was about Ritchie and his best friend Potsie (the name says it all) as they bungle their way through high school in the innocent '50s, trying to meet girls and be cool.

Of course they were hopeless on both counts—until a background character from the pilot episode, Arthur Fonzerelli, better known as Fonzie, got off his motorcycle and made both them and the show popular just by association. After seeing the huge impact of actor Henry Winkler as the motorcycle-riding rebel mechanic, the producers made the Fonzie character more prominent. In the process he became the show's most identifying feature.

Another background character from the pilot who also came into the foreground was a character named Ralph Malph. Ironically, Most got the role of Ralph after originally auditioning for the part of Potsie, which eventually went to Anson Williams. Most was nixed for the Potsie role because of his red hair. Along with the red locks of Ron Howard, the sight of two red-haired best friends would be a bit much. However, his audition went well enough that he still came away with a job.

"Even though I was auditioning for Potsie, my screen test was well-received and I was told later that Michael Eisner, then the head of ABC, saw it and said, 'You should make that guy a regular.' And so they found another part for me."

In the pilot and first couple of episodes, the Ralph Malph character, like Fonzie, is on the sidelines of the central action. He is usually seated in a souped-up jalopy in the parking lot of Arnold's Drive-In and unlike Fonzie, who was more of a lone wolf in those first episodes, it's Ralph Malph who is surrounded by a bunch of adoring girls. For that reason alone, he had ample reason to look down on the obviously hopeless duo of Ritchie and Potsie.

In those first couple of episodes, the Ralph character is pretty undeveloped and like Fonzie, he only has a small number of lines. Not that there was a lot to work with in the character in those early days. "For the first half of that first season, the character wasn't too defined," says Most. Wondering just how to play Ralph, who was a bit of a wiseguy, Most asked the producers and writers what Ralph's background was—"And all they told me was that he was a character who likes cars." So much for backstory. Most had his work cut out for him in bringing this guy to life.

Before the end of that first season, however, Fonzie was established as the audience favorite and Ralph Malph had subtly changed from someone who thought he was better than Ritchie and Potsie to becoming one of them. The trio became best friends and Ralph emerged as the practical joking clown. He may have lost some of his initial cool, but Ralph was the life of the party, Arnold's Drive-In resident bon vivant.

Most credits *Happy Days* director Jerry Paris for the new characterization of Ralph Malph. Prior to *Happy Days*, Paris was probably best known as the next-door neighbor Jerry Helper on *The Dick Van Dyke Show*, where he also worked as director. Most says, "The main influence on my character was from our director, Jerry Paris. His own personality was probably closer to Ralph. He was outgoing and gregarious, a larger-than-life type. He would come up with ideas and bits of schtick for Ralph and I would do them. The producers liked it and that influenced the writers—they saw Jerry acting as Ralph and me bringing it to life. Afterwards, I was able to come up with my own ideas. But originally, to become Ralph, I was basically playing Jerry Paris."

When *Happy Days* debuted on January 15, 1974, the show was centered around Ritchie and Potsie. However, when the overwhelming popularity of the Fonz soon became apparent, the producers switched from the buddy comedy to the unlikely friendship between clean-cut Ritchie and high school dropout Fonzie. Whereas most of the storylines used to revolve around Ritchie, now only about a quarter of the scripts were devoted to that character.

When Howard left in 1980, the series changed its focus again. By now, Fonzie had become owner of his own garage, had an apartment over the Cunningham family's garage and he had taken night school classes. He not only graduated but he also now taught auto shop at the local high school. By this time, Ritchie's kid sister, Joanie (played by Erin Moran), had grown into a teenager and the show revolved around her volatile romance with Fonzie's cousin, Chachi, played by Scott Baio.

It was around this time that Most also packed it in. After six seasons, he wanted to pursue other acting projects and so the producers wrote him off the series by having both Ralph and Ritchie join the Army and being stationed in Greenland.

Although the series enjoyed a decade-long run and would stay on the air until 1984, Most could see the writing on the wall. Or rather, in his weekly scripts. "By the sixth season, I felt the show was deteriorating and the scripts weren't as good," he says. "Part of the problem was that for the third season the show started taping before a studio audience and their presence had a large effect on the performers. It had been a one-camera show and shot like a film for the first two seasons. There was no audience so it was more realistic and low-key. But when we began taping in front of a studio audience with a three-camera set-up, just by the nature of the situation, the comedy becomes broader because you're playing to the audience and that changes the energy. "It's a subtle thing in that you, as an actor start to play it broader in order to get the laugh. You say to yourself, 'Well, it worked when I did this the last time,' and so you do it again and maybe embellish it a bit."

For Ralph Malph, the resident cut-up, going broad for the laugh was only natural for a character who dreamed of becoming a stand-up comic. No joke was too corny and no pun too bad for Ralph. Over the course of the series, Ralph went from being a popular high school jock to barely-tolerated class clown and then a college boy and enlisted man with the Army. His father, Mickey Malph, played by Jack Dodson (Howard Sprague on *The Andy Griffith Show*), was an eye doctor by trade but was a kindred comic spirit. Some of Ralph's more memorable bits were when they teamed up for father-and-son comedy routines.

In 1979, the spinoff happy producers and ABC seriously considered doing a spinoff with the Ralph and Potsie characters to star Most and Williams. *Laverne and Shirley, Mork and Mindy* and *Joanie Loves Chachi* all had their origins on *Happy Days*. As the characters got older and the focus turned to the younger characters, a *Ralph and Potsie* series only seemed natural. It was a logical next step.

Today, Most says he was relieved that it didn't happen. "The talk of a spinoff was a year before I left the show and it was a very close call. The network almost went for it but at the last minute Fred Silverman decided not to do it. And I was not unhappy about that decision. I was kind of relieved. I was not mourning the fact that it did not happen."

One can hardly blame him. Considering the falling standards in the writing, a Ralph-Potsie spinoff was probably not a good idea. You can almost imagine the premise — Ralph, a struggling comic, and Potsie, a struggling singer, would move to New York or Hollywood, share an apartment (naturally with wacky neighbors) and chase starlets. Or else, Ralph would end up being Potsie's manager. Either way it would be just awful. Or a hit. Regardless, Most has no regrets that it all fell through.

Discouraged by the decline in the show and its direction, when Most decided to leave the series in 1980, it was also because of his frustration as a young actor. Having been with the show since the pilot in 1974, he had gotten about as much as he could out of the character and he admits that playing Ralph was starting to feel a bit stifling. The actor was also looking forward to trying on other characters.

"When I left the show, I realized that I hadn't begun to touch my acting skills," he says. "At the time, I was looking to do something different. I had been that character for six years. When I got into acting as a teenager, I had envisioned my entire career being various kinds of characters in a variety of situations, both drama and comedy. So I felt it was time to move on."

Most had been hoping to tackle other kinds of acting challenges—something as far removed from *Happy Days* and his Ralph Malph character as possible. At the time, he could have easily landed a regular role on any number of sitcoms. Instead, Most told his agents not to even ask about sitcom work. "I told my agents that I didn't want to do any TV other than special projects. I wanted to do film and theatre but back then it was hard to make that jump from television to film.

What inspired Most to set his hopes on a movie career was his lead role in *Leo and Loree*, a feature film he did in 1980 right after leaving *Happy Days*. It had begun a few years earlier as a project Ron Howard was to direct but by 1980, Howard wasn't available and so Jerry Paris directed the film. It co-starred Linda Purl, who at various times played two different characters on *Happy Days* as girlfriends of Ritchie and then later Fonzie.

"It was a good movie and I was told that this would be the launch of my movie career," says Most. "But the distributors test-marketed it in Omaha and Nebraska and this was more of an urban movie with lots of Hollywood references and they didn't get it. So it was never released. If it had been seen, it would have hopefully opened some doors and made for more opportunities."

Meanwhile, all television had to offer was work in sitcoms. Typecasting had already become a problem in that he couldn't get any TV work because of his high profile as a sitcom actor. Ironically, Most says that when his agents first told him to audition for *Happy Days* back in 1973, he was hesitant. "At the time, I was more interested in dramatic work but I thought, I guess I could do comedy."

He points out that the jobs he did have on episodic television back then were all vastly different characters on different types of television formats. "I did a *Police Story* back in the early '70s where I played a psychopathic bomber. But after *Happy Days*, I wouldn't have even been considered for a part like that. People on the street would say to me, 'When are we going to see you in something?' They were willing to see me in other shows. But it's the industry. The powers-that-be assumed that the audience wouldn't accept me in other roles."

Of course, not helping matters was his own personal decision not to do any more sitcom work. "It wasn't that I didn't want to do *any* television. Especially a sitcom. I wanted to do serious work. I had offers to do sitcom pilots but I wasn't interested at that time. In retrospect, burning my bridges with television might not have been the best career move. But it was a self-induced hiatus."

Not that Most was idle during his post–*Happy Days* period. In 1981, he was part of a touring production of the musical *Damn Yankees* starring Dick Van Dyke. Although he had officially left *Happy Days,* he rejoined his former co-stars Winkler and Howard by doing the voice of Ralph on the Saturday morning cartoon show *Fonz and the Happy Days Gang.* That experience helped him get a job as a regular voice-over actor in 1983 on the animated fantasy series *Dungeons and Dragons.*

Also in 1983, he was reunited with the entire cast of *Happy Days* when he and all the other originals who had left came back for the series' final episode, "Welcome Home." In that episode, Ralph gives up his stand-up comic aspirations and joins his father in the eye-doctor business.

However, whether by choice or the result of typecasting, Most did little TV work during the 1980s. Like all recognizable TV faces, he took a couple of trips to *Fantasy Island* and on *The Love Boat.* Later he guested on *Murder, She Wrote,* which used the same casting technique.

He also made a memorable appearance in 1982 on what has become a fan favorite of the cops-on-motorcycle series *CHiPS.* Here he played a concert promoter named Moloch in "Rock Devil, Rock." Ponch, played by Erik Estrada, sang a disco tune at a punk rock concert that's about to get out of hand and brings everyone together through music.

But overall, TV and film work was rare and so Most returned to the theatre. He tried to change his image and further distance himself from his *Happy Days* connection by changing his screen name to Donald Most instead of Donny and then just Don Most.

Ironically, it was his *Happy Days* connection that got him a part which in turn got his face out there again and helped jump-start his career. In 1995, he was cast in the touring Broadway production of a revival of *Grease.* He was to play an aging lecherous disc jockey named Vince Fontaine. Again, in typical Most fashion, he was initially hesitant about taking the job. After all, it was a show set in the same time period as his old TV series which he had been trying to distance himself from for so long.

"There was enough of a '50s connection between *Grease* and *Happy Days* that it made sense to the producers to hire me," he says. "I was a bit hesitant about taking the part but it was 15 years after I had left *Happy Days* and I was now playing an adult character instead of a teenager. Also, it was a touring show of the Tommy Tune production from Broadway. On a show like that, no one comes expecting to see me as Ralph Malph. With a familiar musical like that, the show is the real star."

The exposure resulted in an increase in television guest work but at the same time, Most was doing more work in theatre, hoping to establish himself as a director. His long-term goal was to direct films. "Long before I had the chance to direct *The Last Best Sunday*, I had directed four or five plays in Los Angeles," Most explains. "The first was *Doubles* which is a serio-comedy. I had previously acted in it out East at the Westport Playhouse in Connecticut in 1987. So it was a comfortable choice for my first directing job. I directed it at the Tamarend Theatre in Hollywood in 1991. It got good reviews in the *L.A. Times* and that all helped reinforce my sense and belief that I could direct and so it was also a good way to test the waters.

"But all the time during this period, I was looking for the right project to do as a film. I had met a writer, Karen Kelly, who was interested in independent film-making and I optioned a couple of scripts from her. I had also met an experienced producer, Michael Murphey, and he was interested in the same kind of films and subjects as I was. We hit it off and together we optioned Karen's script to *The Last Best Sunday*."

From all accounts, the film is a reflection of the overly thoughtful Most. Reviews praised it for its attention to detail and Most's ability to establish mood and atmosphere. Ron Howard has called the $1 million romantic drama "a gem" and Henry Winkler has said that Most is "very meticulous, which makes him perfect for directing movies."[3]

Most considers directing to be the perfect marriage for his talents. Yet, considering his background he doesn't consider himself to be primarily an "actor's" director. "Well, one of my strengths as a director obviously is in coming from that world as an actor myself. But photography has always been a serious hobby of mine and so I've always been interested in the aesthetics of film and I think I have a very good eye.

"So for me, directing is a nice blend of working with the actors and making each scene work as fast and well as it can and merging that with a good visual sense in being able to bring a sense of composition and light to the film, and I get a big thrill out of it."

While waiting for more directing assignments, he's keeping the doors open for acting jobs. "I'm on a crusade now to get the acting career to where I think it should be," he says.

Unlike the effect of *Happy Days,* the national exposure from *Grease* did not result in more nostalgia job offers. On the contrary, since *Grease,* many of his TV guest appearances have been in cult sci-fi series. They have also required quite different characterizations. On *Dark Skies,* he played 1960s LSD-guru Dr. Timothy Leary. On *The Crow: Stairway to Heaven,* he came up with a new look for his recurring role as an unorthodox psychiatrist.

"The character on *The Crow* was a death-obsessed psychiatrist who specialized in regression therapy and past lives. The producer and I thought a beard would be perfect on that type of character so I grew a beard for the part. I ended up liking it and kept it."

However, his most personally satisfying recent role was when he was reunited with Ron Howard when the now big-time director hired him for his 1999 film *EdTV,* which also happened to be a scathing indictment of network executives and the television industry. Most played a TV network executive who was a yes-man for the head executive, played by Rob Reiner. The character was exactly the type who wouldn't have allowed Most to even audition for a job after his *Happy Days* were over.

"With *EdTV,* Ron was poking fun and satirizing the excesses of television and so there was an awareness of that in how I played my character," says Most. "It was all about the nature of television and the hierarchy at the networks and their emphasis on ratings. But the main part for me on the set was just to be truthful and make it real and be funny.

"But yes, he was the type of executive who wouldn't have even considered me for a job before, so I definitely did get some satisfaction from playing that character — and from the movie as a whole."

Except for reruns of *Happy Days,* Ralph Malph is pretty much a memory these days. The once fiery-red hair has faded to a much lighter strawberry blond over the past 20 years. The beard looks good and helps diminish any resemblance. Only that instantly recognizable goofy impish grin remains.

Notes

1. Nitrate Online; "25th Seattle International Film Festival Reviews"; by Eddie Cockrell.
2. *Ibid.*
3. *People* magazine; "Most Happy"; by Samantha Miller; December 14, 1998.

Don Most Credits

FILM CREDITS

1. *EdTV;* 1999; Benson
2. *Hourglass;* 1995; Andre
3. *Acting on Impulse;* 1993; Leroy
4. *Stewardess School;* 1987; George Bunkle
5. *Leo and Loree;* 1980; Leo
6. *Crazy Mama;* 1975; Shawn

TV CREDITS

1. *Dead Man's Island;* TV movie; 1996; Burton Andrews
2. *Hagar the Horrible;* TV series; 1989; (voice)
3. *Dungeons and Dragons;* TV series; 1983; (voice) Eric Terrence
4. *Fonz and the Happy Days Gang;* TV series; 1980; (voice) Ralph Malph
5. *With This Ring;* TV movie; 1975; James Cutler
6. *Huckleberry Finn;* TV movie; 1975; Tom Sawyer
7. *Happy Days;* TV series; 1974–1980; Ralph Malph

NOTABLE TV GUEST APPEARANCES

1. *Star Trek: Voyager;* Kadan; 2/28/2001
2. *Star Trek: Voyager;* Kadan; 2/21/2001
3. *Yes, Dear;* Professor Rhodes; 12/04/2000
4. *The Crow: Stairway to Heaven;* Dr. John Dorsett; 4/16/1999
5. *The Crow: Stairway to Heaven;* Dr. John Dorsett; 11/20/1998
6. *Diagnosis Murder;* Emerson Horn; 4/30/1998
7. *Dark Skies;* Dr. Timothy Leary; 5/31/1997
8. *Sliders;* Skip Collins; 11/29/1996
9. *Baywatch;* Roger Clark; 11/1/1993
10. *Murder, She Wrote;* Ozzie Gerson; 2/25/1990
11. *Charles in Charge;* Lottery Winner; 1989
12. *Murder, She Wrote;* T.J. Holt; 12/14/1986
13. *Happy Days;* Ralph Malph; 10/25/1983
14. *CHiPS;* Moloch; 10/31/19821
15. *Fantasy Island;* 1/23/1982
16. *Fantasy Island;* 1/17/1981
17. *The Love Boat;* 1980
18. *The Love Boat;* 1979
19. *Police Story;* 12/3/1974
20. *Emergency!;* 12/22/1973

Ken Osmond

Eddie Haskell on *Leave It to Beaver*

"Listen, your parents can't legally throw you out of the house until you're 21. It's true, I read it in a magazine."
— Ken Osmond as Eddie Haskell
on *Leave It to Beaver,* circa 1960

Fast-forward thirty years later to *The New Leave It to Beaver* TV series and a grown-up Eddie Haskell has just sent his 12-year-old son Bomber off to military school for spilling white grapefruit juice on the white carpet.

Eddie, you've changed. What's up, Gertrude?

In black and white, as a kid, for the most part, Eddie was a harmless, overly polite smartass. But in living color on the revived series, he had become nastier and more insensitive with age. On the new series, he played the ponies, cheated on his wife, made his kids call him "sir" and drank beer straight out of the can. What gives, Sam?

Blame it on the producers, suggests Osmond, who played Haskell on both incarnations of the TV series which has come to represent the ideal childhood during the late 1950s and early '60s. Osmond noticed on the new series that "Eddie was more malicious and I voiced my opinion to the contrary to the producers but that's the way they wanted the character to go. However, they reciprocated with scripts showing the tender side of Eddie which gave me a chance to show that there was a *real* Eddie. I mean, he's not a *total* idiot.

"Actually, the tender side of Eddie was seen in the original show too. Not that often but occasionally you would see him in a vulnerable light — just enough to let you know that Eddie was a real person."

Osmond was born June 7, 1943, in Los Angeles and had been working as an actor for a number of years by the time he was signed to *Leave It to Beaver,* when he was 13 years old.

In 1957, when the show's producers, Joe Connelly and Bob Mosher, were looking for someone to play the best friend of Tony Dow's Wally Cleaver character, they were looking for someone who could convincingly play a "bad influence." They wanted someone who could play a cocky, self-assured kid with a natural knack for getting on people's nerves.

Osmond played the part for the next six years until the series was cancelled in 1963. But the show has remained on the air in syndicated reruns ever since and over time, Eddie Haskell has become a bona fide pop-culture icon. "He's become a cult figure," agrees Osmond. "I wish I could explain it — because I'd buy some stock in whatever it is — but I can't explain it."

Actually, the popularity of Eddie Haskell isn't all that hard to understand. On a show as relentlessly wholesome as *Leave It to Beaver,* Eddie was a necessary jolt of irreverence. As a thoroughly unctuous creep, he was a contrast to the clean-cut Cleaver boys, Wally and Theodore, a.k.a. The Beaver. For their parents, Ward and June, Eddie Haskell represented every parent's worst nightmare. He was the kind of kid that an adult didn't trust just on instinct alone. To their faces, he was polite and condescending but they weren't fooled for a moment and saw through his routine attempts to ingratiate himself with his insincere compliments of "My, that's a lovely dress you're wearing, Mrs. Cleaver." As they suspected, as soon as they were out of ear shot, Eddie would be trying to talk Wally and the Beav into some kind of mischief.

Osmond brought a lot to the role — the loose slack posture that straightened up as soon as an adult entered the room, that patented verbal smirk and his infamous wiseguy laugh, "heh, heh, heh," known to fans as "the Eddie Cackle." But Osmond says the most defining aspect of the character was "The ability to change — from being a stone idiot to a sweetheart and to do it instantly. Like when you're telling Beaver, 'Hey squirt, do this,' and at that moment, Mrs. Cleaver walks in — and being able to say in the same breath, 'Good afternoon, Mrs. Cleaver.'"

As for "the Eddie Cackle," Osmond says that it was just part of the growth of the character on the show. "It's not something that just happened overnight. It developed over a period of many, many years. It's never been a part of my own personality in real life, it's strictly Eddie."

Osmond reports that he had a pretty normal life back then. "I went to a public high school and was treated pretty much like any other student. Eddie was just another character on TV back then."

Today, however, is a different story. Although most people are able to separate the actor from his TV character, that's not always the case. "There are exceptions. Occasionally I'll run across a fan who is *amazed* that I am not like Eddie. But most people accept Eddie as just being a character. When they do identify me with Eddie, I take it as a compliment — apparently I've put the character over and so I do take it as such."

However, he's also quick to point out that despite his contributions to the character — "God, I hope that Ken is not like Eddie!"

In fact, Osmond did such a good job at playing Eddie that his acting days were over not many years after *Leave It to Beaver's* cancellation in 1963. There were guest shots on other sitcoms including an episode of the Connelly-Mosher production *The Munsters.* Here he was part of a group of practical-joking frat boys. But Osmond adds that his character was a follower, not the ringleader of the group. There was also a role in the 1967 teen flick *C'Mon, Let's Live a Little,* starring pop singers Bobby Vee and Jackie DeShannon. It was the standard college malt shop stuff and the tag line says it all — "Let's sing! Let's rock! Let's make the scene!" There was also a timely subplot about free speech and student radicals and Osmond was cast as The Beard.

He speculates that his lack of work after *Beaver* probably had more to do with supply and demand than it did with typecasting. "I don't know if it was typecasting or just a lack of parts for someone my age," he says. "But in the mid-sixties, I got totally out of the industry all together for close to 20 years."

For a while, he ran a helicopter business with his brother. Contrary to popular belief, he did not grow up to become shock-rocker Alice Cooper. That 1970s rumor never bothered him. He says, "It was humorous really. I understand that he had a T-shirt made up that said, 'No, I'm not Eddie Haskell.'"

In comparison, that rumor pales next to the reality that in 1970, the guy who played Eddie Haskell, a natural-born scam artist, became a member of the Los Angeles Police Department. "I was 26 when I entered the Police Academy and I was a policeman for 17 years," he says of his time spent on the force as a motorcycle cop and traffic officer. Unfortunately, he reports that he never did get to experience the delicious irony of being recognized as wise-guy Eddie while handing someone a speeding ticket. "When you get pulled over by a policeman, you don't see a face — you see a badge and a gun and a leather jacket. So I wasn't recognized by civilians. As well, not only do people only see the policeman, but in the areas I worked, in East L.A. and South L.A., the economic standard was such that probably half of the people I stopped had never seen a TV set before, let alone *Leave It to Beaver*. Many of them were illegal immigrants and those were really bad neighborhoods.

"Of course, all the other police personnel were well aware of my time as Eddie Haskell and I would get constant ribbing in role call and such. But if I didn't, I'd have thought they didn't like me, so that was fine. That was great."

While in the line of duty, Osmond was shot three times while running after a suspected car thief. He was saved by his bullet-proof vest, a metal belt buckle and a quick-thinking partner. Some time after that, he retired from active duty with the police force.

In 1983, CBS aired a TV reunion movie entitled *Still the Beaver*, which brought back all the principals from the original series including Osmond and of course, Jerry Mathers as the Beaver. Public response was so positive that the Disney Channel brought it back as a series, *Still the Beaver*, in 1985. In 1986, the series moved to superstation TBS and became a syndicated series as *The New Leave It to Beaver* and ran for the next three years.

Eddie Haskell was now a somewhat shady contractor and the Haskell homestead was on the wrong side of the tracks in Mayfield. Eddie was probably the closest the town had to white trash. Osmond's real life sons, Eric and Christian, played his TV sons, Freddie and Bomber. The youngest, Bomber, was off at military school most of the time but Freddie was a regular character who hung around with the teenaged son of Wally Cleaver. He was a chip off the old block but whereas the new Eddie was abrasive, his young lad was smooth as silk.

Osmond says he neither encouraged nor discouraged his son Eric from auditioning for the new show. "As the show went on, I did discourage the notion of the industry as a way of life and as a career because it is so unpredictable. I tried to keep it in perspective for him and his attitude was that it's fun and it will pay for college."

Osmond is a good authority on the usual fate awaiting most child actors. For most of them, there is no reunion series 20 years down the line. Today, Osmond manages several rental companies as well as being the president of his local water company in the small California town in which he lives with his wife, Sandi.

He says that neither acting nor his time on the police force represented the biggest challenge of his life. In real life, he's a conservative family man and the character he most closely resembles from his old show is—dare we say it, Ward Cleaver, the patriarch of the Cleaver clan, who was played by Hugh Beaumont. Undoubtedly a figure worth aspiring to, Ward was a firm but loving father, forever making mistakes as a parent but always willing to admit them.

"I try to be that kind of father," says Osmond. "I'll tell you, there is nothing in the world harder than being a good father — unless it's being a good mother. It's an extremely difficult job and I would like to *think* I'm like Ward Cleaver, but I *know* realistically that I fall very short of it."

You know, that's just how Ward would have put it.

Ken Osmond Credits

Film Credits

1. *Leave It to Beaver;* 1997; Eddie Haskell Sr.
2. *Dead Women in Lingerie;* 1991; David
3. *C'Mon, Let's Live a Little;* 1967; The Beard
4. *Everything But the Truth;* 1956; (uncredited) Oren Cunningham
5. *Good Morning Miss Dove;* 1955; Tommy Baker at age 9
6. *So Big;* 1953; (uncredited) Eugene, age 9

TELEVISION CREDITS

1. *The New Leave It to Beaver;* TV series; 1985–1989; Eddie Haskell
2. *High School U.S.A.;* TV movie; 1983; Baxter Franklin
3. *Still the Beaver;* TV movie; 1983; Eddie Haskell
4. *Leave It to Beaver;* TV series; 1957–1963; Eddie Haskell

NOTABLE TV GUEST APPEARANCES

1. *Parker Lewis Can't Lose;* Eddie Haskell; 8/11/1991
2. *Happy Days;* Freddie Bascomb; 11/22/1983
3. *Lassie;* Motorcyclist; 2/19/1967
4. *The Munsters;* John; 4/14/1966
5. *Petticoat Junction;* Harold Boggs; 6/9/1964
6. *Circus Boy;* 3/24/1957
7. *Annie Oakley;* 8/26/1956
8. *Lassie;* 1954

Ron Palillo

Arnold Horshack on *Welcome Back, Kotter*

The most-feared occupational hazard of all second bananas is type-casting. Sometimes it can work for you — Don Knotts has managed to work steadily throughout his career just by doing variations on Barney Fife. However, most of the really memorable supporting players only see the other side of that double-edged sword known as typecasting — an abrupt end to their career. Ironically, in doing such a good job as an actor, they become so strongly identified with that one role that casting directors are unwilling to try them in anything else.

The effect on their career is immediate. As Barney Fife would have put it, typecasting "nips it in the bud." "Well, it nipped mine," agrees Ron Palillo, who played the reedy nasal-voiced Sweathog, Arnold Horshack, for four seasons on ABC-TV's *Welcome Back Kotter* in the late 1970s.

Following *Kotter's* cancellation in 1979, Palillo found that his agent couldn't even get him auditions for other parts. The rejection hit Palillo hard both emotionally and psychologically. For four years he went into seclusion and at his lowest point was afraid to even leave his apartment building. There was a good chance that Palillo might share the eventual fate of many former second bananas — a self-imposed hiatus from the industry while carrying on a love-hate relationship with the role that was their greatest claim to fame.

Palillo, however, is the exception to that cliché. He snapped out of it, took a good hard look at himself and then took matters into his own hands. He also returned to where he began — working in the theatre. "If you keep your nose to the grindstone and really figure out what it is you *want*, then you can eventually break the typecasting problem — and I have. But it took almost a decade to do it," he says.

He began by ending his physical resemblance to Arnold Horshack. He started working out in the gym and plastic surgery to his nose and chin erased Horshack's recognizable beak. He then made the decision to return to the theatre.

"It was a matter of getting up the guts and just saying, 'I'm getting out of Los Angeles and moving back to New York and finding out why I got into show business in the first place.' And I sold everything I had, moved back to New York and within a year, I was doing all the things I ever wanted to do. During that first year, I played Mozart in *Amadeus*, I did Nathan Detroit in *Guys and Dolls*, I did the lead in a film called *Wind* and I directed a play. But I couldn't have done all that without leaving Los Angeles and that Hollywood mindset."

Palillo was born in Cheshire, Connecticut, on April 2, 1954. As a child he had his first experience with acting. Although the circumstances were tragic, it turned out to be the best thing in the world for him. "When I was 10 years old, my father died of lung cancer. And I started stuttering the very next day," he says.

"To get me to stop stuttering, my mother got me involved in the local Little Theatre company and indeed, the stutter stopped — and I've never left the theatre." That first play was *The Happy Time* and was a coming of age story set in the 1940s. He did more work with that group and then at the age of 14, started his own theatre company, The Blackfriars Summer Theatre. Palillo acted, directed, did the publicity and sold programs. "We put on shows that we had no business doing at that age, but were very successful. One was *Who's Afraid of Virginia Woolf?* I was 17 and still sounded like Mickey Mouse."

The company continued through his high school years. Palillo attended Cheshire High School where he also took part in the drama club annual productions.

He studied drama at the University of Connecticut in the early 1970s. "They waived all their undergraduate requirements for me," he brags. "I was sort of the Boy Wonder of the Drama department." Graduating in 1973, Palillo received a National Endowment of the Arts award and worked in Florida at the Players Theatre in Miami where he performed in Shakespeare's *Twelfth Night*. He also played in their production of *The Last Sweet Days of Isaac* while flying back to Hartford to film a televised version which his university drama class was doing for the local PBS station. "So it was very interesting to be playing the same character simultaneously because he was played in two completely different ways for both productions."

His big break came in 1975, after a year in *The Hot'L Baltimore* in New York's Circle in the Square, when he was signed to *Welcome Back Kotter* starring Gabe Kaplan as a young Brooklyn high school teacher. Palillo, John Travolta, Robert Hegyes and Lawrence Hilton-Jacobs played the Sweathogs— a motley group of inner-city juvenile delinquents who were (and this could only happen in a Hollywood sitcom) still attending school on a daily basis.

Originally the characters were like those in Gabe Kaplan's comedy routines on which the series was based. They were a genuinely tough bunch of hoods and thugs. When ABC saw the pilot they balked at that approach and so someone suggested that the Sweathogs be more like the Marx Brothers. Horshack was the runt of the bunch. A skinny, goofy class clown with a gleeful moronic laugh, he got to hang around the other cooler Sweathogs due to his wit ("Up your nose with a rubber hose") and the fact that he was easy to pick on.

Palillo brought to the role an occasionally lilting voice — modeled after an aunt's speech pattern — and his father's wheezing laugh. Throw in some shameless mugging and you have a guaranteed scene-stealing performance. Palillo was more than able to hold his own in scenes with Travolta or accomplished stand-up comic Kaplan.

"Gabe Kaplan was our Mary Tyler Moore character," points out Palillo. "He was the norm. He certainly had a slant and an edge to him but he was the norm in our little universe of crazy planets that were revolving around him. He was the sun, we were the planets—*oooh*, what a terrible analogy, that *is* awful! But you have to have a norm so that everyone can bounce off him and Gabe was that."

Over the course of the series, Horshack went from boy to something resembling a man. Initially, it seemed that he wasn't too bright and eventually it turned out that he was the smartest kid in class—he only acted stupid as a way of fitting in with his friends. "Originally Horshack was the class loser," says Palillo. "He also had no family life that we saw on the show. Belonging to the Sweathogs gave him security. He began to stand up for himself. He never would have done that in the beginning of the series."

Palillo's Horshack became so popular that the producers of *Kotter* tried him out in a pilot called *Horshack* in 1979. "I think the pilot was a really good show," he says. "It had a good supporting cast. Andrea McArdle who hadn't done *Annie* yet was my little sister, Ellen Travolta played my mother and *Kotter* producer James Komack was my uncle. It was a very cute show. I just saw it again recently on a *Kotter* marathon and I thought, 'Geez, what a funny show!'

"However, in hindsight, if it had been successful, I probably would have been stuck playing Arnold Horshack for the rest of my life. At the time, it would have been a feather in my cap and would have been very lucrative but it would have sealed my fate as an actor. Had it been picked up, I don't think I would have been offered the chance to play Nazi war criminal Adolf Eichmann in a one-man show. So it was probably for the best — but it was certainly a heartbreaker when it happened."

ABC cancelled *Kotter* that same year and that was the end of *Horshack*. But even during *Kotter's* four-year run, Palillo was worried about becoming typecast as the loveable dork and face a future of similar goofy second-banana roles. "That was one of the things I was afraid of when I was on *Kotter*, that I was going to turn into Don Knotts," he admits.

"And I mean that as a compliment because no one does what Don Knotts does better than Don Knotts. I was real skinny at the time and had no body whatsoever. Even the names had a similar vibration. When you play characters named Barney Fife or Arnold Horshack, you pretty much know what you're going to get. But I was brought up to be a lot of other people. It sounds awfully trite and actors are always being made fun of for this, but I really was brought up doing Shakespeare and drama. Comedy was just something that I sort of fell into. I truly, truly, truly didn't want to turn into Don Knotts— and again, I think Don Knotts is brilliant — but I didn't want to turn into him and always have to play Barney. So I've really had to make a concerted effort to show my versatility and it's finally starting to pay off."

Back in New York, Palillo spent a year on the soap *One Life to Live* playing a sleazy blackjack dealer, and still makes the occasional television guest shot. Although he's had major roles in movies with names like *Friday the 13th Part VI*, *Hellgate*, *Skatetown U.S.A.* and the *Snake Eater* series, he doesn't really like to talk about them. "Don't even go there," he cries in mock exasperation when the topic is broached. "Don't go *near* there! There are *no* movies there. No movies!"

He's far more willing to talk about his sometimes career as an artist. He has illustrated two children's books, *The Red Wings of Christmas* by Wesley Eure and *A Gift for the Contessa* by Michael Mele, both for Pelican Publishing.

For his work as an illustrator, he uses the old family name, Ron Paolillo, in memory of his father. "I learned to draw on my father's knees as a kid," he says. But although it has turned into a part-time income at times, it was never anything he considered doing as a living. "Not ever. I always found it boring in the end. It's a facility or talent that I can do well but it's interesting to me for oh, maybe a month out of the year."

Unlike many of his peers, he's not itching to get back on TV. Instead, he has a thriving theatre career and is often on the road nine months out of the year. He's done everything from *Richard III* to *I Hate Hamlet*. He has played the flamboyant and urbane Truman Capote in *Holiday Memories* and also toured the Midwest for nine months with Becky Moran in *The Four-Poster*, a comedy which covers 45 years of a couple's life from 1895 to 1940 and takes place in their bedroom. He's returned to playing George in *Who's Afraid of Virginia Woolf?* He also played the Artful Dodger in *Oliver* as a kid and then later in his career revisited the show as Fagan. There has been a number of musicals and revivals—*Oklahoma!*, *How to Succeed in Business Without Really Trying* and *Guys and Dolls* as Nathan Detroit (can you imagine Horshack in the Frank Sinatra role?).

But these days, the Horshack reference seldom comes up. Part of the credit has to go to the approach he takes in accepting new work. No longer does he purposely take on a role just to further distance himself from Horshack. There's no need for that now. Instead, he likes to do characters which are completely unlike what he was doing in his previous project.

As an example, he points out that his current project is the one-man show about Nazi war criminal Adolf Eichmann. The play he was in before that was Noel Coward's *Blithe Spirit*. After *Eichmann* he will be playing King Arthur in the musical *Camelot*. "And you can't get any further away from Adolf Eichmann than either of those two roles. But why be an actor if you're not going to gamble with the work that you do?"

But to do all of that he had to get out of Los Angeles where theatre is seen as a stepping stone to get into TV or films. "My last year in L.A., I did *P.S. Your Cat is Dead*, which was supposed to run for six weeks but ran for seven months and for which I won a L.A. Dramalogue Best Actor Award. And as far as the movie and television businesses were concerned, they couldn't have cared less.

"And so I said, 'Wait a minute, I didn't get into this for that!' I use theatre not as a stepping stone to an end. It is not a means to an end, it *is* the end. It is the thing that gives me the greatest joy — and hopefully the thing that I do that gives an audience a lot of joy.

"And I'm not going to use it as a means to getting onto a TV series again. Theatre is too important to me. But that's the way I feel and so I had to get out of that town. It took a great deal of guts to do it but it's the smartest thing I ever did."

Like the other Sweathogs, Palillo will probably never make as much money in a lifetime as the former head Sweathog Travolta now makes for one movie, but he says he doesn't mind. "I *love* the theatre," he enthuses. "I adore theatre. That's what I was put on this earth to do."

Palillo is at peace with his television past. He talks about a review for his performance as Eichmann: "The reviewer said something to the effect that, who would have thought that the guy that had the braying laugh on a TV sitcom could be so multi-faceted and give such depth to a performance and that it shows the power of television to eat up actors and spit them out even when they don't deserve it. Well, you know what? I don't feel spat out anymore."

In 1996, Palillo made a number of rare television appearances on *Ellen* — as 'himself.' One of the supporting characters on that show had an obsessive crush on him from his *Kotter* days and so Palillo found himself back in Los Angeles, which is also where the series was set. "I only did three episodes but the Audrey character talked about me for the entire season," he says. "You can't buy better publicity than that."

More satisfying, however, were his last words on the show when he says good-bye to Audrey. "I can't stay here," he tells her. "In New York, I'm considered a serious actor."

Ron Palillo Credits

FILM CREDITS

1. *Wind;* 1992; Tony
2. *Snake Eater II: The Drug Buster;* 1991; Torchy
3. *Snake Eater;* 1990; Torchy
4. *Hellgate;* 1989; Mim
5. *Committed;* 1988; Ronnie
6. *Friday the 13th Part VI: Jason Lives;* 1986; Allen Hewes
7. *Doin' Time;* 1985; Pappion
8. *Skatetown U.S.A.;* 1979; Frankey

TV CREDITS

1. *One Life to Live;* TV series; 1986
2. *Rubik, the Amazing Cube;* TV series; 1983; (voice) Rubik
3. *The Invisible Woman;* TV movie; 1983
4. *Welcome Back, Kotter;* TV series; 1975–1979; Arnold Horshack

NOTABLE TV GUEST APPEARANCES

1. *Ellen;* Himself; 5/15/1996
2. *Ellen;* Himself; 5/8/1996
3. *Ellen;* Himself; 1/3/1996
4. *Mr. Rhodes;* Arnold Horshack; 1996
5. *CHiPS;* Nick; 2/6/1983
6. *The A-Team;* Reporter; 1/23/1983

Tom Poston

George Utley on *Newhart*;
Franklin Delano Bickley on *Mork and Mindy*

255

Don Knotts has this to say about his old colleague from *The Steve Allen Show* — "Tom Poston is a very funny guy, but he can be both funny and serious. Tom's a helluva actor. He's just a good fine actor and whatever you give him, he does well."

He's right. Although Poston is largely known as a supporting comic for his television work, he can and has done everything. He has played the lead in feature films and in Broadway productions. He's done everything from Shakespeare to musicals to game shows. Adept both at comedy and drama, Poston has never been a discriminating show business snob and during the 1960s, as a regular panelist on *To Tell the Truth*, he would often tape the game show during the day and appear in a Broadway show that night.

One of the reasons for Poston's longevity in the business is his innate likeability. With his guileless face and unflappable manner, he is a television Everyman. Today, he is best known in that capacity for his role as the good-natured handyman George Utley on *Newhart*. However, to an earlier generation, he performed the same function as one of the stock company of supporting players on *The Steve Allen Show*. The sad thing is, even though he was rewarded for both those roles by his peers, to the public, his performances seem so effortless that he seldom gets the credit he deserves as an actor. He makes it all look so easy.

Although it was Steve Allen's Sunday night variety show which brought Poston to the attention of the rest of America, before that he had been a familiar face on Broadway for years.

Poston's show business career began early. Born on October 17, 1921, he grew up in Columbus, Ohio, where, at the age of nine, he began performing as a vaudeville tumbler in an acrobatic troupe called The Flying Zebleys. During high school, he did his first acting when he joined the drama club as a way of pleasing a favorite teacher. He didn't consider it as a potential career choice. Instead, he wanted to follow in the footsteps of his father, a noted chemist. With that goal in mind, he enrolled at Bethany College in West Virginia as a chemistry major.

It's very possible that if World War II had not occurred, Poston would have lived out the rest of his life as a chemist. However, when his studies were interrupted by war, Poston and his brother Richard enlisted in the Air Corps in 1941. He served as a combat fighter in Europe and was later awarded for his part in dropping paratroopers in the D-Day invasion. By the time he left the service in 1945, he had risen to the rank of Captain.

Back in the States after the war, Poston and his brother had planned on going into some sort of business together in which they could use their flying skills. Once again, another career option closed when Poston read a magazine article about Charles Jehlinger, then the creative head of the American Academy of Dramatic Arts in New York. Poston was so impressed with the man and his philosophy that he felt he had to study under him no matter what he taught. Thusly inspired, the former Flying Zebley and fighter pilot set his cap on the far more ethereal life of a career actor and began classes at the Academy.

Months later, he made his debut on Broadway by falling down a flight of stairs in *Cyrano de Bergerac*. Luckily, it was a scripted fall and his small role called for him to nightly fall down the stairs on cue. Poston was still in school when the opportunity came up in 1946 to appear in Jose Ferrer's production of *Cyrano*.

It was with the financial assistance of his brother and the G.I. Bill that Poston was able to attend the Academy. In addition to Jehlinger, he studied under Sanford Meisner, Paton Price and Frank Pacelli. Upon graduating in 1948, he was immediately back on Broadway again courtesy of Ferrer in *The Insect Comedy*.

Poston followed that up in 1950 by appearing in the Broadway production of *King Lear*. The same year, he showed his versatility (and willingness to do any type of work) by landing his first job in the new medium of television. His role on the live Saturday afternoon children's sci-fi series *Tom Corbett, Space Cadet* was not only his first TV experience, but his first job as a regular performer on television. He played the Mercurian Leader — bent on conquering Earth for takeover by the planet Mercury.

Although the first year of the decade was one in which he showcased his classical training in Shakespeare as well as a knack for out-of-this-world villainy on television, Poston established himself as a Broadway fixture during the 1950s because of his natural abilities as a light comedian. His affable stage persona made him ideally suited for comedy and producers took advantage of that by casting him in a number of shows throughout the decade.

In 1953 he toured in the Broadway production of *Bell, Book and Candle* and appeared regularly on television in the soap opera *Hawkins Falls, Population 6,200* as Toby Winfield. That experience qualified him for his role in 1955 in *The Grand Prize,* Broadway's take on the lunacy of television. In 1956, he had his first starring role on Broadway as the baggy-pants top banana in *The Best of Burlesque.*

By the time that Poston was lampooning television in *The Grand Prize,* he was a familiar enough face in New York to be asked to host a local TV variety series called *Entertainment.* While hosting the show, he was noticed by television personality Steve Allen and after that, his future on television was assured. In 1956, he joined *The Steve Allen Show* and along with fellow supporting players Louis Nye and Don Knotts, he became a member of the most revered troupe of second bananas in television history.

Legend has it that Poston was so nervous at his audition for the show that he momentarily forgot his own name. Thus was born his best known character on the show — the perennially befuddled amnesiac from The Man on the Street interviews. The character is so surprised at being stopped unawares that he becomes too flustered to even answer the first question, "What is your name, sir?" Poston's response was a moment of genuine puzzlement followed by a look of mild panic and embarrassment and then determination to remember. He had the look of someone who knew the answer was right on the tip of his tongue but before he had a chance to spit it out, Allen would interrupt with something like, "Well, moving right along...."

It's a tribute to Poston's talents as a comic that he was able to keep this recurring gag fresh week after week. Done by anyone else it could easily have been unconvincing, annoying or cartoonish. Poston, however, turned it into his signature piece on the show and it was largely responsible for his Emmy win in 1958 as Best Supporting Actor in a Comedy Series.

His theatrical experience as a light comedian made Poston a natural addition to *The Steve Allen Show*. The genial Poston was mild-mannered, almost unflappable and his presence provided a much needed contrast to his more wild and manic co-stars. Comedy sketches on the show were typically zany and off the wall. Improvisation was encouraged in rehearsals and as long as the performers could pull them off, ad-libs were welcomed during the live show. The show often had the feel of flying-by-the-seat-of-your-pants broadcasting. In spirit, *The Steve Allen Show* most closely resembled the movies of the Marx Brothers.

As a long-time fan of the brothers Marx, Poston fit right in with the show's controlled chaos. He spent three seasons with the New York–based series from 1956 to 1959 and then returned for what proved to be its final season when the show moved to Hollywood in 1961.

With his ready wit and experience working in front of a studio audience, it was inevitable that Poston would become a game-show personality. In 1958, he was invited to be one of the celebrity panelists on *To Tell the Truth* along with Kitty Carlisle, Orson Bean and Peggy Cass. Poston once described his first experience on the popular prime time game show this way — "My first performance on *Truth* was a classic. I spilled a glass of water all over Kitty Carlisle's dress. The audience roared, so I turned and said, 'What's so funny?' I picked up the glass and gestured at them with it, not realizing that the glass was still half-full. The water hit a lady in the front row, and she happened to be the producer's wife. A real classy beginning, eh?"[1]

That inauspicious debut was just the beginning of a 10-year association with the show for Poston. As well, after a few months on *Truth,* he was signed in 1959 to host his own game show, *Split Personality.* The daily afternoon show, which only ran for one season, featured audience participation.

The late 1950s and early '60s were some of the most productive in Poston's career. He was able to show off his versatility in drama as well as comedy while starring in a wide range of entertainment vehicles. While working on *To Tell the Truth* and *The Steve Allen Show,* he was still active on Broadway. In 1958, he played a tipsy attorney in *Drink To Me Only.* The next year he met and co-starred with his future wife, Suzanne Pleshette, in the Broadway farce *The Golden Fleecing,* written by Lorenzo Semple Jr. (best remembered today as the chief writer of the *Batman* TV series). Pleshette played Poston's love interest in the play. In 1961, he starred again on Broadway in the musical comedy *The Conquering Hero,* written by Larry Gelbart (best known for TV's *M*A*S*H*) and choreographed by Bob Fosse. Poston played Woodrow Truesmith, a would-be Marine who missed out on any active participation in World War II because of his hay fever and yet finds himself acclaimed as a returning hero and nominated for Mayor in his hometown.

During this time he also showcased his classical training and theatrical experience on TV by acting in a special television production of Shakespeare's *The Tempest* in 1960 with Richard Burton and Maurice Evans. The following year he was in the Ethel Merman special called *Merman on Broadway.*

Poston's stage persona as the slightly frazzled Everyman made him an ideal choice for his first film work, the starring role in the 1962 movie *Zotz!* As was the case with much of his stage roles, here he played an unlikely hero who is caught up in circumstances beyond his control. The film was produced by William Castle, the B-movie director celebrated for his low-budget horror movies and gimmicky publicity stunts. *Zotz,* however, was a bit of a departure for Castle and is more fantasy instead of horror and the emphasis is on comedy rather than chills.

Poston played Jonathan Jones, a college linguistics professor who finds an ancient coin with magical powers. The coin can slow down time so that people move in slow motion. It can also make someone experience sudden pain and even death if the owner points their finger and says, "Zotz!" By today's standards, these are pretty lame special effects— slowing down the film or instructing the actors to double over as if in pain. Surprisingly, they only add to the film's considerable charm. The professor offers the coin to the U.S. government, but is dismissed as a crank and both he and the coin fall into the hands of foreign enemy agents. Mayhem ensues.

The following year, Poston starred in the Castle-directed film *The Old Dark House,* which was produced by England's Hammer Films. The movie was a remake of the 1932 horror classic of the same name, which itself was a variation on the play *Ten Little Indians.* Poston played Tom Penderel, an American car salesman living in England. He receives a mysterious invitation to spend the weekend at the isolated mansion of an eccentric millionaire. Others have also been invited and they start getting killed off one by one. Poston's easy-going manner is a comic contrast to the escalating death count occurring around him. Again, he is put in the role of the reluctant hero as he tries to figure out who is committing the murders—and why—before he too becomes a victim.

The Castle films were Poston's only work in motion picture lead roles. Fortunately, he was realistic in his expectations regarding a film career and what sort of work he could do. Given his background in comedy, it's not surprising that he once said, "I'd like to do an old-fashioned comedy. I have no ambition to be another Clark Gable, Leslie Howard or John Gilbert. My real dream is to make films like those of Charlie Chaplin, Laurel and Hardy and the Marx Brothers. There's nothing like that around anymore."[2]

He almost got the chance to do that kind of classic slapstick comedy on television when he was cast in Buck Henry and Mel Brooks' TV pilot for their proposed series, *Get Smart*—a spoof of the James Bond spy movies of the time. However, the pilot was being made for ABC-TV and when a short-sighted ABC executive read the script and didn't get the humor, the project was turned down. That ended Poston's involvement. As he explained later, "When ABC rejected the proposal, Mel took it to NBC who liked it and said it would be a good vehicle for Don Adams—who was under contract to them while I wasn't—and the rest as they say, is history."[3]

Poston took it all in stride and has no regrets—in fact, he even appeared on the series as a guest star, playing a mad scientist KAOS agent in one episode. "I have never had anything but admiration for Don and what he did with the show," Poston said. "It was completely different from anything I would have done, I'm sure."[4]

True, it is hard to imagine anyone but Don Adams in the role of Maxwell Smart. However, as in his work with similar material in *Zotz* shows, Poston would have been able to pull it off and make the role his own. Poston's Agent 86 would have probably been more baffled than stupid.

Unfortunately, that was Poston's last shot at the lead role on a television series. The majority of the rest of his roles on television have been in supporting roles. Fortunately, that is a job at which he excels.

Throughout the 1960s and early '70s, Poston continued to work in theatre. He starred in productions of *A Funny Thing Happened on the Way to the Forum*, *Come Blow Your Horn*, *40 Carats* and *Romanoff and Juliet* on Broadway. In regional theatre, he showed he was capable of more than light comedy in productions of *Richard III*, *Romeo and Juliet*, *Mother Courage* and *The Crucible*. He also once again did *Cyrano de Bergerac*—this time in the title role, played Tevye in *Fiddler on the Roof* and has played both Oscar and Felix in productions of *The Odd Couple*.

Theatre would be a constant source of work and personal satisfaction throughout his career. He enjoyed the creative challenge of being a stage actor. As he once put it, "The film process is so powerful that, as you stand and speak, you can't alter the image. But, in a play, the character is very rarely drawn to fit the artist. Almost always, the playwright draws the characters as he sees them through his own imagination and it's up to the actor to portray it that way."[5]

Nonetheless, by the mid–1970s, Poston had made a big return to television and it was largely due to his experience on *The Bob Newhart Show,* guest-starring as Cliff Murdock, a character that had been specifically created with Poston in mind. He had known Newhart since the early '60s when Newhart was working as a nightclub comedian. Their long friendship was wonderfully used to advantage on the show whenever Cliff— Bob Hartley's old college roommate —came to town for a visit.

In college, Cliff had been nicknamed "The Peeper." Hartley's nickname was "Moon." No explanation is really necessary in understanding how they earned these titles while attending college in the late 1950s. However, although Hartley had become a doctor of psychology and had left his past behind, Cliff was still the practical-joking prankster he had been in his school days— he had once filled Bob's socks with pieces of raw chicken. For some reason, Hartley thought Cliff was the funniest guy in the world and during visits by the Peeper, he was constantly cracking up. Those visits brought out a side of Bob that was seldom seen in the normally level-headed psychologist. On the other hand, Bob's wife Emily tried her best to tolerate the Peeper when he and her husband would spend the night reminiscing about the good old days and trying to out-do each other with corny practical jokes.

Poston found the Newhart show experience to be so much fun that he began to concentrate his career on other supporting roles on television. In 1975, in the prison sitcom *On the Rocks,* he played Mr. Sullivan, the easy-going cell block guard. On *We've Got Each Other,* in 1977, he played Damon Jerome, an absent-minded photographer. In 1979, he joined the cast of *Mork and Mindy.* This time he was cast against type and played the cranky next-door neighbor, Franklin Delano Bickley.

Mork and Mindy made a star of Robin Williams. Poston, who doesn't talk much about his own work, once said something about co-star Pam Dawber that speaks volumes about his understanding and insight on how to play a role opposite a more overwhelming and larger-than-life character. It was undoubtedly something he learned years earlier himself on *The Steve Allen Show*. "I tell you, that Pam Dawber is a genius," he said. "She was able to make *Mork and Mindy* be about Mindy and Mork and not just Mork. She didn't do it by being forceful, dynamic or overpowering, she did it by playing Mindy so well."[6]

Poston stayed with the show for three years and went directly from there to be reunited with Bob Newhart on *Newhart* in 1982. Unlike their first collaboration, Poston's role of handyman George Utley had not been written with him in mind. In fact, it had been created for Jerry Van Dyke. Barry Kemp, the creator-producer of *Newhart*, had gotten his start in show business as a writer for Van Dyke years earlier. When he and Newhart came up with the idea of setting the new series in a New England country inn, Kemp created the character of the slow-witted handyman as a way of saying thanks to Van Dyke. However, after being promised the role, either through the wishes of Newhart or the network (no one is saying), the part of George Utley was offered to Poston — much to the extreme displeasure of Van Dyke.

As originally conceived, the role of the country bumpkin caretaker is one that Van Dyke could have done in his sleep. But it's doubtful that the character would have evolved as it did in Poston's hands. Poston brought an intelligence to the character and his George Utley wasn't nearly as thick as you were led to believe. He played someone who was supposed to be a buffoon but did so without being a buffoon. It's doubtful that Van Dyke would have brought the same depth to the character. Poston is a subtle actor; Van Dyke is a broad comedian. For proof, all you have to do is look at Van Dyke's supporting work in Kemp's next series, *Coach*. His character, assistant football coach Luther Van Damme, started out as a fast-food gorging, lazy slob–and remained that way for the entirety of the series' eight-year run. There was no resultant animosity between the two veteran actors— although Poston later guest-starred in an episode of *Coach* as Luther's agent and they had a knock-down fist fight. Van Dyke's approach to comedy might have clashed with Newhart's low-key style. Poston, however, could also be low-key and he and Newhart already had a history of knowing how to play off each other.

On the other hand, Poston's George Utley grew as a character. As the series went on, it was clear that in many ways, George was the smartest guy on the show. He was certainly the most practical, had the most common sense and was a better judge of character than the others. But all of that wasn't conveyed just through the scripts. Poston has the most guileless face on TV and it was often only the twinkle in his eyes that betrayed what George was thinking — or if he was even thinking at all. For someone who was supposedly thick, he could be sharp as a tack — or not. You just never knew with George.

When the character was first introduced on the show, Newhart's character, Dick Loudon and his wife, Joanna, had just moved from New York and bought the Stratford Inn, almost on a whim. They were newcomers and early episodes exploited that fish-out-of-water scenario. One of the wisest decisions the producers made after Poston was cast as the handyman was to keep the relationship between George and Dick as that of employee and boss rather than falling back on their chemistry on *The Bob Newhart Show* and have them be best buddies. There was more comic potential to have the two characters in a workplace setting with one being in a supervisory position over the other.

George was a lifelong Vermont native and his family had taken care of the Stratford Inn for the past 200 years. He came from a long line of handymen who had taken care of the inn. The premise was also a good way of using George as a foil for Dick. It presented many opportunities to set up Dick to look stupid and then get one of Newhart's patented reaction shots. Dick Loudon was the author of a series of "How-To" books — but George was the real thing. Dick may have written the books about repairs and home improvements, but George knew the more easy and practical way of doing things.

In fact, George was a regular Mr. Handyman –and that was his life. The viewer often got the impression that George lived in his own little world. Other than his weekly Lodge meetings, he didn't have much of a social life. He went to bed early and was up early the next morning having breakfast in the dining room with Dick and Joanna and then it was off to work.

The handyman's uniform of denim overalls, tool belt and cap looked natural on George. His father and grandfather and great-grandfather had all been handymen at the Stratford and this was a source of pride for him. He lived for his job. At one point, he invented a board game, "Handyman," in which opponents moved their men around the board, picking up points for various chores. It didn't catch on because it didn't have an ending — you just kept forever going round and round working and working. But as far as George was concerned, everyone was a winner because they were a handyman. In the last episode of the series, a Japanese developer buys up the town and everyone becomes millionaires. With his new riches, George plans to open "Utleyland," a theme park for handymen.

Dick Loudon's biggest complaint and source of frustration with George was that he kept missing the point of things. Dick would explain something and George would just stand there with the same blank look on his face. In that sense, George was a close relation to the character Poston played on *The Steve Allen Show* — the guy who couldn't remember his own name. But with George, you were never quite sure if he genuinely didn't understand Dick's question or if it was just such a stupid request that he took for granted that anyone would know the answer.

The only clues to what George was thinking could be found in that glint in his eyes or on those lips that always seemed to verge on breaking into a sly smile. The role of George Utley could have come off as a dolt in the hands of someone not as deft as Poston. His was a disarming goofiness. He did it by portraying the character in a way that didn't insult the viewer's intelligence.

The producers and Newhart obviously approved of the approach Poston took. After the second season, the entire supporting cast had been changed — only Poston remained. They weren't the only ones who liked his work. Over *Newhart's* eight seasons, he was nominated for Outstanding Supporting Actor in a Comedy Series three times — in 1984, '86 and '87.

Part of the reason Poston looked so happy on the show was that it was a happy set. The star sets the tone on a sitcom and Newhart's sets had a reputation for being tension free. Poston once said of Newhart's sets, "They are the most orderly in town. He absolutely insists that everyone do his job exactly right and with the least fuss."[7]

Like many other co-workers, he also remarked on Newhart's willingness to share laugh lines. "Newhart is generous. He permits everybody to do the job," he once said.[8] On another occasion he simply noted that, "Everything Bob does rings true, both on and off camera. If Bob wants to keep doing *Newhart,* and he wants me to be on it, I'll be happy to do it until we both fade into the sunset."[9]

On the topic of his own work, Poston is notoriously tight-lipped. Just like George Utley, he has always taken a humble attitude towards his considerable achievements. Rather than blow his own horn, he prefers to let the performance speak for itself. He once admitted, "Even my own work, I don't comment on very often. I don't try to figure it out — I try to just do it."[10]

So it is of little surprise that when he was once asked about his characterization on *Newhart,* Poston replied, "George Utley is a leading man, a very heroic, very romantic character."[11] Of course, that's the kind of tongue-in-cheek answer one might expect from the typically droll Poston. Then again, that might be *exactly* how he himself viewed the character. After all, even though George was set in his ways, it was because he was from an earlier time. He had integrity and values— all from the Handyman's Code which had been passed down from his ancestors. So, in that respect, George was indeed a heroic and romantic figure.

After Newhart called it quits on *Newhart* in 1990, Poston played the father of Howie Mandel's character on *Good Grief,* a 1990 sitcom set in a funeral home. Only someone with his innate likeability could have played Ringo Prowley, a con man who schemed widows and the bereaved out of their money.

Poston had appeared in all of Bob Newhart's sitcoms. Even in *George and Leo,* a sitcom where Newhart shared the top billing with Judd Hirsch, Poston took part in the popular "Cameo Episode" which reunited past members of Newhart's two series as well as from Hirsch's *Taxi.* He was back again with Newhart on *Bob,* the short-lived 1992 series where Newhart played a 50-year-old comic book artist. Poston had a recurring role as Newhart's poker buddy, Jerry Fleisher. It was a part as far removed from George Utley as possible. In their first episode together, he made a blatant pass at Bob's wife.

In 1995, Poston joined the cast of *Grace Under Fire.* For three seasons he played Floyd Norton, father of the character played by Dave Thomas from *SCTV.* He continues to work, not only on TV, but in big budget feature films, such as the 1999 Rob Reiner comedy, *The Story of Us,* and the 1998 Richard Dreyfuss film, *Krippendorf's Tribe.*

At the age of 80, Poston shows no signs of slowing down and still shows up at open auditions in the hope of getting a guest shot on a sitcom. Actor Jack Riley, who played Elliot Carlin on *The Bob Newhart Show,* often sees Poston at those auditions and speculates that "With someone like Tom Poston, he just loves working. I can understand that — because it's fun. He loves it, as I do."

Poston has the same attitude about life. At an age where most of his peers are retired and taking it easy, Poston is going strong — doing things like golfing daily, guest starring wherever he can and dating and marrying Suzanne Pleshette. He first met his co-star from *The Bob Newhart Show* in 1959 when they starred together as lovers in *The Golden Fleecing* on Broadway. They dated briefly at the time. On May 16, 2001, they returned to New York to be married. It was the third marriage for the 64-year-old Pleshette and Poston's fourth marriage. His golden years are proving to be the stuff that many younger men dream about — and it couldn't have happened to a nicer guy.

Notes

1. *Gentleman* magazine; December 1963; "Who Put the Wry in Tom Poston's Eye?"; by Gene Feehan.
2. *Gentleman*; December 1963.
3. *TV Times* magazine; August 4, 1989; "George Utley as Agent 86?" by Michael Cunliffe.
4. *TV Times*; August 4, 1989.
5. *Gentleman*; December 1963.
6. *TV Times*; August 4, 1989.
7. *TV Guide*; January 1, 1983; "Bob Newhart's Back"; by Bill O'Hallaran.
8. *New York Post*; January 31, 1983; "Poston's New Show a Hit"; by Martin Burden.
9. *TV Times*; January 1, 1983.
10. *Gentleman*; December 1963.
11. *TV Times*; January 1, 1983.

Tom Poston Credits

FILM CREDITS

1. *The Story of Us;* 1999; Harry
2. *The Mercurian Invasion;* 1998; The Mercurian Leader
3. *Krippendorf's Tribe;* 1998; Gordon Harding
4. *Murphy's Laws of Golf;* 1989
5. *Carbon Copy;* 1981; Reverend Hayworth
6. *Up the Academy;* 1980; Sisson
7. *Rabbit Test;* 1978; The Minister
8. *The Happy Hooker;* 1975; J. Arthur Conrad
9. *Cold Turkey;* 1971; Edgar Stopworth
10. *Soldier in the Rain;* 1963; Lieutenant Magee
11. *The Old Dark House;* 1963; Tom Penderel
12. *Zotz!;* 1962

TV CREDITS

1. *Grace Under Fire;* TV series; 1995–1998; Mr. Norton
2. *Bob;* TV series; 1992; Jerry Fleisher
3. *A Quiet Little Neighborhood, a Perfect Little Murder;* TV movie; 1990; Don Corman
4. *Good Grief;* TV series; 1990–1991; Ringo Prowley
5. *Save the Dog!;* TV movie; 1988
6. *Circus of the Stars #13;* TV special; 1988
7. *Fresno;* TV miniseries; 1986; Doc Parseghian
8. *Newhart;* TV series;1982–1990; George Utley

9. *The Girl, the Gold Watch and Dynamite;* TV movie; 1981; Omar
10. *Mork and Mindy;* TV series; 1979–1982; Franklin Delano Bickley
11. *A Guide for the Married Woman;* TV movie; 1978; Marty Gibson
12. *We've Got Each Other;* TV series; 1977; Damon Jerome
13. *The Magnificent Magical Magnet of Santa Mesa;* TV movie; 1977; William Bensinger
14. *On the Rocks;* TV series; 1975; Mr. Sullivan
15. *Steve Allen's Laugh Back;* TV series; 1975; Various characters
16. *That Was the Week That Was;* TV series; 1964; Himself
17. *Merman on Broadway;* TV special; 1961
18. *Showcase Theatre: The Tempest;* TV special; 1960; Trinculo
19. *Split Personality;* TV series; 1959; Host
20. *To Tell the Truth;* TV series; 1958–1968; Panelist
21. *The Steve Allen Show;* TV series; 1956–1961; Various characters
22. *Hawkins Falls, Population 6,200;* TV series; 1953; Toby Winfield
23. *Tom Corbett, Space Cadet;* TV series; 1950; The Mercurian

NOTABLE TV GUEST APPEARANCES

1. *The Lone Gunmen;* Cap'n Toby/Fred Tabalowski; 6/1/2001
2. *ER;* Earl; 5/3/2001
3. *ER;* Earl (combative old man); 2/1/2001
4. *Dharma and Greg;* Dr. Gillespie; 2/22/2000
5. *Malcolm and Eddie;* Garth; 2/21/2000
6. *Diagnosis Murder;* Tom Porter; 9/23/1999
7. *Malcolm and Eddie;* Garth; 9/20/1999
8. *Honey, I Shrunk the Kids;* Uncle Cosmo; 1997
9. *Cosby;* Tim; 4/5/1999
10. *Cosby;* Tim; 2/15/1999
11. *Maggie Winters;* Lester Mulford; 10/21/1998
12. *Touched by an Angel;* Ed; 4/12/1998
13. *Just Shoot Me;* Herb; 4/9/1998
14. *Home Improvement;* Ted; 11/25/1997
15. *Sabrina, the Teenage Witch;* Mortgage Broker; 11/14/1997
16. *George and Leo;* Traffic cop; 11/3/1997
17. *Dr. Quinn, Medicine Woman;* 2/8/1997
18. *The Larry Sanders Show;* Himself; 11/20/1996
19. *Home Improvement;* Ned; 11/19/1996
20. *Murphy Brown;* Old Man Swenson; 10/14/1996
21. *Home Improvement;* The Clerk; 12/12/1995
22. *Coach;* Art Hibke; 11/14/1995
23. *Coach;* Art Hibke; 4/5/1995
24. *Grace Under Fire;* Floyd Norman; 3/14/1995
25. *Grace Under Fire;* Floyd Norton; 3/14/1995
26. *Family Matters;* Mr. Looney; 2/17/1995
27. *Family Matters;* Mr. Looney; 10/14/1994
28. *Murphy Brown;* Old Man Swenson; 2/28/1994

29. *Family Matters;* Mr. Looney; 2/4/1994
30. *Dr. Quinn, Medicine Woman;* 10/30/1993
31. *Dream On;* Sidney "Uncle Bouncy" Barish; 6/2/1993
32. *Coach;* Dr. Hibke; 4/9/1991
33. *The Simpsons;* Capital City Goofball (voice); 11/8/1990
34. *St. Elsewhere;* 5/18/1988
35. *Crazy Like a Fox;* 5/3/1986
36. *CHiPS;* Bill Connor; 2/24/1979
37. *Mork and Mindy;* 1978
38. *The Love Boat;* Mickey O'Day; 12/24/1977
39. *The Bob Newhart Show;* Cliff Murdock; 3/19/1977
40. *Alice;* Jerry; 12/25/1976
41. *The Bob Newhart Show;* Cliff Murdock; 11/20/1976
42. *The Bob Newhart Show;* Cliff Murdock; 9/25/1976
43. *The Bob Newhart Show;* Cliff Murdock; 2/28/1976
44. *The Bob Newhart Show;* Cliff Murdock; 9/13/1975
45. *Get Smart;* Dr. Zharko; 3/1/1969
46. *The Defenders;* 10/1/1964
47. *The Defenders;* 9/24/1964
48. *Thriller;* Charlie Denham; 10/30/1961
49. *The U.S. Steel Hour;* 7/31/1957
50. *The Phil Silvers Show;* Lieutenant; 10/6/1956
51. *Goodyear Television Playhouse;* 7/3/1955

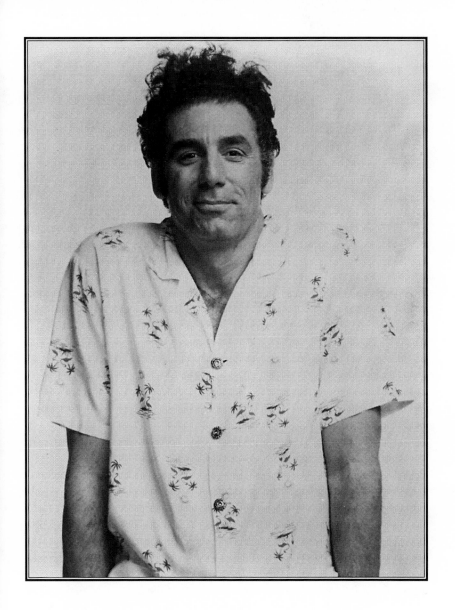

Michael Richards

Cosmo Kramer on *Seinfeld*

In an industry celebrated for having more than its share of egoma-niacs, Michael Richards is a true rarity — an actor who doesn't want to talk about himself. When asked for an interview for this book — a *biographical* study of memorable television sitcom actors— Richards isn't too keen on sharing his life story. "I'm afraid there's not enough material to fill your pages," he apologizes.

Instead of Michael Richards, the man — he wants to talk about Cosmo Kramer, the man. Kramer was the three-dimensional, very "real" human being that he gave life to on *Seinfeld*. Richards says that he is far more interested in discussing the neglected topic of the craft of creating a char-acter.

So be it.

Still, just for the record, let it be known that Michael Richards was born July 23, 1948, in Los Angeles. His father died when he was two years old and he was raised in the L.A. suburb of Culver City by his mother, Phyllis, who worked as a medical records librarian. At the age of 12, Richards realized that he wanted to be an actor when he took his first act-ing classes in school and then played Caliban in a school production of *The Tempest*. After graduating high school in 1967, he studied drama at Los Angeles Valley College and teamed up with classmate Ed Begley Jr. to do improvisational comedy in between rock bands at The Troubadour on the Sunset Strip.

In 1970, he was drafted and spent two years in West Germany as a medic and also working with an entertainment unit. Upon his return to the States, he studied drama at the California Institute of the Arts and spent a few years in San Diego, performing with the San Diego Repertory Company. In 1979, he returned to Los Angeles and stand-up comedy and within a year was signed up for *Fridays,* a late night variety and sketch com-edy show. When it was cancelled in 1982, Richards returned to the theatre in a series of dramatic roles, took acting lessons from Stella Adler and worked on a number of TV cop shows. In 1989, Larry David, an old col-league from *Fridays,* was creating a sitcom with comedian Jerry Seinfeld and Richards was hired to play the wacky next door neighbor on *Seinfeld*. And the rest is history.

That's the bare bones of Richards' life story. However, any bio-graphical study of the man requires some information about the birth of Michael Richards, *the actor.* Not much digging is required and one early artifact is Richards' 1967 yearbook from Thousand Oaks High School.

The yearbook contains three telling photos of Richards. In one, he is standing on the school's front steps wearing sunglasses and a blanket draped over his head like a shawl. A second photo is the cast of the drama club's production of *The Wizard of Oz.* Richards played The Scarecrow. The third is his individual graduation photo of a pleasant, somewhat serious-looking young lad. Beneath the photo is the caption, "Voted Most Humorous."

The yearbook almost seems like a glimpse into Richards' future. He would become an actor noted for his willingness to do almost anything in creating a character. He would become an actor who was adept at physical comedy. And as any *Seinfeld* fan will attest, it was Kramer who was not only the most humorous, but also the most popular character on that show.

As proud as he is of his high school achievements, Richards cautions against reading too much into them. "The thing is— that even though I was named Most Humorous and I guess that the Scarecrow in *The Wizard of Oz* is a comedic role — even back then, I was an *actor.* I didn't consider myself a comedian.

"In high school I was in all the school plays and I did plays in town as well. So I had done a lot of plays— one of which, yes— was *The Wizard of Oz.* I also did *Arsenic and Old Lace, Kiss and Tell* and *The Crucible.* In university, we did a production of *Tartouffe, Street Scene* by Elmer Rice, *Antigone,* a number of classical plays and Shakespeare, *Marat/Sade* and if you look at all that and ask, 'Where's Kramer in this?' you aren't going to find it.

"Looking for signs of Kramer in my past is kind of narrow because it doesn't see me as an *actor.* It doesn't take into consideration my classical training. It doesn't take into consideration the work I recently did as McCawber in the TV movie *David Copperfield* and the fact that I'm doing an English accent and moving in a manner that is completely contrary to everything I did as Kramer.

"Another issue is that in the 1980s, after *Fridays,* I guest-starred on every dramatic show that was on the air —*Hill Street Blues, St. Elsewhere, Miami Vice, The Scarecrow and Mrs. King*— and in all of those shows, I was playing heavies. And a number of other things. If you look at Stanley Spadowski in the movie *UHF,* that has nothing to do with what I was doing in *Trial and Error* and you won't even notice anything about Kramer in that.

"It's just that people lose sight of the actor and because *Seinfeld* was so successful and went on for 10 years, *everybody* can only see me as that — until I emerge in other parts. For a while there, until he did *The World According to Garp,* nobody could see Robin Williams except as Mork from *Mork and Mindy.* They related everything he did to that Morkish mentality, 'Oh, he's just doing Mork.' It's a narrow-minded form of journalism that doesn't know how to approach an actor *as* an actor. It's like saying Ben Kingsley *is* Ghandi."

In case you missed the point — Michael Richards is *not* Kramer. He has done a wide variety of roles, both comedic and dramatic and had played about 100 different characters before bursting through Jerry Seinfeld's apartment door as what has turned out to be his most famous and best-known character.

"The fact is," he says, "Within the range of what I do, there aren't that many actors who could even do that. They're very limited, they can only do one thing because they're not actors. Period. They just play themselves."

"Being an actor, you have to play *characters*," he says and that brings us to the creation, interpretation and evolution of Kramer.

Richards was hired for the role of Jerry Seinfeld's offbeat next door neighbor because of his talent for creating eccentric characters. It was something he had been doing since his stand-up days in 1979, performing an almost surreal kind of act. One routine he did back then involved dragging a very large branch onto the stage and pretending to be a guy who lived in a tree. Another bit was one he later used in *Trial and Error* as his character's "audition" piece in which an unseen assailant beats him up. It's a brilliant piece of physical comedy and in the original conception was about how people beat themselves up when they drink too much.

Part of the reason he was asked to join the ensemble cast of *Fridays* was because of his ability to create characters and he brought some from his stand-up act — a self-destructive kid named Battle Boy and an open-shirted greaseball named Vinnie. So by the time *Seinfeld* came along, Richards had already established a reputation in the industry for his ability to come up with unique characters. "I was hired to develop eccentricity," he says. "Larry and Jerry already knew me. That's my past. I'm sort of a specialist in the field of creating eccentric characters."

Yet, when you are given your first script or it's your first day on the set and you have been hired to play "eccentric," as an actor, just what does that mean? It could mean anything.

That's why, when we first met Kramer in the first "season," a four-episode run during the spring of 1990, the character in no way resembles the gregarious extrovert that we would come to know. In those early episodes, the character is written as a guy who's not too bright and is portrayed as a slack-jawed dolt. His hair is normal and his wardrobe is relatively sedate. His appearances in Jerry's apartment are limited to those of a very minor character.

"In the beginning, Larry David really didn't know what the Kramer character was all about," says Richards. "The direction that I was given was that the character suffered from agoraphobia — he *could not* go outside. That's where they wanted to go with him, that he had a mental problem and was afraid of going outside. That's all I had to go on. When I did my background — that's my training, from studying with Stella Adler — I wanted to know his history. Like how does he pay for his apartment, what kind of car does he drive, where does he work — and *none* of that was provided for me.

"So I had to kind of go in my head and think, 'What would the guy be like if he doesn't leave the apartment building and only goes into Jerry's place across the hall and this is his world?' So I really just played him like a dog. You know, 'Oh, Jerry's home. I'm not alone now.'

"Also, the way I was written, I had no real intentional life, there was not much to go on and so it kind of caused me to be slow and behind what everybody else was doing. Other people on the show had stories, life was going on outside Jerry's apartment. But I wasn't going out, I wasn't getting into those stories. I wasn't extroverted in any way, shape or form. It was simply that the writers didn't know what to write. The character just simply wasn't being written more at that time.

"So what you've got in those early episodes is an embryonic character who is usually overshadowed each week by the guest talent who at least had greater motivation and intentional life insofar as their characters knew where they were going and how they played into the story as a whole. I was purely a plot device. The character was really just a device to come in, say something wrong that would shift the story or give some bit of information that would send one of the characters in a different direction of the story. But that's all. He was just a device. He wasn't even a human being.

"I was concerned that the character was actually going to be cut from the show. The writing was getting smaller and smaller and I felt less applicable to the course of the show as a whole. And when I wasn't getting answers from Larry or Jerry or any of the writers as to who this Kramer character was ... well, as far as I was concerned, we had no character at all."

Although he was creatively frustrated, Richards came to accept what he perceived to be his role on the show. However, on a show that prided itself on being an anti-sitcom, the wacky next door neighbor was a standard sitcom convention. Richards was used much in the same way as Pat Harrington as Schneider on *One Day at a Time* — come in, do a few jokes and leave.

"Yes, I was in that place and I embraced it," agrees Richards. "I felt that my job really was to come in, lay down a couple of lines— what I called 'the blows'; get a few laughs by saying this or that and then go back out the door and let the story go on. And because I'd been around television and sketch comedy, I knew my place so I just took the money home. I didn't really fight too hard to become more than that because I felt in essence that this character, as a device, was my contribution to the show.

"So my job — and I took pride in it — was to make sure that when I came through that door, that I hit my mark and I got out and if I got the blows and the laughs on all of what I was supposed to deliver, then my job was done. I felt good about that."

Part of Richards' ambivalence about his place on the show was the fact that early on he didn't think the show was going to last. The fact that it would go on for almost a decade would have seemed unfathomable at the time. Of that first four-episode season, Richards says, "I didn't have a lot of work to do and I didn't mind that — because I really didn't think that the show was going to be picked up."

He recalls that when the pilot was aired in the summer of 1989, the show was not picked up to become a series. Being brought back in mid-season the following spring for only four episodes wasn't exactly a vote of confidence by the network either — but it was more than Richards had expected. "When I got a call that the show had been picked up for four episodes, I didn't even know that the show was still on the boards at that point. I thought, 'This is a joke. This thing's going nowhere.' So when we came back for the four episodes, I didn't make too much of it — just did what was written and went home. Still, comparatively speaking, they were pretty good episodes. It wasn't a bad show. But I have to say that it was the critics who actually kept that show on the air because it got some good notices after that first episode.

"On the other hand, some critics also said that the supporting cast should be completely replaced, particularly my character — *and I agreed with them!* He was just a nuisance to it all. I didn't see the overall purpose of my character to begin with — because he had no purpose. So I thought the critics were right in a sense that there really was no *character* here. I didn't know what they could relate to here."

Even when the show was brought back six months later for its second "season" — an order of only 12 episodes, its future was still iffy, at best. After that first season, who would have guessed that it would go on for another 164 episodes and for the better part of the 1990s, single-handedly define the term "Must See-TV"?

However, the second season was to be the show's turning point — both creatively and in the ratings. This was the season where everything started to gel. The actors were able to get a handle on their characters and during that season, Richards discovered the key to playing Kramer and finally became comfortable with the role.

"With each new script, starting in that second season, they started to take the characters more and more into something that we, as actors could really begin to work with," he says. "I always felt the character had much to offer the other characters and the writing started to reflect that. Jerry would ask me a question and Elaine would want to get my beat on it and George was so at odds with himself that even he would stop to listen to what Kramer had to say. So that sort of thing started coming about and really helped me know where I stood with the cast in this whole Seinfeldian world. Originally, we played him as stupid. That he didn't know what anybody was talking about. It wasn't until later on that we came up with the hook that he was a hipster doofus."

To help make the character stand out, Richards began to create and incorporate defining details about the character and that led him to come up with the key for how he should play Kramer. Although he invented a number of little bits of business that could be identified as Kramerisms, his first major contribution was his way of sliding into Jerry's apartment seemingly out of nowhere. Just bam! He's there. "I had to infuse what little material I had with something that would make it interesting. There were all sorts of devices I used to make the character interesting — starting with the look and his way of coming through the door."

"When I came through that door, I came through in that way because I'm stepping *into* a story on the move so I've got to cut it quick. I have to come in, I have to move right into something that's already in motion. I never walked into that room and everything was at a standstill. There was always a story on the go and so I *swung* into it.

"And that helped define a direction for the character for me because I began to feel that this is a guy who really comes into the swing of things, comes into life, he comes right into it and wants to become part of it right away. He's *not* slow. He's not two steps behind everybody else. He's not stuck in a building or afraid to go outside. It's vice versa. Jerry's apartment *is* the outside world to him. It's not the totality of his universe.

"To keep the character fresh, I would come up with new bits of business. But I knew that the door should become a trademark because some people do that kind of thing. They have a little tic or personal little thing that they do — like say someone who whistles each time he leaves for work. I felt I wanted that kind of hook for Kramer. I wanted to give him certain identifiable traits that the audience would all come to know on him. That's why I also came up with the hair and the retro clothing."

However, in creating those identifying features, given that he was hired to create eccentricity, Richards ran into the problem of how to balance the character's extreme personality and still keep him real. For himself he solved the problem by going back to his theatrical training and figuring out what the reasons would be for Kramer's somewhat strange behavior.

"I always used to say that I fought against caricature — which was my worst fear. When I came to the show, that was my biggest problem. I saw that Jerry and Jason Alexander as George were playing pretty close to themselves. But I was hired because I specialized in creating eccentric characters."

The normally soft-spoken Richards explains, "I had to change the register of my voice; the way I moved and walked and so I was inventing something other than myself. And in the course of doing that, I was afraid that it might appear artificial. So I would start with my inner life of the character. You know, stuff like — 'Why is he wearing this style of clothing?' So I'd have to find a justification for it and it was by finding justifications that I felt real. Because *I* had to know too. I mean, we're in New York and that's a very *real* city and so this is a guy that you have to be able to see on the streets of New York.

"I would ask myself — 'Who is this Kramer? How does he support himself? What's his angle? What's he doing in New York?' And none of that was on paper in the beginning. How does this guy pay for his apartment? We know how Jerry does — he's a comedian. But Kramer was *ethereal*, footless. So I had to invent an inner life to this character and that's how the hair and the look and everything else came about."

But all that stuff has to be natural or it doesn't work. The flying-through-the door routine, the almost-spastic reaction shots, the finger-snap and pointing gesture which accompanied his catchphrase "Giddy-up," the self-conscious goofy grin when he's cocky — they were all established identifiable Kramerisms.

"All those things have to fit into the nature of the character's presence within the story," says Richards. "Otherwise it seems artificial or put on. It's very tricky. It has to be *organically* acceptable. It has to be as natural as if you'd just looked at somebody walking down the street and there's something *odd* but *real* about that person."

Undeniably, Richards' Kramer was both odd and real. In creating the character's look, he had to work from the ground up — from the shoes to the hair. Like the entrances into Jerry's apartment, Richards says both the vintage clothes and the loaf of hair were ways to give the character distinctive identifying features. To satisfy himself and create more back story, he also had to find reasons *why* Kramer wore his hair and those fashions like he did.

"The clothing came about quite naturally," he says. "In the beginning, he was already wearing '60s-style shirts and pants which were a bit too short. I went to a second-hand store and found these shirts from 1966 still in the packages and I thought that this was something that this guy would wear. They're just part of his old wardrobe — particularly since it was a guy who never went outside. I presumed that this was a guy who would be wearing the same clothes from years ago over and over again. This is all he's got. He doesn't go out and buy new clothes and so it had to be older clothing."

Gradually, the clothes became more cool-looking while still being from another era. Since the character now had an outside life, the reasoning for still wearing the vintage clothing was that since Kramer was a man of limited income, it was only logical that he would shop in second-hand stores. The fact that he was proof that you didn't have to spend a lot of money to look good was a bonus. Kramer had great taste in clothes— in the jargon of the sixties hipsters he resembled, the look was so cool it was "straight from the fridge, Dad."

Richards, however denies intentionally trying to come up with a cool look — it was just because that was what he reasoned the character would wear. If Kramer was the type of guy who would wear overalls or Brooks Brothers suits, he would have worn them. "I didn't deliberately choose those '60s clothes for any sort of retro-cool attitude," he says. "I just felt those were his clothes. In the beginning, I was heading in that direction. That was the one thing that was already sort of established. Everyone thought that it was such a cool choice and activated him in such a hip way — but no, that wasn't the reason for it. And at the time, none of that stuff was even on board. No one was wearing clothes from the sixties then."

It was a similar situation with the hair. No one was wearing their hair pulled up like that at the time — or even since then, for that matter. During the second season Richards came up with that hairstyle and he confesses that it all came about by accident. "The hair came about because of a bad haircut I had been given," he says. "My hair got cut too short and so I was trying to pull it up on top to make it look a little longer. But as I was pulling it up, I could see that it could become a 'look.' Radical hair in 1989 really wasn't happening so I was kind of fortunate to get in on the cutting edge. As I started pulling the hair up, it felt like it accentuated the kind of eccentricity I was looking for."

Of course there had to be a reason for it. "I noticed one time in a James Dean movie that the hair looked a little too up and it was because of the wind. So I felt that it was possible that Kramer just needs a haircut. And that's how I thought of it — it's just getting a little too long on top and he hasn't gotten a haircut yet."

Probably the hardest aspect of Kramer's life to justify was his apartment and how he could afford it since he seldom seemed to do anything which would generate an income. It helped that his apartment was only seen on rare occasions and when it was, you were never given much of a look at it. Given that lack of details, Richards could envision what kind of apartment it was that Kramer could afford. Since he was always mooching food from Jerry, you could also assume that he didn't even cook in there. In the first season episodes, the slow-thinking and introverted Kramer seemed like he would have been a hot-plate kind of guy.

"I always thought that it was a rent-controlled apartment and that Kramer had got it for cheap and it stays cheap until he moves out and then the rent will go higher," he says. "In my own mind, I always assumed that it was one of those apartments that had no windows because you never saw any windows whenever they shot a scene in his apartment. I figured that it's not really like Jerry's apartment — it's smaller. There's no windows and there might not even be a kitchen. These are the ways I would justify its expense because there's no way Kramer could afford something like Jerry's apartment in New York."

Originally, Kramer's apartment was never shown and that helped Richards in his conception of the character. "There was a lot of controversy about my apartment," he says. "People were always wondering what it was like and early on we had decided that we were never going to show his apartment."

That, in turn, helped him to get into character before he would burst through that door into Jerry's room. Richards says that by taking the method approach to acting, he would integrate the unknown aspects of Kramer's apartment with his own need to get into character and what was going on in Kramer's mind wouldn't necessarily have anything to do with what was in that week's script.

"I liked the idea of the mystery from not showing his apartment," says Richards. "I liked the idea of him being like a fourth element, just coming in from nowhere. Yet, I had enough internal life and what I had made up about this character so that I was always coming from somewhere. I had things going on in my mind — previous situations that the character had been in that had nothing to do with the story but would at least make me feel more present.

"A lot of times, I'd come in, in a hurry and I'd be saying something and get some paper towels and go back out. Like that was my motivation for coming in. Or I went to the refrigerator and was looking for something because I was thinking of making a pie. Now, that may not have even been in the script. So I was always filling my entrances with something that had nothing to do with the story. Again — entrances, looks. It's all make-believe, man."

Over the series' nine-year run, Richards made close to 300 of those patented entrances. Each one further connected the character with the audience. They came to expect it. In fact, at one point, the studio audience had to be told before each taping not to burst into applause every time Kramer burst into Jerry's apartment. It was holding up the show.

Once Richards had established the character, it was no trouble for the audience to accept Kramer's other eccentricities. Coming from anyone else, his hare-brained schemes might have been greeted with skepticism, but with Kramer being the source, they somehow made sense. A coffee table book about coffee tables? With a built-in coaster, no less. What an inspired idea! A pizza restaurant where the customer creates his own pie? Surely someone has picked up on that idea by now. A bra for out-of-shape middle-aged men? Well, there is definitely a need for such a product. A perfume that smells like the beach? Sounds romantic.

It's ironic that on a series where initially, he was the most slow-witted one of the bunch, over time, as the other characters de-evolved, Kramer of all people ended up being the one with the most common sense and being the most on the ball.

Richards, however, cautions against giving the character too much credit for brains. "It was about midway through the series when we came up with the idea that he was a hipster-doofus— that he was hip to what everybody else was saying," Richards asserts. "But if you listen closely, he doesn't really know what he's talking about. You gotta be careful because if you follow his directions, most likely you're going to end up in trouble!"

He's probably right. As inspired as Kramer's business ideas truly are, they aren't really potential money-makers. A coffee table book about coffee tables? Sure, it has lots of novelty appeal but how many copies would it actually sell? And what self-respecting member of the male species would walk into a store and buy a bra for himself — let alone be caught wearing one? A perfume that smells like the beach? Does that include the scent of dead fish and pollution?

Yet all of that is another key to the character. He is definitely operating on a different wavelength than the rest of the world — but he's totally grounded in reality. He's self-sufficient. He has his own social circle beyond Jerry's core group and a whole network of acquaintances who do favors for each other. He's self-assured, confident and very successful when it comes to women. In short, he's his own man. All of that gives the character *credibility*. The audience is willing to accept any looney idea he comes up with, no matter how ludicrous it may seem.

Richards credits the writers for a lot of the growth in the character. "As I got more inspired and with what I was coming up with for the character, it started to get the writers to thinking and so it was just a wonderful meeting of the minds and the creativity just started to occur and everybody got on to it. That's what was nice about *Seinfeld,* for the most part, the run of the show was very organic. There wasn't a lot of pulling teeth or struggles about what direction the show should go. Everybody just *got* it."

As an example he cites an episode from the second season in which he first felt in tune with the character. There was a scene set in a laundromat where Kramer is bouncing around carrying a big, heavy bag of cement mix. It was the first time he did a lengthy bit of physical comedy shtick on the show. "I asked for that scene," Richards points out. "Originally I was just supposed to come into Jerry's apartment and say what I had done with the bag of cement mix. But I asked the writers if I could act that out because actions speak louder than words and I thought it would be more interesting to *see* Kramer put that cement in the washing machine rather than just have me come in the apartment and say that's what I did.

"So we tried it and it worked and I always thought that was the real way to go with Kramer. I thought at times that Kramer talked too much and I like to 'show' rather than 'tell.'"

Over the course of the series, plots and storylines were tweaked to the point where what originally was a show about somewhat ordinary people became increasingly broader and even absurd in its approach to comedy. In the beginning, the characters of Jerry, Elaine and George were basically pleasant, down-to-earth types and Kramer was the only extreme character. However, eventually the others became extreme characters and in comparison, Kramer was the only "normal" one.

"Yes, he seemed a bit more on top of things, whereas everyone else was pretty screwed up," Richards agrees. He adds that much of the show's development was out of the actors' hands. "That all comes out of the writing," he explains. "If you follow the course of the writing, a lot of the changes are due to the way the writers started moving with the show. There's an autonomy to that which is difficult to control. You have to just go along with it. A lot of the time I was just adjusting to material and not that capable of directing the course of the character from season to season where I could overview or envision how the character should behave."

In the 1997–98 season, when everyone knew it was to be the final season, the writers pulled out all the stops and the show probably reached its most surreal peak with an episode where Kramer hauls the set to the old *Merv Griffin Show* out of a dumpster, sets it up in his apartment and when friends drop by, their visit turns into a talk show appearance with Kramer as host and his friend Newman (played by Wayne Knight) as his sidekick.

In that episode alone, the series confirmed that it had lost all touch with reality. Richards admits that "What was beginning to happen was that in the last year of the series, we were doing caricatures of the characters—which was okay because we had been on for years, everyone knew these characters and we all had the background and had the feet of our characters so we were able to go in that direction. But if we had started the show out on that level, I don't think we would have made it."

Undeniably, Kramer was the most popular character on *Seinfeld*. TV viewers didn't tire of him because he kept the character fresh with all the small touches and bits of business Richards came up with for the character. He also may have reminded people of the other great second bananas. Art Carney as Ed Norton also had a way of bursting into the Kramdens' apartment on *The Honeymooners*—albeit in a much different and more intrusive fashion. Kramer's almost spastic horrified reaction shots were reminiscent of Shemp Howard on *The Three Stooges*. Richard's work on the show as a physical comedian was on a par with all the great masters of the art, from Buster Keaton to Dick Van Dyke. But in whatever he was doing on the show, all those physical bits were only springboards for Richards. If he was conscious of any similarity to others, it didn't show in the work. He put his own stamp on everything he did and that's what made Kramer such a unique creation.

Audiences also responded to the character because he was always such an "up" and optimistic fellow. While everyone else on the show were fundamentally pessimists and miserable at heart, it seemed like nothing could get Kramer down for long. You had the feeling that everywhere he went, he had a good time.

"He *was* an upbeat character," agrees Richards. "Sometimes, he'd complain about something but in the next scene he'd come back in with some new idea and he'd be up an' at 'em again. I played him with a full optimism. I felt that was very, very important and thank God that Larry and Jerry and the rest of the writers felt the same way. I do believe he was one of the most optimistic characters there ever was."

Fans weren't the only ones to agree with Richards' contribution to the show. He won the Emmy Award for Outstanding Supporting Actor in a Comedy Series three times—for 1992–'93; 1993–'94 and 1996–'97.

When Jerry Seinfeld decided to pull the plug on the show and *Seinfeld* went off the air in 1998, Richards took it easy for a year and then began planning his return to television.

As far back as 1995, he had been talking about wanting to do a TV series about an Inspector Clouseau–type private detective. He had always enjoyed those episodes of *Seinfeld* where Kramer went "undercover" and wore a disguise, spoke with a foreign accent and tried to pass himself off as Doctor Martin Von Nostrand. During *Seinfeld's* run, he had even made a series of slapstick television commercials for Clorets (only shown in Canada) in which he played a bumbling private eye.

When Richards signed with NBC in 1999 to play private detective Vic Nardozza in *The Michael Richards Show,* he had ambitious plans. Inspired by Jacques Tati's pantomime and slapstick classic, *Hulot's Holiday,* Richards envisioned a television series shot film-style with one camera as his character investigated crimes in Los Angeles. "I always thought that if I ever got back on television, I'd like to have a comedic romp through the world of private investigation. We had no supporting cast. Like *Hulot's Holiday,* you really have just one person in the midst of a situation. I wanted to use Los Angeles as one big pratfall. That's how we originally tackled it but it was so different that it actually scared the network. They couldn't see a show without a supporting cast because all shows are ensemble shows."

It also proved too costly and time consuming. "There was no way I was going to be able to put in the 16-hour days needed to do a filmed show week after week so we decided to go back to a four-camera in-studio show with a supporting cast — and that turned everything into a sitcom. We were far removed from getting into the kind of work I originally wanted to do with this character and that was very disheartening to me."

If the critics were responsible for keeping *Seinfeld* on the air in its first year, they were also certainly partly responsible for the cancellation of *The Michael Richards Show.* Long before the first episode was even aired, there were reports that the pilot had been scrapped and the series was labeled as "troubled." When the series debuted, whenever Vic tripped or did a pratfall, they only saw Kramer.

When the show was cancelled after only a handful of episodes, Richards says he was relieved. "The show clearly wasn't a big hit. They would have had to really work at it but I had lost heart anyway. After a few shows in, I realized that I didn't even have the stamina to carry through with it all. It wasn't running smoothly, I disagreed with most of the writing and I was so grateful that NBC decided to pull the plug on it. They had me for six years and I was scared they were just going to keep me on TV. I was so miserable with it all."

In reality, Vic Nardozza and Cosmo Kramer didn't have too much in common other than a propensity for pratfalls. "But even when I did Kramer, I didn't do that many falls," asserts Richards.

So he is understandably offended whenever one of his characters — or he, himself is compared to Kramer. Whenever *Seinfeld* was on its summer hiatus, Richards deliberately chose projects that would help him escape the inevitable typecasting.

In Diane Keaton's 1995 film, *Unstrung Heroes,* he played a sweet and gentle mentally unstable man. He was also eccentric. In *Trial and Error,* during the first five minutes of the movie he did a bit of physical comedy and that was it. With both movies, reviews compared his characters to his role on *Seinfeld.* As he points out, critics often forget that he's an *actor.*

"I'm concerned about the narrowness of that kind of thing because it just relates to the physical comedy or Kramer and suggests that that's the extent of this guy's range. The issue of accentuating more of this Kramer thing is quite repulsive to me."

Unfortunately, that's very likely to happen for the rest of his career. Every character he takes on will be compared to Kramer. However, unlike many actors, Richards doesn't harbor any ill will towards the role for which he will always be best remembered. "I was quite happy doing *Seinfeld.* It was a wonderful experience," he says. "I never had any problems keeping the character fresh. Right up to the last show, I always felt fresh and capable. I could have gone on for years with that character," he says and then laughs—"But I didn't want to!"

He speaks with genuine affection and admiration when he talks of Kramer as being a one-of-a-kind original. "But as far as inventiveness, that guy could have been anywhere. He could say he's going to Los Angeles and wants to be a surfer. You could go on that. That character could go *anywhere.*"

Michael Richards Credits

FILM CREDITS

1. *Redux Riding Hood;* 1997; (voice) The Wolf
2. *Trial and Error;* 1997; Richard "Ricky" Rietti
3. *Ellen's Energy Adventure;* 1996; (uncredited) Caveman discovering fire
4. *Unstrung Heroes;* 1995; Danny Lidz
5. *Airheads;* 1994; Doug Beech
6. *So I Married an Axe Murderer;* 1993; Obit writer
7. *Coneheads;* 1993; Motel Clerk
8. *Problem Child;* 1990; Martin Beck
9. *UHF;* 1989; Stanley Spadowski
10. *Choice Chance Control;* 1987
11. *Whoops Apocalypse;* 1986; Lacrobat
12. *Transylvania 6-5000;* 1985; Fejos
13. *The House of God;* 1984; Dr. Pinkus
14. *Young Doctors in Love;* 1982; Malamud

TV CREDITS

1. *The Michael Richards Show;* TV series; 2000; Vic Nardozza
2. *David Copperfield;* TV movie; 2000; Mr. Wilkins Micawber
3. *Neil Simon's London Suite;* TV movie; 1996; Mark Ferris
4. *A Comedy Salute to Andy Kaufman;* TV special; 1995; Himself
5. *Seinfeld;* TV series; 1989–1998; Cosmo Kramer
6. *Marblehead Manor;* TV series; 1987; Rick the Gardener
7. *Fresno;* TV mini-series; 1986; 2nd Henchman
8. *The Ratings Game;* TV movie; 1984; Sal
9. *Faerie Tale Theatre: Pinocchio;* TV special; 1983; Mario's Friend
10. *Fridays;* TV series; 1980–1982; Various characters

NOTABLE TV GUEST APPEARANCES

1. *The Larry Sanders Show;* Himself; 10/12/1994
2. *Mad About You;* Kramer; 11/11/1992
3. *The Larry Sanders Show;* Himself; 9/19/1992
4. *Miami Vice;* Pagone; 3/7/1986
5. *Hill Street Blues;* Special Agent Dupre; 11/14/1985
6. *Scarecrow and Mrs. King;* 3/11/1985
7. *Cheers;* Eddie Gordon; 2/14/1985
8. *Night Court;* Eugene Sleighbough; 12/13/1984
9. *St. Elsewhere;* 2/15/1984
10. *St. Elsewhere;* 3/7/1983

Jack Riley

Elliot Carlin on *The Bob Newhart Show*

TV Guide once compiled a list of the Top 50 most memorable television characters of all time. There were the usual suspects—Barney Fife, Ralph Kramden and of course Archie Bunker. And there was also Mr. Carlin from *The Bob Newhart Show*, who was played by Jack Riley. What's impressive about his inclusion on this list is that Riley wasn't the star of the show or a co-star. His name didn't even appear in the opening credits. Mr. Carlin was a recurring character. Undeniably, however, he was a memorable one.

If the goal of any actor doing a guest shot on a TV series is to make enough of an impression to be invited back, then Riley was certainly successful. He was cast in the series' first episode in 1972 as just another member of a therapy group. It was supposed to be a one-shot for all involved but Riley was asked back as a solo patient. Before long, he was the show's most utilized recurring character.

On this series in which Bob Newhart played psychologist Dr. Robert Hartley, Elliot Carlin was Hartley's most regular patient and was the show's resident neurotic. In addition to his private sessions, he was also a member of all of Hartley's therapy groups—including two of which he wasn't even eligible for—the unemployment workshop and the support group for senior citizens. Dr. Hartley explained the exception this way, "Mr. Carlin has trouble relating to people of all ages."

No kidding. Carlin had problems with people because he was a maladjusted anti-social nasty little paranoid completely lacking in people skills. His most striking quality was that he was a master of sarcasm — no one was immune to his caustic one-liners and succinct put-downs. It was that knack for acerbic barbs that made Carlin so memorable and popular — with TV audiences if not the other characters on the show.

It's not too surprising to learn that prior to *The Bob Newhart Show,* Jack Riley had once worked as a writer for insult king Don Rickles. But unlike the brash, aggressive Rickles, Riley's low-key and understated style of comedy was much like the star of the show (and coincidently, Rickles' best friend), Bob Newhart.

Making an impression is something Riley has done throughout his career. As a member of his high school Glee Club, he and the others sometimes performed as tuxedo-clad cheerleaders at school sporting events. While serving in the Army, he was assigned to the special forces' entertainment unit and was part of an all-soldier musical revue which was put together by a former member of The Rockettes. They were a line of trained killers dancing and kicking up a storm in the tradition of Radio City Music Hall. While working at his first job, in the record library of a radio station in his hometown of Cleveland, disc jockeys picked up on his keen sense of humor and hired him to write comedy sketches to perform with them on their shows. Soon he had his own show. By that time, a career in show business was all that Riley would consider. He eventually moved to California and after a couple of standout guest shots on *The Mary Tyler Moore Show*, he was noticed by the producers of *The Bob Newhart Show*, which was also an MTM Production.

Riley was born in Cleveland on December 30, 1935. As a child he developed an eye for observing the unintentionally funny things in life. He didn't have to look much further than his own father.

"My father was a real character," says Riley. "He was one of the first do-it-yourselfers. Our house was about three feet lower than the other houses in the neighborhood and he was always trying ways to raise it. Whenever he saw a truck go by from a construction site, he'd pay the driver a few bucks to dump the dirt in our yard. So I spent most of my childhood digging the dirt from the front yard and taking it around back. He did the same thing with bricks and trying to jack the garage up. These projects never got finished. It was always an ongoing thing. He also found out that he could get some paint from the city for a cheap price and so everything in our basement was painted bright orange. It was bridge paint.

"So a lot of my humor came from my father. He was just living his life and it was funny to observe — but he didn't know it was funny. He was very serious about his home-improvement projects. But they were done with a sense of absurdity that kind of crept into my life at an early age."

Of course it seems like no one in Cleveland has a normal childhood. It is also the home of Riley's old friend Tim Conway, Fred Willard, Martin Mull and Pat McCormick. As Riley says, Cleveland is a natural target for jokes and as an example, he points out that one of its rivers once caught on fire.

Riley spent his high school years in the early 1950s at St. Ignatius High School, an all-male school run by the Jesuits. "I was one of the class clowns," he confesses. "I spent a lot of time in the hallways." Although he didn't study theatre or belong to the Drama Club, it was in high school that Riley got his start as a performer. He and five other class clowns formed an informal Glee Club and would put on theatrical comic pep rallies. "Before the football games, we would dress up as the opposing team and their coaches— or their girl cheerleaders— and do little skits and comedy sketches and that's when I first got into getting laughs," says Riley.

"For the basketball games, we really got elaborate for the half-time shows. It was at a time when Jackie Gleason was really popular. He had a character called Reggie Van Gleason who was a 'ne'er do-well' high-society rich-boy drunk. So as the cheerleaders for the basketball team, we did a blatant imitation of Gleason. We dressed up like Reggie in top hats and capes and whenever our team got a basket, we would come out and go, 'Ooooohhh, that was a *good* one!' And that's how I got into comedy."

After high school, Riley attended night courses at John Carroll University where he was an English major. During the day, he began working in the record library of KYW, a Cleveland television and radio station. Pulling and filing records, he got to know the disc jockeys and became friends with Big Wilson, the most popular local DJ at that time. "He was the top morning man but he also had a radio show on Saturday nights and he would just screw around with it and would let me on to do voices and Bob and Ray–type sketches that I would write for us. He also did a nightly bit on TV that came on at 11:20. For some reason, they did the 11:00 news for 20 minutes and then had 10 minutes to fill before *The Steve Allen Tonight Show* came on and so they filled it with Big Wilson and we would do comedy sketches I would write for it. That was how I got my start in the business. He asked me to write material for him and so I quit my job in the record library and went pro."

In 1958, Riley was drafted. While he was about to go into the Army, Tim Conway was just then getting out of the Army and ended up replacing Riley as a writer-performer for Big Wilson.

"I had first met Tim Conway in the Christmas of 1956," remembers Riley. "He had a big reputation as the campus clown at Bowling Green University where had had a radio show. We invited him to take part in a benefit show and we became good friends. Later, when I was going into the Army, he replaced me at my job at the station. I remember that there was a big meeting as to whether Tim Conway was funny enough to follow me. I guess that's been proven over the years."

Once in the Army, Riley auditioned for the Entertainment Unit of the Special Forces. This was the quiet period between the Korean War and the conflict in Vietnam and Riley calls it one of the best times of his life. "I auditioned for the touring military show *Rolling Along of 1960*. It was an all-soldier show — 25 guys, and we toured every U.S. Army base in the world. We got three-day passes in Tokyo, Paris, London and Berlin and so it was a great way to see the world in nine months. It was great! It was like being an officer. We had special quarters and it was all very cushy."

The show itself was remarkable in its own way. "A former Rockette from Radio City Music Hall named Skippy Lynne was hired by the Army as the choreographer and director of the show. So the result was 25 guys doing lots of kicking and dancing just like the Rockettes. My big bit was — whatever big production number they did, I couldn't do it and so I'd come out and fall on my ass. It was like a musical revue with comedy. There were big sets and good lighting equipment. The Army really did it up right."

The experience helped make up Riley's mind as to what he wanted to do when his two-year hitch was up. Forget Cleveland, he was going to New York. "*Rolling Along* was like being in vaudeville. We were doing sometimes two shows a day. It almost felt like being in a Broadway show and so I thought, 'Well, I'm going to go to New York and that will be it. All of which I did and lasted there about a year and didn't get anywhere so I went back to Cleveland — which was probably the most stupid thing I ever did in my life."

Although Riley regrets his decision not to stay in New York, his time there was actually productive. When his time in the Army was up in late 1960, Big Wilson had moved on to radio station WNEW in New York and offered Riley a writing job. Once there, he was making $100 a week writing for Big Wilson and was also hired by two other DJs to write for each of them for the same amount of money. He also began taking acting classes, one of which was taught by Nancy Walker, as well as voice lessons in between auditioning for Broadway plays.

"I really could have gone that way if I had stayed and I often think about it and wish I had, but a radio station back in Cleveland, WERE, offered me the unbelievable amount of $12,000 a year to go back and do a radio show with another guy and that kind of money was too much of a draw. But I do regret missing out on that New York acting thing — doing off–Broadway and really connecting."

If he had stayed in New York, it may have fast-tracked his career. Then again, he may have remained just another struggling actor in the Big Apple. On the other hand, in going back to Cleveland he was able to develop the skills which have kept him employed in the business for all of his career. "Other than the money, part of my reasoning for going back to Cleveland was that I thought, 'Well, I still don't have enough of an on-air personality myself or radio technique to be able to just sit there and bull-shit,' and I thought this would be a good chance to work on that. In retrospect, I've always made a good living doing voice-overs — that has saved me many, many years in a row. So maybe I got that training in Cleveland radio and moving back was the right thing to do."

At WERE, Riley was teamed up with another DJ, Jeff Baxter, and they did a popular three-hour afternoon drive-home show for four years until Riley ended up heading for California. "We were both fans of Bob and Ray and Jonathan Winters and we did those kinds of sketches. Jeff was mostly the straight man and I did a lot of the characters. For every 15-minute segment, we tried to have at least some kind of notion of something funny —

and that would be our writing session. The rest was mostly improvised. We had an old-lady character like Jonathan Winters' Granny Frickett and we had her living in the attic of the radio station and we had a character named Billy Broadway who was a very 'Nu Yawk' kind of guy. And we sometimes made fun of the music we played. WERE was a middle-of-the-road music station and we had one character named Robert Koolaid, who couldn't even *talk* on key."

In his off hours, Riley began doing community theatre. "I think I got the acting bug then and started working with some pretty good groups. I studied voice with a woman named Marietta Richards and then auditioned for *Kiss Me Kate* at the Music Carnival out in Warrensville, Ohio. I did *Kiss Me Kate* out there with a lot of New York actors and that's when I connected with real pros." He also did *Once Upon a Mattress* at the Chagrin Valley Playhouse as well as *Mr. Roberts* with Tim Conway, who was then home on his summer hiatus from *McHale's Navy.*

During the same period, he also hooked up with Bill Daily, his future co-worker on *The Bob Newhart Show.* "I used to go to Chicago on weekends and Bill had a little improv group with the actress Ann Elder. When one of their group couldn't make it, I'd take his place and it was a lot of fun."

Improv seems like a natural choice for a team which included Riley and Daily. Riley admits that neither was overly exceptional at memorizing lines. "Bill always struggled with that but luckily when we did the TV show together, Newhart thought it was funny. And I'm not exactly Mr. Memory myself and so we'd always wonder which of us would be the first to go 'up' on our lines and Newhart would always laugh. And then I went to other shows after that and they didn't think it was so funny."

In 1965, at Tim Conway's suggestion, Riley made the move to California. "He was performing and writing on *The Hollywood Palace* and said, 'Why don't you come out here and help me write some sketches and we'll see what happens?' It had always been in the back of my mind to go out there and be an actor and this was a nice way of doing it. I lived at his house for the first few months and that was the first impression I got of California — living in a house with Tim Conway!"

At the same time, Riley was making the rounds of auditions and also working as a writer for other people. "Bill Daily was connected with a company that did commercials and they were always looking for ideas and writers and Bill took me down there, and I clicked really well with them and worked for them off and on for years, writing and performing in their commercials. As a matter of fact, I had been working steadily for them when I got the *Newhart* show in 1972."

He also worked as a writer of special material for Rowan and Martin in their pre-*Laugh-In* days and for comic Mort Sahl. "Mort had a Los Angeles TV show and Ann Elder was a friend of his and the two of us were the sketch comedians for his show."

But the most fun he had as a writer in Hollywood was in working on the short-lived ABC series *The Don Rickles Show* in 1968. "I was a writer and performer on that show and Rickles still talks about it as being the most fun he's ever had on television," says Riley. "Pat McCormick, another friend from Ohio, was his foil as an Ed McMahon–type and we did all kinds of wild sketches.

"Originally it was supposed to be a game show like *You Bet Your Life* only with Rickles instead of Groucho Marx, but that turned out to be total chaos. Rickles couldn't do it, he was too wild and so the producers, Mark Goodson and Bill Todman, decided to keep the time slot and turn it into a half-hour variety show instead of a game show.

"But they kept the same budget as the game show and so we had no money at all — ever. They were very cheap. If a sketch called for oranges, we had to go out and buy them ourselves. The deal was that Rickles would bring a friend of his from the business in on a Sunday morning and in return for doing the show, they'd get a big-screen TV set or something. So we had some big name guests. We had Lorne Greene, David Janssen, Mickey Rooney and Don Adams. We'd have one big sketch and if we got tired of writing or ran out of ideas and still had to fill space we'd just write down something like, 'Lorne Greene comes in dressed like an Indian and Don does tirade.'

"This was at a time when ABC was a very weak network. It was supposed to be on Saturday night at eight o'clock but some of the affiliates would put us on Saturday afternoons opposite the football game. It was just horrific. I think we did about 17 of those shows before getting cancelled."

But Riley didn't head West to be a writer and he kept busy seeking out acting gigs. "I wanted to keep my performing jobs going because I didn't want to be a writer. I never have, even though I've done it several times. I was always happier being out there doing it. I hate being on the sidelines." He's maintained that attitude to this day and talks of going to auditions and seeing who else is up for the part. "It's unbelievable who you see there just for a guest shot on a sitcom with a couple of scenes with five lines in each. You'll see Tom Poston, Dan Castellaneta, Alex Rocco — I keep expecting to see Sean Connery walk in. With someone like Tom Poston, he just loves working and I can understand that — because it's fun. He loves it, as I do. I like to keep going with this stuff and so I do a fair bit of theatre because I have the bug still."

Riley's first regular job on a network series came in 1966 on *Occasional Wife,* a romantic comedy on NBC starring Michael Callan and Patricia Harty. It was set in a baby food company and Callan played a swinging single junior executive. To get a promotion, he pretends to be married and hires his upstairs neighbor to pretend to be his wife.

"I played a recurring character named Wally Frick," says Riley. "He was one of the guys in the office of the baby food company and was also the nephew of the owner of the company. The kind of character I played in that show really set my career because he was really a forerunner of Mr. Carlin. Wally Frick was a back-stabbing guy and always pulling rank. He was a nasty little person and for some reason that's how Hollywood saw me after that. I don't play too many characters on TV who smile a lot. They don't hire me for that. It doesn't ring the cash register. *Occasional Wife* only ran the one season though — which was too bad. It was a hair's breadth away from getting renewed and would have really changed everybody's life."

However, as he said, the role did give him his first experience with typecasting and that led to more work. Screen Gems, the company which produced *Occasional Wife,* found him more work on their other series. On *Hogan's Heroes,* he made three appearances as a Nazi soldier; he did a couple of episodes on *Gomer Pyle* as the barrack's wiseguy and he also worked again with Bill Daily on an episode of *I Dream of Jeannie.*

It was while working with another company, MTM Productions, that Riley hatched his greatest claim to fame. In 1971, he played Eldon Golfax in an episode of *The Mary Tyler Moore Show.* Mary goes back to her hometown for her high school reunion and Riley's character asks if she remembers him. When she can't place his face, Eldon starts bragging about all his plastic surgery and his toupee. The next season he was back playing Barry Barlow, a strutting, swinging single who was about as cocky as Elliot Carlin. In fact, both characters had elements of Mr. Carlin and in 1972, when MTM Productions were casting for *The Bob Newhart Show,* they remembered Riley's appearances on *Mary Tyler Moore.* He read for the part of Carlin and got it. Originally, it was only to be a one-shot guest appearance. The first episode of the series was about a fear-of-flying group therapy workshop and Carlin was just another member of the group. The character is only slightly different from the acerbic bully he would later become. His big scene is a warm moment when he and group member Michelle Nardo (played by Renee Lippin) have a breakthrough and bond. The warm fuzzy moment, however, is undercut when Carlin immediately turns on her.

Riley says of that first episode, "If anything, I was more timid, more like a guy who was unable to function because he was so shy and retiring." But in the way Carlin and Michelle cooed one minute and were at each others' throats in the next breath, the producers saw the possibilities and he was invited back. He ended up playing in half of the series' 135 episodes.

"When they got the therapy group together for that first episode, there was never any plan for that group to ever do anything but that one episode," recalls Riley. "But I got a few laughs so they brought my character back again and they also brought all five characters back and put them in a group." In addition to Carlin, the rest of the group consisted of Michelle, who was afraid of her father; mousy Mr. Peterson (played by John Fiedler), who was afraid of his wife; brash and abrasive Mr. Gianelli (played by Noam Pitlik), who was afraid of intimacy; and the sweet, scatterbrained Mrs. Bakerman (played by Florida Friebus), who probably didn't have any psychological problems and was only there because she was a lonely widow.

In the early group sessions, Carlin was more neurotic than sarcastic. In these episodes, Mr. Gianelli was the bully of the group and was always picking on Mr. Peterson, whom he nicknamed The Twerp. But after the classic episode where produce vendor Gianelli was crushed to death by a truckload of zucchinis, the writers began to give the put-down lines to Carlin.

Riley says that the character really came together for him in an episode in the second season where he went on a date with Dr. Hartley's receptionist, Carol Kester, played by Marcia Wallace. "That episode was one of the big turning points," he says. "That was the first time the character was really focused on. What happened was, in that episode, we went to a Japanese restaurant and they wrote me some zingers where I was insulting people. They saw that this kind of acerbic zinging worked with the character and after that they kind of sailed with it. They made him to be an almost Don Rickles kind of character."

That was also the episode in which they gave Carlin a background. He may have been the patient with the most problems—but he was also the most successful. He was a real estate tycoon and apparently his cold, calculating mind and lack of people skills made him ideally suited for that profession. Riley recalls that Carlin's background partly came about just through the wardrobe he had chosen to wear. "Originally they wanted the character to dress almost like a guy living under the freeway and wearing the same suit all the time. But they had all these clothes in wardrobe that I wanted to wear—I was a big Ralph Lauren fan and so I decided that I wanted to dress well. From that I think they realized that Carlin could be a rich guy and that he didn't necessarily have to be down and out to be insecure."

The other part of Carlin's look which was his most commented-upon feature was his bad hairpiece. It was like a sculpted furry bowl, every hair in place. Riley insists that he wasn't wearing a bad toupee. "It was my own hair — but they would comb it down and use lots of hair spray and that's the one thing about the character that people really remember. For some reason, people in New York particularly love the show and for years afterwards if I was in New York and walking down the street, people would want to touch my hair to see if it was real."

Riley's first inkling that his character was a success happened when he realized how popular The Group had become. "I think what happened was that the group caught on first. I remember one night for the taping, the group came out to get into our chairs on the office set and the studio audience started cheering. That was really thrilling."

The Carlin character started to take off in that second season and he made just as many solo visits to Dr. Hartley's office as he did with The Group. Soon Riley was averaging about 12 appearances a year and eventually he almost became one of the Hartleys' inner circle of friends — being invited almost out of guilt to join them for Thanksgiving dinners and parties. He was also the only patient with whom Hartley ever went out drinking. "It all started very small, but they gave me bigger parts because the character was going over so well. Towards the end, there were a few episodes where Newhart couldn't be on the show and they wrote an episode where I took Suzanne Pleshette to my high school reunion and passed her off as my wife."

Carlin's popularity isn't too hard to understand. On a show full of nice guys, he was a refreshing contrast in being the only character who was thoroughly negative. Audiences also responded to his honesty. Carlin would say exactly what was on his mind and was brutally blunt. In group, he would quietly sit there with a permanent smirk on his face just waiting for someone to say something stupid and worthy of ridicule. There were no exceptions to who was a potential target for a zinger. He would go after anybody — his few "friends" (the other people in group who had to tolerate his presence) and even complete strangers. As a result, Carlin was probably the kind of guy who got beaten up a lot.

Not even Dr. Hartley was immune to Carlin's sarcasm. In fact, it was Carlin who gets credit for pointing out that Hartley probably wasn't a very good psychologist. Whenever Hartley would make a point by using a cliché or corny platitude, Carlin would cut through all that with a succinct and incisive putdown. Sometimes he didn't even have to open his mouth to show his disdain — all it would take would be a raised eyebrow, an upwards roll of the eyeballs or a slight bit more curl on his ever-present smirk.

As good as his insult scenes were in group, Riley's best work was in the quiet scenes done with Newhart in the office. They would invariably open with Carlin sitting on the couch, looking down at his hands and in an almost hopeless-sounding voice, say, "I don't know, Dr. Hartley," and then go on to tell about his latest problem. The resigned tone in his voice was undercut by the absurdity of his troubles. With his usual deadpan expression he would say something like, "I only have one problem this week. Last night I was possessed by the Devil." It was the perfect blend of the banal and the bizarre.

"Those scenes were so low-key," remembers Riley. "I'd say something and then Newhart would say something and then there'd be no laugh and then he'd blink 17 times and bring the house down. It was all about trusting the silence and getting laughs that way. That's a way of working that I always felt comfortable with and I think that's why Newhart and I hit it off so great."

Riley knew that he was working with the master and says, "I was a fan of his style and his timing in the way he would stretch out the quiet and I think I did imitate that style on the show. I had always been a big fan of his. When I was in Cleveland, we used to have parties and listen to his records and I loved his timing and that underplaying that he does. Everybody else back then was doing 'big' like Gleason, but Newhart was always understated. I always loved that because I think it comes naturally to me. I think it might have something to do with my Irish background — people would just sit around and zing each other quietly. I always understood his timing and admired it because I thought it was something I could do — and then to be on the show and doing it with him was unbelievable. We always understood each other.

"The greatest thing about him is that he trusts silence so much — like Jack Benny did — where what happens in the pauses is really what the funniest part is with Newhart.

"Lorenzo Music, one of the producers of the show, told me that when he and David Davis were trying to come up with the premise of the show, the main thing that they thought of was that Newhart is the kind of guy who *listens* funny. And that's so true if you remember his telephone routines from his stand-up comedy days. They thought that if they made him a shrink, it would be a perfect opportunity for him to listen funny and that's what he does."

In the mid–1970s, *The Bob Newhart Show* stood out because of that low-key approach to comedy. At the time, most other comedy shows consisted of people yelling at each other. But in those scenes in the office between Newhart and Carlin, both were allowed to underplay the scene and react off each other using the same subtle style. Riley credits all that to the show's star. "Newhart set the tone and he allowed that kind of acting on the show. He understood it — a lot of people wouldn't. I've been on shows where they'd say, 'You've gotta come in with the line — boom — because there's too much space in there.' That happens a lot. Or I'll be on a show and put out my normal energy and they'll complain that it was underplayed — as opposed to trying to be Dom DeLuise, I suppose. But there's other ways of getting laughs than being big, loud and brash."

As an example, Riley cites his appearance on Newhart's subsequent series, *Newhart*. "They brought me in for one episode where Newhart's character and his wife went to a marriage counselor. They're waiting in the outer lobby and I'm coming out of the office and the doctor says, 'Thanks Mr. Carlin, I'll see you in another week.' And I walk out of the office and he stares at me and I say, 'What are you looking at?' And he's all flustered and starts stammering — 'Oh, I'm really sorry ... you look sort of like ...' And I say, 'Gee, I'd like to stand around here all night and listen to you stutter, but I have a life,' and then I leave. The psychiatrist says to Newhart, 'You'll have to excuse Mr. Carlin. I'm trying to undo the damage that some quack in Chicago did to him 10 years ago.'

"Now *that* was a roof-raiser! I used to call them 17-blinkers. Newhart blinks 17 times and every time he gets a bigger laugh. That was great. They did it with taste and brevity and it worked." Riley also resurrected the character for a *Bob Newhart Show Reunion Retrospective* in 1993 as well as Newhart's 1997 series, *George and Leo*, and an MTM-themed episode of *St. Elsewhere*.

After Newhart pulled the plug on the series in 1978 after its sixth season, Riley found himself typecast as the grim, neurotic Mr. Carlin. "Right after the show, I was miserably typecast for a while," he says. "I was a comedy sore thumb for a long time. As they told my agent once, 'We can't have Mr. Carlin, the nut from the *Newhart Show* coming on a courtroom scene of *L.A. Law*. They actually said that. But eventually that all fades. But if it's that versus being unknown, I'll take being known anytime."

One of the benefits of being known was that it resulted in Riley being cast in the low-budget cult-movie spoof, *Attack of the Killer Tomatoes*, made in 1978 on a shoestring budget about the same size of the movies it was lampooning. The movie's producers had budgeted $1,000 for a brief appearance by a "name" actor since the rest of the cast were unknown amateurs. They chose to blow their whole wad on the guy who played their favorite character on *The Bob Newhart Show*.

"My agent told me that it would be $1,000 for a day's work and to just go down to San Diego and do it and nobody will ever hear about it," says Riley. "So I went down there and in the scene I was in, the helicopter crashed and it was all over the news."

During the post–*Bob Newhart Show* years, Riley has done numerous guest shots on a variety of sitcoms but during those times when he wasn't on television as much as he may have liked, he was able to fall back on his already-established career in the voice-over field. For the past 10 years, he has worked on the animated *Rugrats* series, which has also spawned two feature films. It is a role Riley's own do-it-yourself father would likely appreciate — he plays Stu Pickles, a stay-at-home dad and inventor.

In the advertising area, for the past 15 years he has done voice-overs with Casey DiFranco in an ongoing series of television ads for Chef's Brand Country Crock margarine. Says Riley, "I do a lot of auditioning for voice-over commercials because that's like winning the lottery when you get one of those."

He is also very active in the Los Angeles theatre scene. "I try to do at least one play a year," he says. In 2001, he appeared in *Jubilee*, a spoof of musicals which was written by Lloyd Schwartz, former writer-producer of *The Brady Bunch*. "It's a send-up of every movie musical cliché you've ever seen. My big number is a take-off on 'I've Gotta Be Me' — and it's titled, 'I Don't Want to be Me' — as in, who would want to be me?"

Sounds just like the sort of song Mr. Carlin might sing, but Riley's stage career is far removed from that character. Other theatre credits include *Twelve Angry Men, Small Craft Warnings, The Fantasticks, Zeitgeist, Inherit the Wind* and *House of Blue Leaves.*

Television is a different story and it's harder to avoid the Carlinesque roles. "I try to stay clear of it but they want that irascible type for a lot of the stuff that I'm up for," he says. However, one television venue where he is cast in roles with no resemblance to Elliot Carlin is his regular sketch-comedy work with Jay Leno on *The Tonight Show*. For a long time he played Marshall Applewhite — the fruitcake leader of the Heaven's Gate cult responsible for the mass suicide of his followers, who believed they were all going to join a UFO following in the tail of Comet Hale-Bopp. Since this was television in the 1990s, good taste was not an issue and they had Riley appearing as Applewhite *after* the suicide, giving updates from the UFO. When they cast him as Mother Theresa, however, her death ended any further appearances in that role. Even *The Tonight Show* wouldn't dare risk the public outrage if that running gag hadn't been dropped.

In conversation with Riley, it's clear that he got his greatest kick from playing the unforgettable Elliot Carlin, whom *TV Guide* put on their list of "TV's 50 Greatest Characters Ever!" in their October 16, 1999, issue. They praised Carlin as "The most neurotic man on TV." Riley still finds himself awed at being included in such a select list. "To be on the same list as Jackie Gleason and Art Carney — it was unbelievable," he says.

What made Carlin such a memorable character and worthy of inclusion in such a stellar group is that he became a fan favorite while showing absolutely no redeeming qualities — and therein lies his appeal. To TV audiences, that was his charm. Although that didn't make him unlikable, Carlin wasn't easy to warm up to. So much so, in fact that no one — not even the guy who knew him best — called him by his first name or as Elliot Carlin. Whenever Riley refers to his favorite character, it's always as "Mr. Carlin."

Jack Riley Credits

FILM CREDITS

1. *Recess: School's Out;* 2001; (voice) Golfer #1
2. *Rugrats in Paris: The Movie;* 2000; (voice) Stu Pickles
3. *The Rugrats Movie;* 1998; (voice) Stu Pickles
4. *Chairman of the Board;* 1998; Condom Boss
5. *Boogie Nights;* 1997; Amber Waves' ex-husband's lawyer
6. *Theodore Rex;* 1995; Alaric
7. *A Dangerous Woman;* 1993; Bandleader
8. *The Player;* 1992; Himself
9. *C.H.U.D. II;* 1989; Bud the Chud
10. *Gleaming the Cube;* 1989; Homeowner
11. *Spaceballs;* 1987; TV Newsman
12. *Finders Keepers;* 1984; Ormond
13. *Night Patrol;* 1984; Doctor Ziegler
14. *To Be or Not to Be;* 1983; Dobish
15. *Frances;* 1982; Bob Barnes
16. *History of the World: Part I;* 1981; Stoned Soldier
17. *Butch and Sundance: The Early Days;* 1979; Messenger
18. *Attack of the Killer Tomatoes!;* 1978; Salesman
19. *High Anxiety;* 1977; The Desk Clerk
20. *The World's Greatest Lover;* 1977; Projectionist
21. *Silent Movie;* 1976; Executive
22. *California Split;* 1974; Second Bartender
23. *Bank Shot;* 1974; Jackson
24. *The Long Goodbye;* 1973; Riley
25. *McCabe and Mrs. Miller;* 1971; Riley Quinn
26. *Catch-22;* 1970; Doctor

TV CREDITS

1. *Rugrats;* TV series; 1991– ; (voice) Stu Pickles
2. *Portrait of a White Marriage;* TV movie; 1988
3. *Roxie;* TV series; 1987; Leon Buchanan
4. *The History of White People in America, Part 2;* TV special; 1986; Scientist
5. *The History of White People in America, Part 1;* TV special; 1985; Scientist
6. *Brothers-in-Law;* TV movie; 1985; Freeman
7. *Lots of Luck;* TV movie; 1985; Marvin
8. *When Your Lover Leaves;* TV movie; 1983; Ralph
9. *Marriage Is Alive and Well;* TV movie; 1980; Owen
10. *The Tim Conway Show;* TV series; 1980–1981; various characters
11. *The Bob Newhart Show;* TV series; 1972–1978; Elliot Carlin
12. *Occasional Wife;* TV series; 1966; Wally Frick

NOTABLE TV GUEST APPEARANCES

1. *Son of the Beach;* Chappy; 8/8/2000
2. *Son of the Beach;* Chappy; 4/18/2000
3. *Son of the Beach;* Chappy; 3/28/2000
4. *Touched by an Angel;* Leo; 11/28/1997
5. *Baywatch;* 11/10/1997
6. *George and Leo;* Elliot Carlin; 11/3/1997
7. *Seinfeld;* Rider; 5/8/1997
8. *The Drew Carey Show;* Mr. Jones; 11/13/1996
9. *Coach;* Oliver; 10/5/1996
10. *Hudson Street;* Howie; 10/31/1995
11. *Friends;* Airline Passenger; 5/18/1995
12. *Too Something;* 1995
13. *Married ... with Children;* Wendell; 10/2/1994
14. *Family Matters;* Wayne; 1/22/1993
15. *Night Court;* Jim Wimberly; 1991
16. *Night Court;* Beepo; 1989
17. *Night Court;* Beepo; 1989
18. *Charles in Charge;* Professor Kleeman; 1989
19. *Newhart;* Elliot Carlin; 11/16/1988
20. *Punky Brewster;* Director; 5/3/1988
21. *Night Court;* Dr. Flick; 1987
22. *Night Court;* Dr. Flick; 1987
23. *St. Elsewhere;* Elliot Carlin; 11/20/85
24. *Night Court;* Warren Wilson; 12/6/1984
25. *Night Court;* Emil Dutton; 3/7/1984
26. *Family Ties;* Earl; 12/8/1982
27. *Eight Is Enough;* Joe Roth; 1980
28. *Barney Miller;* Robert Lovell; 2/8/1979
29. *Diff'rent Strokes;* Miles Monroe; 1978
30. *Alice;* Richard Atkins; 10/20/1976

31. *Barney Miller;* 1/29/1976
32. *Harry O;* Eddie Stern; 2 /6/1975
33. *Happy Days;* Officer O'Reilly; 2/19/1974
34. *Kung Fu;* Royal; 1/3/1974
35. *Cannon;* Programmer; 5/7/1973
36. *The Mary Tyler Moore Show;* Barry Barlow; 12/16/1972
37. *M*A*S*H;* Capt. Kaplan; 10/8/1972
38. *The Mary Tyler Moore Show;* Eldon Golfax; 10/30/1971
39. *Hogan's Heroes;* S.S. Man; 11/15/1970
40. *Hogan's Heroes;* Guard; 12/26/1969
41. *Hogan's Heroes;* Captain; 1/18/1969
42. *I Dream of Jeannie;* Frank; 10/14/1968
43. *Gomer Pyle, U.S.M.C.;* Larry; 10/13/1967
44. *Gomer Pyle, U.S.M.C.;* Larry; 10/6/1967

Ronnie Schell

Duke Slater on *Gomer Pyle, U.S.M.C.*

Ronnie Schell wears his second-banana badge with honor. He jokes that his friend Harvey Korman once kidded him at a roast: "Every time a top-flight comedian dies, Ronnie Schell moves up a banana."

"Being a second banana was always fine with me," insists Schell. He explains that he was always content playing support and letting the star deal with the pressure of carrying the show. Not that he was without ambition. He proudly points out that during almost 40 years of continuing employment in the entertainment industry, the longest time he has ever been out of work was for two weeks.

Schell's name may not be known to everyone, but his face certainly is—there was a time in the 1960s on television that he seemed to be *everywhere*. And he was—one season on *Gomer Pyle*, the next season on *That Girl*, the following season starring in his own series, *Good Morning, World* and then back to *Gomer Pyle*, where he spent a number of seasons playing Duke Slater, the barracks' wise guy who ended up as Gomer's buddy.

Schell's naturally outgoing personality and that distinctive voice which has snared him more than his share of voice-over work helped to establish his TV persona. He usually plays an overly confident eager beaver with a smooth line of patter. He's never an out-and-out con man but there's usually a bit of a hustler in his character.

Over his career, he's played lots of salesmen and sleazy executives. That glib, superficial quality also makes him ideally suited for playing show business types. On *That Girl*, he played Marlo Thomas' agent. On his own series, *Good Morning, World*, he was an AM-radio morning disc jockey and he seems so well-suited for the role that it's almost disappointing to learn that he was never involved in radio. In *The Shaggy D.A.*, one of many family films he did for Disney, he was a harried television director. In all these roles, there's something likeable about him. The character is usually a first-rate phony, but his one redeeming quality is that he doesn't know any better; he just can't help himself. No matter how shallow or despicable the character, you always get the feeling that they always actually believe whatever line of guff they're selling. Many actors can play a cliché—but Schell always injects a humanity into his roles by embracing the character's self-delusions.

Schell sums up his standard character type this way—"He's usually something like a likeable antagonist. Most of the roles I do are negative people but with a likeability to them."

That quality comes from Schell's own personality—as does the fast-talking glibness of most of his characters. "That comes from my nightclub days as a stand-up comic," he says. "My onstage persona was a sort of a smart-aleck but it was tempered with self-deprecation because I called myself 'America's Slowest-Rising Young Comedian.' When I first started in the business, I didn't have any ambitions to be a 'big' star. I always knew I had a knack for comedy because I used it in high school and college to get out of various situations, so when I got the chance to audition at the Purple Onion in San Francisco, I took it because the money was pretty good at that time. So I started out as a nightclub comedian and then I started opening for big stars and I toured with the Kingston Trio for a couple of years and they were *huge* stars. It was a wonderful job for me because there was no pressure on me. If the venue we played was packed, I would jokingly say, 'Well fellas, I told you I'd pack the place.' And if it was less than that, I would just tell myself, 'Well, it's not me — I'm just the supporting act.' I got to like that sort of groove and so when people would ask about my career, I'd say, 'It's lonely in the middle.'

"So when I got into television and movies I really had no ambition to be the big star. I enjoyed being in that groove and liked where I was— and I've never lacked for work."

Schell began entertaining at an early age. As a child, his parents would wake him up to perform and play piano at late night parties. He was born in Richmond, California, in the San Francisco Bay area on December 23 in a year during the 1940s which he will not disclose. "If people ask, I say, 'Oh, I must be in my mid-fifties.' I'm really in my sixties but I don't look it. Hollywood loves to stereotype and if they know your age, they'll say you're either too young or too old for a part just based on what it says on your birth certificate." His father, Dave, worked for a naval supply center and his mother, Marguerite, was a waitress.

An admitted class clown, Schell says he was often kicked out of class for attention-seeking antics during his days at Richmond Union High School. After graduating in the mid–1950s, he decided to go into the far more disciplined environment of the Air Force. Luckily, his superior officers found a way to harness his energy and put his natural comedic gifts to good use. After winning a few base talent contests doing record pantomimes, he was transferred to an entertainment unit and began touring airbases with a variety show and working as an emcee and stand-up comic for the force's travelling dance band, The Airmen of Note.

When his hitch was up, Schell enrolled in San Francisco State University and eventually graduated with a liberal arts degree. At the time, his studies were the last thing on his mind. "I went to college with *no* ambition other than to meet ladies," he says. "But during my senior year, I got into the drama department and I did a few plays and I got a little interested in that. There was going to be a comedy show called Campus Capers and so this other fella and I got up an act together and it absolutely brought down the house."

After that, Schell went solo and began working around town and went moving up to the Purple Onion and then to The Hungry I — the hippest room in town. In 1960, he hooked up with The Kingston Trio, toured on and off with them for three years and that led to more nightclub engagements out of town.

In those days, as today, Schell wrote his own material. But he admits that when he began, a lot of his act was borrowed. "When I started, I 'borrowed' like most young comedians do. But I wasn't stealing from other young comics. I'd steal from the big ones and I used a lot of joke books. Eventually I began putting my own attitudes and observations into my act and it seemed to work well. I might do something off-stage and someone would say that I should put it into my act. After a while, you develop your own on-stage persona.

"But I had an advantage over other comics in that I could play both kinds of clubs. I could do the hip clubs like The Hungry I or The Playboy Club but also the more mainstream clubs. If I saw that I was going to be working The Colony Club in Omaha, Nebraska, I would temper my material towards a more commercial vein. That's why I consider myself a chameleon comedian. I still do it today. Some comedians can't do it or won't do it and that's why they get reputations for saying the wrong things to the wrong audience."

It was while being out on the road working as a stand-up comic that Schell got the news which changed the direction of his career. "It was in 1964 and I was working the Hacienda Club in Fresno, California, when I got a call from my manager and he told me they were spinning off Jim Nabors' Gomer character from *The Andy Griffith Show* into his own series called *Gomer Pyle, U.S.M.C.* and they needed someone to play Gomer's best buddy. He told me that if I got the part, not to expect to do a lot of comedy because the philosophy of the producer, Aaron Ruben, was that the two main characters, Gomer and Frank Sutton's Sergeant Carter, were bigger than life and they want someone who is fairly normal and looks at both of these two people and says, 'Hey, what's going on here?' So, I sort of represented the audience."

Schell auditioned for the job and despite having no real television experience to speak of — other than being a contestant on Groucho Marx's *You Bet Your Life* while still in university, and a cameo on the syndicated 1957 police drama *Harbor Patrol* with Wendell Corey — he was cast as Private Gilbert "Duke" Slater.

He admits that he was a bit nervous for the first few episodes. "I had done some plays in college but none of them were in leading roles. So, for me it was all on-the-job training. That's where I learned as an actor how to play support and set up the situation. Whenever we had a veteran actor come on, I would observe him. Frank Sutton, who played Sgt. Carter, was the pro in our group because the rest of us were all kids. I watched him a lot and tried to learn from him because he had a lot of experience from having done Broadway and movies. He helped me a lot. Whenever I went over the top, he would always say to me, 'Hey, bring it down a little bit, you're getting too sketchy.'"

For the most part, Schell came across quite naturally despite his lack of experience. "I don't know what to attribute that to, other than the fact that as an actor in those first episodes, there wasn't that much for me to do. So I just reacted as myself to the lines that were written and that made it easy."

Originally, Schell's Duke Slater character was the ringleader of the barracks gang who would try to get naïve Gomer into some kind of trouble with Sgt. Carter. Eventually he became Gomer's friend and protector. As the series went along, Sgt. Carter, of all people, took on that role. Schell, who left the show after the third year to work on his own series, *Good Morning, World,* returned the next season as a Corporal and sharing an office with Carter.

In the first season, Ted Bessell's Frankie Lombardi character was more of a true friend of Gomer and Schell's Duke character was the Marine barracks' resident wise guy. "In the first six episodes, I'm basically a guy who's looking at Gomer and every time he does something stupid, Duke says to his buddies, 'What's with this guy?!' or he says to the Sergeant, 'Let's get rid of this loser,'" says Schell. It was in the seventh episode where the character took on his own personality. "For the first six, I just stood around googly-eyed in reaction to Gomer. But after a while, I guess Aaron Ruben got to know me a little better and started injecting more sarcasm.

"But the seventh episode, called 'Gomer and the Dragon Lady,' was my first real episode. It was about Gomer's first kiss and I con Gomer into thinking that he's going to get a kiss from a lady who runs a restaurant — knowing that she beats up everyone who puts the make on her. It ends up that she thinks Gomer is sweet and gives him a big kiss. So Sgt. Carter and Duke try it and they still get beaten up.

"I remember at the time that Aaron Ruben said to me, 'When you approach the girl, just use some lines that you would use yourself.' So I said, 'Hey baby, give me a kiss and let's go to the moon.' He liked that and put it in. The bottom line is that she did some judo moves on Duke. But that was my first real episode."

Schell was a regular on *Gomer Pyle* for the first three seasons. In 1966, while still working on the show, he also spent a season in a recurring role on *That Girl*, where he played Harvey Peck, the agent of Marlo Thomas' character. Schell's slick, fast-talking TV persona made him a natural choice to play a talent agent. "According to comedy writers, agents don't have that good of an image and they stereotype them and my character was written as one of those agents who say 'Sweetie' and 'baby' at the end of every sentence," says Schell. "But I was always in Marlo Thomas' corner, rooting for her and trying to get the character acting jobs — so that at least made me a likeable agent.

"George Carlin had played her agent before me and believe it or not, they didn't think he was right for the part. I was on the lot doing *Gomer* for the same studio and they liked what I did as Duke Slater so they put me into it as Harvey Peck."

In 1967, Schell left both *Gomer Pyle* and *That Girl* when he was offered his own series, *Good Morning, World*. The CBS sitcom was about a morning radio disc jockey team called Lewis and Clarke. Schell played Larry Clarke, a swinging single. Joby Baker was Dave Lewis, the married member of the team. Plots involved Dave's family life and Larry's interest in their neighbor, Sandy Kramer, who was played by Goldie Hawn in her pre–*Laugh-In* days.

Although it was a big jump from playing support to a co-starring lead role, Schell says he didn't feel intimidated at the time. "Surprisingly, I took it for granted. I thought of it as just part of the business. I was just moving on to the next phase in my career. I didn't take it as a big promotion because my co-star was still sort of the lead and I was more of the comic top-banana on the show.

"I never felt any pressure because it was usually about Joby's character and his problems because he was the one with the marital situation. He was the straight guy and I was more like, well, Duke Slater. I was single and loved girls and Goldie Hawn was sort of my girl in this series. The character was a bit of a deluded swinger because he always went back to Goldie. But he was definitely one of those guys who thinks he's pretty hot stuff."

Although the series was produced by Sheldon Leonard and written by Carl Reiner, who had just finished *The Dick Van Dyke Show*, it only lasted one season. "It was a show that couldn't miss and yet it did," says Schell. "At the end of the season, CBS was thinking of renewing it but Joby Baker didn't like working in front of a studio audience and he wanted out. They were thinking of replacing him with Bill Bixby but nothing came of that. But it was really the time slot that killed us. We were on opposite *Tuesday Night at the Movies* which was always really strong in the ratings."

With typical self-deprecating humor, Schell adds, "I used to say that the reason we didn't score high in the ratings was because every Tuesday night, people would look in their *TV Guides* and ask themselves, 'Well, what should we watch tonight — Ronnie Schell or Cary Grant?' And guess who won?"

He wasn't too upset or heartbroken by the news of the cancellation because he returned to *Gomer Pyle*, where he was not only welcomed back but his character was given a promotion. "The moment my show was cancelled, I was asked back to *Gomer Pyle*, which I was very happy about because it was a Top 10 show. It surprised me that it was such a hit and so when *Good Morning, World* was cancelled, it was actually thrilling to go back and be seen again on *Gomer Pyle*. I was thrilled to go back. That show was *huge*."

"The character changed quite a bit when I returned. They made him a corporal and put him in an office with Sgt. Carter," says Schell. "So now he had more responsibility and was more like Sgt. Carter's buddy. But I always favored Gomer in any situation — you know, like 'Don't be so hard on Gomer, sarge.'"

During the series' seven-year run, the character went from initially trying to get Gomer into trouble to taking a liking to him and trying to keep him out of trouble. Schell points out, "When they made me a corporal and put me in the same office with Carter, that softened my con man image a lot."

After 7 years, the writers had explored just about every situation they possibly could on *Gomer Pyle*, having taken the title character from boot camp to re-enlistment. The series ended in 1969 to make way for *The Jim Nabors Hour*, which debuted that fall. It was a variety show and Nabors brought his pals Frank Sutton and Schell along. "We did that show for two seasons and I was the main sketch comedian on there because Frank, being more of an actor, skits and sketches wasn't really his thing. So I did most of the main comedy characters — again, patterned on my own personality."

When the show was cancelled in 1971, it was due to Fred Silverman's infamous purge of all of CBS's stable of rural-appealing shows. Despite solid ratings, shows like *The Jim Nabors Hour, The Beverly Hillbillies* and *Mayberry R.F.D.* were all axed in an attempt to woo big-city audiences.

Since then, Schell has kept his hand in every form of the entertainment business. He does voice-over work for commercials, feature films and television cartoons. He's been playing Las Vegas twice a year for the past 25 years. He does the occasional guest shot on television and has been in seven Disney family films. Then there's also the corporate entertainment he does for companies like IBM.

"Early on, I diversified," he explains. "I thought it was important for longevity. And it's paid off because I'd been very fortunate in that I work all the time. Mostly I do corporate entertainment these days. I write and perform at their annual conferences and conventions. When I do the corporate stuff, there are certain rules you have to follow and you write your material to reflect their corporate philosophy so that the audience can identify with it.

"The entertainment industry has changed a lot with the times and if you want to work, you have to change with them. Not long ago, I played a crooked politician on *The Wayans Brothers*. Now, that's a TV show that's different from the sitcoms I used to do. And it's a style of comedy I don't understand. But when I was offered a guest shot, I took it — it was a very popular show.

"So I'm very lucky in that with everything that I do, I'm always working. Still, like most people in this business, every time I get a job, I worry that it's going to be my last. I just signed to do 10 concerts in Florida a year and a half from now. And that's great, but I was immediately wondering what I'm going to be doing the week after all that. But that comes with the territory."

In his downtime, Schell stays pretty close to the business. He plays softball at charity events on a team called The Re-Runs which includes Fred Willard and Jack Riley. Every Thursday, he and Riley, Pat Harrington and Harvey Korman get together in an Encino coffee shop. "I enjoy being a second banana and us bananas hang out together," says Schell. "We get together and talk about what happens in our end of the business."

The coffee shop group is a side group of the larger "Yarmy's Army," named after the late comic Dick Yarmy and the group of comedians who would go visit him in the hospital to cheer him up when he was dying of cancer. "There are about 36 of us in Yarmy's Army," Schell elaborates. "It's mostly second bananas — but lots of big stars, too. People like Tim Conway, Don Knotts and Louis Nye — those are all certainly top bananas. We get together once a month for dinner and we do shows around the country. I'm always on those tours because I'm one of the few bananas in the bunch who still has a nightclub act. A lot of the guys started out as comics but ended up as actors."

Schell puts his second-banana status to good use as the honorary Mayor of Encino, the unofficial home of all hard-working Hollywood bananas. "The Encino Chamber of Commerce has named me the Honorary Mayor for the past 12 years," he says. "I've recently moved to the west side just because of the weather but since it's all part of Los Angeles, I still get to be Mayor.

With his trademark humor, he speculates, "The real reason they make me Mayor is because I attract all the stalkers at our public events."

Ronnie Schell Credits

FILM CREDITS

1. *Pride and Peril;* 2000; Bill Taller
2. *The Good Bad Guy;* 1997; Police Chief
3. *Revenge of the Red Baron;* 1994; Lou
4. *Fatal Instinct;* 1993; Conductor
5. *Rover Dangerfield;* 1991; (voice) Eddie
6. *Jetsons: The Movie;* 1990; (voice) Rudy 2
7. *The Check Is in the Mail;* 1986; Dr. Brannigan
8. *Dutch Treat;* 1986; Lou Winters
9. *The Devil and Max Devlin;* 1981; Greg Weems
10. *How to Beat the High Cost of Living;* 1980; Bill
11. *Love at First Bite;* 1979; Gay in Elevator
12. *The Cat from Outer Space;* 1978; Sergeant Duffy/Voice of "Jake" the cat
13. *Gus;* 1976; Joe Barnsdale
14. *The Shaggy D.A.;* 1976; TV Director
15. *The Strongest Man in the World;* 1975; Referee

TV CREDITS

1. *Family Album;* TV miniseries; 1994; The Emcee
2. *Leisure Suit Larry 6: Shape Up or Slip Out!* TV special; 1993; (voice) Jimmy the Bartender/Kenny
3. *Hollyrock-a-Bye Baby;* TV movie; 1993; (voice)
4. *I Yabba-Dabba Do!;* TV movie; 1993; (voice)
5. *Perfect People;* TV movie; 1988; Dr. Stroud
6. *Scooby Doo Meets the Boo Brothers;* TV movie; 1987; (voice) Freako
7. *Santa Barbara;* TV series; 1985; 1988; Frank Armsted
8. *Down to Earth;* TV series; 1984; Lester Luster
9. *The Smurfs;* TV series; 1981; (voice)
10. *Kraft Salutes Disneyland's 25th Anniversary;* TV special; 1980; Himself
11. *Casper and the Angels;* TV series; 1979; (voice)
12. *Battle of the Planets;* TV series; 1978; Jason
13. *The Mouseketeers at Walt Disney World;* TV special; 1978
14. *Forever Fernwood;* TV series; 1977; Piersall
15. *Fred Flintstone and Friends;* TV series; 1977; (voice)
16. *The Whiz Kid and the Carnival Caper;* TV movie; 1976; Deputy Scruff
17. *The Imposter;* TV movie; 1975; Dance director
18. *Butch Cassidy and the Sundance Kids;* TV series; 1973; (voice)
19. *Goober and the Ghost-Chasers;* TV series; 1973; (voice) Gilly
20. *The Jim Nabors Hour;* TV series; 1969–1971; Himself
21. *Good Morning, World,* TV series; 1967; Larry Clarke
22. *That Girl;* TV series; 1966–67; Harvey Peck

23. *Gomer Pyle, U.S.M.C.;* TV series; 1964–1967; 1968–1969; Gilbert "Duke" Slater

NOTABLE TV GUEST APPEARANCES

1. *The Wayans Brothers;* Councilman Ted McKay; 10/1/1998
2. *Coach;* Dr. Howard; 11/14/1995
3. *Step by Step;* 1991
4. *The Golden Girls;* Thomas; 1/23/1990
5. *Saved by the Bell;* Elliot Stingwell; 1989
6. *Mathnet;* Art Fraud; 1987
7. *The New Love, American Style;* 1/6/1986
8. *Sledge Hammer!;* Reporter; 1986
9. *Shadow Chasers;* Mel Ferdman; 1985
10. *Too Close for Comfort;* 1982
11. *Alice;* Ken Baldwin; 11/18/1979
12. *Mork and Mindy;* Bob Faith; 9/23/1979
13. *Mork and Mindy;* Bob Faith; 9/16/1979
14. *Charlie's Angels;* Ernie Flack; 3/7/1979
15. *The Dukes of Hazzard;* Lester Starr; 2/2/1979
16. *Alice;* Buck; 3/26/1977
17. *Emergency!;* Allan Hendricks; 10/23/1976
18. *Emergency!;* Jasper, the drunk; 1/17/1976
19. *Emergency!;* Harold Peterson; 2/8/1975
20. *Happy Days;* Monty Miller; 12/5/1974
21. *Adam-12;* Jack Hofstead; 9/24/1974
22. *Happy Days;* Ernie; 5/7/1974
23. *Adam-12;* Henry Klemp; 12/15/1973
24. *Temperature's Rising;* 11/20/1973
25. *Emergency!;* Fred; 11/10/1973
26. *The Andy Griffith Show;* Bernie, the furrier; 2/26/1968
27. *The Andy Griffith Show;* Jim Martin; 3/21/1966

Rose Marie

Sally Rogers on *The Dick Van Dyke Show*
(shown with Morey Amsterdam as Buddy Sorrell)

Rose Marie has no problem with the term second banana. After all, that was her billing when she was second on the bill in the Broadway production of Phil Silvers' *Top Banana* in 1951.

The musical comedy featured Silvers in the title role as Jerry Biffle, a Milton Berle–like television comic. Rose Marie played Betty Dillon, a girl with her own showbiz dreams. Her big solo in the show, "I Fought Every Step of the Way," could be considered an anthem for all second bananas.

"In that show, it wasn't a matter of the rest of us playing straight man to Phil," explains Rose Marie. "It was like, after Phil, I was the next one. Not co-star, but almost co-star. The term 'top banana' came from burlesque. The star was the top banana and all the other comics were second bananas. It never went to the third or fourth banana. And in that show, we had all the best ones—Herbie Faye, Joey Faye, Jack Albertson.

"When they were casting the show, Phil told the producer, Jack Donohue, to get all the best guys from burlesque because they were the ones who *knew*. And I said to him, 'You know Phil, to be truthful, all of these people can steal the show from you.' And he said, 'Good. Because they will only make me work harder and they will only make me look better.' I never forgot that. That attitude comes from the big people. They know it's for the good of the show."

Other than Silvers, she cites Jackie Gleason and Dick Van Dyke as two of the "big ones" who recognized the importance of surrounding themselves with people steeped in the second-banana tradition.

Of her years co-starring with Morey Amsterdam on *The Dick Van Dyke Show*, she says, "I'm not thrilled with the title 'second banana' but the thing of it is, the second banana *makes* the show—no matter what it is. I mean, with our show, how many times can you hear Mary Tyler Moore say, 'Oh, Rob!'? You've got to have some diversion and Morey and I were that—as were Art Carney and Audrey Meadows on *The Honeymooners*. Gleason was the greatest thing in the world, but you *need* that help."

When she was cast in *Top Banana* at the age of 28, Rose Marie was already a show business veteran and had turned professional a quarter of a century earlier.

Born Rose Marie Mazzetta on August 15, 1923, in New York, she won her first singing contest on the radio at the age of three. At five, she had her own national radio program on NBC following *Amos and Andy* and titled *Baby Rose Marie*. Her singing voice was the same deep husky voice that she used as an adult in musical numbers on *The Dick Van Dyke Show*. When she was seven, NBC sent her on a publicity tour of all the major cities, accompanied by her father and her own band, so the public could see that the voice of Baby Rose Marie did indeed belong to a child.

Her film career began at the age of six in the 1929 musical short *Baby Rose Marie: The Child Wonder*. She appeared in other musical shorts between 1932 and '34. Her first feature-length film was *International House*, starring W.C. Fields in 1933. Her next feature movie wouldn't be until 1953 in the film version of *Top Banana*. "Oh, that was terrible," she says of the film. "They just filmed it as it was played on-stage." Even stranger, it was filmed in 3-D for no other apparent reason than it was the latest fad.

At the age of 11, she dropped the "Baby" from her name and was simply billed as "Rose Marie." Long before Cher and Madonna, she was a woman singer who was known by her first name alone. As a teenager, she was a headliner on the nightclub circuit at upscale clubs like The Copacabana and the Latin Quarter in New York. By the end of the 1940s, she was a well-known radio, nightclub and recording star. In 1946, mobster Bugsy Siegel hired her and Jimmy Durante and Xavier Cugat to open Las Vegas' first luxury casino-nightclub, The Flamingo. Of her two weeks there, she says, "For the opening of The Flamingo, the place was packed with everyone from Hollywood. But by the second week, everyone had gone back home and we were playing for nine and ten people a night." As the Strip grew, she would be back many times as a headliner.

During the 1940s, Rose Marie married musician Bobby Guy, who later worked as first trumpet player with the NBC orchestra. She says that they were a very social couple and this indirectly led to a job on *The Dick Van Dyke Show* in 1960 because it was produced by an old pal, Sheldon Leonard, who was also the producer of *The Andy Griffith Show* and *The Danny Thomas Show*.

"I had been friendly with Danny Thomas and Sheldon Leonard for years before *The Dick Van Dyke Show*," she explains. "When Danny came from Chicago to New York, I was his opening act when he played The Martinique and was the Great White Hope of the nightclub business and we became friends at that time. And when I came out here to California, I worked on the radio as Sheldon Leonard's sister on *The Phil Harris Show*. So when Danny was doing *The Danny Thomas Show*, my husband played first trumpet on the show and I kept saying to Danny, 'When are you going to use me on the show?' And Sheldon would always say, 'Don't worry, your time will come.'

"In the meantime, they'd come over to the house for dinner or we'd go to their homes and when I worked Vegas, they'd come down and see the show. So anyway, one day I get a call from the casting director of the production company and I said, 'Well, finally—I get a shot on Danny's show,' and she said, 'No, this is for a new show called *The Dick Van Dyke Show*.' And I said, 'What's a Dick Van Dyke?'

"Dick was well-known back East. But out here and back East are two different worlds and neither one knows what's going on at the other coast."

As executive producer, Sheldon Leonard thought that the role of TV comedy writer Sally Rogers was a part that Rose Marie was born to play. Writer-producer Carl Reiner had created the character partly based on the writer and actress Selma Diamond, whom he had worked with on Sid Caesar's *Your Show of Shows*. Originally, he had based the other writer in the script, Buddy Sorrell, on another writer from the show, Mel Brooks.

Rose Marie continues, "So I went down and I met Carl Reiner and Sheldon said, 'If you want the best, get Rose Marie,' and I was very flattered that he said that because after the show went on, Carl sent me a wire saying, 'Sheldon was right,' and I treasure that very much. Anyway, I said, 'What's the show about' and they said, 'Writers, blah, blah, blah ...' and I asked them, 'Well, do you have a third writer yet?' And they said no, so I said, 'Well, what about Morey Amsterdam?' And they just looked at me. So I said, 'Well, he's a writer and he's a comic,' and they *all* knew him.

"This business is so funny. You can be friendly with someone and have dinner with them all the time but they wouldn't think of you for a part unless you said to them, 'What about me?!' Out here, your whole career can be summed up in The Legend of Show Business. It's a series of questions over the years and goes like this, 'Who is Rose Marie?' 'Get me Rose Marie.' 'Get me a Rose Marie type.' 'Who is Rose Marie?'

"Well, they asked me if I knew where they could reach him and I said, 'Sure. I've known him since I was 11 years old' and I gave them his phone number because he was living in Yonkers, New York. So I went home and called Morey and told him that they were going to call him about a new show called *The Dick Van Dyke Show*.' And *he* said, 'What's a Dick Van Dyke?'"

The fact that both Rose Marie and Amsterdam separately came up with the same punch line says a lot about their relationship both on and off *The Dick Van Dyke Show*. She had first met him in 1935 on radio's *Al Pierce and His Gang*. During the 1950s, he wrote material for her nightclub act. Years after the *Van Dyke Show*, they played an old long-married couple on a 1996 episode of the sitcom *Caroline in the City* in what would be Amsterdam's last television appearance.

On *The Dick Van Dyke Show*, Sally Rogers was single and always looking for a potential husband. Buddy was married to the seldom-seen "Pickles." When Van Dyke and Mary Tyler Moore's characters Rob and Laura Petrie were having the gang over for dinner or a party, Buddy and Sally would usually show up together and without dates. It might have been because of frugality on the part of the producers, who didn't want to hire a couple of actors for just one scene. Or maybe it was because Pickles—who was the subject of many of Buddy's jokes—was best imagined than actually seen, much like Norm's wife Vera on *Cheers* or Maris, the unseen wife of Niles Crane on *Frasier*.

Whatever the reason for Pickles' frequent absence from all those parties, it helped establish the notion that Buddy and Sally were just like a married couple. They got along but argued and were on the same wavelength—and like any long married couple, they were so in tune with each other that, just like the actors playing them, they finished each others' sentences and could simultaneously arrive at the same punch line to a joke.

They were a "couple" in every sense of the word, except for romance. Marriage would never have even been a consideration. That would have eliminated half of their material. Sally was always doing bits about her bad dates and trying to trap a man and Buddy had just as many one-liners about Pickles as he did about Richard Deacon's Mel Cooley character, whenever he had the misfortune of walking into the writers' office.

"I thought it would be perfect if they could utilize Morey just the way he was," says Rose Marie. "Morey also wrote a lot of our stuff on the show. If they were stuck for a joke or an idea, he'd say, 'Wait a minute, I'll write something.'"

It was not unusual for Amsterdam to come up with a number of jokes for any situation. He was known in the business as The Human Joke-Machine. He had written for all the greats—Jack Benny, Milton Berle, Henny Youngman—and he had an encyclopedic knowledge of jokes, having begun in vaudeville as a teenager in the 1920s. Not all of them were good but they were all readily available, on the tip of his tongue.

Amsterdam's first television job was on a panel of "experts" on the 1948 quiz show *Stop Me If You've Heard This One*. The same year, he was given his own variety hour, *The Morey Amsterdam Show*, with Art Carney as his sidekick. It lasted two years, first on CBS and then on the Du Mont network. In 1950, he was one of the rotating hosts of *Broadway Open House*, a late night variety program. He was also a regular panelist on the quiz show *Who Said That* and the 1958 celebrity game shows *Make Me Laugh* and *Keep Talking*, which was hosted by Carl Reiner. By the time *The Dick Van Dyke Show* came along, Amsterdam, like his character, was an authentic show business veteran.

Of the differences between Buddy Sorrell and Morey Amsterdam, Rose Marie says, "Morey was playing himself to a degree. He was a little overboard on the show because in real life, Morey was never 'on.' He wasn't full of jokes all the time. He wasn't loud. At parties, he was full of stories and he had a comic's license to use a one-liner on occasion. But he was never 'on' to the point where you would have to say, 'Shut up! Just shut up!'

"He was married and had a wonderful family, lived very well and was a very sweet, dear man. Let me tell you one thing about Morey — he never talked badly about *anybody*. I never heard him criticize anyone. He was a much beloved member of our industry."

The high esteem with which Amsterdam was held in his profession can be seen with a glimpse at the cast list of his self-penned 1966 movie, *Don't Worry, We'll Think of a Title Later.* It starred himself, Rose Marie and Richard Deacon from *The Dick Van Dyke Show.* The cast was made up of a who's who of comedy with cameos by the big names like Steve Allen, Milton Berle and Danny Thomas, as well as old friends like head Stooge Moe Howard, Irene ("Granny Clampett") Ryan, Carl Reiner and Cliff ("Charlie Weaver") Arquette.

When Amsterdam died of a heart attack at the age of 88 in 1996, that respect was still there. "Morey's funeral was the best show in town," says Rose Marie. "Every comic in Hollywood was there and everybody had something to say and there was one laugh after another — which is what Morey would have wanted."

Rose Marie says that like Amsterdam playing Buddy, playing Sally Rogers wasn't much of a stretch for her. "I just sort of played myself," she admits. "*But,* I was happily married. That was the difference. I *am* an actress, don't forget. But basically, I'm a performer. I started in radio when I was five years old, so I've been in this business a very long time. I enjoy my work. I love what I do — but basically, I'm a performer."

What Sally Rogers and Rose Marie had most in common was that they were both career girls long before that became common. At the time, most women stayed home and raised the kids. In the writers' room, Sally was treated like an equal and that was the same situation with Rose Marie on the set. Quite often, *The Dick Van Dyke Show* was a workplace comedy, as was *The Mary Tyler Moore Show.* In the first half of the century, women like Sally Rogers and Rose Marie were pioneers. Without them, there may not have been a *Mary Tyler Moore Show* in the 1970s.

Says Rose Marie, "Carl Reiner somewhat based Sally Rogers on Selma Diamond, a writer he worked with on Sid Caesar's show. So that's where the attitude of Sally just being one of the boys comes from. Basically, I was one of the first women on TV who was treated equally. As for myself, they sort of took all that for granted because I was working alongside friends I had known for years. I was there, I worked with the guys, I was treated like an equal and I was making the same money so I think that sort of broke down some barriers. I've had so many letters where people tell me, 'Because of *you* I became a writer,' or 'I was treated differently, you set the pace for the rest of us.'"

In a long and varied career, Rose Marie counts *The Dick Van Dyke Show* as five of the happiest years of her life. "We all enjoyed our jobs there," she says. "Dick was the easiest guy in the world to get along with. He'd sit in the corner and doodle all day. But that man is so talented, he doesn't even know how talented he is.

"Everyone looked up to Sheldon Leonard with the greatest respect. In his comments during the script readings, he'd know exactly what was wrong. But he'd also say, 'This is bad, but I'll tell you how to fix it.' You don't mind if someone criticizes if they can tell you how to fix the problem. Sheldon was a genius that way and he was doing the same on other shows and going from one set to the next. He'd come in, make his suggestions and then he'd be gone. His nickname on the set was 'Lamont Cranston' because he was like The Shadow."

When the series went off the air in 1966, Rose Marie continued working with more of her friends on the celebrity game show *Hollywood Squares,* where she was the only regular to appear on both the first and last episodes of that series' original run. Over the years, she has starred in her own short-lived series, the baseball comedy *Hardball* in 1994 and the fantasy sitcom *Scorch* in 1992. Prior to the *Van Dyke Show,* she had also been a regular supporting player for three years on *The Bob Cummings Show* in the mid–1950s and on the one-year run of *My Sister Eileen* in 1960.

But her most fond memories are from the CBS series for which she is best remembered. "When the show came to an end, we were all very sad," she says of the last days of *The Dick Van Dyke Show.* "We didn't want it to come to an end. We thought we could do another two or three years. But Dick wanted to do movies and Carl thought he was all dried up so it was a case of 'Let's quit while we're ahead.'"

Rose Marie Credits

FILM CREDITS

1. *Shriek If You Know What I Did Last Friday the 13th;* 2000; Mrs. Tingle
2. *Lost and Found;* 1999; Clara
3. *Sandman;* 1993; Car Saleswoman
4. *Witchboard;* 1985; Mrs. Moses
5. *Bruce's Fingers;* 1980
6. *Cheaper to Keep Her;* 1980; Ida Bracken

7. *Lunch Wagon;* 1980; Mrs. Schmeckler
8. *The Honey Cup;* 1975
9. *The Man from Clover Grove;* 1975; Sister Mary
10. *Memory of Us;* 1974; Housekeeper
11. *Dead Heat on a Merry-Go-Round;* 1966; Margaret Kirby
12. *Don't Worry, We'll Think of a Title Later;* 1966; Annie
13. *The Big Beat;* 1958; May Gordon
14. *Top Banana;* 1953; Betty Dillon
15. *Rambling 'Round Radio Row 1934;* 1934; Herself — Baby Rose Marie
16. *Back in '23;* 1933; Herself — Baby Rose Marie
17. *Sing, Babies, Sing;* 1933; Herself — Baby Rose Marie
18. *International House;* 1933; Herself — Baby Rose Marie
19. *Rambling 'Round Radio Row 1932;* 1932; Herself — Baby Rose Marie
20. *Baby Rose Marie, the Child Wonder;* 1929; Herself — Baby Rose Marie

TV CREDITS

1. *Cagney and Lacey: Together Again;* TV movie; 1995; Mitzi Glass
2. *Hardball;* TV series; 1994; Mitzi Balzer
3. *Scorch;* TV series; 1992; Edna Bracken
4. *Bridge Across Time;* TV movie; 1985; Alma Bellock
5. *Honeymoon Suite;* TV series; 1973
6. *The Doris Day Show;* TV series; 1969–1971; Myrna Gibbons
7. *The Hollywood Squares;* TV series; 1966–1981; Herself
8. *The Dick Van Dyke Show;* TV series; 1961–1966; Sally Rogers
9. *My Sister Eileen;* TV series; 1960; Bertha
10. *The Bob Cummings Show;* TV series; 1955–1959

NOTABLE TV GUEST APPEARANCES

1. *The Hughleys;* Edna, Sally's mother; 3/19/2001
2. *Suddenly Susan;* 11/24/1997
3. *Wings;* Eleanor Bluto Biggins; 4/16/1997
4. *Caroline in the City;* Stella Dawson; 1/21/1997
5. *Caroline in the City;* Stella Dawson; 2/1/1996
6. *Herman's Head;* Sally; 10/7/1993
7. *Ultraman: The Ultimate Hero;* 1993
8. *Murphy Brown;* Frank's Mother; 2/25/1991
9. *Murphy Brown;* Rose Fontana; 10/1/1990
10. *Remington Steele;* Billie Young; 3/8/1986
11. *The Real Ghostbusters;* (voice) Mrs. Spengler; 1986
12. *CHiPS;* Herself; 12/7/1980
13. *The Love Boat;* 1977
14. *Chico and the Man;* Kissy Face; 12/24/1976
15. *S.W.A.T.;* Hilda; 12/13/1975
16. *S.W.A.T.;* Hilda; 4/28/1975
17. *Kojak;* Mrs. Tildon; 2/23/1975

18. *Petrocelli;* 9/11/1974
19. *Adam-12;* Jean Wagner; 1/17/1973
20. *Adam-12;* Woman at Bus Depot; 1/19/1972
21. *My Three Sons;* Genevieve Goodbody; 12/7/1968
22. *The Virginian;* The Lady from Wichita; 9/27/1967
23. *Hey, Landlord;* Aunt Harriet; 4/23/1967
24. *The Monkees;* Millie Rudnick; 3/20/1967
25. *The Monkees;* Bessie Kowalski; 10/24/1966
26. *The Adventures of Jim Bowie;* 1/3/1958
27. *Gunsmoke;* Mrs. Monger; 12/28/1957

Larry Storch

Corporal Randolph Agarn on *F Troop*

As a teenager growing up in the Bronx borough of New York during the first part of the 20th century, Larry Storch would go to weekend parties with neighborhood pals like the Yarmy boys, the Karvelas brothers and Jimmy Komack. Instead of sitting around talking about girls and sports or telling jokes and spinning records, their gang would try to top each other in doing impersonations of various celebrities.

Most of them would go on to careers in show business. Komack would become a producer of TV shows like *Get Smart, The Courtship of Eddie's Father* and *Welcome Back, Kotter.* Dick Yarmy would become a stand-up comic famous on the nightclub circuit and beloved by his peers. His brother Don would change his name to Don Adams and star as Secret Agent Maxwell Smart on *Get Smart,* where he would occasionally employ his Bogie imitation. He also employed his cousin, Robert Karvelas, to play Larabee, the Chief's assistant and the only Control agent dumber than Max.

But without question, the best mimic of the bunch was Larry Storch and his imitations would be his entry into show business. Since the age of 14, he had been making the rounds of amateur talent contests and picking up the prize money for his dead-on impressions of movie stars. When he was 17, he made his professional debut at New York's Paramount Theatre on the same bill as Benny Goodman and Peggy Lee. Over the years, celebrity impersonations and his ability to do foreign dialects would be his trademark and he gained a reputation as "The Greatest Ear in the Business." He once spent three days in 1947 in Las Vegas teaching Sammy Davis Jr. the fundamentals of the art and Cary Grant credited him with being the originator of the oft-repeated "Judy, Judy, Judy," line.

Storch's talent for dialects was put to good use on the TV series he is best known for — *F Troop,* where he played the Irish New Jersey post–Civil War cavalryman Corporal Randolph Agarn. On the 1960s sitcom, the writers took advantage of his knack with accents and wrote episodes featuring the actor as visiting overseas members of the Agarn family. The French branch was represented by Lucky Pierre Agarniere and *F Troop's* Fort Courage was also visited by the Russian Dmitri Agarnoff.

Impersonations and dialects are still such a big part of Storch that in conversation with the man, you never know just who you will be talking to from one minute to the next. It could be Cary Grant, Edward Everett Horton or any number of ethnic variations of Joe Sixpack. Impersonations flow out of Storch as naturally as bad jokes from Morey Amsterdam.

Professionally as well, Storch is still getting work from his talent with dialects. After years of living in California, he and his wife returned to New York in the 1980s hoping to retire and take it easy in his old home town. Instead, he's been active in plays ever since, getting back in a wide variety of ethnic roles—an Italian gangster, a German scientist, an old–South riverboat captain. In his latest play, the Broadway touring production of *Annie Get Your Gun*, the 78-year-old Storch played Chief Sitting Bull. "It's a bit of a stretch for me," he jokes. "After having been a cavalry soldier on *F Troop*, to now run over to the Indian side, that's a stretch—but I can do it."

Storch credits growing up in the great melting pot that was New York City back in the Depression for his ability to mimic various races and celebrities. Born on January 8, 1923, Storch admits that he spent as little time in school as possible. Instead, he went to the movies and would study the mannerisms and vocal stylings of the people up on the screen. As well, he lived in an area which saw lots of newly landed immigrants passing through and he was fascinated by their accents.

"Being able to do dialects was a blessing," he says. "Throughout my career I've done Oriental roles, Russians, Germans, almost every nationality you can imagine—and now Sitting Bull, a Native-American.

"I grew up in the Bronx but when I really picked up on the dialects was about 1933 or so when I was living in New York City. When the immigrants came off the boat in those days, it was a real accent, pure and hadn't been watered down and I was able to imitate that. They all came through the house I was living in—the Spanish, Germans, French, Japanese, and I glommed right onto it. Their voices absolutely enthralled me.

"I always had a gift for imitating. I could do my parents and grandparents and the neighbors around us. Gradually, I began doing people on the movie screen."

At the age of 14, Storch entered a talent contest at a local movie theatre, did his impersonations of Edward G. Robinson, James Cagney and Lionel Barrymore and walked off with the $2 prize. Knowing he was on to a good thing, he began going to other theatres and entering their amateur contests. Before long he had a whole circuit of New York area movie theatres which he worked as a way of picking up the easy winnings. "I did a good Lionel Barrymore," remembers Storch. "And he was a big star at the time and for a young kid to be able to do that kind of stuff was very odd for the audience—so I won my share of $2 or $5 bills in the process."

He also made a reputation for himself and when he was only 17, he was invited to join a group of professional impersonators at the Paramount Theatre on the same bill as Benny Goodman and Peggy Lee. Storch explains, "It was 1940 when I got my first salary for a week's work on the stage. There was a trio of impersonators called The Radio Rogues. They were about 10 years older than me and between the three of them they did all the big names of the time. One guy did the politicians, another did musicians like Louis Armstrong and another did movie stars. Well, the fellow who specialized in actors came down with laryngitis and they had this big gig coming up at the Paramount. They knew that I could do Jimmy Cagney, Edward G. Robinson, Cary Grant and all of that and so the one fellow says to me, 'Listen kid, until the other guy gets back on his feet, we'll give you a tuxedo, so skip school and come on down and get your feet wet.' Which I did — and here I was on the stage of the Paramount with Benny Goodman and Peggy Lee. You can imagine what a rush that was for a young kid like myself."

Indeed. It made such an impact on young Storch that it was the end of his time in school. "After my first show, my mother said, 'Well, what's going to happen now?' And I told her, 'Momma, I'm through conjugating verbs. This is *it!* My school days are over.'"

By Storch's own admission, it was just a matter of time anyway and he sums up his scholastic career by saying, "I went to high school for about 20 minutes." He says that he spent so much time skipping school and hanging out in movie theatres that he was actually "encouraged" by his principal at Clinton High School not to return. He was labeled "incorrigible" and his mother was called in for a meeting to discuss his future.

"I was called 'useless' by the principal," recalls Storch. "'Oh, he's a storyteller and a joke-teller, Mrs. Storch. He's useless here and if he wants to get out and make it in the world, I think that's a good idea.' This is the principal talking! And my mother is wringing her hands and pleading, 'Oh please take him back! Take him back, he'll be good.' And I'm going, 'No, no Momma. Listen to the principal. He knows what he's talking about.' And that's how my school days ended. And I've never looked back."

Indeed, he hasn't. Following his week at the Paramount, Storch was approached by an agent who promised him jobs that would get him $125 a week. As it turned out, his first job paid somewhat less. "I remember going out for my first job out of high school and it was at Ye Olde Tavern in West Brookfield, Massachusetts. My pay was $35 a week and I said a little prayer, 'Lord, if you boost me to $50 a week, I'll never ask for anything else again. Just get me $50, Lord and I'll be satisfied.' That's the way we worked in those days. Salaries were very low."

In fact, during his early days, Storch would occasionally augment his income by doing the talent shows and amateur contests. "They paid a five dollar prize a night if you won and that was a good deal of money in those days because it was hard and tough times. So I would work during the week and pick up a little extra on the weekends at those contests— anything where I could pick up an extra dollar here or there."

Storch says he was able to get steady work because he had no trouble coming up with an act. "If you could do impersonations, it was the easiest way to get yourself on stage. You could put an act together in half an hour—'And look who's coming down the street, why it's Jimmy Cagney! Hello Mr. Cagney,' and then 'You dirty rat, I'm gonna give it to you just like you gave it to my brother...' 'And now who's coming down the street? Why it's Edward G. Robinson ...' So it was very easy to put an act together and get yourself on stage immediately back then."

Instead of relying on just the big names, the Cagneys and Robinsons of show business, Storch began to specialize in the lesser-known character actors. "People like Edward Everett Horton and Frank Morgan—even though they weren't as famous as the big stars, they had distinct voices which were instantly recognizable," says Storch. Character actors like Guy Kibbee and Charles Grapewin may not be remembered today but in the early 1940s, Storch's take on them helped set him apart from the other impersonators.

However, sometimes specialization isn't such a good thing. He tells the story of how he learned this the hard way. "I was very ambitious at one time and I had billed myself as 'The Rembrandt of impressionists.' I had recently seen a Claude Raines movie and had gotten his voice down and shortly afterwards opened up at a place in Massachusetts and said, 'My first impression will be Claude Raines.' After the show, the owner says, 'Hey kid, c'mere. My customers don't know who Rembrandt is—you're fired.'"

In his first couple of years on the nightclub circuit, Storch worked a lot of burlesque theatres. "'And here she is now, the buxom Letitia,' I'd say and then I would stand back and out would come the striptease dancer," says Storch of his main function on the bill. "Then I'd do some impersonations and tell Irish jokes between their acts. Nobody ever gave me a hard time. I did an interesting act and you can't get mad at an impersonator. For the audience, they figured, 'What the hell.' My show helped pass the time of day until the girls came out. It was all experience and between the stories and the impressions, I earned my $35 a week."

In 1942, Storch joined the Navy and was assigned to a Special Forces entertainment unit run by musician Commander Eddie Peabody. He remembers, "They put me in the band and said, 'Listen, do you think you can play the cymbals without lousing up the national anthem?' And I said, 'Sure,' and they made me a cymbal player and I became a Musician—Second Class."

He may have been officially listed as a "cymbal player," but his main role was that of comedian. "We were sent overseas in '43 to Hawaii and then Okinawa to tour naval bases. We went to all the remote little islands and the big ships—we played them all. Peabody took a magician, me and a trio of musicians. Our audiences were a captive audience but they were so grateful to hear any kind of live music on those isolated islands."

While in the Navy, Storch made a lifelong friend in Bernie Schwartz, who was working as a crew member on a submarine tender. Both men had an interest in show business and when Storch was working nightclubs like The Copacabana after the war, he hired Schwartz as a personal assistant for a time. A few years later, after Schwartz had changed his name to Tony Curtis, he helped Storch break into the movies.

Following the war, Storch slowly began to change his act to include more comedy. "It was a gradual sort of thing," he says in describing the evolution of his act. "Originally I would open with an Irish joke and then gradually I put in a few quick little jokes in between the impressions and then little by little, I was doing more jokes. Finally I started doing other things like eccentric dancing—I did a take-off on The Tango—and some physical comedy. I had a yoga routine where I got myself all twisted up and couldn't untie myself and the stage hands would have to come and carry me off the stage. Back then, we rehearsed like mad and also we all had a few songs in our acts."

With the change he began getting booked into better clubs and also began working the Catskills circuit. "That's what we all did back then. Morey Amsterdam, Jack Carter, Henny Youngman, they all did the same as I did. It was constant touring and sometimes you would get stranded while out on the road."

It was while out on the road and hitchhiking after getting back from the war that Storch ran into an old friend, Stan Davis, who was a writer on Bing Crosby's *Kraft Music Hall* radio program. Storch began working on the show as a writer. But because of his background as an impersonator, he would occasionally be asked to imitate on the air one of the show's stars, Frank Morgan, if he wasn't around. Morgan is best known today as the Wizard in *The Wizard of Oz*. Years later, when Storch and his childhood friend, Don Adams, were doing voice-over work for the cartoon series *Tennessee Tuxedo*, Storch would do his Frank Morgan voice for the character of Mr. Whoopee.

While doing the radio show, Storch met the influential newspaper columnist Hedda Hopper in 1945 and she liked him so much that she got him into The Copacabana in New York. "Hedda Hopper, she's my fairy godmother," says Storch. "She got in back of me and gave me all the help in the world."

Hopper arranged an audition for Storch out West at a new nightclub and this resulted in meeting another powerful woman. "Desi Arnaz was opening a nightclub in Hollywood called Ciro's. I wasn't sure that I would be a hit so I packed my navy uniform in case I had to hitchhike back to New York. I auditioned for Lucille Ball and did my impersonations and she said, 'Fine. You can open for Desi and his band and do 15 minutes before he comes out and does Babaloo.' And I was there for 11 weeks. So Lucy played a big role in my career."

After that, Storch was booked solid in many of the better clubs in the big cities. "By the time I got into the New York rooms like the Copa, my days at the Catskills were numbered. After that, you didn't like to drive to those places." It was while working in the more upscale clubs that Storch was noticed in 1952 by the producers of the television show *Cavalcade of Stars*, which was on the Dumont network. Jackie Gleason had just finished his first season and they needed a host for the replacement summer series while Gleason was on vacation.

By this point, Storch's nightclub act had evolved considerably. He still did celebrity impersonations but he now used his gift for dialects in creating a number of stock characters. This is what impressed the producers of *Cavalcade*. In hiring Storch, they were hiring someone who brought with him a number of diverse, already fully created characters who could be used in any number of sketches as well as routines from Storch's act. They had also known of Storch's work in a Chicago revue called *Red, White and Blue* and knew that even though he was only 29 years old, he was already a show business veteran and a well-rounded entertainer who could sing, dance, tell jokes and act. In other words, he was the ideal host for a variety series.

There was no audition for the job as host of *Cavalcade*. The producers hand-picked him and Gleason gave him his blessing. Storch remembers getting the job this way: "The Great One called me up to his office which was in his hotel suite and he comes out in a bathrobe and says, 'All right, Larry. I'm going to let you take over for the summer. I'm leaving Art Carney with you. My advice to you is this—We're *live*, Larry. Hundreds, maybe even thousands of people watch this show and they'll be watching you, you know that don't you? So just don't use any four-letter words—can you remember that?' I said, 'Yes sir,' and he said, 'Goodbye and good luck,' and that's how I got the show."

The show's writers capitalized on Storch's talent for dialects and wrote sketches in which he spoke in whatever accent the situation called for — Cockney, French, East Side New York. Storch contributed to the writing of the show and also did recurring characters week to week. There was Victor, a 10-year-old brat; Smiley Higgins, a TV cowboy and Railroad Jack, a philosophical hobo.

Another was Barrington Darvey, a proper English gentleman who worked for the BBC as a reluctant boxing commentator. The sport was all too much for Darvey, who was repulsed by the whole exhibition and could barely force himself to look at the fight he was covering. Storch gave him lines like, "My, but that one chap seems to have utter disregard for the other. Another crack in the ribs, oh dear me! Oh, that *was* a blow. Thank heavens it's all over!"

One of his most popular characters was Willie, the teenaged zoot-suiter from New Jersey. Many of his routines as Willie were monologues done as telephone conversations. In one, he complained about his mother — "What am I going to do wit my mudder? Today she throws the blanket back from my sack, calls me a bum and tells me to get a job. Imagine that? Four o'clock in de afternoon and my old lady wants me to run out and look for a job!"

"I got along very well with the writers on the show," says Storch. "They had a streak of Nat Hiken about them — he was the genius who created *Car 54, Where Are You?* They had that kind of comedic style which I liked very much and they also took advantage of various dialects I could do."

He also enjoyed working with Art Carney. "He was the greatest. There was nobody in the world like Art Carney. There was a streak of madness about him. He would erupt into things that were just hysterical and you had to be on your toes with him because it was live. It was a delight just being with Art Carney. You see, Gleason wouldn't work with anybody who wasn't a genius."

When Gleason moved the show's production team from Du Mont to the CBS network the next season, Storch was again asked back as a summer replacement for *The Jackie Gleason Show*. The format was the same as it had been on *Cavalcade of Stars*, but now it was on a bigger network, reached more people and was titled *The Larry Storch Show*.

Storch recalls how television changed show business in its early years. "You became famous in twenty minutes," he says. "The day after a show, people would be spotting you on the street." But it also meant that people began to stay home more often to watch TV instead of going to the nightclubs. Eventually, everyone ended up on television, but at the time Storch wanted to do it all — TV, nightclubs, theatre and movies.

"You did whatever came along," he explains. "Whatever was good that came along, that's what I'd take. I really had no big dream about Broadway or the movies. I just wanted to work. I had no set plan at all, I just wanted to get out in front of an audience and do my act and get a weekly salary. I had no big dreams *at all.*"

Storch had done live theatre long before *Cavalcade* came along, but when Broadway beckoned, he couldn't turn it down. "Broadway validates you," he says. "Just being on the stage validates you." The call came in 1956 when he was cast in the comedy *Who Was That Lady?* He played an overly emotional Russian spy and was able to put both his talent for dialects and broad comedy to use.

That role led to his debut in movies. Hollywood bought the rights to the play in 1959. Storch's old friend Tony Curtis had gone on to become a big movie star and had been cast as the lead in the movie version of *Who Was That Lady?* Curtis insisted that Storch reprise the role he had created on Broadway. "Tony Curtis gave me a call to come out there and do the same part I had done on Broadway," says Storch. "I was the only one from the original Broadway show who was asked to be in the movie and that was only because of my friendship with Tony C. Whenever Hollywood gets its hands on a successful play, they cast it with movie stars. That happens a lot. If you say, 'Well, I originated the part on Broadway, why didn't you cast me?' They'll say, 'Oh, no. You're not the type.'"

The small part the movie version of the play launched Storch's movie career and in the early 1960s, he did four movies with Curtis—*Captain Newman, M.D.* (1963), *Wild and Wonderful* (1964), *Sex and the Single Girl* (1964) and *The Great Race* (1965).

During those same years, Storch was back on TV as a recurring character on *Car 54, Where Are You?* He played Charlie the Drunk. Unlike, say, Otis the town drunk on *The Andy Griffith Show,* Charlie was a dry drunk and would become intoxicated just by *talking* about booze — particularly the drinks at his favorite bar where you could get two shots for a quarter. Storch had previously done a couple of guest shots on *The Phil Silvers Show,* which had also been done by *Car 54's* writer-producer Nat Hiken.

The format of *Car 54* was a lot like the set-up Storch would find on his next series, *F Troop. Car* 54 featured a classic team-up of the comic and the straight man — Joe E. Ross and Fred Gwynne — whereas *F Troop* had Storch and straight man Forrest Tucker. *F Troop* had a similarity to another Nat Hiken series, Phil Silvers' *Bilko,* about a con man sergeant in the army. *McHale's Navy* would use the same premise in a World War II setting. *F Troop* took the idea back in time to the post–Civil War Old West.

When Storch was asked to audition for *F Troop* in 1965, he was initially reluctant. "I had been making movies up to then and I was afraid that another TV series might hold me back. But it turned out to be one of the best things I ever did."

Storch points out that his real concern about doing *F Troop* was that it meant working with horses. "Nobody knew that I was scared to death of horses," he says. "I'm from Brooklyn. I had been in the Navy. What did I know about horses? When the producers asked me what I knew about them, I said, 'Well, I know they give milk and can bite from both ends.' I'd have much rather been driving a police car and I was afraid the horse would just run off and I wouldn't be able to stop it. Well, the first day of shooting, that's exactly what happened. The horse ran away with me on it and they found us half a mile away over a hill.

"But I did learn to ride. Well, at least to the point where I could defend myself and I never fell off. I held on and I'd grab ahold of the mane and I'd keep up as best as I could."

Although he got to the point where he felt comfortable on his horse, "Barney," when you see the opening credits of *F Troop*, it's surprising that Storch even went through with an audition considering everything else that was involved. In addition to the sight of star Ken Berry riding his horse backwards, there was a shot of Storch kicking the wheel of a cannon. The wheel falls off and the cannon accidentally goes off and knocks down the support of the watchtower which then collapses. "As well as horses, I also didn't like the sound of guns shooting off," he confesses. "But it turned out to be a great experience and the highlight of my life on TV. I'll never be lucky enough to do anything like that again."

The plots of *F Troop* revolved around the problems encountered by Captain William Parmenter, played by Ken Berry. During the last days of the Civil War, he had accidentally led a charge in the wrong direction and instead of retreating, his troops advanced. After the unexpected victory, he was rewarded for his unintentional valor with a promotion to commanding officer of the outpost Fort Courage.

Parmenter was to settle the Indian problem in that territory west of the Missouri River. However, unknown to the military, Sergeant Morgan O'Rourke (played by Forrest Tucker) and his sidekick, Corporal Randolph Agarn (Storch), had already secretly negotiated a treaty with the Hekawi Indians. Both parties realized that there was a lot of money to be made selling Indian souvenirs to tourists—especially if those Indians were still considered to be a threat.

With the arrival of Parmenter, there was little danger of O'Rourke's racket being discovered. Parmenter turned out to be as incompetent as the rest of the troop under his command. They included a tone-deaf bugler and a near-blind lookout in the watchtower. Not only was Parmenter blind to the rampant larceny going on around him, but he barely even noticed that the sole woman in the whole territory, Wrangler Jane (played by Melody Patterson), was out to seduce him. O'Rourke and Agarn were free to carry on the Bilkoesque schemes without interruption — except for hijackings and thievery from the Shug Indians, the only genuinely hostile tribe in the area.

As the CEO of O'Rourke Enterprises, strong and tall O'Rourke was solid as a rock. He was the smooth-talking "idea man." He was obviously the one with the brains. His partner in crime was a contrast. Whereas O'Rourke was low-key, Agarn was downright manic. He was a crafty schemer and was more than a bit of a con man. Over-emotional and bois-terous with a hair-trigger temper, Agarn was a pint-sized bundle of energy and when in character, Storch was able to chew up the scenery.

"*F Troop* was one of the few shows where I got to be really raucous," says Storch. "Most of my other roles have been somewhat subdued in com-parison. But that was the one where I was allowed to really go crazy and do things off the wall. I played Agarn as if he was out of Passaic, New Jer-sey, and was really dragged kicking and screaming into the Cavalry. I was grounded in New York and my approach was more of an Eastern rounded character, a New York guy playing the angles."

Originally, Storch had auditioned for the role of Sergeant O'Rourke. But he says, "When I showed up for the audition and there was Forrest Tucker — the size of a polar bear, I said to myself, 'I'm never going to get this role as sergeant.' And then Tucker said to me, 'Now, wait a minute, they must need a corporal around here,' and he made it known that he wanted me to be on the show and that's how I got the job."

They had never met before that day but there was an instant chem-istry between them. "Tucker just said, 'We'll make them laugh — you and I.' *He* knew we were going to be funny," says Storch. "Tucker was the most generous actor in the world. If there was a scene where you could be funny, he would let you and encourage you and even get the director to give you the punch line." Years after *F Troop*, they teamed up again for the Saturday morning live-action kids' show, *The Ghost Busters*, in 1975.

If Tucker played straight man to Storch, Ken Berry played straight man to the entire cast. As the wholesome, clean-cut Parmenter, it could have been a thankless role but Storch has only praise for his former co-star. "Oh, he was head and shoulders above everybody else. Even today, I can't speak too highly of that guy and his talent. He has a laid-back qual-ity that was just wonderful on that show — here he was, he kept turning down the advances of this sex-pot, this Jezebel of the fort, because he had that righteous background. His character was from Philadelphia and he went by the book. But Ken Berry could do anything. He was an actor, a song-and-dance man and he's a naturally funny guy. He has a dry sense of humor which I adore."

F Troop on the whole had a very weird sense of humor. It may have been a sitcom originally created in the *Bilko* mold, but it was often absurd and surreal and had more in common with shows like *Get Smart* and *Green Acres* than it did with *McHale's Navy*. Although it was set in the 1860s and looked like a western, it was full of topical references to 1960s pop-culture. For instance, the son of Hekawi Chief Wild Eagle was a beatnik-hippie named Crazy Cat and hung out at the Playbrave Club. In one episode, Henry Gibson turned up as an accident-prone trooper named Wrongo Starr. There was even one surreal episode where Tucker, Storch, Berry and Patterson did a spoof of a rock band and performed an electrified version of Bob Dylan's "Hey, Mr. Tambourine Man."

Those modern references accompanied by a knowing wink to the audience were coupled with lots of vaudeville-type schtick. Television and movie veterans guest-starred as visiting Indians. Edward Everett Horton appeared as Chief Running Chicken; Don Rickles as Bald Eagle; Milton Berle as an Indian detective, Wise Owl; Phil Silvers as 147-year-old Flaming Arrow. On those occasions, no joke was considered too old or too corny.

"We had all manner of Indians," recalls Storch. "All the actors may have been white, but we had Mexican Indians, Hawaiian Indians, Italian Indians. Anybody who could put on a pair of moccasins and some feathers was certainly welcome."

Without question, the show was different. The mix of camp and vaudeville was best seen in an episode where Paul Lynde showed up at Fort Courage as a singing Mountie, Sergeant Ramsden, pulled by a dog sled on wheels pulled by 10 Huskies. "That was marvelous," says Storch. "He pulls in singing and gets off and says in that voice of his, 'I always get my man!' Yes, the show was pretty off the wall."

That unique blend of comedy styles explains the show's enduring popularity in syndication today. Even though it was set in the 1800s, even though its humor was from the 1960s and vaudeville, somehow its appeal is timeless. At the time, however, it wasn't so richly appreciated and was cancelled in 1967 after only its second season.

Storch had been nominated for a Best Supporting Actor in a Comedy Series in 1967 for his work on *F Troop*. When the show ended, he hoped the nomination might open the doors for more challenging work — particularly drama. "I had decided that I could use a recess from comedy and I was hankering for more gritty Peter Falk–type parts. I thought the Emmy candidacy would help me get them. Then, the first thing I was offered was a one-shot television role as a chimpanzee. I laughed hysterically at the idea, but I wound up playing a chimpanzee. I wasn't surprised when my next part was on *Garrison's Gorillas*.

That show in which he played a chimp was *I Dream of Jeannie*. However, *Garrison's Gorillas* was a war-time drama and Storch's first dramatic role on television was that of a nervous little convict recruited to help the war effort in World War II. It was the first of many dramatic roles to come over the years. The reasons behind the move were easy to understand — to show people that he could do roles unlike the boisterous Corporal Agarn. "My wife and I talked over the idea of doing drama and decided that people should know that I can do more than jump up and down and make loud noises," he says. "Another dramatic role that I did was in an episode of *The Alfred Hitchcock Hour*. I was the good-natured villain. You couldn't tell that I had engineered a killing. It was Hitchcock at his best."

Someone must have been impressed with Storch's talent because the next time he was back on TV, it was as the lead in the CBS sitcom *The Queen and I* in 1969. He played Charles Duffy, the purser of *The Amsterdam Queen*, an ocean-liner that had seen better days and whose owners were considering selling for scrap. Duffy was a bit of a schemer and episodes focused on his attempts to save the ship — and in the process, his job. Storch says that, "Although Duffy was a guy who liked to work the angles like Agarn did, he was a lot more subdued." Unfortunately, the series was a mid-season replacement and was not picked up for the next season.

Over the next 15 years, Storch did a lot of guest shots on episodic television — often cast as a foreigner — and TV movies and voice-over work.

In 1985, he and his wife, Norma, returned to live in New York and he has been active on the stage ever since. Shortly after arriving back home, he was cast in the Broadway touring production of *Arsenic and Old Lace* and toured with that for two years as the German plastic surgeon, Dr. Einstein. The same producers cast him in *Breaking Legs*, a comedy about the Mafia. He also played in *Purlie* in 1988 as an old Southern gentleman named Cap'n Cotchipee.

However, the work of which he is most proud is his acting in *Porgy and Bess* in 1983 on Broadway. "I think that was the most important thing I ever did as an actor," he says. "I was with them for three years and we went to Europe, Canada and toured throughout the States and I was the only white actor in it. Ironically, I was playing a redneck in it and I've worked with and being friends with blacks all my life. In show business, talent is a great leveler."

Moving back to New York was the best thing that could have happened to his career. "You get up to bat more often if you're here in New York," he says. "You audition more often and even if you get turned down, at least people see you." Not that he gets to spend much time in town. At the age of 77, he was cast in the touring Broadway production of *Annie Get Your Gun.* "Now, it seems like I'm an actor who's always on the road," he says. Storch shows no signs of slowing down and has no interest in retiring. To what does he owe his long life and career? His marriage is one thing. He met his wife Norma in 1946. They dated for 15 years before finally marrying in 1961. They have been inseparable ever since.

The other secret to a good long life is standing on your head. Says Storch, "Once a day, usually in the morning, I stand on my head for 10 to 15 minutes. It's for circulation and I've been doing it for about 45 years. My teacher told me that if you do nothing else, this is one of the best exercises you can do for the body."

If that had been a bit of dialogue from *F Troop,* you could almost imagine someone next being hit over the head with a hat.

Larry Storch Credits

FILM CREDITS

1. *The Secret Daughter;* 1996; Himself
2. *The Silence of the Hams;* 1994; Sergeant
3. *I Don't Buy Kisses Anymore;* 1992; Giora
4. *Adventures Beyond Belief;* 1987 5. *A Fine Mess;* 1986; Leopold Klop
6. *The Perils of P.K.;* 1986
7. *Fake-Out;* 1982
8. *The Flight of Dragons;* 1982; Pawnbroker
9. *S.O.B.;* 1981; Guru
10. *Sweet Sixteen;* 1981; Earl
11. *Without Warning;* 1980; The Scoutmaster
12. *Airport 1975;* 1974; Purcell
13. *Journey Back to OZ;* 1971; (voice) Amos
14. *The Great Bank Robbery;* 1969; Juan
15. *The Monitors;* 1969; Colonel Stutz
16. *A Very Special Favor;* 1965; Harry the Taxi Driver
17. *The Great Race;* 1965; Texas Jack
18. *Bus Riley's Back in Town;* 1965; Howie
19. *Sex and the Single Girl;* 1965; Motorcycle Cop
20. *Wild and Wonderful;* 1964; Rufus Gibbs
21. *Captain Newman, M.D.;* 1963; Corporal Gavoni
22. *Who Was That Lady?;* 1960; Orenov
23. *Gun Fever;* 1958; Amigo
24. *The Last Blitzkrieg;* 1958; Ennis

TV CREDITS

1. *The Adventures of Huckleberry Finn;* TV movie; 1981; Dauphin
2. *Better Late Than Never;* TV movie; 1979

3. *Scooby and Scrappy-Doo;* TV series; 1979; various voices
4. *Jack Frost;* TV special; 1979; (voice)
5. *Incredible Rocky Mountain Race;* TV movie; 1977; Eagle Feather
6. *Joys;* TV movie; 1976
7. *The Ghost Busters;* TV series; 1975–1976; Eddie Spenser
8. *Columbo: Negative Reaction;* TV movie; 1974; Mr. Weekly
9. *The Couple Takes a Wife;* TV movie; 1972; David
10. *The Woman Hunter;* TV movie; 1972; Raconteur
11. *The Brady Kids;* TV series; 1972; (voice) Marlon, the Magic Bird
12. *Sabrina, the Teenage Witch;* TV series; 1971; various voices
13. *Sabrina and the Groovy Ghoulies;* TV series; 1970; various voices
14. *Hunters Are for Killing;* TV movie; 1970; Rudy LeRoy
15. *The Queen and I;* TV series; 1969; Mr. Duffy
16. *The Pink Panther Show;* TV series; 1969; various voices
17. *F Troop;* TV series; 1965–1967; Corporal Randolph Agarn
18. *That Was the Week That Was;* TV series; 1964
19. *Tennessee Tuxedo and His Tales;* TV series; 1963; Phineas J. Whoopee
20. *Out of the Inkwell;* TV series; 1961–1963; (voice) Koko the Clown
21. *The Larry Storch Show;* TV series; 1953
22. *Cavalcade of Stars;* TV series; 1952; host

NOTABLE TV GUEST APPEARANCES

1. *Land's End;* Bobby Forrest; 2/17/1996
2. *Married … With Children;* Himself; 3/12/1995
3. *Ghostbusters;* (voice) Eddie's Dad; 1986
4. *The Fall Guy;* Theo; 9/19/1984
5. *Harper Valley P.T.A.;* 1982
6. *CHiPS;* Chub; 9/21/1980
7. *Fantasy Island;* The Eagleman; 5/17/1980
8. *CHiPS;* Franco; 9/22/1979
9. *CHiPS;* Franco; 9/15/1979
10. *The Hardy Boys/Nancy Drew Mysteries;* 11/27/1977
11. *Kolchak: The Night Stalker;* Jim "The Swede" Brytowski; 10/4/1974
12. *All in the Family;* Bill Mulhoren; 1/20/1973
13. *Emergency!;* 10/21/1972
14. *Alias Smith and Jones;* Mugs McGeehu; 9/16/1972
15. *The Persuaders;* Angie; 11/19/1971
16. *Gomer Pyle, U.S.M.C.;* Gen. Manuel Cortez; 1970
17. *The Doris Day Show;* Duke; 1970
18. *Get Smart;* The Groovy Guru; 1/13/1968
19. *Garrison's Gorillas;* Clarence Dorn; 12/19/1967
20. *The Mothers-in-Law;* Ralph; 11/12/1967
21. *I Dream of Jeannie;* Sam, the chimp; 9/12/1967
22. *The Andy Williams Show;* 12/4/1966
23. *That Girl;* John MacKenzie; 1966
24. *Gilligan's Island;* Jackson Farrell; 1/23/1965

25. *Gomer Pyle, U.S.M.C.;* Gen. Manuel Cortez; 1964
26. *The Alfred Hitchock Hour;* Oscar Blenny; 4/5/1963
27. *Car 54, Where Are You?;* Charlie; 2/24/1963
28. *Car 54, Where Are You?;* Charlie; 12/2/1962
29. *Car 54, Where Are You?;* Charlie; 11/4/1962
30. *Car 54, Where Are You?;* Charlie; 10/28/1962
31. *The Phil Silvers Show;* Bopster; 1/1/1959
32. *The Phil Silvers Show;* The Crying Sailor; 10/28/1958
33. *Your Show of Shows;* 3/8/1952

Vivian Vance

Ethel Mertz on *I Love Lucy*

When people think of the great second bananas of television, the usual suspects come to mind — Art Carney, Don Knotts and Michael Richards. However, one of the pioneers in the business was Vivian Vance, who played Ethel Mertz on *I Love Lucy*. Perhaps she doesn't spring so readily to mind as the others because contrary to them, she was playing "straight" to the star — who happened to be the broad and extreme character.

Just the same, her legacy is that you can see her influence on a number of sitcoms over the years. You can find it on *Roseanne* in the relationship between the main character and her sister Jackie. It can be seen on *The Mary Tyler Moore Show* spinoffs *Rhoda* and *Phyllis*. Certainly *Laverne and Shirley* owes a lot to the spirit of the work of Vance and Lucille Ball on their first series and then on *The Lucy Show*.

If Vance has been underrated and hasn't been given her due credit over the years, it may be because Ball was such an overwhelming presence that all eyes were on her. Or maybe it's because she did it with such ease. Her reactions to whatever mayhem Lucy was concocting was the same response felt by the audience. Or maybe it's because she's a woman.

Vance was born Vivian Roberta Jones on July 26, 1909, in Cherryvale, Kansas. Her family moved shortly afterwards to Independence, Kansas, and later settled in Albuquerque, New Mexico.

During high school, she studied drama and was a cheerleader. After graduating, she worked briefly singing in the chorus of a couple of touring musicals and also sang torch songs in a travelling revue show. Returning home, she became involved in the Albuquerque Little Theatre, which had just been founded. She appeared in their first play, *This Thing Called Love*, as a vamp. Over the next two years, she appeared in all of the theatre's productions in comedic roles ranging from "the wronged woman" to a nun.

Her first starring role came in 1932 as the title character in the courtroom drama *The Trial of Mary Duggan*. Vance was on stage for the entire play and had a couple of emotionally charged scenes. Her performance in the play, coupled with her previous work, so impressed the local theatre community that a benefit performance of the play was staged to raise funds to send Vance to New York to study professionally and embark on a career in the theatre.

Vance set off to New York after that benefit show pressured not only by her own expectations–but her hometown had financed her dream and was counting on her to be a success.

Upon her arrival in New York, she first found work by singing torch songs in Manhattan nightclubs and in the chorus of Broadway musicals. Her first job on Broadway came in 1933 in the Jerome Kern and Oscar

Hammerstein production *Music in the Air*. The audition for chorus girls was only supposed to be for those with voices trained in operetta. Instead of leaving, Vance got up and belted out Sophie Tucker's "After You're Gone." While she was being shown the door, Kern called her back and gave her a job in the chorus.

In 1934, she went from the chorus to understudying Ethel Merman in the lead role of *Anything Goes!* When the play went on the road in 1935, Vance inherited the role. The next year she sang in the chorus and again was the understudy for Merman in *Red, Hot and Blue!*

Five years after her arrival in New York, she had her first starring role on Broadway in a musical starring Ed Wynn, called *Hurray for What!* She next toured in the Broadway production of *Kiss the Boys Goodbye* by Clare Booth. It was a supporting role in which she played a starlet who was willing to do anything to get to the top. She also played support to Gertrude Lawrence in *Skylark* in 1939 and for Danny Kaye in 1941 in his first starring musical, *Let's Face It*. In 1944, she and her new husband, actor Phil Ober, performed with the USO overseas entertaining the troops in Italy and North Africa in a production of Ruth Gordon's *Over Twenty-One*.

In 1945, she joined the tour of Mel Ferrer's production of *Voice of the Turtle* and traveled with them to Chicago and San Francisco. During the tour, she suffered a nervous breakdown and was hospitalized for months. She didn't return to the stage for almost three years. Part of Vance's emotional problems was due to her drive for success and the pressure she felt in not wanting to let down the folks back home.

Some years later she talked about her early days and the price she eventually had to pay. "When I got to New York, I found I wasn't as good as I thought I was. But of course I couldn't go back." So she had to try that much harder than most others and a decade in the competitive theatre world of New York eventually took its toll. "Whenever my sisters sigh about the glamour of the life I live, I remind them what it cost. After all, I'm the one who had the crack-up."[1]

In 1947, legendary Broadway producer George Abbott brought her back to the Great White Way in *It Takes Two*. After that show, she was back on Broadway in a short-lived but critically acclaimed revival of *The Cradle Will Rock*. Both of these experiences helped restore Vance's self-confidence sufficiently enough that she agreed to Mel Ferrer's invitation to join him at the La Jolla Playhouse in southern California in a new production of *Voice of the Turtle* — the play she had been in when she had her breakdown five years earlier.

If Vance had turned down Ferrer's offer because of bad memories associated with her breakdown, she likely would have remained unknown to television audiences for all the years to come. As it happens, Desi Arnaz was casting for someone to play a supporting role on his and his wife's new TV series, *I Love Lucy*. The show's director had worked with Vance in the theatre not long before and had taken Arnaz out to La Jolla to consider putting her in the TV show.

That night, Arnaz made the decision to cast Vance in the role of Ethel Mertz on the new show. The rest is history. *I Love Lucy* premiered on October 15, 1951, on CBS, ran for 10 years and hasn't been off the air since.

Although it was originally conceived of as a husband and wife series and patterned after Ball's radio show, *My Favorite Husband*, the series soon evolved into a show about the interplay between the two couples on the show — Lucy and her husband, Ricky Ricardo, and their neighbors Fred and Ethel Mertz, played by William Frawley and Vance. Before long, plots would be centered around the schemes Lucy would dream up to "get even" with "the boys." Ethel was her reluctant partner. Anytime you heard Lucy utter the phrase, "Ethel, I've got an idea!" you just knew that slapstick hijinks were soon to follow as they got themselves into some outlandish, embarrassing predicament.

The expressions on Vance's face — which could be anything from serious doubt to horror and disbelief — were the same feelings the audience experienced when Lucy came up with a dubious-sounding ruse behind her husband's back. Wackiness alone does not make great comedy. It's the reactions of the others in the scene which give a reality to the most ludicrous of scenarios. Vance, Frawley and Arnaz had their work cut out for them in playing opposite Ball. It was the same challenge Gale Gordon and Ball's own children, Lucie and Desi Junior, would face on *Here's Lucy.*

Lucie Arnaz, who played Lucy's daughter Kim on *Here's Lucy*, worked with both Vance and Gordon and says she learned a lot about the art of playing support from them but also just from doing the work. "I learned from doing and trying to respond in a believable manner. That is what I always felt Vivian and Bill and my father and mother were doing — being believable and not 'acting.' Putting themselves in the situations and asking themselves what would I do here, how would I respond to this if it were really happening.

"On *Here's Lucy*, we always represented how 'normal' people would view the situation, as did my father on *I Love Lucy*. Most of the audience would probably have the same kind of reactions in similar circumstances."

Arnaz continues, "It is always more of a thankless job to play the straight man to outrageous characters. But without that person's reaction, the audience doesn't laugh nearly as much. The reactions that Viv had to

Lucy's antics doubled and often tripled the laughs that Lucy got. Remember her trepidatious reaction when Lucy was tangoing with all those eggs in her blouse? And the editors were the first to realize it. As you will notice, they always cut to the reactions of those witnessing the behavior.

"Now, the show was always filmed in front of a live audience and they weren't able to be influenced by a close-up of one of the other characters to tell you to notice their reaction, but, they always did. You just do that. You check out how the other person feels about what you have just seen and by their facial responses, you click in deeper to what has really taken place and what the depth of the situation is. Vivian and Bill's and my father's reactions to the situations they witnessed were crucial to the comedy of that show."

Playing second banana to "Big Red" wasn't always a thankless job. Vance won the Emmy Award for the new category of Best Supporting Actress in a Comedy in 1954. When she accepted, she thanked Ball by joking, "I want to thank the greatest straight woman in show business."[2] She would also be nominated in 1955, '57 and '58.

Although there were aspects of her character that Vance personally didn't like, she loved working on the show. In Ball, she found a perfect partner who shared the same work ethic. Since the slapstick scenes usually involved the two of them, they would rehearse and carefully choreograph every little detail.

However, she wasn't happy about playing an "older" woman, someone who would be married to the 64-year-old Frawley, and thus was expected to appear on television looking like a frumpy housefrau. Hairdressers and make-up artists were instructed to give Ethel an older woman's look, and eyelashes, lipstick and more youthful make-up were not allowed. Whereas Lucy always dressed smartly, Ethel's wardrobe consisted of simple dreary housedresses or a ratty-looking terrycloth bathrobe.

Her resentment of the older-woman look was understandable considering that Ball was only two years younger than Vance. Still, she knew it was all part of the character and accepted it. However, the one aspect of Ethel Mertz which absolutely galled her was the fact that people thought she was old enough to be married to William Frawley. She and Frawley were from different worlds and had little in common. Vance had come from the theatre and enjoyed the freedom that Ball and Arnaz gave her in encouraging her when she wanted to talk about her character's "motivation" in a scene. Although Frawley had also trod the boards on the Great White Way, he had spent the last two decades in Hollywood making movies that were often cranked out on a weekly basis and he preferred to just say his lines and get it over with in one take.

Even worse than the notion that her character was married to someone old enough to be her father was the fact that since this was the early days of the new medium called television, some people actually thought that she and Frawley *were* married and even asked about her husband, Fred, when they saw her out in public.

Of the infamous feud between the two co-stars, Lucie Arnaz says, "Honestly, I never knew they were fighting. So, either they were very professional about the way they handled it with people off the show or it was all a hyped-up controversy. I know she didn't want to be seen as frumpy and she couldn't believe that people would believe that someone as young as she was could be married to such an 'old goat.' But, beyond that, I don't think it was personal ... and you know what? I personally don't care. They did a very professional job of playing a battling couple of lovebirds for eight years and I think that is all they could be expected to do and the rest is nobody's business."

Regardless of their personal feelings, there was definitely no lost love between them and when *I Love Lucy* stopped filming, although Vance went on to work for Ball and Arnaz again in *The Lucy Show* and *Here's Lucy* — there would be no professional reunions between her and Frawley.

When *I Love Lucy* stopped filming in 1959, Vance tried to distance herself from Ethel Mertz. "I did everything I could," she said. "I played *The Jack Paar Show* and did summer stock. I kept as busy as possible. There was a special reason for this. I had to find my own identity. I was so submerged in Ethel Mertz that I was afraid I would never again be recognized for my own self. Oh, I was grateful for her for the biggest success I had ever known. But being a creative person, I was worried that I would be stuck doing the same role all my life. Well, I found myself. I found people to be amazingly receptive. Many critics said of my summer theatre work: 'I went expecting to see Ethel Mertz, but after the first two minutes, I wasn't aware that she was anyone but Vivian Vance.'"[3]

Yet when Ball wanted her to play her sidekick on *The Lucy Show* when it began in 1962, Vance immediately signed on. But it was not without reservations. This time she made sure she didn't have to play an older woman and this time she was billed as co-star, not a supporting player. On the series, Ball was a widower and Vance played her divorcee friend, Vivian Bagley.

It was a much different character than what she played on *I Love Lucy*. She once described Ethel as a "Dowdy, competitive snoopy 'older woman' who mercilessly picked on her husband. She was everything I didn't want to be."[4]

Part of the appeal of working on *The Lucy Show* was that Vance insisted that her character would not be anything like Ethel Mertz. "I wanted her to have my own name. That's how 'Viv Bagley' came about. I wanted her to be more like me, to get to wear pretty clothes, to smile and laugh a lot, to be open and objective and *not* older than I."[5]

It is probably no small coincidence that on *The Lucy Show*, Vance — like Frawley on *My Three Sons* — is noticeably more relaxed and carefree. Whether it was just the way the character was written or was due to the absence of her old sparring partner is anybody's guess.

Although her character was somewhat different, the situations the two women found themselves in on *The Lucy Show* were very much the same as on the old show. Lucy would concoct some hare-brained scheme and Vance would be dragged along against her better judgement.

Vance and Ball were more like friends both on and off the show. Since the end of *I Love Lucy*, both had divorced and remarried. In 1961, Vance married John Dodds, who was a book editor in New York. They bought a house in Connecticut and after three years of commuting between the two coasts, Vance bowed out of *The Lucy Show* in 1965 and limited herself to the occasional "special guest appearance."

In 1974, she and her husband moved to the San Francisco Bay area. The next year she did a guest appearance on *Rhoda* and there was talk of making her a regular character. It was a nice gesture by the producers of the show as an acknowledgement of Vance's importance to situation comedies about women. On the episode, Vance again played an upstairs neighbor in a small New York apartment building. But this time she was an urbane and sophisticated woman of the world.

During her post–*Lucy Show* years, Vance devoted herself to her home life and stage work. Working in the theatre was the one constant throughout her life. Even when *I Love Lucy* went on its first summer hiatus in 1953, she did summer stock. When she returned to La Jolla Playhouse that summer to work again with Mel Ferrer in *Pal Joey*, it wasn't as supporting player, but as co-star.

From that point on, whenever Vance did summer stock, *she* was the lead. Ironically, after all her years on the legitimate stage in New York and in tours across the country, it took television and the name of Ethel Mertz — a character she often despised — to make Vivian Vance a *star*.

Due to her television success and with her huge name recognition as a box-office draw, Vance was able to support the Albuquerque Little Theatre with frequent benefit performances. It was a way of repaying the folks back home who had helped her get started by sending her to New York all those years earlier.

She was also invited back to Broadway and performed there in the short-lived *My Daughter, Your Son* in 1968. It was her first time back since *The Cradle Will Rock* twenty years earlier.

A few years later she was diagnosed with breast cancer and was ill off and on for many years before dying on August 17, 1979.

In her last few years, she kept busy with theatre projects and television appearances. She last worked with Ball on a TV special in 1977 titled *Lucy Calls the President*.

Lucille Ball had long acknowledged Vance's contribution to her shows and their success. But Vance also had an indelible influence on her daughter, Lucie Arnaz. Their connection was through Vance's first love, the theatre. Arnaz had been born just months before *I Love Lucy* went on the air and Vance watched her grow up. She went to see her in high school plays and later when Arnaz was working on *Here's Lucy*, Vance would encourage her to do more work on stage.

Arnaz recalls, "My friendship with Viv was that of a real great Auntie Mame type, but, someone that you'd only see once in a while and I was pretty young at the time and we didn't talk a lot. But, as a small child, I remember that she never would 'talk down' to you and she had a great sense of humor and mischief. I think kids are attracted to and feel safe around adults like that.

"I have always said that one of the main reasons that I drifted towards the live theatre instead of staying with television after *Here's Lucy* was because Viv took me aside one afternoon while she was guesting on our show and told me to 'get back to the stage' every chance I got and not to get stuck on a sitcom for the rest of my life. She knew I loved the work I had done in theatre and she didn't want the same thing to happen to me that happened to her. She may have been offered leads in theatre after *I Love Lucy*, but she did tell me that she had been typecast for so long as Ethel Mertz that it was difficult for her to get back to playing the more challenging roles she enjoyed."

Arnaz's most treasured memory of Vance came on the opening night of her first starring role on the legitimate stage in a production of *See-Saw* in 1974. Vance had been ill at the time and had gone out of her way to be there on opening night, although Arnaz didn't even know she was there until the curtain call.

"It absolutely stunned me," recalls Arnaz. "I looked off stage-left after the curtain came down on my last big number. I was all alone on stage opening night in Boston at the Colonial Theatre and there was Viv standing in the stage-left wings applauding and yelling bravos. I remember being absolutely floored and hugging her for what seemed forever. I had to go on to take my bows with the rest of the company and when I came back, she was gone. My guardian angel, as ever."

It was a touching gesture of affirmation which was bound to have a profound effect on a young actress just starting out on what would be a long and successful career in the theatre. It was not unlike the gesture made by the members of the Albuquerque Little Theatre to another young actress whom they thought had "what it takes," many years earlier. Like the best of all of Vance's work, it was a strong show of support.

Notes

1. *Good Housekeeping*, "TV's Favorite Comedy Team Breaks Up"; by Rollie Hochstein; October 1965.
2. *The Other Side of Ethel Mertz: The Life Story of Vivian Vance*; by Frank Castelluccio and Alvin Walker; Manchester, CT; Knowledge, Ideas and Trends Publishing; 1988; page 191.
3. *Newsday*; "Lucy and Ethel Team Up Again"; Associated Press; August 30, 1961.
4. *Good Housekeeping*; October 1965.
5. *Ibid.*

Vivian Vance Credits

FILM CREDITS

1. *The Great Race*; 1965; Hester Goodbody
2. *The Blue Veil*; 1951; Alicia
3. *The Secret Fury*; 1950; Leah

TV CREDITS

1. *Lucy Calls the President*; TV special; 1977
2. *CBS Salutes Lucy: The First 25 Years*; TV special; 1976; Herself
3. *The Great Houdini*; TV movie; 1976; Minnie
4. *Getting Away from It All*; TV movie; 1976; May Brodey
5. *Here's Lucy*; TV series; 1968; Vivian Jones
6. *The Lucy Show*; TV series; 1962–1966; Vivian Bagley
7. *I Love Lucy*; TV series; 1951–1959; Ethel Mertz

NOTABLE TV GUEST APPEARANCES

1. *Rhoda*; Maggie Cummings; 11/24/1975
2. *Here's Lucy*; Vivian Jones; 2/21/1972
3. *Here's Lucy*; Vivian Jones; 2/22/1971
4. *Here's Lucy*; Vivian Jones; 2/15/1971
5. *Here's Lucy*; Vivian Jones; 1/26/1970
6. *Here's Lucy*; Vivian Jones; 1/19/1970
7. *Love, American Style*; Zimia, the medium; 1969
8. *Here's Lucy*; Vivian Jones; 12/16/1968
9. *The Deputy*; Emma Gant; 12/12/1959
10. *Westinghouse Desilu Playhouse*; 12/11/1959
11. *Shower of Stars*; Herself; 1955

Sincerely, Walker
Jimmie

Jimmie Walker

"J.J." Evans on *Good Times*

A stock gimmick in the creation of any memorable second-banana character is the frequent use of a snappy catch phrase. Nothing can establish a character on a sitcom quicker and if the show is popular enough, it will even become a part of everyday speech and make the actor a household name in the process.

As a result, the actor will forever be identified with it. Jaleel White will never be able to go out in public without someone asking, "Did I do that?" in a simulation of Steve Urkel's high-pitched voice from *Family Matters*. Ron Palillo will always have to answer for Arnold Horshack's all-purpose insult, "Up your nose with a rubber hose," from *Welcome Back, Kotter*. In the case of Jimmie Walker, he will always be associated with the catch phrase of his character, J.J. Evans from *Good Times*. Ever since the mid–1970s, Walker has been linked to just one word — "*Dyn-o-mite!*"

It all came about innocuously enough. In the series' second episode, the word appeared in one of J.J.'s lines of dialogue. The script didn't call for any special reading for that particular word. There was no emphasis on it in the sentence. It was just another word in the script. J.J. was to enter the Evanses' apartment after a brief run-in with the law. J.J., in the tradition of all great second-banana characters, had an over-inflated ego and he explained how he turned the tables on the police — "They knew they were in trouble once they realized they were dealing with Kid *Dyn-o-mite!*"

The emphasis on the last word was put there by Walker and he delivered the line with all the style and panache of a seasoned stand-up comic who knew how to drive home a punch line. When he punctuated the sentence with the explosive, eye-popping "Dyn-o-mite!" the studio audience went wild.

The next week, the producers recalled the audience reaction and had "dynamite" written into the script again. Walker, however, just read it like any other word. They told him to read it the way he had the week before but he had forgotten just how he had put his own spin on the word. Luckily it didn't take him long to remember and once again the crowd roared its approval.

Naturally, "dynamite" showed up in the following episode. And every subsequent episode after that for a number of months. Despite limiting its use to only once an episode or sometimes not at all, it didn't take long for the expression to catch on. The word was a perfect match for Walker. Not only was he about as thin as a stick of dynamite, but his line readings could be just as explosive. Before long, ratings for *Good Times* quickly went sky-high and as a result, the producers expanded J.J.'s role.

"Dyn-o-mite" became a part of the common vernacular. There was a time in the 1970s when it was impossible to walk by a school yard and not hear kids using the word — either in imitation of Walker or in having appropriated it as their own new word for "cool." The word also showed up in print on "J.J." T-shirts, socks, suspenders and lunchboxes. If you owned a "J.J." doll, "dyn-o-mite" is what you heard when you pulled the string to make him talk.

Walker himself capitalized on its popularity. He quickly recorded his first comedy record, for Buddah Records in 1975, and titled it *Dyn-o-mite!* The phrase has remained with him and 25 years later, his official web-site is named "dynomitejj.com." Some performers have been horrified that a silly catch phrase has followed them around for their entire career, but Walker doesn't mind. His post–*Good Times* career has been a continuation of what he was doing before the series began and as a stand-up comic he still often gets billed as Jimmie "J.J." Walker with the word "Dynomite" appearing below his photo. For Walker, "Dyn-o-mite!" has become just as effective as a piece of identification as a business card.

James Walker Junior was born June 25, 1947, in New York. Like his character on *Good Times*, the real James Junior grew up in a housing project, this being the Melrose Project of the South Bronx. During his childhood it was an area of neglected and burnt-out buildings, unemployment and street gangs. Walker later described the area as looking "like a scene from World War III," and opportunities to get out were very limited. "I'll tell you about Morris Avenue," he once said. "There were like 20 guys I hung out with on the street. Five of them were dead before they were old enough to vote. The rest of 'em? If they aren't in the slam, or 'away for a rest' someplace else, they're still on the street hustlin'."[1]

Despite how bleak the area looked, for the young Walker, who spent his entire youth there, it was just "the neighborhood." "When you're in the ghetto, you don't know you're in the ghetto because you never leave."[2]

Walker's father, James, worked as a baggage clerk at New York's Penn Station. His mother Lorena worked as a school lunchroom aide and so there was not a lot of money in the household for any luxuries or spending money for James Jr. and his younger sister, Beverly. When his parents divorced when Walker was a teenager, there was even less money although his mother had gone back to school and became a registered nurse.

James Jr.'s early academic accomplishments were not as impressive. He attended De Witt Clinton High School in the Bronx but dropped out at the age of 15 due to boredom. After working as a delivery boy for the Grand Union Market, he realized that $47 a week wouldn't get him too far and he began taking night school classes at Theodore Roosevelt High School to get his high school diploma.

At night school, he learned about a government program which would pay him to go to school and continue his education. Through SEEK (Search for Elevation, Escalation and Knowledge), an educational program for lower-income kids, he studied radio engineering and announcing at the RCA Technical Institute in Manhattan. His first real job was as a part-time engineer at WRBR, a small New York radio station.

He worked nights at the school and enrolled in another SEEK program to study as a speech and drama major at City College of New York in 1966. It was in a freshman class called Oral Interpretation that Walker was first bit by the show business bug. Each student was to do a three-minute speech without using notes. Walker chose to do a Dick Gregory comedy routine. He had first seen Gregory when the influential black comedian had done a talk at Walker's high school and not only told jokes but talked about growing up in the ghetto. Walker admired Gregory's ability to find comedy in such a setting and turn it into political and social commentary. That combination would also become Walker's approach to comedy throughout his career.

When Walker got up to do his borrowed Gregory material in front of the class, he finally saw his future and a way out of the ghetto. "I was rappin' on and on, and the whole class really dug it," he later said. "The teacher dug it too but she wrote on my critique: 'This is not a nightclub stage; this is a classroom.'"[3]

Nonetheless, the response from his classroom audience had an immediate effect—"That did it. The germ hit me. Those three minutes turned me on, and I knew what I wanted to do."[4]

Walker began writing an act, working up "chunks" (as he called them) of comedy about various themes— school, television, politics, the ghetto— and began performing every place he could. He worked talent shows, schools, community centers— any place that would have him. He stayed in college for a year and a half before leaving to pursue comedy full time. He did a brief stint as a DJ in Norfolk, West Virginia, but missed the immediacy of a live audience.

Back in New York in 1967, he took an engineering job at radio station WMCA and also got his first break when he was asked to open for the Last Poets, a group of black poets who did readings in the New York area. The group, which specialized in militant political and social commentary, were in need of a funny opening act to relax the audience in preparation for the heaviness to follow.

His first gig with the Last Poets was New Year's Eve 1967 at the East Wind club in Harlem. He did five minutes of material, floored the crowd of 350 and spent the next 18 months touring with the group along the East

Coast. During that time, he was writing more material, perfecting his stage persona and trying it out wherever he could.

Walker's act was initially aimed at black audiences but he began to broaden his material so that it would have more universal appeal. He still talked from a black perspective but his humor was never bitter or militant. He became popular with white audiences by putting both blacks and whites up for ridicule without seeming to overtly put down either group.

Walker found regular work in Harlem at the Apollo Theatre and other venues with the Last Poets. But in 1969, he landed his first racially mixed gig at a downtown club with the misleading name of The African Room. He shared the bill with other up-and-coming talents like David Brenner, Steve Landesberg and singer Bette Midler. Of the group, Brenner was the most experienced comic and he got them all into Budd Friedman's comedy club, The Improv, where they all became regulars.

By 1972, all of the group had appeared on the revived *Jack Paar Show*, except Walker, who was still waiting for his break on late night national television. Midler, Brenner and Landesberg told the show's booking agent that they would no longer appear unless Walker was given a chance. Thus, Walker made his television debut and was immediately booked for a second appearance and did one more guest shot before the show was cancelled in 1973. The show was just what he needed to launch his television career. Dan Rowan had seen him on the *Paar* show and booked him for a *Laugh-In* TV special. More importantly, in September 1973, CBS offered him a contract to warm up the studio audience before their tapings of the short-lived sitcom *Calucci's Department*.

At the same time, Norman Lear was creating a new series, *Good Times*, which was a spinoff of *Maude*. It was to star Esther Rolle, who played Florida Evans, the opinionated black maid on that series, and the new show would be about her family life. A CBS casting director had noticed Walker's rapport with an audience as the warm-up act for *Calucci's Department*. A tape of one of his Paar appearances was set for Lear to look at. Allan Mannings, a producer for *Good Times*, recalled seeing Walker years earlier at The Improv and then later on the *Paar* show.

"I forgot about him until I caught him one night on the *Paar* show and he broke me up all over again," Manning later said. "Absolutely wiped me out. I tucked him away in my mind for future reference — and when I got involved with Norman Lear in the new series, Jimmie was my first and only choice for J.J."[5]

Lear concurred with Mannings' assessment and Walker, who had never acted in anything before this, let alone a television show, was cast as Florida and James Evans' eldest son, James Junior (or 'J.J.' for short)—

without even having to do an audition. Within weeks, "Dyn-o-mite!" would make J.J. Walker a household name. With only four guest shots as a stand-up comic on his television resume, Walker had become an overnight sensation—after seven years of working the comedy clubs.

Good Times was a spinoff from the Norman Lear production line of sitcoms. In this case, it was a spinoff of a spinoff. Good Times was a spinoff of Maude which was a spinoff of All in the Family—which in turn had been based on a popular British series, Till Death Do Us Part. Although he used the same technique with Sanford and Son (with Redd Foxx playing a black Archie Bunker), and it had spinoffs of its own, Lear's production company really hit a gold mine with All in the Family. In addition to Maude, it also spun off The Jeffersons, which in turn gave up a sitcom about their maid, with 227, starring Marla Gibbs.

On Maude, Florida Evans was a proud and strong-willed black maid who worked in the suburban home of white upper-class liberals Maude and Walter Findley. She was a scene-stealer with her droll sarcastic remarks and ability to manipulate and exploit the Findleys' liberal sensibilities and two hundred years of white man's guilt. When Florida was given a show of her own, it was set in a Chicago housing project and episodes originally revolved around the constant struggle for Florida and her husband James to feed their family while dealing with unemployment, an economic recession and life in the ghetto. The show could have just as easily been called "Hard Times" if not for the way the parents didn't let poverty prevent them from having a close family. The efforts of the uneducated father to get a good job and the stoic strength of the long-suffering mother was what held this family together. Their attitude about their sorry predicament was one of "grin and bear it" because we're all in this together.

Good Times and two other Lear programs, The Jeffersons and Sanford and Son, were among the first occasions that life in a black household was seen on network television. As such, Good Times was a pretty sanitized representation of life in an inner-city ghetto. As can be expected when a show about black people is written and produced by well-intentioned white people, the Evanses' apartment was a nice, tastefully furnished lower-middle class apartment and although there was talk about neighborhood hookers, pimps, drug pushers and winos, they were seldom seen. If anything, with their modest apartment and financial woes, Good Times was not much different in tone from the feminist sitcom One Day at a Time from the same era.

The Evans children included 12-year-old Michael, played by Ralph Carter. Michael was one of those kids only found in TV sitcoms who are smarter, more mature and more insightful than the adults on the show. He was also the show's most vocal proponent of black rights and whenever the plight of the black race was brought up, it was usually Michael who would back it up with statistics. Middle child Thelma was both intelligent and pretty. But her main role on the show was to provoke and trade insults with big brother J.J. As played by BernNadette Stanis, she gave as good as she got. But it was usually Walker as the eldest child who was the center of attention.

Even by sitcom standards, J.J. stood out as a unique character. Over six feet tall and weighing 125 pounds, he was probably the most authentic stringbean in second-banana history. Like other TV stooges, he was a boastful braggart and had a big ego to compensate for his small brain.

He called himself "The Black Prince" and indeed, he strutted about the Evans household as if he was some form of royalty. With his back arched, his arms held akimbo and his head held high and proud bobbing in synch with his steps, he looked more like a skinny ostrich with a prima donna complex. J.J. may have thought of himself as the Black Prince but with his ever-present floppy-brimmed denim hat, he was actually the Court Jester of the Evans residence. Truth be told, it was Florida who had all the real power and authority.

As he did with his trademark line reading of "dyn-o-mite," he used the same exaggerated enunciation whenever he referred to himself as the "eb-o-ny genius." But the audience would have laughed at anything he said. They even laughed when he said nothing at all. His wide goofy grin displayed a mouthful of teeth; his eyes could pop out in mock expressions of surprise or shock. His reaction shots were written into the scripts simply as "J.J. reacts."

Indeed, Walker's repertoire of facial expressions made him one of the most expressive of the cast members. He easily stood out with his winning collection of eccentric affectations. Early on, *TV Guide* noted, "J.J. is one of the few fully realized originals to have come to life on the small screen in recent years."[6] That's not bad praise for someone who made his acting debut on that very show just months earlier. *Good Times* was the scene of not only his television acting debut but his first acting of any kind. Even in high school and college, he wasn't interested in theatre or drama club. His focus had always been on stand-up comedy.

To his credit, Walker had no delusions about his acting abilities. Right from the start, he maintained that in his ambitions and talent, he was a comic first, not an actor. "I'm no actor," he explained during the first season of *Good Times*. "I'm a comic who lucked into a good thing."[7]

On another occasion, he admitted, "Until this show came along, I'd only done stand-up stuff, but I wasn't afraid of acting or playing a character. I didn't even think about it. They gave me the script and I ran with it."[8]

It was true — all his facial expressions and technique with line readings had all been perfected through years of performing stand-up comedy in front of live audiences and gauging their immediate response to determine what worked and what didn't. It had all been solitary training. He didn't even have any experience doing sketch comedy in which he would have to play off partner. He had no background in helping to build a scene, handing off a joke or punch line or knowing the basics of how to play a second banana. Not too surprisingly, he became the star.

It was inevitable that with such a strong characterization, J.J. would eventually become the dominant character. As a result, the older, experienced actors became resentful. Esther Rolle was frequently vocal about her objections to the J.J. character. She once complained, "Negative images have been quietly slipped in on us through the character of the oldest child. I resent the imagery that says to black kids that you can make it by standing on the corner saying 'Dyn-o-mite!'" She continued, "He's 18 and he doesn't work. He can't read and write. He doesn't think. The show didn't start out to be like that."[9]

No, the show sure didn't start out like that. It was conceived as a vehicle for Florida, the maid from *Maude*, with Rolle as the star. Her objections may have more to do with sour grapes than concerns about negative black images. Early episodes were about Florida and husband James trying to run a household in bad economic times. The kids were just kids and mostly in the background. But from the first utterance of "Dynomite," in the second episode, it was obvious who was the real crowd favorite with the studio audience. J.J.'s role was soon expanded and he became the focal point of many episodes. Just like "The Fonz" on *Happy Days*, a minor character became an unexpected favorite and the producers changed the show's tone and focus to take advantage of that and in the process, cash in on the ratings-winning popularity of the character. It's no wonder that Rolle had her nose out of joint.

At one point, late in the series' run, she left the show for a year and only returned on the condition that J.J.'s character would be toned down and be less cartoonish. In the interim, much had been done to change J.J. and him put him through a maturing process. Before the third season, actor John Amos, who played James Senior, had left the show in a contract dispute over money. J.J. became the man of the house and as such, he was given more responsibilities. That was a big change from how the character was originally represented. In the first few episodes it was implied that J.J. was a shoplifter and had problems with the police. That aspect was quickly dropped once his popularity became apparent and he was seen as potential role-model material.

As early as the second season, he was helping support the family by working after school as a delivery boy for The Chicken Shack, a chicken and ribs restaurant. In keeping with his role as a walking sight-gag, his uniform included a cap with a bobbing rubber chicken on top. As for Rolle's complaints that he didn't read or write or think, well, right from the start it was clear that J.J. still attended school on an almost daily basis—which in reality, may have been a stretch to believe in any ghetto teen, especially in light of the fact that Walker himself had dropped out of school when he was a kid. However, J.J. not only graduated from high school but also attended art school as a means to accomplish his dream of becoming an artist—again, a commendable but unlikely goal for someone growing up in an inner-city ghetto. Paintings attributed to J.J. showed his obvious talent and with typical J.J. modesty, he often referred to himself as the "Van Gogh of the ghet-to." So very early on, it was apparent that even though he may not have been as smart as his siblings, despite his superficial goofiness, he had many good qualities and was a fine role model for kids of any race. Besides, anyone that quick-witted couldn't be that stupid.

Walker personally was puzzled by the criticisms pointed at his character by the elder cast members. Rolle's objections were common knowledge and Walker eventually responded by saying, "I don't know how it all started. The series is in its fifth year and all of a sudden these people are finding fault with my character. Where have they been all these years? He's not supposed to be a genius. And he's not supposed to be dumb.

"All I do is deliver the lines the writers turn out for the series. They seem to be acceptable to most people or we wouldn't be in the top twenty in the Neilsen ratings. I mean, is The Fonz on *Happy Days* representative of white teenagers? Are the sweathogs in *Welcome Back, Kotter* a reflection of young whites? I surely don't feel guilty or apologize for the character I portray. Many of the scripts deal with real-life topics such as my hatred of narcotics, which I think is healthy for my young viewers."[10]

By its sixth season, *Good Times* had fallen on bad times with a significant drop in the ratings, from a respectable position in the twenties to #53. Amos had left the show in 1976, Rolle had quit the series twice and had missed entire seasons. New cast members were brought in to fill the void but it was not enough to return the show to its roots of being about a struggling black family. It became just another sitcom where the storylines all revolved around the kids and the show was cancelled by CBS in 1979.

Walker almost immediately returned to series television in January 1980 in the ABC cop show *B.A.D. Cats*. He played the comic relief character, Rodney Washington—a car thief who had become an auto repossessor. The series, which also starred LaWanda Page (*Sanford and Son's* Aunt Esther), *Combat's* Vic Morrow and a young Michelle Pfeiffer, only lasted a month.

His next full-time job came in 1983 with the lead role in *At Ease,* an ABC sitcom which was a remake of *Bilko,* featuring Walker in the Phil Silvers role. Walker played Sgt. Val Valentine, a scheming hustler at a peacetime Army post in small-town Texas. This series lasted four months.

In 1987, he was back on TV — for an entire season this time — in the syndicated comedy *Bustin' Loose.* Again he played a hustler. Based loosely on the 1981 Richard Pryor movie of the same name, Walker played Sonny Barnes, a con man and teller of tall tales. Serving a five-year sentence of community service, Sonny was put to work cleaning up after and taking care of five orphans, all of whom were crazy about the braggart Sonny's colorful but imaginary exploits.

Throughout his post–*Good Times* career, Walker appeared in numerous films and guest shots on television, but primarily he concentrated on his stand-up comedy career. As he told *TV Guide* back in 1974, *Good Times* was just a vehicle to get him where he wanted to go a lot quicker. He wanted a career as a comedian that would see him performing in front of not just black audiences but racially mixed rooms. During his years on *Good Times,* he hired a couple of little-known comics named Jay Leno and David Letterman to write material for him that would appeal to white middle-class America. "I want everybody to dig me. Young, old, black, white, Eastern, Midwestern," he said. "Universality is what I work at hardest. I booked myself 65 dates solid in North Dakota to prove I wasn't just a ghetto comic."[11]

That's all paid off in that today he still works six months a year traveling on the comedy club circuit. However, although he is often a welcome guest on the late night talk shows of his former writers, Leno and Letterman, Walker's best and most-frequent late night guest shots are on Bill Maher's current events TV roundtable, *Politically Incorrect.*

Walker is a natural for a show like *Politically Incorrect.* In addition to doing jokes about politics in his nightclub act, for the past 25 years he has hosted a number of open-line talk radio programs throughout the country. He has worked at "710 Talk in L.A.," WHIO in Dayton, Ohio, WOAI in San Antonio, WLS in Chicago and KKAR in Omaha, Nebraska.

As did his early idol, Dick Gregory, Walker uses humor to make his point. His talk radio work is political and issue oriented. His opinions come from the perspective of a black who grew up in an inner-city ghetto. However, they aren't stridently linked to any racial group.

Although people may come out to see his show or tune in to him on the radio expecting to hear "the black perspective," what they get instead is the voice of common sense. He is the voice of a thoughtful Everyman — that is, if Joe Lunchbox had a sense of humor. Walker is a moderate with no political affiliations. He distrusts both political parties and all lobby groups equally.

Universality is indeed the secret to Walker's long-running popularity. His appeal reaches all races and he can back up his jokes and opinions from having lived in both the black and white man's worlds. It's true that he got his start performing with black militants, but he also points out that many of the people who helped him early in his career were white.

It's no act either. Walker judges people on their own merits, not their skin color. Although his list of favorite musicians includes Motown greats like Stevie Wonder, the Temptations and the Four Tops, he is also probably the only black person to ever publicly admit to being a lifelong fan of James Taylor. Now, *that* is *dyn-o-mite!*

Notes

1. *TV Guide*; December 14, 1974; "No Time for Jivin'"; by Rowland Barber.
2. *Jimmie Walker, the Dyn-o-mite Kid*; by Joel H. Cohen; Scholastic Books; New York; 1976; page 8.
3. *Ibid.*; page 18.
4. *TV Guide*; December 14, 1974.
5. *TV Guide*; December 14, 1974.
6. *TV Guide*; December 14, 1974.
7. *TV Guide*; December 14, 1974.
8. *Jimmy Walker, the Dyn-o-mite Kid*; by Joel H. Cohen; page 29.
9. *Jimmy Walker, the Dyn-o-mite Kid*; by Joel H. Cohen; page 35.
10. *The Great TV Sitcom Book*; by Rick Mitz; Putnam Publishing, New York; 1980; page 260.
11. *TV Guide*; December 14, 1974.

Jimmie Walker Credits

FILM CREDITS

1. *Shriek If You Know What I Did Last Friday the 13th*; 2000; Pimp
2. *Plump Fiction*; 1997; Stingy Customer
3. *Ripper*; 1996; Soap Beatty
4. *Open Season*; 1996; Homer
5. *Monster Mash: The Movie*; 1995; Hathaway
6. *Home Alone 2: Lost in New York*; 1992; Celebrity

7. *The Guyver;* 1991; Striker
8. *Invasion of the Space Preachers;* 1990; Himself
9. *Goin' Bananas;* 1987; Mozambo
10. *Kidnapped;* 1986; Chester
11. *Water;* 1985; Jay Jay
12. *Doin' Time;* 1985; Shaker
13. *Airplane!;* 1980; Windshield Wiper Man
14. *The Concorde: Airport '79;* 1979; Boisie
15. *Rabbit Test;* 1978; Umbuto
16. *Let's Do It Again;* 1975; Bootney Farnsworth
17. *Sing Sing Thanksgiving;* 1974; Himself

TV CREDITS

1. *Chienne de Vie;* TV movie; 1996
2. *Bustin' Loose;* TV series; 1987; Sonny Barnes
3. *The Jerk, Too;* TV movie; 1984; Card Player
4. *At Ease;* TV series; 1983; Sergeant Val Valentine
5. *Murder Can Hurt You;* TV movie; 1980; Parks the Pusher
6. *B.A.D. Cats;* TV series; 1980; Rodney Washington
7. *Telethon;* 1977; TV movie; Himself
8. *The Greatest Thing That Almost Happened;* TV movie; 1977; Morris Bird III
9. *Good Times;* TV series; 1974–1979; James "J.J." Evans, Jr.

NOTABLE TV GUEST APPEARANCES

1. *The Drew Carey Show;* Lewis' Double; 3/28/2001
2. *Night Stand;* Himself; 1997
3. *The John Larroquette Show;* Slyde Wilson; 10/16/1996
4. *Space Ghost Coast to Coast;* Himself; 6/19/1996
5. *In the House;* Darryl; 11/13/1995
6. *Deadly Games;* Talk Show Host; 1995
7. *The Larry Sanders Show;* Himself; 7/13/1994
8. *Blossom;* Himself; 2/21/1994
9. *The Love Boat;* 1985
10. *The Fall Guy;* John; 9/19/1984
11. *Cagney and Lacey;* 1983
12. *The White Shadow;* Himself; 12/16/1980
13. *The Love Boat;* Marvin Jones; 11/22/1980
14. *The Love Boat;* Marvin Jones; 11/15/1980
15. *The Love Boat;* 11/17/1979
16. *The Love Boat;* 11/11/1978
17. *The Love Boat;* Ronald; 9/24/1977

Fred Willard

Jerry Hubbard on *Fernwood 2-Night*

No one plays Fred Willard better than Fred Willard.

Over the years, Willard has created and developed one of the most recognizable character types to be found in movies and on television. It is a guileless type who has a knack for sticking his foot in his mouth. Whenever he does so—which can be quite frequently—he is usually blissfully unaware of the fact.

The character was seen for the first time as Martin Mull's sidekick, Jerry Hubbard, on Norman Lear's talk show parody *Fernwood 2-Night* back in the late 1970s. That same persona has shown up under different names over the years in other projects with Mull, as well as those by writer-director Christopher Guest, who cast Willard in his films *Waiting for Guffman* and *Best in Show*.

By now, almost everyone in Hollywood is aware of the Fred Willard character and specifically what Willard can bring to a role. Incredibly enough, however, after 30 years in show business and 20 years spent defining that character, Willard still has to go to auditions.

Casting agents and producers get younger all the time and many simply don't know his body of work or haven't even seen *Fernwood 2-Nite* because they're unaware of any cultural event prior to the Beastie Boys.

Willard, now in his early sixties, takes it all in stride. He laughs when he tells the story of going to an audition not too long ago. "I went to the Warner Bros. lot for a job a couple of years ago and the guard at the gate said, 'You know, I don't think you still have to audition for these things.' And I told him, 'Not only do I have to audition but they'll take a long time telling me why I was wrong for the part.' It never ends."

Ah, if only security guards ran the studios.

In a way, Willard has gotten his revenge by playing a sitcom producer in the 1998 film *Permanent Midnight*. It was a true story of a young man who "toils" away as a screenwriter on a thinly disguised version of *ALF*. Willard played a laid back but brutally honest producer and brought many of his own touches to the performance. Although the man was a fool, Willard doesn't want to take the credit for that. He says the character was written that way. Still, he played the part with great relish.

The character differed from Willard's familiar Jerry Hubbard–types in that he *knew* the *ALF*–like show they were doing was garbage—but just didn't care. On *Fernwood 2-Night*, Jerry Hubbard, on the other hand, had no idea that the low-budget talk show he co-hosted was so cheesy. In fact, he thought they were putting on a great show of first-rate entertainment. Even if Mull's character pointed out the truth to him, he probably still wouldn't care—he was only on it because he was the station owner's brother-in-law.

That lack of a definite career objective might also describe how Willard himself ended up in show business. Although he has worked hard and consistently over the years, as a young man, his early career choices seem whimsical.

Born September 18, 1939, in Shaker Heights, Ohio, Willard attended Shaker Heights High School for a couple of years until his mother decided that military school might be a good idea. After leafing through all the catalogues for various military academies, most of which featured pictures of "little military guys jumping horses or marching through the snow," according to Willard, he settled on the Kentucky Military Institute outside of Louisville.

The decision was easy, admits Willard. "The entire school moved to Venice, Florida, for the winter. After Christmas vacation, we spent three months on the west coast of Florida. It was much more relaxed and really a lot of fun. The actual school is no longer in existence. Ironically, now it's a drug and alcohol rehabilitation farm."

After a brief stint in the Army, Willard had no real career goals. "Now what am I going to do, I thought. And at the time, I thought I'd be a disc jockey," he recalls.

"I'm from Cleveland—which was a very progressive rock and roll city at that time. I loved music and I thought, 'Boy, it would be great being a disc jockey and picking out all the songs I wanted to play.'"

When asked if he had ever had any experience in radio, Willard quickly admits, "Never."

He was also vaguely interested in other aspects of show business—he had always liked the comedy films of Bob Hope and Abbott and Costello. "Back then, I'd go to the movies and I had no idea how much work they took. I'd see a two-hour movie and figure that they probably spent a week filming it, so I thought this would be a wonderful life."

He never studied drama in high school or took part in any school theatrical productions, Willard says. "No. I wasn't interested in drama during high school. I was more interested in sports. I wanted to be a baseball player."

In the end, he wound up going to acting school in New York. "It was called Showcase Theatre and strangely enough, it's still there," says Willard. "It was run by a married couple who were both kind of like frustrated actors. The woman was kind of like Blanche from *A Streetcar Named Desire* and the man reminded me of a John Barrymore wanna-be. They were both very theatrical.

"But the reason I went there was because it was the only school I found where they put on a showcase. For 10 weeks you would rehearse scenes with a partner and at the end of that period, you would put on a show for two nights and they'd invite an audience. I think that really is the best way to do it—just the fact of getting up on stage and doing a scene with a partner in front of an audience is just invaluable."

Willard's move towards comedy came about after striking up a friendship with fellow student Vic Greco. They eventually became a comedy team. "Vic was a very funny guy and we started kidding and joking around together. One day we saw an ad in the trade papers that said a variety show was casting and looking for comic actors. So we went down and the producer said, 'Do you have any sketches?' Of course we didn't and he said, 'Well, come back with a sketch and I'll look at it.' So we went and wrote a whole bunch of sketches and kept going in every week with more and more sketches and finally he gave us work. But he didn't put us in his show—he put on a show of just the two of us. An evening of our sketches."

That set the pattern of work for the next decade for Willard—writing and then performing up on stage, first with Greco and then other comedy troupes. Greco and Willard worked together sporadically for the next few years and even spent a summer working at Green Mansions, the theatre resort in upstate New York. While there, Willard performed in the world premiere of Jules Ffeiffer's play *Crawling Arnold.*

At the time, the early 1960s, comedy teams traditionally consisted of a funny guy and the good-looking straight man who also doubled as a singer. Willard and Greco were contrary to that norm and he describes them as being more like Wayne and Shuster—just two comic actors. "We had an unusual act for back then in that all we did was our comedy sketches. We had no interplay with the audience.

"As a result, we'd play a place like The Hungry I in San Francisco, which was a very hip place. We did *so* well there—there were times that the laughter was so loud and so long that we couldn't continue our scenes. Then we'd go to the next club and just bomb. You couldn't figure it out—it was the same act. But the more mainstream clubs expected a comic and a singer and a bit of patter with the audience. And we didn't do that. We'd just come out and start from the very beginning doing sketch comedy."

From that strong beginning in sketch comedy, after splitting up with Greco, Willard soon established himself as one of the finest working in the then-new field of improvisational comedy during the late 1960s and early '70s. Working first with Second City in New York and then Chicago, and then as a founding member of the famed improv group Ace Trucking Company, the switch to improv was a career-defining move for Willard.

However, Willard explains that his work at Second City wasn't all that different from the meticulously worked-out sketches he and Greco had been doing. "It's all improvisational," he says. "But what they do is improvise and then finalize it. When you go see a Second City show, you're seeing a scripted show but almost all of it came out of improvisation."

The Ace Trucking Company was formed in 1969 after Willard had left Second City and was performing in New York in the off–Broadway production of another Jules Ffeiffer play, the black comedy *Little Murders*, also starring Alan Arkin, Linda Lavin and Paul Benedict.

"A friend called me and said, 'We're doing a little comedy show after the regular show ends at a club called The Bitter End.' I still had some sketch ideas left over from Second City so I wrote up a couple of ideas and we would just improvise and as that went on, the improvs would become sketches."

The loose group of friends eventually chose the name Ace Trucking Company. For Willard, it was different from his improv experience at Second City. This was more like working without a net. "It ended up that we would do a 45 minute show. And of that we'd do 20 minutes of scripted material and then 20 minutes of improvisation and then close the show with a set piece.

"One hundred percent improvisation always scares me. I don't even particularly like to watch it. But it's kind of fun in the middle of a show. It was almost foolproof. There were five of us so there was always someone jumping in with an idea. And if it was bombing, we'd have one of the guys come out with a little crown and a wand and he'd say, 'I'm the Bad-Scene Fairy and this scene is finished'—and at least that would get a laugh. But as we got better, and went on more and more, he would never show up because we'd always be doing something funny. By our second year we really had a dynamite act."

The troupe cut a record—all improv, made up on the spot in the recording studio—a decision Willard now questions. They became regulars on the *Tom Jones* ABC variety show as well as appearing as "themselves" in the popular "racy" film about college life, *The Harrad Experiment*.

Willard says that the Ace Trucking experience differed from Second City in many ways. "With Second City, you were in a theatre and the audience coming to see you knew what to expect. With Ace Trucking, we were in nightclubs and you have college students and drunks so you've got to go *right* to a joke. So you'd go for jokes which you did not do at Second City. They frowned on that over there. The emphasis was more on scene and character development.

"In a nightclub, you went quickly for a joke and if you got a little 'blue' that was fine. It was good training and once you get into the swing of it, it's not hard at all. If you're improvising every night, it's quite easy."

Willard spent four years based in New York. After *Little Murders*, he also appeared in an evening presentation of *Arf* and *The Great Airplane Smash*, one act plays starring Paula Prentice and directed by her husband, Richard Benjamin.

He also appeared in his first movie, *Teenage Mother*, in 1966. It was an exploitation flick about an unwed teenage new mother. If the tagline "She was a motorcycle mama" wasn't enough to lure people into the theatres, the film also included an actual birthing scene of a real baby being born. Set in an inner-city high school, Willard played the baseball coach who was also dating a young, blonde sex-education teacher from Sweden.

"There's a funny story about that film," offers Willard. "There was a scene where I'm walking down the hall with some kids and I hear a scream because the sex-education teacher was being pulled into the boiler room and some guy was trying to rape her. Anyway, I hear the scream and run down the hall and burst into the boiler room and stop the rape.

"So when the movie came out, my wife and I went to the opening in Staten Island, and we take the ferry across to the theatre and when my big scene comes up, the bad guy had dragged the sexy girl into the boiler room and was pulling her clothes off. I ran into the boiler room to stop him *and the whole audience booed!* They wanted to see some sex, so I was actually the bad guy. And that was the first movie I ever did."

In 1973, Willard and his wife Mary returned to Los Angeles where he became one of the regulars on ABC-TV's summer variety series, *The Burns and Schreiber Comedy Hour,* starring the comedy team of Jack Burns and Avery Schreiber. "At the time, I was getting $270 a week and to be getting that kind of money each week, I thought that was just golden."

He liked it so much, in fact, that when *Burns and Schreiber* ended its summer run, he found other jobs in television and has been working regularly in Hollywood ever since.

Until he created the quintessential Fred Willard–type character with Jerry Hubbard when *Fernwood 2-Night* came along in 1977, Willard seemed to specialize in another kind of role on TV sitcoms. He was often cast as the vain, loudmouth type. His first work in that area was a 1975 episode of *The Bob Newhart Show* where he played an old boyfriend of Bob's sister, Ellen, in an episode called "Tobin's Back in Town." His character tried to impress her and woo her back from Bill Daily's Howard Borden character.

"I kind of fell into a lot of those roles around that time," he recalls. "The same kind of character, the guy who has no self-awareness and is full of himself."

He landed a similar role in 1976 as a regular on the short-lived NBC sitcom *Sirota's Court.* A forerunner of *Night Court*, Willard played assistant district attorney Bud Nugent. Willard sums up the character as "Vain and bumbling and I was always putting my foot in my mouth. After they bought the pilot, there was a whole change of command at the network and they didn't want to put it on and so they buried the show and put it on opposite Christmas specials where even *I'd* rather watch the Christmas specials. But Michael Constantine was the star of the show and doing it was a lot of fun."

Sirota's Court could have been a turning point in Willard's career. He had been building a reputation on television for playing incompetent braggarts.

He played a similar type role as an officious officer in the 1977 pilot for a comedy series called *Space Force*, a parody of *Star Wars* and *Star Trek*. The timing was right for such a show and Willard says he thought, "Oh boy, here's my break. I'm going to be a sitcom star!"

However, while waiting for word that *Space Force* had been picked up as a series, Willard was approached by the producers of Norman Lear's late night soap opera parody, *Mary Hartman, Mary Hartman*. They were doing a summer series called *Fernwood 2-Night* which was to be a spoof on a small-market variety talk show and were interested in Willard playing Martin Mull's co-host, a low-rent Ed McMahon named Jerry Hubbard.

Willard was reluctant to get involved with the summer series because he was banking on *Space Force* being picked up and he had his heart set on that show making him a sitcom star. Still, he went to a meeting with *Fernwood's* producers and began naming other actors he thought would be good for the part. "And they said, 'No, no—don't give us all these names, we're interested in *you*,'" Willard recalls. "And I said, 'Well no, I did this pilot and I really want to be a sitcom star.' And they said, 'Well, do us a favor. Will you just come in and meet Martin and we're just going to have a few run-throughs so will you just help us out until we find someone because we can't find the right guy.'

"So I went in and we did a few run-throughs and I found Martin to be *so* funny and I had so much fun that after a few days, I said, 'You know, I'm kind of enjoying this. I think I'd like to do this!' And I still don't know whether I could have been a big sitcom star, but that show turned out to be two years of the most fun I've ever had."

Fun aside, being cast as Jerry Hubbard was a turning point in Willard's career. It could have continued in the direction of the vain, smug sort of character he played on *Sirota's Court*—but many actors could have played that role. On the other hand, fatuous Jerry Hubbard was a far more unique character. The role represented the birth of the Fred Willard–type character.

On *Fernwood 2-Night*, Willard did a variation on yet another incompetent. Jerry Hubbard only had the job of co-host because he was the TV station owner's brother-in-law. One suspects that if his sister's husband owned a car dealership, Jerry would most likely be the sales team manager. He would probably be good at it too. Jerry was one of those naturally friendly types who end up gravitating to careers in car sales or real estate. Not because he was a sharp salesman but because he had a pleasant personality and the gift of gab. People liked him.

Jerry Hubbard is the kind of guy who could be *your* brother-in-law. Or next-door neighbor out in the suburbs. Someone to talk about golf scores and barbequing techniques over the backyard fence and over a beer after a long, hard week of selling aluminum siding.

As such, he was the perfect foil for Martin Mull's Barth Gimble character. Whereas Barth was glib, Jerry was guileless. Barth was quick-witted and Jerry was a bit slow on the uptake. Barth was shallow and phony but Jerry was bluntly honest.

The most important difference between the two characters, however, was that Barth was sarcastic and smug but Jerry was too good-natured for put-down humor. In fact, Jerry was often on the receiving end of Barth's barbs. Long before David Letterman officially brought the Age of Irony to late night television, the folks at *Fernwood 2-Night* were already mining gold in that vein of comedy. The young urban audience tuned in to laugh *with* Barth Gimble and his caustic one-liners, but they laughed *at* Jerry Hubbard—who as usual, was completely oblivious that anyone was laughing at *him*.

Although the audience may have been laughing at Jerry, it was he, not Barth, that people warmed up to—he was one of *us*. In short, he was loveable. One could appreciate Barth's cynical witticisms but you wouldn't necessarily want to go out for a drink with him. You would have to be on your guard while having a Tom Collins with the acerbic Mr. Gimble. You wouldn't feel uncomfortable around Jerry Hubbard, though, you could relax.

Not that Jerry was immune to rubbing people the wrong way. He had a knack for infuriating guests by inadvertently offending them. But he was always unaware of any boorishness on his part. People would put up with Jerry and respond to him as you might a feeble-minded person — as if he just couldn't help it.

Whenever a guest of any particular ethnic or religious background came on the show, Jerry managed to nail every cultural cliché right on the head. Not in a malicious way, but in his usual blundering and earnest fashion. Luckily, being offensive was one of *Fernwood 2-Night's* trademarks. It was a Norman Lear production and Lear was no stranger to controversy and tackling taboo subjects on his sitcoms *All in the Family, Maude* and *The Jeffersons.* On those shows he upset people simply by showing the offensiveness of bigotry and racism.

Fernwood 2-Night, however, was often offensive just for the sake of being offensive. And proud of it. At the time, producer Alan Thicke bragged, "We will offend the sensibilities of a number of Americans, for which we apologize out front. But we're discriminating in our satire, we're offending everybody, regardless of race, creed, color or income level."[1]

By today's television standards, the show still holds its own on the bad-taste barometer. Yet it may seem a bit tame when compared to today's real talk shows. In that sense, the show was ahead of its time.

Jerry Hubbard, however, didn't have a mean-spirited bone in his body. Part of the reason people were willing to tolerate him was because like many second-banana characters, he was somewhat childlike. He had a child's curiosity and would ask questions like a child would — just blurt it out, without any thought that he might be trampling on a delicate subject.

The key to Jerry Hubbard — indeed to all the characters yet to come in that Fred Williard–type mold — is that he is basically clueless. Jerry is the kind of guy who if he walked into a roomful of people and everyone was laughing, even though he didn't know why they were laughing, he would start laughing himself. Willard himself laughs in recognition when asked about this aspect of the character he created. He then goes on to elaborate, "When I played Jerry, I had to make an effort to not censor any of my thoughts, just to say the first thing that came to my mind. I had a mother and a grandmother who were like that and would come up with some of the dumbest statements that almost *seemed* to make sense."

Jerry's interests and concerns were also childlike. On one episode, as was his wont, he went off topic and began getting quite upset about television evangelists. After a few minutes of this ad-lib rant, he finally arrived at the point: there were now so many of them that it was almost impossible to find any good cartoon shows anymore on a Sunday morning.

"A lot of times, when you're on television on a talk show, you might think of something to say right then and you think, 'Am I going to sound stupid if I say this?' — and if you do, you just don't say it," explains Willard. "But as Jerry, I would just get rid of that fear so that it was almost like a stream of consciousness sort of thing. If something came to me, I would just open the door and let it out. It's like those people who don't really think before they open their mouths. And if I could think of a way for Jerry to misunderstand something, it was all the better."

Such scenes, although they put the spotlight on Willard, worked so well because of Mull's bored, incredulous or exasperated reaction shots. "And then Martin's character would get mad and in being mad at me, he would start off on something that was just as stupid," notes Willard.

Those scenes were often improvised and they show just how well the two comics could work together. They were often each other's straight man. According to Willard, they just naturally clicked when they met for the first time, and they continued to work together off and on for the next two decades in their post–*Fernwood* careers.

Although Willard had not met Mull prior to the show, he had seen him in concert performing his off-beat and whimsical original songs. At the time, Willard's peers didn't know whether to consider Mull a fellow comic or a singer of funny songs. "I had seen Martin in a club once. I thought he was a very unique talent and was really amazed at how he didn't take aim at easy targets.

"And later — but before *Fernwood 2-Night* — I had seen him do one of the funniest things I'd ever seen. It was on *Mary Hartman, Mary Hartman*. There was a scene where Mary Kay Place was a country and western singer and Martin and her husband are watching her sing when she collapsed and fell over in a faint. Her husband jumped up and ran over to her and Martin stood up, stopped and lit a cigarette — and *then* went over to help. And I know that was all *his* invention. That was his character, just so self-centered.

"When we met on *Fernwood 2-Night* and they did the first show, I was originally to sit next to Martin but on the couch and as the guests came out, I would keep moving down the couch. But the first show went so well that they re-shot it and got me a chair next to Martin and said, 'We want to keep you next to Martin because you two guys have such good interplay.'

"It was a perfect match because I was a big fan of Martin's humor and he seemed to like mine. So we'd say to each other during the breaks — 'Okay, in the next segment I thought I'd do this and then ...' and the other person would invariably laugh and say, 'Oh, that's great, do it!' So it was a very good mutual support. The show was scripted but after the first two weeks they welcomed us to go off the script and they would overshoot or cut down later."

For viewers, it was obvious that both Willard and Mull were having fun. In one episode, both they and their guest, Kenneth Mars, who played William W.D. "Bud" Prize, couldn't even keep a straight face. "There were some segments, like the ones with Bud Prize, the guy who wore the chinstrap. He'd come out and they would have a whole segment written for him but Kenneth Mars would usually come on with his own material and so we'd just improvise the whole 10-minute segment with him.

"One time he came on and his character was quite upset about something or other and he was yelling and spouting this anger and then after the commercial break, Martin and I are talking and I looked over and he was sitting there asleep. And I thought, 'This is so perfect for his character — that he would go from those two extremes,' and so *I* started to laugh and that started *him* laughing — while still pretending to be asleep.

"There were about two times in the whole two years that Martin and I got laughing and couldn't stop and I think they were both in shows with Kenneth Mars."

Fernwood 2-Night was to be just a summer series but it proved to be so popular that it came back in April 1978 as *America 2-Night*. The producers had Barth, Jerry and the house band, Happy Kyne and his Mirth Makers (led by big-band veteran Frank DeVol), move the show to Alta Coma, California — "the unfinished furniture capital of the world," and do the show for the fledgling low-budget UTN network.

The change in locale allowed the series to take advantage of Hollywood celebrities who normally wouldn't be passing through Fernwood, Ohio. On *America 2-Night*, big names like Charlton Heston and Carol Burnett would come on and happily make fun of themselves, just as 20 years later, real-life celebrities would beg to spoof themselves on the talk show parody *The Larry Sanders Show*.

In retrospect, the first season seems more pure as just a spoof of a local TV show. Although the fictional UTN network was still low-budget and they retained the old set's cheesiness, the series lost a bit of its charm in going Hollywood. Not that there was ever any danger of it being confused with Johnny Carson's *Tonight Show*. "It was never meant to be a *Tonight Show* parody," says Willard. "As Martin once said, 'If we wanted to do a spoof on *The Tonight Show*, it would have been very funny — but it would have lasted about two episodes.'"

As fate would have it, Willard and Mull's series lasted two seasons — but they've teamed up and worked together on a regular basis ever since the last *America 2-Night*. The first collaboration was Mull's critically acclaimed PBS series, the "mockumentary" *History of White People in America*. Mull co-wrote, produced and hosted the 1985 two-part series which examined what it meant to be white and middle-class in the post–*Roots* United States. The saga was largely seen through the eyes of the Harrison family, an average white family living in suburban Ohio. Willard played patriarch Hal Harrison and Mary Kay Place was his wife, Joyce. They had two teenaged children.

Hal Harrison was the next stage in the evolution of the Fred Willard–type character — good-natured and ineffective. Willard readily admits that Hal could be considered a slightly older Jerry Hubbard — "Sure, if Jerry ever got it together enough where he could get married and have a family." Hal also shared Jerry's uncanny ability to always say just the wrong thing. One scene showed him in conversation with an Orthodox Jew, played by Harry Shearer. With his childlike natural curiosity, Hal asked about yarmulkes, the hair and beard and Jewish tradition, and while doing so, he managed to drag every known Jewish cliché into the conversation.

"That series was also set in Ohio and I'm from there so I kind of know the mentality. That kind of person isn't mean-spirited, they just don't know any better," explains Willard.

In 1986, they did another installment of the *History of White People* series which examined democracy as Hal ran for the office of water commissioner. In 1988, they concluded the series with *Portrait of a White Marriage*.

The last major pairing between the two actors occurred on *Roseanne*. Mull was a regular character as Roseanne's homosexual boss at the diner where she worked. He was also on staff as the show's "creative consultant." Roseanne and Tom Arnold offered Willard the chance to guest as the lover of Martin's character. "And I said, 'You know, it makes me uneasy. We had done so many things together and have such a history that people are going to wonder if we *were* lovers,' so I told them no, I don't really want to do it.

"I started to regret it and then one day Martin called and asked, 'What if you were to come on as my significant other, we get married on the show and adopt a baby?' And I said, 'Oh, that's hilarious, let's do it!' I think we did about six or seven *Roseannes* after that."

Willard starred in a number of other series— as a host on *Real People* and *Access America*, a bizarre look at community access television shows, and *D.C. Follies*, where he played The Bartender of a Washington, D.C., club peopled by life-size puppets of well-known celebrities and political figures. On the ABC political satire series, this time Willard played the straight man.

His current most regular gig is on Jay Leno's *Tonight Show*. It represents a return to sketch comedy because he plays whatever character the writers come up with from that week's news stories. "Those are really fun to do because I'm really the clown and Jay is the straight man."

Another return to his roots is evident in the work he has been doing over the years with comic writer/producers Christopher Guest and Eugene Levy. He first met Guest in 1969 when both were in the off–Broadway production of *Little Murders*.

He also worked with Guest on Rob Reiner's 1984 mockumentary, *This is Spinal Tap,* about a fictional heavy-metal band. In the film, from a script co-written by Guest, Willard played Lieutenant Hookstratten, who had booked the band into his Air Force base's Officers Club for its Saturday night get-together. In Jerry Hubbard fashion, he clearly has no conception of the inappropriateness of his poor choice in musical acts. Willard later revived the character for the *Spinal Tap Reunion* TV movie in 1992.

He had first worked with Eugene Levy as a guest on Levy's *SCTV*— the Second City comedy series from Canada in the early 1980s. Years later, when Levy had established himself as a writer and director in Hollywood, he cast Willard in his made-for-TV western spoof, *Sodbusters.*

Willard's best known work in a Guest and Levy collaboration is the 1996 feature film *Waiting for Guffman,* directed by Guest and written by himself and Levy. Set in the Midwestern town of Blaine, Missouri, it features an ensemble cast including Guest's character, Corky St. Clair. He is a transplanted "very theatrical" New Yorker who puts on an amateur revue to celebrate the sesquicentennial (150-year anniversary) of the founding of Blaine, the stool capital of America. Willard and ex–*SCTV*er Catharine O'Hara play Ron and Sheila Albertson, a married couple who run the town's sole travel agency (they've never been out of state themselves). They are also the only ones in town with any acting experience. They had worked with Corky in his musical adaptation of *Backdraft* the previous summer until the theatre accidentally burned down during one performance. Of course, these two deluded, self-styled thespians are just awful hams, but Corky, who should know better, thinks they are fabulous and real troopers. He likes to call them "the Lunts of Blaine." The movie's advertising tagline says everything you need to know about Ron and Sheila and the others—"There's a good reason some talent remains undiscovered."

For Willard, his Ron Albertson role was another chance to explore that Fred Willard–type character. More importantly, to the actor, *Waiting for Guffman* was a rare opportunity to work in improvisation. Guest likes to use improv and so he surrounds himself with actors who are up to the task. For the actors, working in improvisation on a feature film gives them the best of both worlds. It's creatively liberating and yet without the pressure of doing it live on stage and possibly bombing. Most importantly, it gives them far more freedom to be creative than is offered in most other working situations. They get to breathe life into their characters because everything they say comes from being in character. All they initially have to go on is the character's name and a bit of background.

"*Guffman* was 100 percent improvised," Willard explains. "We had a structure and we knew what each scene was about. It wasn't like we started the cameras rolling and just improvised and didn't know where it was going to go. It was quite closely structured, but all the dialogue was ours."

This creative situation is where Willard gets to strut his stuff and further define the Fred Willard–type. One of his best lines in *Guffman* comes when Ron is advising one of the amateurs in the Blaine theatre group: "If there's an empty space, just fill it with a line. That's what I do—even if it's from another show." The line is pure Willard. It's the sort of thing you can easily imagine coming out of the mouth of Fernwood's Jerry Hubbard.

Willard has described the type of character he is best known for playing this way: "I think it's kind of broad. A guy who doesn't conceal his thoughts, who has a lack of self-awareness. A blunderer. A guy who, if his pants were on fire, would carry on as if he didn't notice."[2]

It should be pointed out that Willard has also played many different characters and is certainly versatile. However, since Ron Albertson bears more than a passing resemblance to Jerry Hubbard and Hal Harrison, and since much of these characters were created by him in improv situations, the question has to be asked: is there very much of these characters in Fred Willard? And vice-versa. "Oh yes," he readily admits. "There must be. I'm sure there is."

Waiting for Guffman and the most recent Guest-Levy collaboration, *Best in Show,* a spoof of pedigreed dog shows, are the sort of projects where Willard gets to excel at what he does best—create sketch comedy with other people and you share the laughs. It's a creative environment, not a competitive situation where the actors are more worried about their allotted number of lines and laughs. In a movie like *Guffman,* despite Guest's strong presence, there are no real stars and no supporting actors. Certainly no second bananas. *Everyone* gets a chance to shine.

Willard takes the same approach in some of his other work. You can even see it in the humble title of a live show he occasionally puts on — "Alone at Last — Fred Willard's One-Man Show — With a Cast of 12." "When I finished working with Ace Trucking Company, we still had a lot of wonderful sketches that had never been on TV and so I thought I would take the most theatrical stuff and put it in a show. I have a lot of friends who are very funny actors and so the more the merrier.

"At the time, there were a *lot* of one-man shows in L.A., and that's how the title popped into my mind. My first line when I came out to talk to the audience was, 'I talked to a lot of people about doing a one-man show and they said that the most important thing is to surround yourself with the best actors possible and I think I have that.'"

So Willard is still doing what he did right from the beginning of his career with Showcase Theatre — rehearsing a scene, performing it in front of people and working with a partner. Working with others has always been an integral part of Willard's longevity in show business. He needs a partner and whether it's Martin Mull or Jay Leno, he needs someone not just to react to him but for him to reciprocate.

His generous nature can be seen in his own philosophy regarding the art of the second banana. "I think what makes a good straight man is someone who loves comedy and loves jokes and so you give everything you have, knowing that the other guy is going to do the joke. You want to do everything you can — to then hear the joke and then hear the audience laugh."

The kid who once dreamed of being a baseball player uses a baseball analogy to describe his team-player approach to comedy. "It's like a baseball player. The second baseman gets the ball hit to him, he throws it to the short stop, the short stop makes the pivot and completes the double play. But *you* started it. And you know, although you aren't getting the laugh. You do it because you *enjoy* the laughter so much. And you have to be a big comedy *fan*."

Notes

1. *The Complete Directory to Prime Time TV Shows*; by Tim Brooks and Earle Marsh; Ballantine Books; New York; 1999; page 341.
2. *Metro Weekly News*; San Jose, CA; "Waiting for Willard"; by Richard von Busack; March 20, 1997.

Fred Willard Credits

FILM CREDITS

1. *Teddy Bears' Picnic*; 2001
2. *Chump Change*; 2001
3. *Dropping Out*; 2000; Paul Blanchard
4. *Best in Show*; 2000; Buck Laughlin
5. *The Pooch and the Pauper*; 1999; The President
6. *Austin Powers: The Spy Who Shagged Me*; 1999; Mission Commander
7. *Idle Hands*; 1999; Dad
8. *Can't Stop Dancing*; 1999; Chester
9. *Permanent Midnight*; 1998; Craig Ziffer
10. *Waiting for Guffman*; 1996; Ron Albertson
11. *Prehysteria 3*; 1995; Thomas MacGregor

12. *High Strung;* 1994; Insurance Salesman
13. *Ray's Male Heterosexual Dance Hall;* 1987; Tom Osborne
14. *Roxanne;* 1987; Mayor Deebs
15. *Moving Violations;* 1985; Terrence "Doc" Williams
16. *This Is Spinal Tap;* 1984; Lt. Hookstratten
17. *National Lampoon Goes to the Movies;* 1981; President Fogerty
18. *First Family;* 1980; Presidential Assistant Feebleman
19. *How to Beat the High Co$t of Living;* 1980; Robert
20. *Americathon;* 1979; Vincent Vanderhoff
21. *Fun with Dick and Jane;* 1977; Bob
22. *Cracking Up;* 1977
23. *Chesty Anderson, USN;* 1976; FBI agent
24. *Silver Streak;* 1976; Jerry Jarvis
25. *Hustle;* 1975; Interrogator
26. *Harrad Summer;* 1974; member, The Ace Trucking Company
27. *The Harrad Experiment;* 1973; member, The Ace Trucking Company
28. *Jenny;* 1969
29. *Teenage Mother;* 1966

TV CREDITS

1. *Maybe I'm Adopted;* TV series; 2001; Jerry Stages
2. *When Billie Beat Bobby;* TV movie; 2001; Howard
3. *Back to Back;* TV movie; 1996; Loan Officer
4. *Sodbusters;* TV movie; 1994; Clarence
5. *Hart to Hart: Old Friends Never Die;* TV movie; 1994
6. *The Tonight Show with Jay Leno;* TV series; 1992 to present; various characters
7. *Spinal Tap Reunion: The 25th Anniversary London Sell-Out;* TV movie; 1992; Lt. Hookstratten
8. *Access America;* TV series; 1990; Host.
9. *I, Martin Short, Goes Hollywood;* TV special; 1989; Psychiatrist
10. *Portrait of a White Marriage;* TV movie; 1988; Hal Harrison
11. *D.C. Follies;* TV series; 1987–1989; The Bartender
12. *Big City Comedy;* TV special; 1986
13. *The History of White People in America: Volume II;* TV movie; 1986; Hal Harrison
14. *Lots of Luck;* TV movie; 1985; A.J. Foley
15. *The History of White People in America;* TV movie; 1985; Hal Harrison
16. *Thicke of the Night;* TV series; 1983; Himself
17. *'Salem's Lot;* TV movie; 1979; Larry Crockett
18. *Real People;* TV series; 1979–1983; Himself
19. *Flatbed Annie & Sweetie Pie: Lady Truckers;* TV movie; 1979; Jack
20. *America 2-Night;* TV series; 1978; Jerry Hubbard
21. *Fernwood 2-Night;* TV series; 1977; Jerry Hubbard
22. *Forever Fernwood;* TV series; 1977; Jerry Hubbard
23. *Escape from Bogen County;* TV movie; 1977

24. *How to Break Up a Happy Divorce;* TV movie; 1976; Lance Coulson
25. *Sirota's Court;* TV series; 1976; Bud Nugent
26. *The Burns and Schreiber Comedy Hour;* TV series; 1973; Regular

NOTABLE TV GUEST APPEARANCES

1. *Ally McBeal;* Dr. Harold Madison; 2/26/2001
2. *Ally McBeal;* Dr. Harold Madison; 2/19/2001
3. *Bette;* Jasper Perkins; 1/24/2001
4. *Buzz Lightyear of Star Command;* (voice) Pa; 2000
5. *The Hughleys;* Applegate; 4/21/2000
6. *Ladies Man;* Larry Little; 1/17/2000
7. *Ladies Man;* Larry Little; 11/15/1999
8. *Love and Money;* Dr. Fielding; 10/29/1999
9. *Just Shoot Me;* Larry; 2/23/1999
10. *The Simpsons;* Wally; 1/31/1999
11. *Two Guys, a Girl and a Pizza Place;* Frank Farber; 9/30/1998
12. *Mad About You;* Henry; 5/19/1998
13. *Sabrina, the Teenage Witch;* Bobby Calzone; 5/8/1998
14. *Mad About You;* Henry; 4/28/1998
15. *The Weird Al Show;* Award Show Host; 11/22/1997
16. *Diagnosis Murder;* Harry Fellows; 10/30/1997
17. *Space Ghost Coast to Coast;* Himself; 10/10/1997
18. *Lois and Clark: The New Adventures of Superman;* President Garner; 3/9/1997
19. *Lois and Clark: The New Adventures of Superman;* President Garner; 3/2/1997
20. *Clueless;* Joe Pasadine; 10/6/1996
21. *Roseanne;* Scott; 5/7/1996
22. *Sister, Sister;* Mr. Mitushka; 5/1/1996
23. *Sister, Sister;* Mr. Mitushka; 2/28/1996
24. *Lois and Clark: The New Adventures of Superman;* The President; 2/11/1996
25. *Roseanne;* Scott; 2/6/1996
26. *Friends;* Mr. Lipson; 1/28/1996
27. *Roseanne;* Scott; 12/12/1995
28. *Murphy Brown;* Dick; 11/27/1995
29. *Family Matters;* Vice Principal Mallet; 10/14/1994
30. *The Jackie Thomas Show;* Hatfield Walker; 1/12/1993
31. *The Ben Stiller Show;* 1/3/1993
32. *Dream On;* Fenton Harley; 9/19/1992
33. *Married ... with Children;* Stan; 2/23/1992
34. *Mad About You;* Henry Vincent; 1992
35. *The Golden Girls;* Bob; 11/2/1991
36. *Murder, She Wrote;* Lt. Phillips; 2/17/1991
37. *My Secret Identity;* 11/14/1988
38. *New Love, American Style;* 1/8/1986
39. *SCTV;* Fred Winston; 2/14/1984
40. *Mama's Family;* Willie Potts; 184

41. *SCTV;* Himself; 11/12/1982
42. *Fame;* Al Stefano; 1982
43. *Laverne and Shirley;* 1976
44. *Laverne and Shirley;* 1976
45. *The Bob Newhart Show;* John Tobin; 1/4/1975
46. *Get Smart;* Agent 198; 11/2/1968
47. *Hey, Landlord;* Danny Subanski; 12/11/1966
48. *Pistols n' Petticoats;* Ben; 11/26/1966

Index